QSB+ VERSION 3.0

Yih-Long Chang
Georgia Institute of Technology

Prentice Hall, Englewood Cliffs, New Jersey 07632

Editorial/Production Supervision: Lisa Kinne
Electronic Consultant: Yvette Raven
Acquisitions Editor: Valerie Ashton
Production Coordinator: Herb Klein
Copy Editor: Nancy Marcello
Interior, Cover, and Box Design: Sue Behnke
Front Matter and Back Matter Design: Meryl Poweski
Editorial Assistant: Eileen Deguzman
Production Assistant: Renee Pelletier

Printed in the United States of America
10 9 8 7 6 5 4 3 2 1

ISBN 0-13-045873-2

Prentice-Hall International (UK) Limited, *London*
Prentice-Hall of Australia Pty. Limited, *Sydney*
Prentice-Hall Canada Inc., *Toronto*
Prentice-Hall Hispanoamericana, S.A., *Mexico*
Prentice-Hall of India Private Limited, *New Delhi*
Prentice-Hall of Japan, Inc., *Tokyo*
Simon & Schuster Asia Pte. Ltd., *Singapore*
Editora Prentice-Hall do Brasil, Ltda., *Rio de Janeiro*

To My Family

CONTENTS

PREFACE

QSB+ 3.0 (Quantitative Systems for Business Plus, Version 3.0) is a software package that contains the most popular problem-solving algorithms in management science and operations research (MS/OR). The topics and programs (in parentheses) in QSB+ 3.0 are listed as follows:

1. Linear programming (LP)
2. Integer linear programming (ILP)
3. Linear goal programming (GP)
4. Quadratic programming (QP)
5. Nonlinear programming (NLP)
6. Dynamic programming (DP)
7. Transportation and transshipment problems (TRP)
8. Assignment and traveling salesman problems (ASTS)
9. Specialized network modeling (SNET)
10. Capacitated network flow modeling (CNET)
11. Project scheduling: CPM/PERT (CPM)
12. Inventory theory (INVT)
13. Inventory theory 2 (INVT2)
14. Queuing theory (QUEUE)
15. Queuing system simulation (QSIM)
16. Decision analysis (DA)
17. Markov process (MKV)
18. Time series and forecasting (TSFC)
19. Financial analysis (FA)

QSB+ 3.0 can help an instructor explain how a scientific algorithm works. Students will find that learning management science and operations research (MS/OR) through the use of QSB+ 3.0 is interesting and less intimidating. Practitioners may use QSB+ 3.0 in their decision-making processes. Because of the friendliness of this microcomputer software, the user will not encounter the difficulty of using a mainframe. QSB+ 3.0 also demonstrates the power of the microcomputer in problem solving.

Since so many professors, students, and practitioners have enjoyed using QSB+

in their MS/OR instruction, learning, and application processes, we are committed to making the programs with the best quality. QSB+ 3.0 is another step to achieve this purpose. Besides making the software more comprehensive, we have greatly improved the QSB+ 3.0. The difference and improvement of the QSB+ 3.0 over the earlier versions are briefly described below.

Enhanced User Interface: QSB+ 3.0 uses four basic interface mechanisms to run the programs: *pull-down menu, dialog window, spreadsheet window,* and *list box*. The pull-down menu is used for operation selection, the dialog window is used for problem specification and parameter assignment, the spreadsheet window is used for problem data entry, and the list box is used for multiple choice situation. The *mouse* and *keyboard* are the designated operational devices. If your computer is equipped with only a keyboard, you will have no problem running the programs. Refer to Chapter 2 for the description of the user interface.

More Useful Modules: Four useful modules have been added to QSB+ 3.0 to enhance the coverage. They are nonlinear programming (NLP), capacitated network flow modeling (CNET), inventory systems (INVT2), and financial analysis (FA). NLP solves unconstrained and constrained problems with general nonlinear functions, CNET solves capacitated network flow problems, INVT2 analyzes the three typical inventory systems: fixed-order-quantity, fixed-order-interval, and optional replenishment (s, S) systems, and FA performs investment, annuity, compounding, and loan/annuity payment analyses. In addition, all programs are enhanced with better solution methods, display, and printing. For example, numerous probability functions are added in the programs such as INVT, INVT2, and QSIM. QSIM now handles multi-stage, multi-customer, and multi-channel queuing systems. QUEUE not only computes queuing performance but also analyzes costs. TSFC now performs time series forecasting and general linear regression.

Uniform Spreadsheet-type Data Entry: All programs use a uniform spreadsheet-type format to enter the problem. Now you can enter variable names, node names, matrix-type data, network connections, and so on with a uniform spreadsheet format that uses a consistent control mechanism.

We have tried to organize the software and manual with a more logical sequence. Mathematical programming methods including LP, ILP, GP, QP, NLP, and DP programs are presented first, followed by network-type algorithms including TRP, ASTS, SNET, CNET, and CPM programs. The probabilistic models including INVT, INVT2, QUEUE, QSIM, DA, MKV, TSFC, and FA programs are presented in the last chapters.

For the manual, Chapter 1 introduces the QSB+ 3.0, and Chapter 2 describes the user interface. If you are not familiar with QSB+ and/or window-type interface, we highly recommend you walk through the tutorial sections in Chapter 2. Chapters 3 to 21 present each individual program module. We have tried to describe each module as independently as possible so that you don't need to cross-refer to other chapters. However, we have also tried to omit redundant information as much as we can. Each module-related chapter contains the program introduction, technical information, brief tutorial examples, and exercises. Selected exercise solutions are listed in the Appendix.

We are certainly indebted to many professors and users who provided valuable suggestions and comments from using the earlier versions of QSB and QSB+ programs. The quality of the product is dedicated to them. We would like to thank Valerie Ashton, Editor-in-Chief at Prentice Hall, for her efforts and arrangement to improve the quality and the speed of the publication of QSB+ 3.0. We also would like to thank Lisa Kinne and the entire Production team for careful preparation of the final product.

1

INTRODUCTION TO QSB+ 3.0

QSB+ 3.0 (Quantitative Systems for Business Plus, Version 3.0) is an interactive, user-friendly decision support system that covers most topics and methods in management science. The primary purpose of QSB+ 3.0 is to assist the instructor in teaching these topics and to provide the student with a friendly way to learn and solve problems. QSB+ 3.0 makes these topics less intimidating by letting students gain hands-on experience in problem solving. However, QSB+ 3.0 also has the capacity to assist practitioners in addressing problems of moderate size.

SPECIAL FEATURES

User-friendly: QSB+ 3.0 is specially designed both for those who have no experience in solving quantitative business problems on a personal computer as well as for those who are familiar with personal computers but do not want to do any computer programming. The information and messages presented in QSB+ 3.0 are easy to understand. For the decision maker, QSB+ 3.0 displays brief solutions to the problems; for management scientists and students, QSB+ 3.0 can display detailed and understandable intermediate steps in the solution of problems.

Menu-driven: QSB+ 3.0 uses a menu-driven structure that enables users to recognize the options available to address a problem. By using a mouse or keyboard, users can pull down menus to enter a new problem, read an existing problem, modify an existing problem, solve a problem, display the solution, change setup, or choose another program. Several options also have associated submenus to direct the user.

Easy data entry and modification: QSB+ 3.0 enables users to enter data from the keyboard or read data from a disk(ette) if the data have been stored. Spreadsheet full-screen editing is employed for the problem data entry. Therefore, users who have studied the basic concepts of management science will find that problem structuring and data entry are easy with QSB+ 3.0. Every program has the capacity to modify or save an existing problem.

CONTENTS OF QSB+ 3.0

QSB+ 3.0 covers the majority of popular topics in management science. The problem size that can be handled by QSB+ 3.0 depends on the memory in your computer. The following provides an overview of the topics (programs) and capabilities covered by QSB+ 3.0.

1. Linear programming (LP):

Uses the revised simplex method to solve, for example, 100 by 100 linear programming problems with 20% nonzero coefficients. Special features of LP are:

- **a.** Spreadsheet or free-format data entry
- **b.** Graphic solution and sensitivity analysis for two-variable problems
- **c.** Upper-bounding method when bounds exist
- **d.** Re-inversion to reduce rounded error
- **e.** Scaling data to reduce rounded error
- **f.** Displaying detailed simplex tableaus
- **g.** Displaying sensitivity analysis

2. Integer linear programming (ILP):

Uses the branch-and-bound procedure to solve, for example, 100 by 100 linear mixed integer programming problems with 10% nonzero coefficients. Special features of ILP are:

- **a.** Spreadsheet or free-format data entry
- **b.** Newest and best bounds for branch selection
- **c.** Upper-bounding method when bounds exist
- **d.** Re-inversion to reduce rounded error
- **e.** Scaling data to reduce rounded error
- **f.** Displaying detailed branching nodes and bounds

3. Goal programming (GP):

Uses the multiphase simplex method to solve linear systems with prioritized multiple objective functions. Special features of GP are:

- **a.** Spreadsheet or free-format data entry
- **b.** Upper-bounding method when bounds exist
- **c.** Re-inversion to reduce rounded error
- **d.** Scaling data to reduce rounded error
- **e.** Displaying sensitivity analysis

4. Quadratic programming (QP):

Uses the modified simplex method to solve linear systems with quadratic objective function. Special features of QP are:

a. Spreadsheet or free-format data entry
b. Upper-bounding method when bounds exist
c. Re-inversion to reduce rounded error
d. Scaling data to reduce rounded error
e. Analyzing the objective function matrix

5. Nonlinear programming (NLP):

Solves nonlinear problems with or without constraints. Special features of NLP are:

a. Spreadsheet and free-format data entry
b. Line search for unconstrained problems
c. Penalty function method for constrained problems

6. Dynamic programming (DP):

Solves the stagecoach, knapsack, and production and inventory control problems. Special features of DP are:

a. Spreadsheet format for data entry
b. Displaying solution steps

7. Transportation and transshipment problems (TRP):

Uses the modified distribution method to solve transportation and transshipment problems. Special features of TRP are:

a. Spreadsheet or free-format data entry
b. Maximizing or minimizing objective
c. Eight initial solution methods
d. Fractional supplies or demands are allowed
e. Displaying detailed tableaus

8. Assignment and traveling salesman problems (ASTS):

Uses the Hungarian method to solve assignment problems, and uses branch-and-bound procedure to solve traveling salesman problems. Special features of ASTS are:

a. Spreadsheet or free-format data entry
b. Maximizing or minimizing objective

- **c.** Displaying detailed tableaus
- **d.** Quick heuristic method for solving traveling salesman problems
- **e.** Displaying branching nodes for traveling salesman problems

9. Specialized network modeling (SNET):

Solves the shortest route, minimal spanning tree, and maximal flow problems. Special features of SNET are:

- **a.** Spreadsheet format for data entry
- **b.** Special and efficient algorithms for different problem types
- **c.** Displaying detailed solution steps

10. Capacitated network modeling (CNET):

Solves general capacitated network problems. Special features of CNET are:

- **a.** Spreadsheet format for data entry
- **b.** Maximizing or minimizing objective
- **c.** Special network simplex for solving problems
- **d.** Allows flow capacities, that is, lower and upper bounds

11. Project scheduling - CPM/PERT:

Solves project scheduling with up to 1500 activities. Special features are:

- **a.** Spreadsheet matrix format for data entry
- **b.** Solves multiple critical path project scheduling (CPM/PERT)
- **c.** Performs crashing analysis for certain activity duration projects
- **d.** Simplex method to solve the optimal crashing schedule
- **e.** Performs probability analysis for uncertain activity duration projects
- **f.** Allows specifying different distributions for activity durations
- **g.** Allows multiple starts or endings

12. Inventory theory (INVT):

Solves EOQ, EOQ with discount, and newsboy problems. Special features of INVT are:

- **a.** Displaying inventory cost curve
- **b.** Incremental or total unit discounts
- **c.** Discounted or constant holding cost
- **d.** Nine distributions or discrete values for newsboy stochastic demands

13. Inventory theory 2 (INVT2):

Solves fixed-order-quantity (FOQ), fixed-order-interval (FOI), and optional replenishment (OR) inventory systems. Special features of INVT2 are:

- **a.** Searches for the best solution to minimize the related costs
- **b.** Detailed cost analysis
- **c.** Nine distributions or discrete values for the stochastic demands

14. Queuing theory (QUEUE):

Analyzes queuing problems such as *M/M/1, M/G/1, D/M/1, M/M/s, M/M/s/N, M/M/s//K, M/M/s/N/K, M/G/infinity, M(b)/M/1,* and *M/M/s/s* problems. Special features of QUEUE are:

- **a.** Pressure services and discouraged arrivals for the M/M systems
- **b.** Displaying popular performance data
- **c.** Displaying probabilities

15. Queuing system simulation (QSIM):

Simulates multiple-stage queuing systems. Special features of QSIM are:

- **a.** Multiple-stage service and queuing systems with discrete events
- **b.** Allows assembly or split operations
- **c.** Thirteen distributions for arrival, service, and batch-size patterns
- **d.** Bulk arrival is allowed
- **e.** User specification for simulation time, data collection starting time, number of observations, and random number
- **f.** Spreadsheet format for data entry
- **g.** Displaying popular performance data

16. Decision analysis (DA):

Solves Bayesian analysis, payoff analysis, and decision tree. Special features are:

- **a.** Spreadsheet format for data entry
- **b.** Displaying solution steps
- **c.** Six criteria for payoff analysis

17. Markov process (MKV):

Performs Markov process. Special features of MKV are:

a. Spreadsheet format for data entry
b. Displaying each Markov step

18. Time series forecasting (TSFC):

Performs time series forecasting using different methods. Special features are:

a. Methods such as simple average, weighted moving average, moving average with linear trend, single exponential smoothing, exponential smoothing with linear trend, double exponential smoothing, double exponential smoothing with linear trend, adaptive exponential smoothing, linear regression, and Winter's model
b. Graphic display for the forecasting results
c. Detailed analysis for the model
d. Optimal search for the model parameters
e. Four performance measures

19. Financial analysis (FA):

Performs investment analysis, annuity, compounding, and loan annuity payment. Special features of FA are:

a. Spreadsheet format for data entry
b. Six popular criteria for investment analysis
c. Allows continuous compounding
d. Displaying cash flow

QSB+ 3.0 IN INSTRUCTION AND LEARNING

Most of the programs in QSB+ 3.0 have an optional ability to display detailed solution procedures. This option can help both instructors and students by making algorithms easier to explain and understand. For example, when using the simplex method to solve the following linear programming model, the LP program can display every simplex tableau, and the associated entering and leaving variables. Fig. 1-1 shows the first iteration of the simplex method to solve the following problem. (For more information, see Chapter 3, "Linear Programming.")

Maximize: $4\ X_1 + 6\ X_2 + 3\ X_3$
Subject to:

$$1.5\ X_1 + 2\ X_2 + 4\ X_3 \leq 550$$
$$2\ X_1 + 3\ X_2 + 1\ X_3 \leq 300$$

X_1, X_2 and X_3 are nonnegative.

Iteration 1

		X1	X2	X3	S1	S2	
Basis	c(j)	4	6	3	0	0	RHS
S1	0	1.5	2	4	1	0	550
S2	0	2	3	1	0	1	300
c(j)-Z(j)		4	6	3	0	0	0
* Big M		0	0	0	0	0	0

Current OBJ (Max.) = 0 IN: X2 OUT: S2

< Next > < Skip > < PgLt > < PgRt > < HardCopy > < Cancel >

Figure 1-1. Simplex iteration 1 for the sample LP problem.

QSB+ 3.0 IN DECISION MAKING

Management science is widely used in business decision making. Consider the following example: ABC Oil Company has three oil storage depots and four demand points for oil. Management wants a shipping schedule that minimizes the total transportation cost and does not exceed storage capacities. Assume that capacities and cost information are given as shown in Table 1-1. The modified distribution method (transportation simplex) is usually used to solve this type of problem. By using the TRP program of QSB+ 3.0, management can determine the optimal shipping schedule very quickly. Fig. 1-2 displays the solution for the ABC shipping problem.

Table 1-1. Capacities and unit costs for ABC Company.

	Demand point				
Storage	Dallas	Kansas	Tampa	Miami	Supply
Boston	5	4	5	6	100
Denver	3	3	6	6	200
Austin	2	5	7	8	400
Demand	200	100	150	250	

Solution for ABC

08-22-1993 22:44:53 Page: 1 of 1

From	To	Shipment	@ Cost/Profit	Opport. Cost
Boston	Tampa	100	5	0
Denver	Kansas	100	3	0
Denver	Miami	100	6	0
Austin	Dallas	200	2	0
Austin	Tampa	50	7	0
Austin	Miami	150	8	0

Minimized OBJ = 3350 Iteration = 4 Elapsed CPU seconds = 0

< PageDown > < PageUp > < Hardcopy > < Cancel >

Figure 1-2. Solution for the ABC shipping problem.

GETTING STARTED WITH QSB+ 3.0

These sections cover the conventions and procedures you need to get started. It is important to follow the information below if you are a first-time user of QSB+ 3.0.

Required Equipment

QSB+ 3.0 is designed to run on the IBM personal computer and compatibles with the DOS or MS DOS operating system. It requires 640K memory and at least one disk(ette) drive. A printer needs to be connected if you will print the output. A color graphic monitor is preferred. A higher version of DOS or MS DOS is recommended.

QSB+ 3.0 Diskettes

QSB+ 3.0 is shipped with two 3.5" high-density floppy diskettes. The following lists the programs in each disk.

QSB+ 3.0 (1):

1. TMSRE.FON (Font file)
2. QSBSETUP.XXX (Printer and display setup file)
3. QSRTEFR.EXE (Run time module for all programs)
4. QSB.EXE (Main Program)

5. LP.EXE (Linear Programming)
6. ILP.EXE (Integer Linear Programming)
7. GP.EXE (Goal Programming)
8. QP.EXE (Quadratic Programming)
9. NLP.EXE (Nonlinear Programming)
10. DP.EXE (Dynamic Programming)
11. TRP.EXE (Transportation and Transshipment Problems)
12. ASTS.EXE (Assignment and Traveling Salesman Problems)
13. SNET.EXE (Specialized Network Modeling)
14. CNET.EXE (Capacitated Network Flow Modeling)
15. CPM.EXE (Project Scheduling: CPM/PERT)

QSB+ 3.0 (2):

1. TMSRE.FON (Font file)
2. QSBSETUP.XXX (Printer and display setup file)
3. QSRTEFR.EXE (Run time module for all programs)
4. QSB.EXE (Main Program)
5. INVT.EXE (Inventory Theory)
6. INVT2.EXE (Inventory Theory 2)
7. QUEUE.EXE (Queuing Theory)
8. QSIM.EXE (Queuing System Simulation)
9. DA.EXE (Decision Analysis)
10. MKV.EXE (Markov Process)
11. TSFC.EXE (Time Series Forecasting)
12. FA.EXE (Financial Analysis)

Making a Backup

If you just purchased QSB+ 3.0, you should make a backup copy by following the user's guide of your computer. Always keep the original in a safe place.

Copying QSB+ 3.0 to Your Hard Disk

If you have a hard disk in your computer, load the whole QSB+ 3.0 onto your hard disk and then use it from the hard disk. Here is the general procedure.

1. Create a new directory called "QSB".
2. Copy all files in QSB+ 3.0 (1) and QSB+ 3.0 (2) into the new directory.

Running QSB+ 3.0

If you have made the backup copy and are ready to use QSB+ 3.0, just type "QSB" from the DOS prompt and press the "Return" or the "Enter" key, and the QSB+ 3.0 will be loaded. You will be able to perform the desired tasks by following the instruction from the screen. In Chapter 2, we will provide detailed information of the QSB+ 3.0 user interface. A first-time user of QSB+ 3.0 is recommended to walk through Chapter 2.

2

USER INTERFACE AND TUTORIAL

This chapter covers the user interface used in QSB+ 3.0. If you are a first-time user of QSB+ 3.0, try the tutorial at the end of this chapter, which will quickly get you started.

USER INTERFACE

In the following sections, we will describe the basic mechanism to run programs, select items, enter data, and solve problems with QSB+ 3.0. We assume your computer is equipped with a mouse and a keyboard; however, if you have only a keyboard, that is fine. In the later sections, we will point out how to use the program when you have only a keyboard.

Interface Elements

QSB+ 3.0 uses four basic interface mechanisms to run the programs: pull-down menu, dialog window, spreadsheet window, and list box. They are described as follows. The detail of pull-down menu structure will be provided in the later section.

Pull-down menus: These contain the menu bar and the submenu elements. Fig. 2-1 displays the general menu bar for all modules, and Fig. 2-2 illustrates a submenu for input data. Menu items can be accessed using a mouse, access keys, or a combination of the "Alt", "Tab", and arrow keys. If your system is equipped with a mouse, drag the mouse cursor to whatever you want to select and press the left button to make the selection. Access keys are the keys on the menu bar that are highlighted when you press the "Alt" key. If you press a letter that is highlighted in a menu title, that menu will be selected. Once a pull-down menu is displayed, each menu item also has a highlighted letter associated with each choice. Press the letter that corresponds to the menu item you want to select. Once a menu is shown, you may also use arrow keys to move the selection and press the "Enter" key to select the item. If you change your mind after pressing "Alt", press the "Alt" key again or the "Esc" key to cancel.

Figure 2-1. General menu bar.

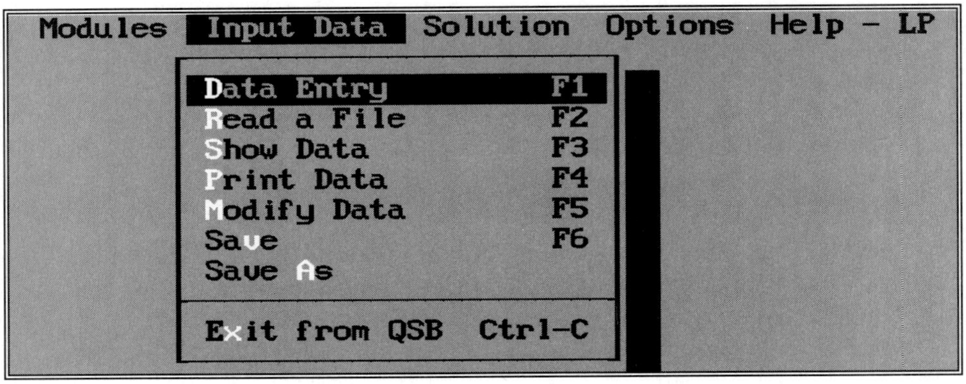

Figure 2-2. Input data submenu.

Dialog window: This may contain instructional or output information, edit fields (data fields), option buttons, and command buttons. Fig. 2-3 illustrates the instructional window which describes the edit keys for data entry. Fig. 2-4 shows a problem specification dialog window which contains information, data fields, and buttons. Fig. 2-5 displays a solution output dialog window. The basic components in a dialog window are described as follows.

- *Instructional or output information:* The instructional message tells about the data entry fields. The output information usually displays the problem solution. The top part of Fig. 2-4 illustrates the instructional information.
- *Edit field (data field):* It is contained by "[ ]" in which you can enter the data for that particular field. Use the "Tab", "shift+Tab", or "Enter" key or the mouse to move along the edit fields. Problem name, number of variables, and number of constraints of Fig. 2-4 are edit (data) fields.
- *Option button:* "( )" is followed by the option. You may click a particular option by using the mouse or the arrow keys to choose among different options. The "Tab", "shift+Tab", or "Enter" key or the mouse will let you move along different optional areas. Note that the selected option is presented by the "(*)" button. Objective function in Fig. 2-4 has two options: ( ) Maximization or ( ) Minimization. Only one can be chosen.
- *Command button:* "< >" contains the commands. Use the "Tab" key or "shift+Tab" key or the mouse to move along different command buttons. Press the "Enter" key or double click the selected button for the desired command. Note that the selected command button is usually highlighted. Fig. 2-4 has three command buttons: < OK >, < Print >, and < Cancel >.

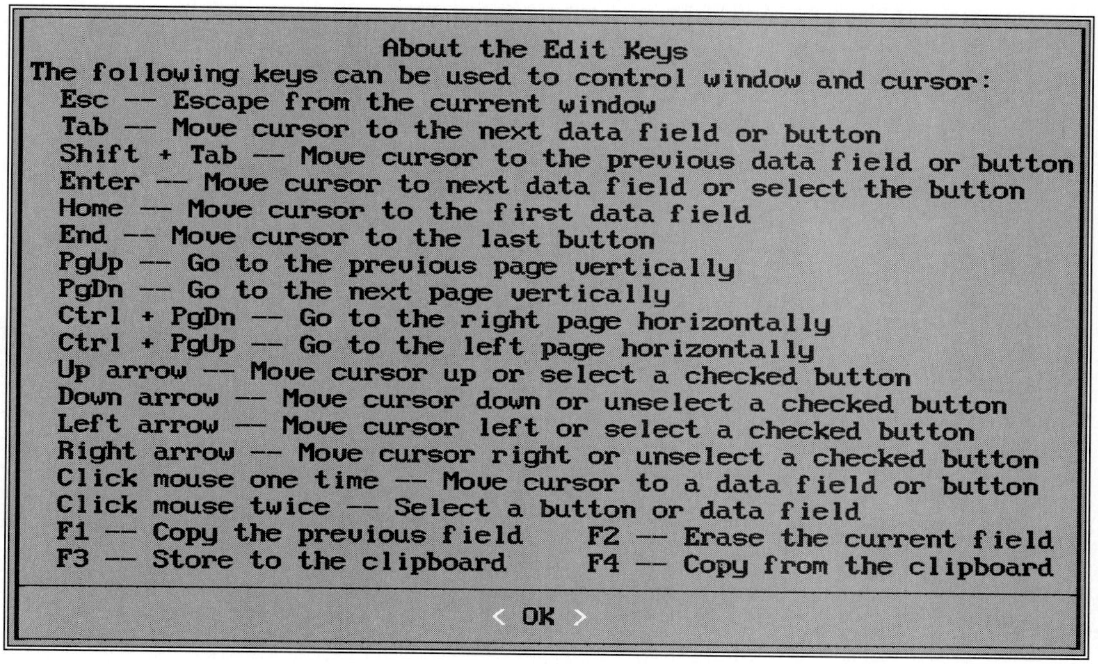

Figure 2-3. An example dialog window - the keys used for editing.

In the following list are the keys used to control cursor, data entry, and to select buttons in the QSB+ 3.0 windows. "+" means to press the keys simultaneously.

Esc:	Escape from the current window
Tab:	Move cursor to the next data field or button
Shift + Tab:	Move cursor to the previous data field or button
Enter:	Move cursor to next data field or select the button
Home:	Move cursor to the first data field
End:	Move cursor to the last button
PgUp:	Go to the previous page vertically
PgDn:	Go to the next page vertically
Ctrl + PgDn:	Go to the right page horizontally
Ctrl + PgUp:	Go to the left page horizontally
Up arrow:	Move cursor up or select a checked button
Down arrow:	Move cursor down or unselect a checked button
Left arrow:	Move cursor left or select a checked button
Right arrow:	Move cursor right or unselect a checked button
Click mouse one time:	Move cursor to a data field or button

Click mouse twice:	Select a button or data field
F1:	Copy the previous data field
F2:	Erase the current data field
F3:	Store the current data field to the clipboard
F4:	Copy from the clipboard to the current data field

```
Problem Specification

 · Enter the following fields to define your problem and
   specify the entry format for your model.
 · The default constraint directions are < (≤) for maximization
   problems and > (≥) for minimization problems.  However, you
   may enter any of ≤, <, <=, =<, ≥, >, >=, =>, and = to
   specify a particular constraint's direction.
 · The default variables' bounds are from 0 to infinity.

Problem Name?                                      [LPExample          ]
Number of variables (excluding slacks/artificials)?   [3               ]
Number of constraints (excluding bounds)?             [2               ]

Objective function:    (•) Maximization          ( ) Minimization

Variable name:         (•) Default (X1,...,Xn)   ( ) You define

Data entry format:     (•) Spreadsheet format    ( ) Free format

Variables' bounds:     (•) Default               ( ) You specify

        < OK >              < Print >             < Cancel >
```

Figure 2-4. An example dialog window - problem specification.

```
Solution Summary for LPExample
08-22-1993 22:53:13                                          Page: 1 of 1
```

Variable Number	Variable Name	Solution	Opportunity Cost	Minimum Obj. Coef.	Current Obj. Coef.	Maximum Obj. Coef.
2	X2	65	0	5.923077	6	9
3	X3	105	0	2	3	12

```
Maximized OBJ = 705  Iteration = 2  Elapsed CPU seconds = 0

   < PageDown >     < PageUp >      < Hardcopy >      < Cancel >
```

Figure 2-5. An example dialog window - solution output.

Spreadsheet window: This is the data input format for your problem. The spreadsheet window is a matrix format to contain your problem data. You may have multiple spreadsheet windows for different problem types when you use different program modules in QSB+ 3.0. A spreadsheet window contains edit (data) fields and command buttons. Fig. 2-6 illustrates the spreadsheet data entry for example LP constraints. Use the command buttons to control the spreadsheet. The control commands in a spreadsheet window are described as follows.

- PgDn (or OK): to go to the next page or next spreadsheet matrix
- PgUp: to go to the previous page
- PgLt: to go to the left side of the spreadsheet
- PgRt: to go to the right side of the spreadsheet
- Help: to recall the help information of the editing keys
- Print: to print the current screen of the spreadsheet
- Cancel: to leave the spreadsheet entry

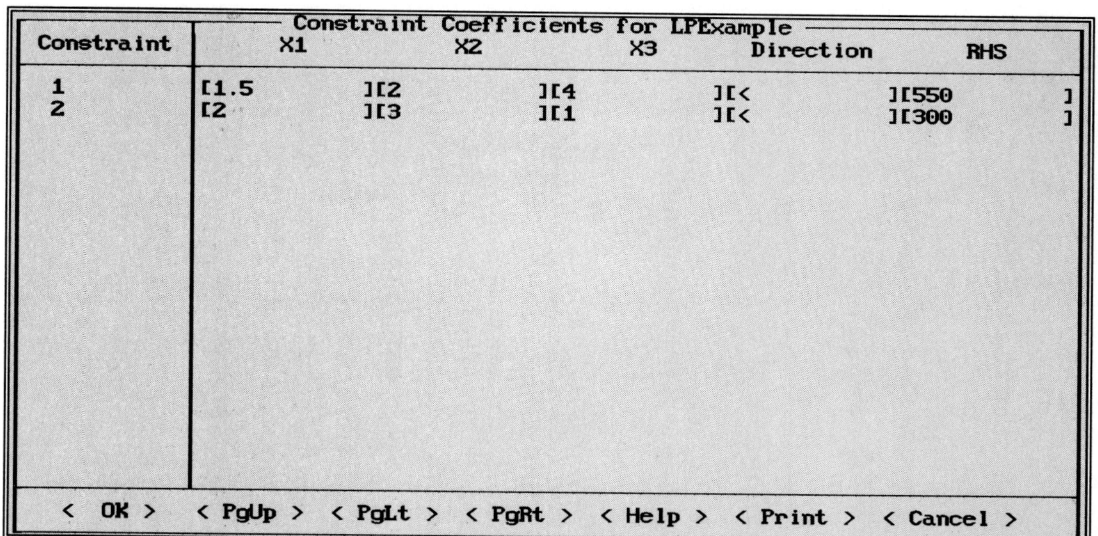

Figure 2-6. An example spreadsheet window - LP constraints.

List box: This is a list of items for selection. In QSB+ 3.0, it is used only for choosing a file name from a list. For example, if you choose option 2 from the input data menu in Fig. 2-3 to read a problem data from a file, the dialog window of Fig. 2-7 will be displayed. You may enter a particular file name and press the "Enter" key. The specified data file will then be read. Or you may use the wild card such as "*.DAT" and choose the "Select" command option and the program will give you a list of the file names such as shown in Fig. 2-8. Use the mouse or the "Tab" key to move to the file list, and use the mouse or up and down arrow keys to choose a file name and press the "Enter" key at the option you choose. The data of the specified file name will be read.

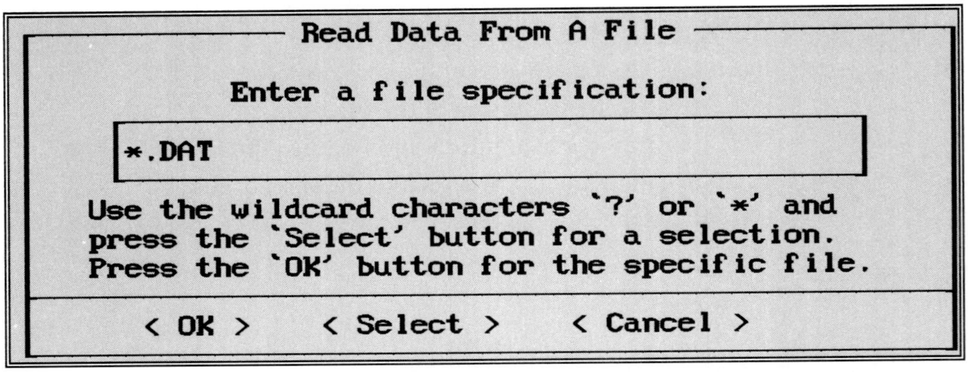

Figure 2-7. The dialog window for entering file name.

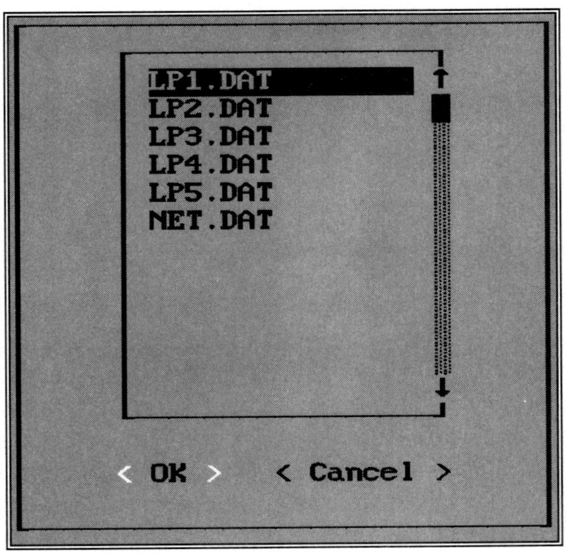

Figure 2-8. The list box for the possible data file names.

Menu Structure

QSB+ 3.0 incorporates the advantages of a pull-down menu structure so that users can follow the instructions on the screen without memorizing command names. This makes QSB+ 3.0 very user-friendly. The menu bar shown in Fig. 2-1 has the same items in all program modules. Each menu has the same subitems except solution. The solution submenu may be slightly different among modules because different modules may require a little bit different setups to solve different types of problems. Note that when a menu item is dim, it is not available at that moment. The menus are demonstrated as follows.

Modules: Fig. 2-9 shows the module menu. You may click an item from this menu to go to another program module. Note that you should use the "Alt" key and the highlighted letter or the combination of arrow keys and the "Enter" key to choose a particular module if you do not have a mouse.

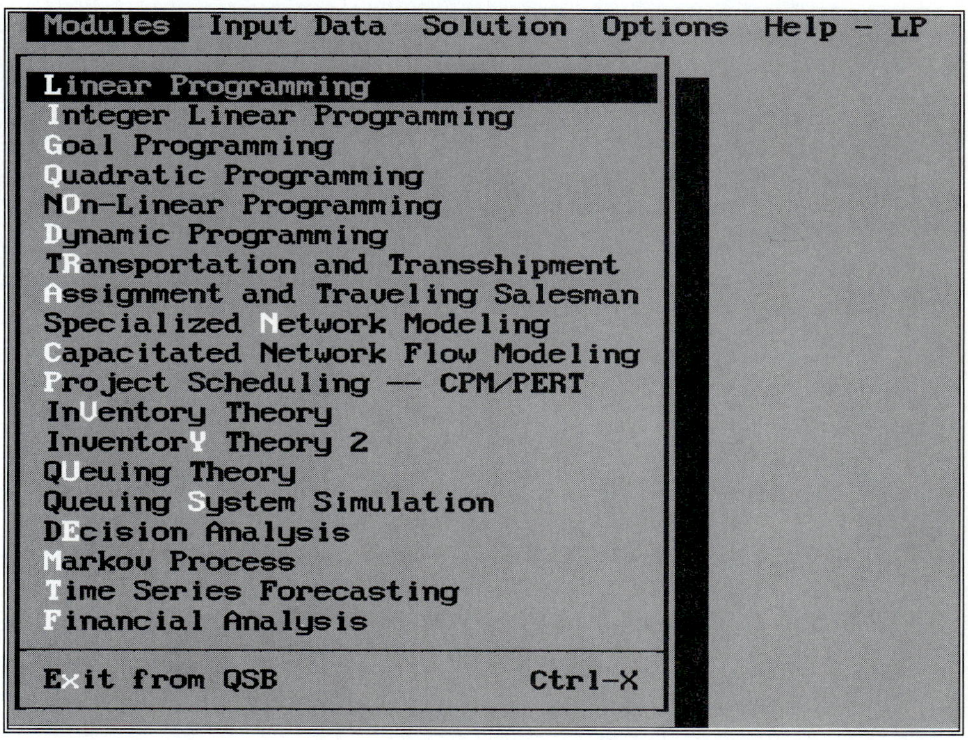

Figure 2-9. Module menu.

Input Data: Fig. 2-2 shows the input menu before entering a problem. You may click "Data Entry" to enter data from scratch or click "Read File" to read an existing problem from a file. After the problem has been entered or read, the input menu will look like Fig. 2-10. From that you may choose to modify, display, print, or save the problem. Again, use the "Alt" key and the highlighted letter or the combination of arrow keys and the "Enter" key to choose a particular option if you do not have a mouse. Input data menu includes the following items:

- Data Entry: Enter data from scratch.
- Read a File: Retrieve problem data from an ASCII file.
- Show Data: Show the problem data.
- Print Data: Print the problem to the specified output device.
- Modify Data: Modify the problem data.
- Save: Save the problem with the original file name.
- Save As: Save the problem with a specified file name.
- Exit from QSB: Quit the program.

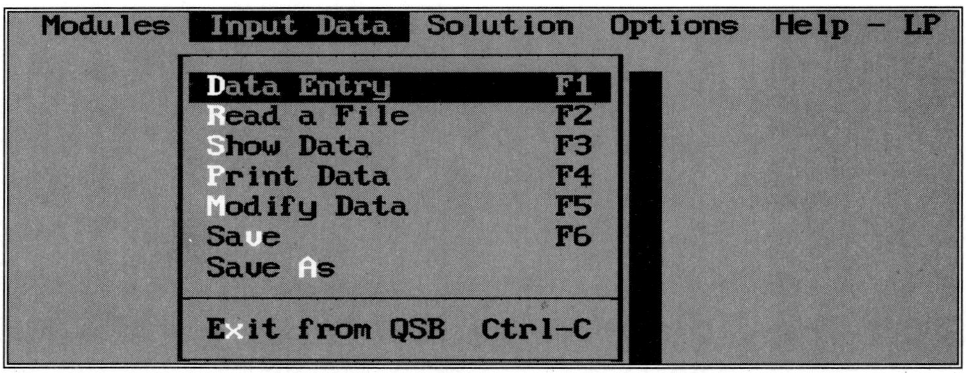

Figure 2-10. Input data menu after data entry.

Solution: After the problem has been entered, the solution menu will look like Fig. 2-11. From that you may choose to solve the problem. In most modules, the option to solve a problem in detailed steps is provided. After the problem has been solved, the solution menu will look like Fig. 2-12. From that you may choose to display, print, or save the solution. The basic items in the solution menu usually include:

- Solve the Problem.
- Show the Solution.
- Print the Solution.
- Save the Solution. Save the solution in an ASCII file.

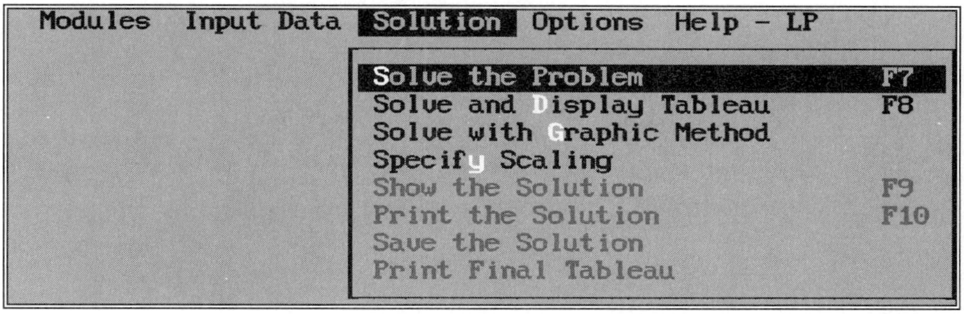

Figure 2-11. Solution menu before solving the problem.

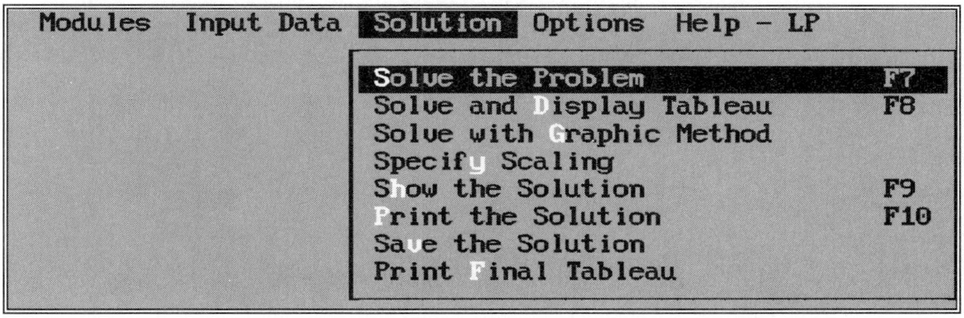

Figure 2-12. Solution menu after solving the problem.

Options: This includes the option to change the screen mode to either color or monochrome and to specify the printer type. Fig. 2-13 shows the options. The options include:

- Color: Change the screen to color mode.
- Monochrome: Change the screen to monochrome mode.
- Printer Selection: Specify the printing device.
- Refresh the Module Menu: It is important to refresh the module menu when you switch from QSB+(1) disk to QSB+(2) disk and vice versa.

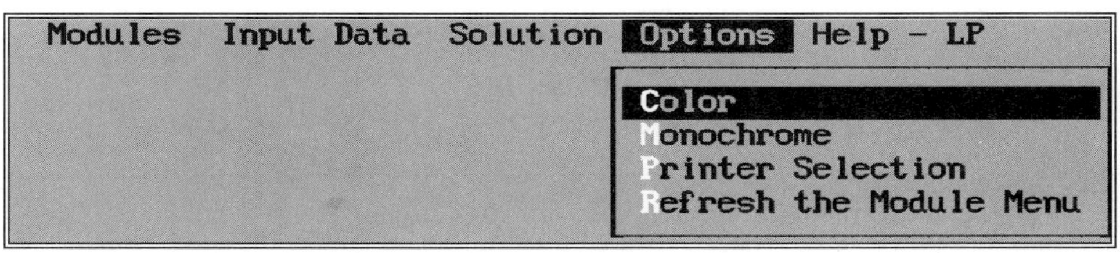

Figure 2-13. Option menu.

Help: This includes the overview information of the particular module, user interface, and edit keys. Fig. 2-14 shows the options. The options include:

- Help about the module: Show the basic information of the module.
- About the User Interface: Describe how to use menus, windows, boxes, and so on.
- About the Edit Keys: Describe the keys used for data entry.

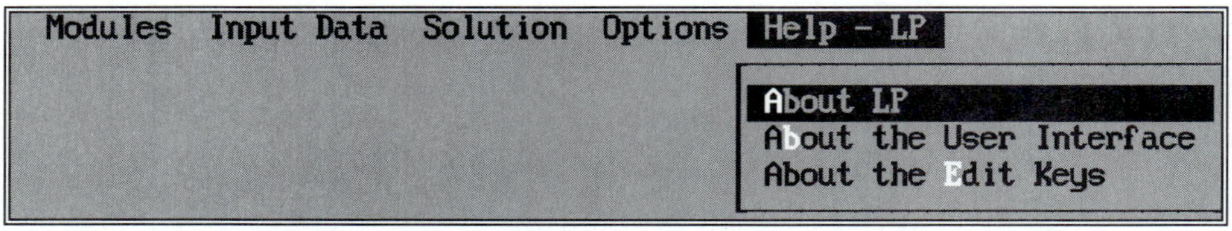

Figure 2-14. Help menu.

Shortcut Keys to Select Menu Item

QSB+ 3.0 provides some shortcut keys to speed up the menu item selection. The shortcut keys are described as follows.

- Ctrl + X: Press the "Ctrl" and "X" keys simultaneously to quit the program.
- Ctrl + C: Press the "Ctrl" and "C" keys simultaneously to quit the program.
- F1: Press the "F1" key to start the data entry.
- F2: Press the "F2" key to read the problem data from a file.
- F3: Press the "F3" key to show the problem data.
- F4: Press the "F4" key to print the problem data.
- F5: Press the "F5" key to modify the problem data.
- F6: Press the "F6" key to save the problem data.
- F7: Press the "F7" key to solve the problem.
- F8: Press the "F8" key to solve the problem and display steps.
- F9: Press the "F9" key to show the problem solution.
- F10: Press the "F10" key to print the problem solution.

TUTORIAL

In the following sections, we will use the LP module as an example to "tour" the user interface of QSB+ 3.0. The procedure will be the same or very similar for the rest of the modules. Therefore, the detailed tutorial will not be repeated in the later chapters. First, we describe the general steps using QSB+ 3.0 to solve a problem.

Problem Solving with QSB+ 3.0

The following procedure describes the general steps when you use QSB+ 3.0 to solve a problem:

Step 1. Prepare the problem and start the program: Understand and formulate your problem and load the QSB+ 3.0 program.

Step 2. Enter or read a problem through the input data menu.

Step 3. Save the problem through the input data menu for later use.

Step 4. Display or print the problem through the input data menu to verify it.

Step 5. Modify the problem through the input data menu if necessary. You may perform several kinds of modifications, such as changing the number of variables and changing the number of constraints on your problem when necessary. Each module of QSB+ 3.0 generally supports many options to change the problem data.

Step 6. Solve the problem through the solution menu. You may choose to display the solution steps such as the simplex tableau of the linear programming. Multiple alternatives are generally available in each module of QSB+ 3.0 to solve problems.

Step 7. Display, print, or save the solution through the solution menu.

Step 8. Leave the program. After you finish solving the problem, quit the program through the "Modules" or "Input Data" menu.

Tutorial Example

We will use the following LP problem to demonstrate the process of running QSB+ 3.0 program modules. The tutorial procedure described below can be generalized to all modules.

Maximize: $4\ X_1 + 6\ X_2 + 3\ X_3$

Subject to:

$$1.5\ X_1 + 2\ X_2 + 4\ X_3 \leq 550$$
$$2\ X_1 + 3\ X_2 + 1\ X_3 \leq 300$$

X_1, X_2, and X_3 are nonnegative.

Step 1. Prepare the Problem and Start the Program

a. If QSB+ 3.0 has been stored in the hard disk, go to the subdirectory that contains QSB+ 3.0; otherwise, insert QSB+ 3.0 disk 1 (which contains the LP module) into drive A, and change to drive A by typing "A:" and pressing the "Enter" key.

b. Type "QSB" and press the "Enter" key. The QSB+ 3.0 welcome logo (Fig. 2-15) will be displayed in a few seconds. Press any key, and the introduction of QSB+ 3.0 will be shown as in Fig. 2-16. Press the Space Bar or "Enter" key, and the menu bar of Fig. 2-17 will be available for selecting the program. Note that you may also choose the items in the submenu of "Options" to change display and printer options or choose the items in the submenu of "Help" to obtain more information.

Figure 2-15. QSB+ 3.0 logo.

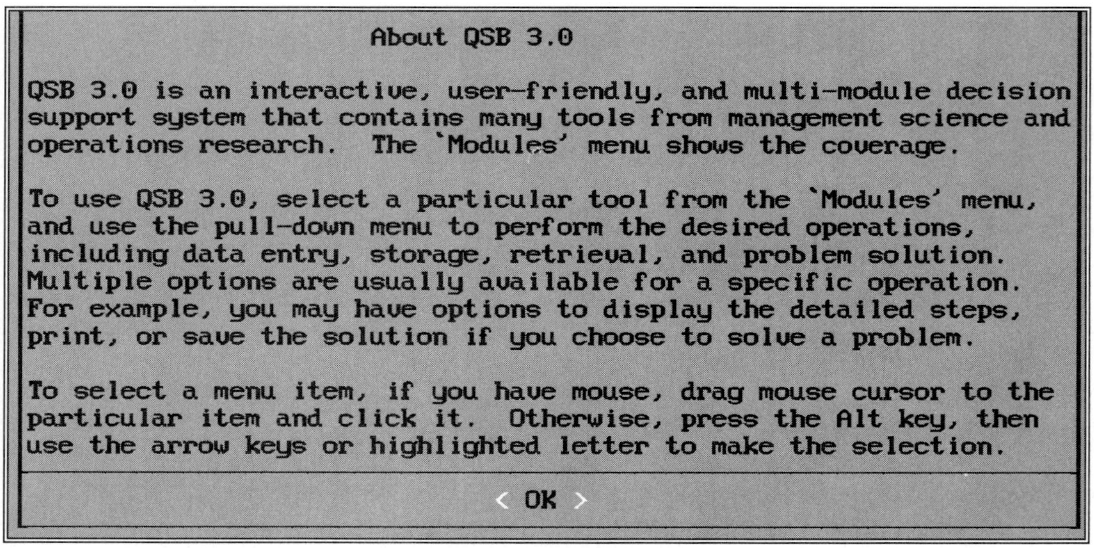
About QSB 3.0

QSB 3.0 is an interactive, user-friendly, and multi-module decision support system that contains many tools from management science and operations research. The 'Modules' menu shows the coverage.

To use QSB 3.0, select a particular tool from the 'Modules' menu, and use the pull-down menu to perform the desired operations, including data entry, storage, retrieval, and problem solution. Multiple options are usually available for a specific operation. For example, you may have options to display the detailed steps, print, or save the solution if you choose to solve a problem.

To select a menu item, if you have mouse, drag mouse cursor to the particular item and click it. Otherwise, press the Alt key, then use the arrow keys or highlighted letter to make the selection.

< OK >

Figure 2-16. QSB+ 3.0 introduction.

Figure 2-17. Main program menu bar.

c. Select the program module LP as shown in Fig. 2-18. Refer to previous sections for how to select an item from a pull-down menu. After choosing the LP program, the LP welcome logo will be displayed as shown in Fig. 2-19. Press any key, and the menu bar of Fig. 2-20 will become available.

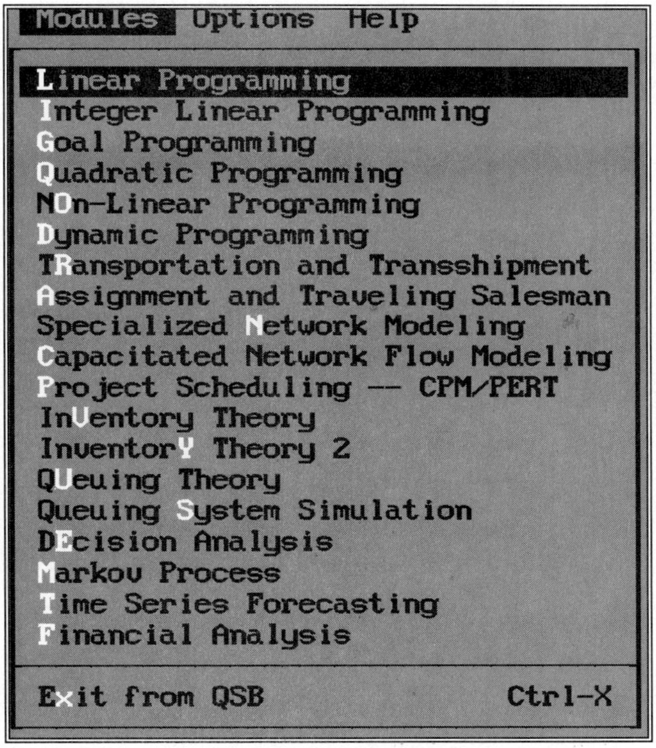

Figure 2-18. Select the LP module.

Figure 2-19. LP logo.

Figure 2-20. QSB+ 3.0 program module menu bar.

Step 2. Enter the Problem

a. Select "Data Entry" from the "Input Data" menu for entering the LP problem. Fig. 2-21 shows the selection. Note that you can also press the shortcut key F1 to select "Data Entry" from the menu bar. After "Data Entry" is selected, the data entry specification for the LP problem will be shown as in Fig. 2-22.

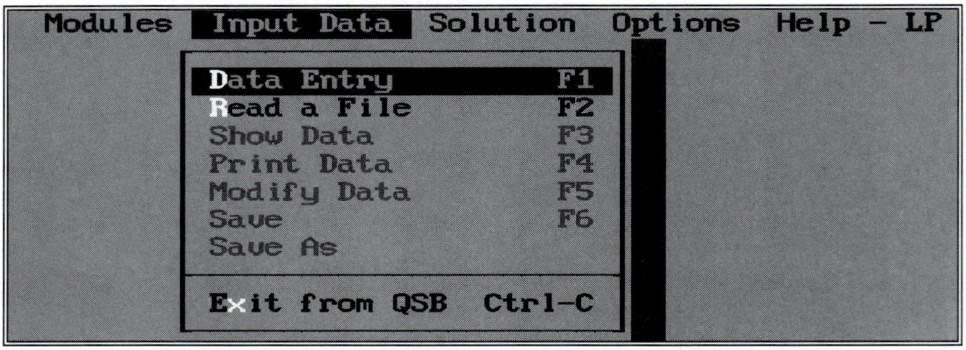

Figure 2-21. Select "Data Entry".

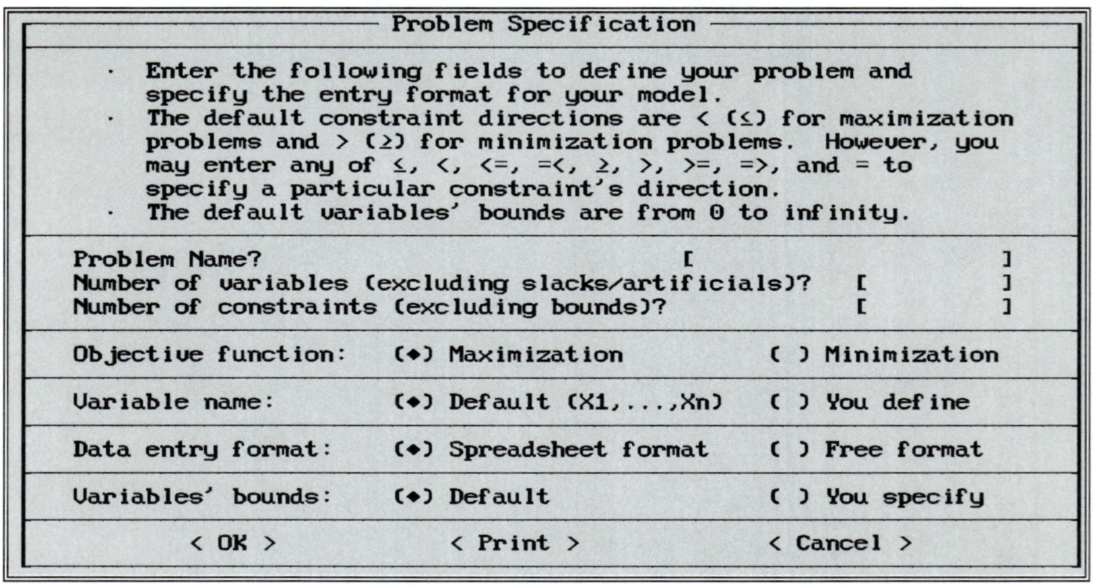

Figure 2-22. LP problem specification form.

b. Enter the required data and options to define the LP problem. Assume "Example" is the problem name. Fig. 2-23 shows the problem definition. Note that you may use the "Tab" and arrow keys in combination or use the mouse to specify an option button (e.g., < > Maximization or < > Minimization). When the entry is done, click "OK" to go to the next step.

c. Enter the objective function coefficients for "Example". Fig. 2-24 shows the entry. Note that the spreadsheet has seven command buttons:

- OK/PgDn: Finish the current page or go to next page vertically.
- PgUp: Go to previous page vertically.
- PgLt: Go to the left page horizontally.
- PgRt: Go to the right page horizontally.
- Help: Show the help information of the edit keys.
- Print: Print the current screen to the printer.
- Cancel: Quit the data entry.

When the entry is done, click "OK" to go to the next step.

d. Enter the constraint coefficients for "Example". Fig. 2-25 shows the entry. When the entry is done, click "OK".

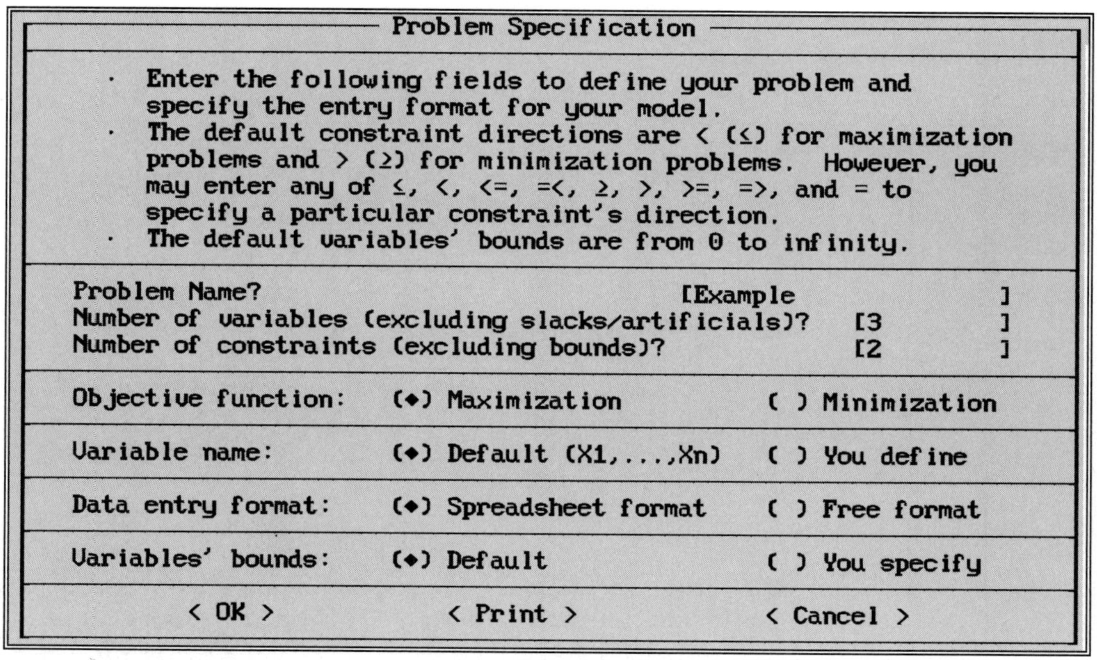

Figure 2-23. LP problem specification for the "Example".

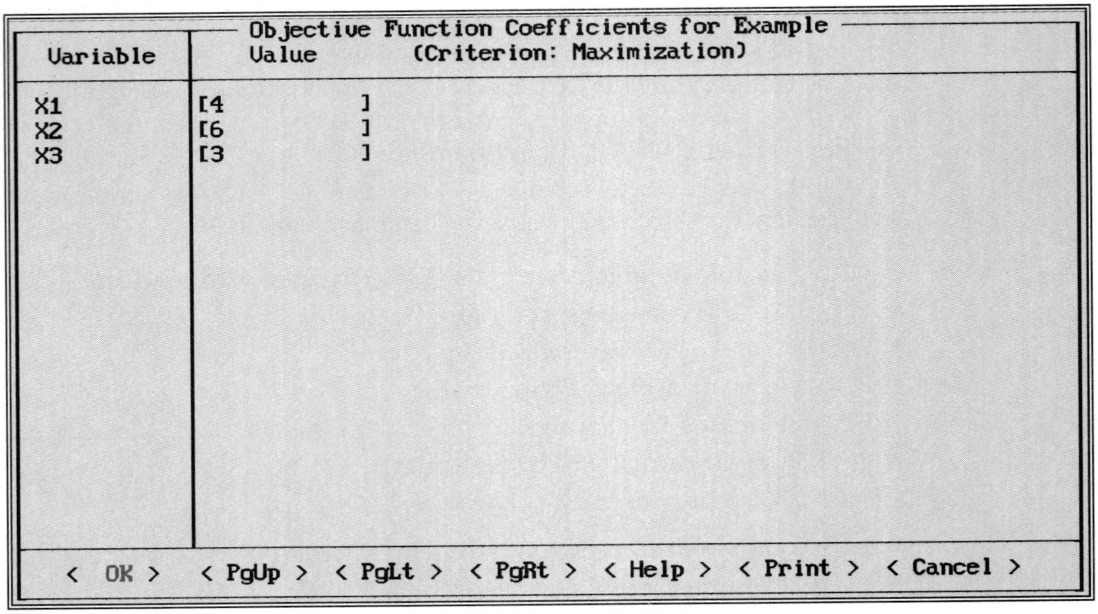

Figure 2-24. Coefficients of the objective function for "Example".

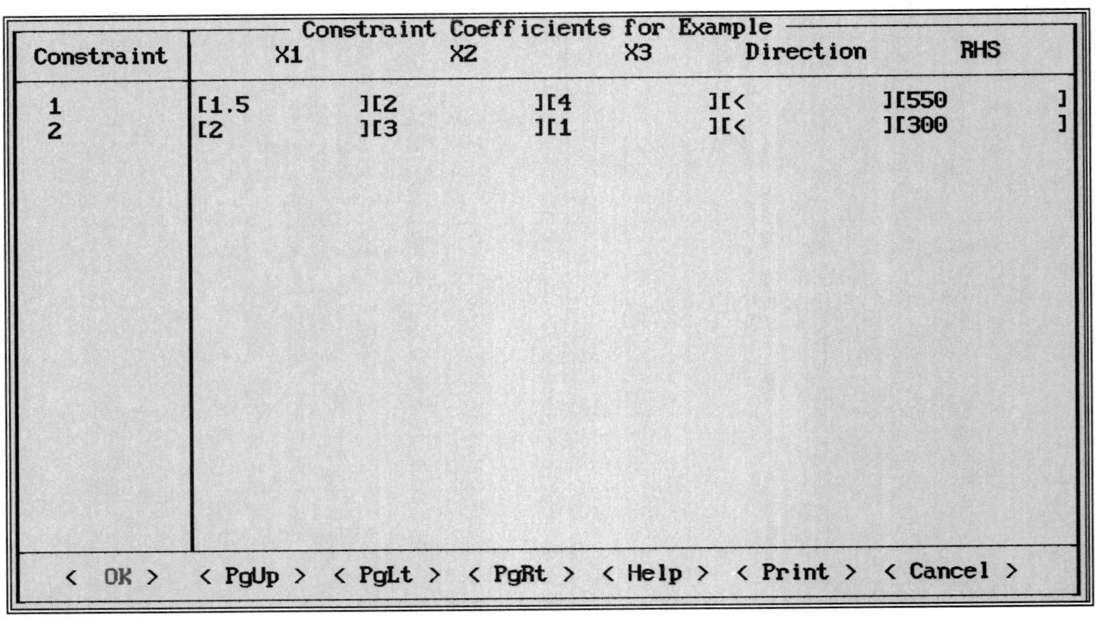

Figure 2-25. Coefficients of the constraints for "Example".

Step 3. Save the Problem (Optional)

After the problem has been entered into the program, it is a good idea to save it in a file in case you want to read it back through the option "Read a File". (You do not need to save the problem in order to solve it.) Fig. 2-26 shows the selection to save the problem. Fig. 2-27 shows the entry of a file name for the problem "Example". Click "OK" if the name is all right. The "Save" option differs from the "Save As" option. It will not ask a file name if it has been entered before and has saved the problem with that name. Note that the file name has two parts: at most eight characters before the period "." and at most three characters after the period.

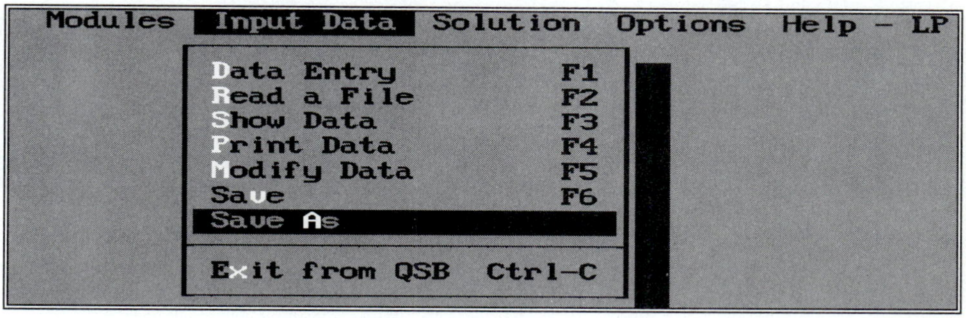

Figure 2-26. Select the "Save As" option.

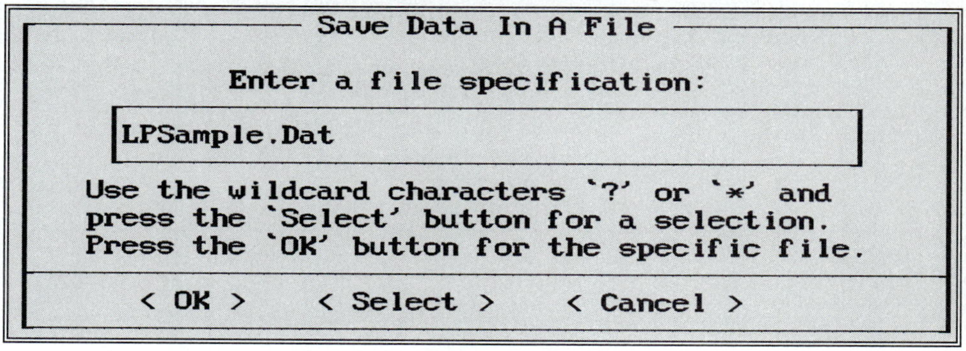

Figure 2-27. Enter the file name "LPSample.Dat".

Step 4. Display or Print the Problem (Optional)

After the problem has been entered into the program, you may want to display or print the problem and check if it has been entered correctly.

Step 5. Modify the Problem (Optional)

You may want to modify the problem after it has been entered into the program. Fig. 2-28 shows the selection to modify the problem. After choosing "Modify Data", Fig. 2-29 shows the options of modifying the problem "Example". Use the "Tab" and/or arrow keys or use the mouse to select the option and Click "OK"; otherwise, click "Cancel" to exit the menu.

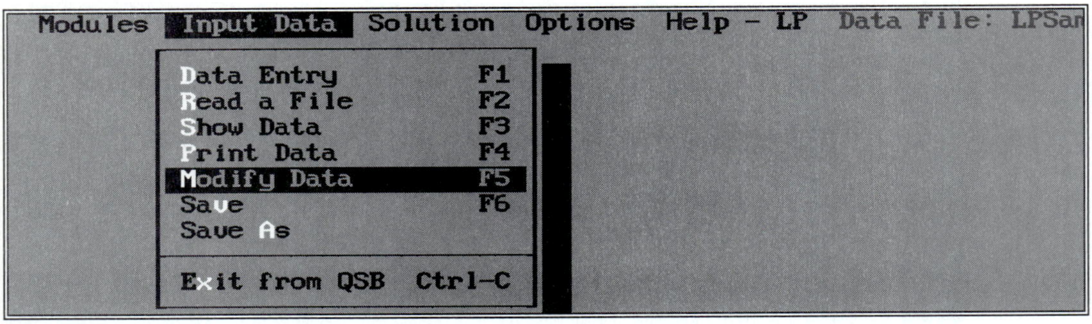

Figure 2-28. Select the "Modify Data" option.

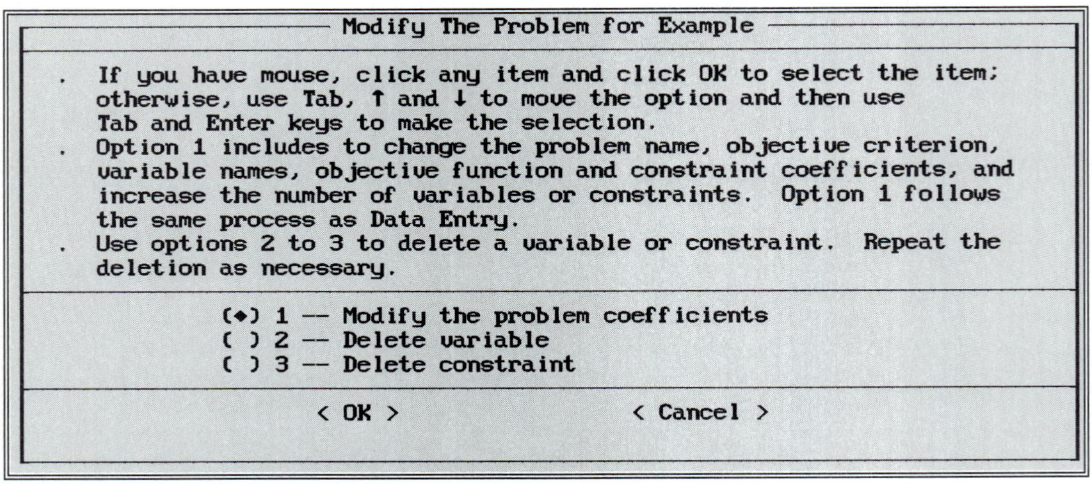

Figure 2-29. Menu for modifying LP problem.

Step 6. Solve the Problem

You can solve the problem after it has been entered into the program. Fig. 2-30 shows the options of solving the problem. In most of QSB+ 3.0 modules, there is an option of solving problems with a display of steps. If you choose to display the solution steps for this LP problem, the simplex tableau will be displayed. If "Solve the Problem" is selected, the message "Please standby . . ." will be shown as the problem is being solved.

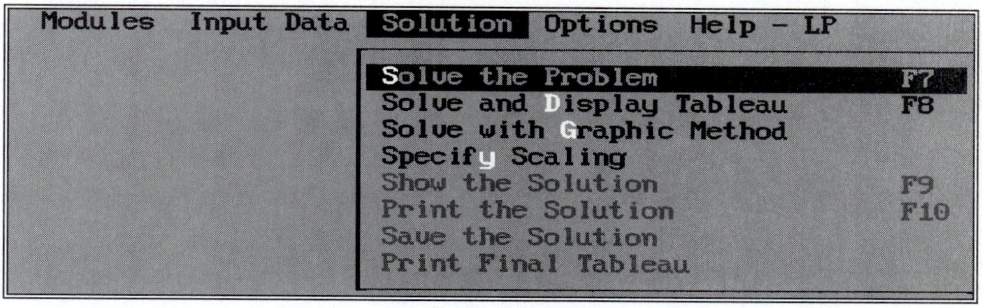

Fig. 2-30. Menu for solving the LP problem.

Step 7. Display, Print, or Save the Solution

After the problem has been solved, you can display, print, or save the solution. Fig. 2-31 shows the option to show the solution. The window in Fig. 2-32 lets you specify to display all or nonzero solution only. Fig. 2-33 and Fig. 2-34 show the solution of the "Example" LP problem. Note that there are four command options to control the display when the solution is being shown:

- PageDown: next page.
- PageUp: previous page.
- Hardcopy: copy the current screen to printer or a file.
- Cancel: quit display.

Step 8. Leave the Program

If you finish all tasks and want to quit the program, you may choose the last option of the "Modules" menu (Fig. 2-18) or the "Input Data" menu (Fig. 2-26), or press the shortcut key "Ctrl+X" or "Ctrl+C" to quit the program. If the problem data has not been saved, the program will confirm whether to save the data or not before it quits. Note that you may also choose any option in the "Modules" menu (Fig. 2-18) to go to another program module.

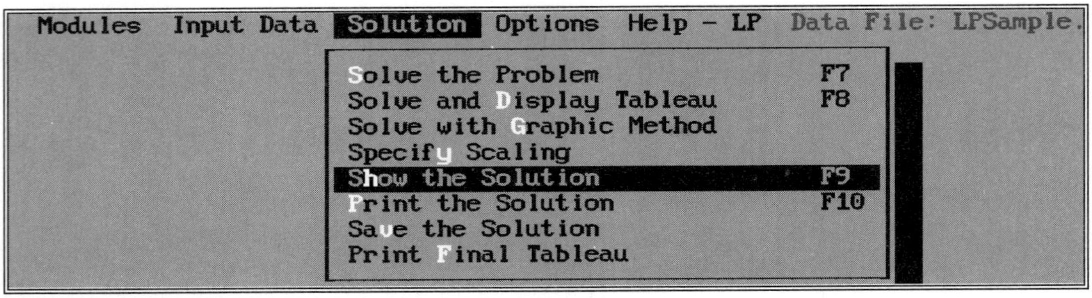

Figure 2-31. Select the option to display the solution.

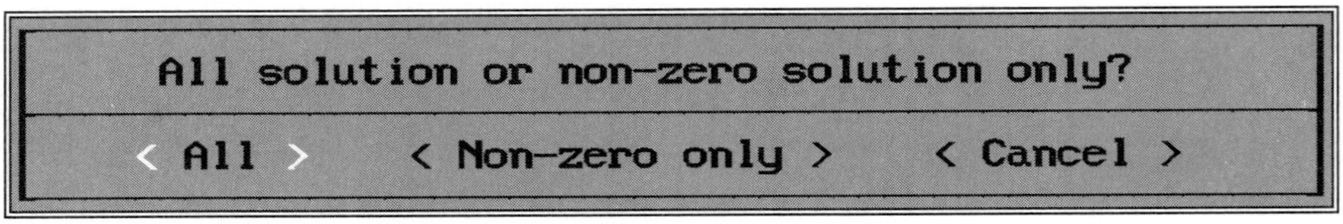

Figure 2-32. Options to specify displaying all or nonzero solution.

Solution Summary for Example

08-22-1993 23:28:28 Page: 1 of 1

Variable Number	Variable Name	Solution	Opportunity Cost	Minimum Obj. Coef.	Current Obj. Coef.	Maximum Obj. Coef.
1	X1	0	.05	-M	4	4.05
2	X2	65	0	5.923077	6	9
3	X3	105	0	2	3	12

Maximized OBJ = 705 Iteration = 2 Elapsed CPU seconds = 0

< PageDown > < PageUp > < Hardcopy > < Cancel >

Figure 2-33. The solution of "Example".

Constraint Summary for Example

08-22-1993 23:29:02 Page: 1 of 1

Constraint Number	Constraint Status	Shadow Price	Surplus	Minimum R. H. S.	Current R. H. S.	Maximum R. H. S.
1	Tight (≤)	.3	0	200	550	1200
2	Tight (≤)	1.8	0	137.5	300	825

Maximized OBJ = 705 Iteration = 2 Elapsed CPU seconds = 0

< PageDown > < PageUp > < Hardcopy > < Cancel >

Figure 2-34. Constraint analysis of "Example".

3

LINEAR PROGRAMMING (LP)

OVERVIEW OF THE LP DECISION SUPPORT SYSTEM

This program solves linear programming problems. You may set up the problem using the following format for data entry:

$$
\begin{array}{llllllllllll}
\text{Maximize:} & 3.2 & \text{GID1} & + & 4.0 & \text{GID2} & - & 5.0 & \text{GID3} & & \\
\text{Subject to:} & 4.0 & \text{GID1} & + & 2.5 & \text{GID2} & + & 3.0 & \text{GID3} & \leq & 50.0 \\
 & 3.6 & \text{GID1} & + & 7.0 & \text{GID2} & - & 2.5 & \text{GID3} & \leq & 86.9 \\
 & 15.7 & \text{GID1} & & & & + & 9.0 & \text{GID3} & = & 20.0
\end{array}
$$

All variables are assumed to be nonnegative.

You may specify free or spreadsheet format to enter your formulation and bounds. You can define variables with up to ten characters. Defaults are $X_1, X_2, \ldots,$ Xn. Problems can be saved on or read from a disk(ette). You can also display or print your problem and modify it as necessary. Furthermore, you can choose to display the detailed steps of the simplex method as the problem is being solved. The graphic solution and graphic sensitivity analysis are provided if the problem has only two variables. You may choose to print out the final solution and the sensitivity analysis.

TECHNICAL NOTES ON THE LP PROGRAM

1. The LP program uses the revised simplex method to solve problems. The upper-bounding method will be used to solve problems with specified upper or lower bounds of variables.
2. "Big M" will be used when you have "equality" or "greater than or equal to" constraints in your problem. LP does not give M a specific value but treats it as a false number and keeps updating the coefficients of M in the objective function.
3. If you choose to solve the problem with displaying tableau, the program will display the simplex tableau by iteration.

4. If the data in your problem have very wide-range values (e.g., 0.0001 and 10000), you may normalize some of the data. Otherwise, round-off errors may occur. LP does allow you to scale the model data in order to avoid round-off errors. However, the results including the final solution and sensitivity analysis are based on the original data.
5. Variables may have upper and lower bounds that can be entered as constraints or pure bounded values. The default bounds for each variable are 0 to infinity, which is represented by "M" in LP. However, the sensitivity analysis may produce slightly different results if you entered the bounds as constraints rather than as pure bounds.
6. All variables are assumed to be nonnegative. If you have some variables with nonpositive values in your problem, you should transform them to nonnegative variables. Bounds can be negative. In the case of a negative lower bound, the correspondent variable will be shifted left before the model is solved.
7. The LP and ILP programs use the same data file format to store or retrieve data. The LP program will skip the identification of the integer variables.
8. The size of problems that can be solved by LP depends on the problem structure. One example is that a 100 by 100 problem with 20% nonzero can be solved by QSB+ 3.0.
9. Besides the spreadsheet for data entry, LP also provides a free format to enter the model by commands. Help information is available. Select the spreadsheet or free-format data entry at the problem specification.
10. Some notations are used in displaying the intermediate steps and final results. They are as follows:

Sn:	Slack variable corresponds to constraint *n*
An:	Artificial variable corresponds to constraint *n*
RHS:	Right-hand side of a constraint
C(j):	Objective function coefficient of variable *j*
M:	Non-Archimedean large number
C(j)−Z(j):	Reduced cost (opportunity cost) of variable *j*

MENU STRUCTURE

The functions and options in each of the pull-down menus are hierarchically listed as follows:

Modules

- Linear Programming (LP)
- Integer Linear Programming (ILP)
- Goal Programming (GP)

- Quadratic Programming (QP)
- Nonlinear Programming (NLP)
- Dynamic Programming (DP)
- Transportation and Transshipment (TRP)
- Assignment and Traveling Salesman (ASTS)
- Specialized Network Modeling (SNET)
- Capacitated Network Flow Modeling (CNET)
- Project Scheduling: CPM/PERT
- Inventory Theory (INVT)
- Inventory Theory 2 (INVT2)
- Queuing Theory (QUEUE)
- Queuing System Simulation (QSIM)
- Decision Analysis (DA)
- Markov Process (MKV)
- Time Series Forecasting (TSFC)
- Financial Analysis (FA)
- Exit from QSB

Input Data

- Data Entry
- Read a File
- Show Data
- Print Data
- Modify Data
  - Modify the problem coefficients
  - Delete variable
  - Delete constraint
- Save
- Save As
- Exit from QSB

Solution

- Solve the Problem
- Solve and Display Tableau
- Solve with Graphic Method
- Specify Scaling
- Show the Solution
- Print the Solution
- Save the Solution
- Print Final Tableau

Options
- Color
- Monochrome
- Printer Selection

Help - LP
- About LP
- About the User Interface
- About the Edit Keys

SOLVING PROBLEMS WITH LP

In the following sections, we will use an example problem to show how to enter and solve the problem. The general procedure and menu options are described in detail in the tutorial sections of Chapter 2.

Example

To demonstrate the use of LP, consider the following problem. Austin Manufacturing Company (AMC) has two machines to make products A and B. Each product requires operation time on each machine. Table 3-1 shows these operation requirements and the total available times on both machines in one month. Considering the current market, AMC can sell as much as it can produce of products A and B. The market prices for each product are $50 and $60, respectively. Management would like to determine the best production plan to maximize the total revenue for the coming month.

Table 3-1. Unit operation times and machine capacities in hours.

Machine	Product A	Product B	Capacity in hours
1	2	3	180
2	3	2	150

The problem is modeled as follows.

Let A = number of product A produced in one month
B = number of product B produced in one month

The LP model is:

$$
\begin{aligned}
\text{Maximize:} \quad & 50\,A + 60\,B \\
\text{Subject to:} \quad & 2\,A + 3\,B \leq 180 \\
& 3\,A + 2\,B \leq 150 \\
& A,\ B \geq 0
\end{aligned}
$$

Enter the Problem

Select “Data Entry” from the “Input Data” menu (refer to Chapter 2 for selecting a menu item). Figs. 3-1 to 3-4 show the data entry of this problem. Note that the “You define” option of the variable names is selected in the problem specification of Fig. 3-1. The default value is specified for variable bounds, and spreadsheet is chosen for model entry. When you enter the direction for a constraint such as in Fig. 3-4, “>”, “>=”, and “≥” all represent “greater than or equal to,” and “<”, “<=”, and “≤” all represent “less than or equal to.”

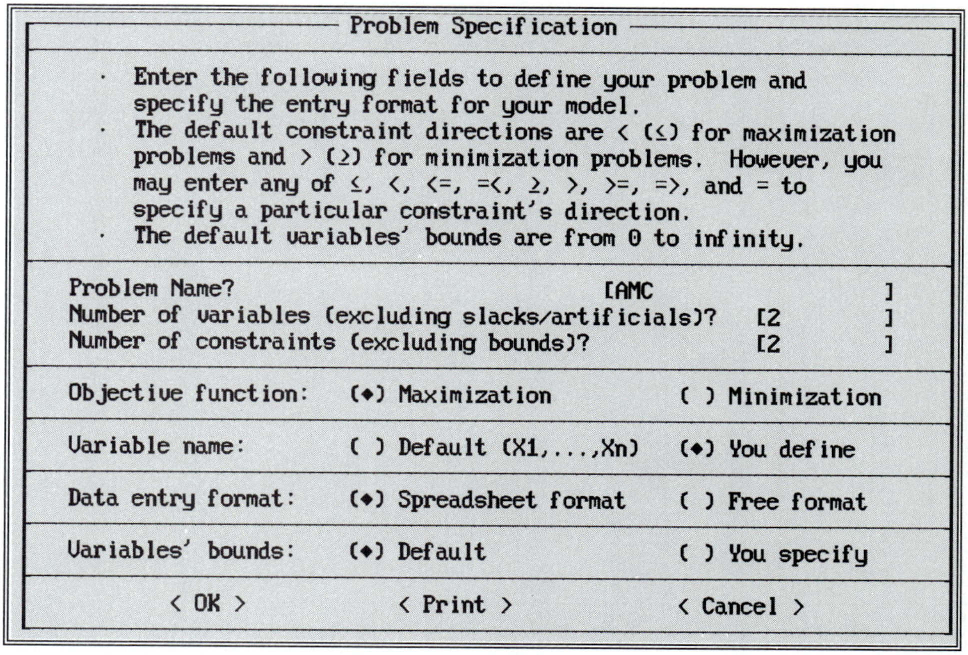

Figure 3-1. Problem specification for AMC.

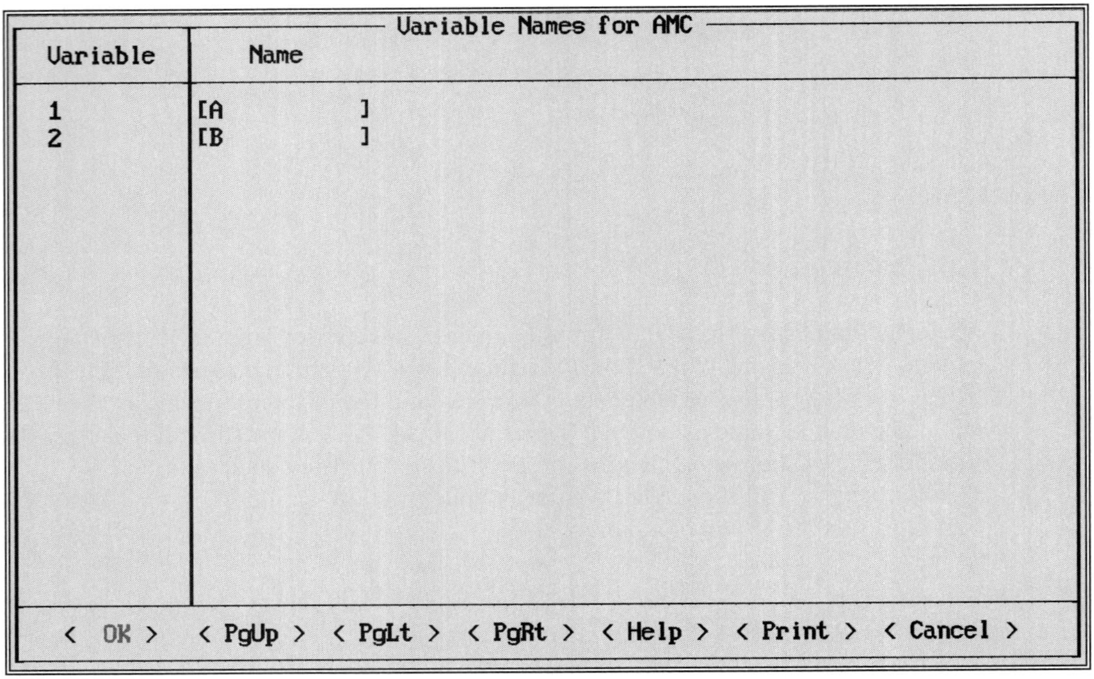

Figure 3-2. Variable names for AMC.

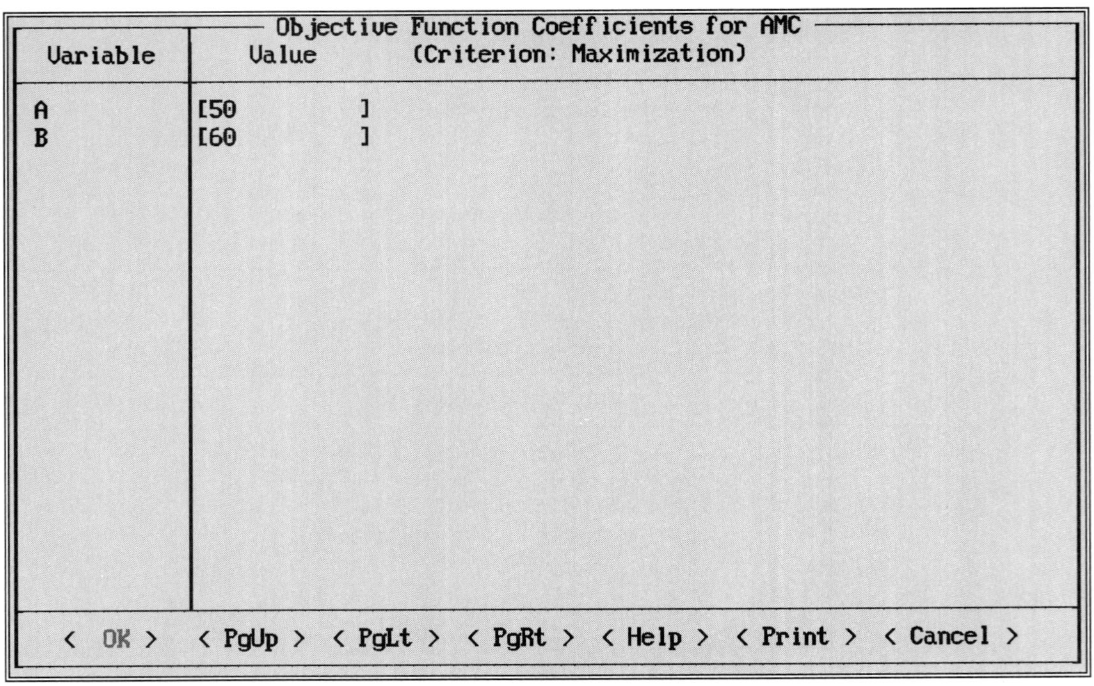

Figure 3-3. Objective function coefficients for AMC.

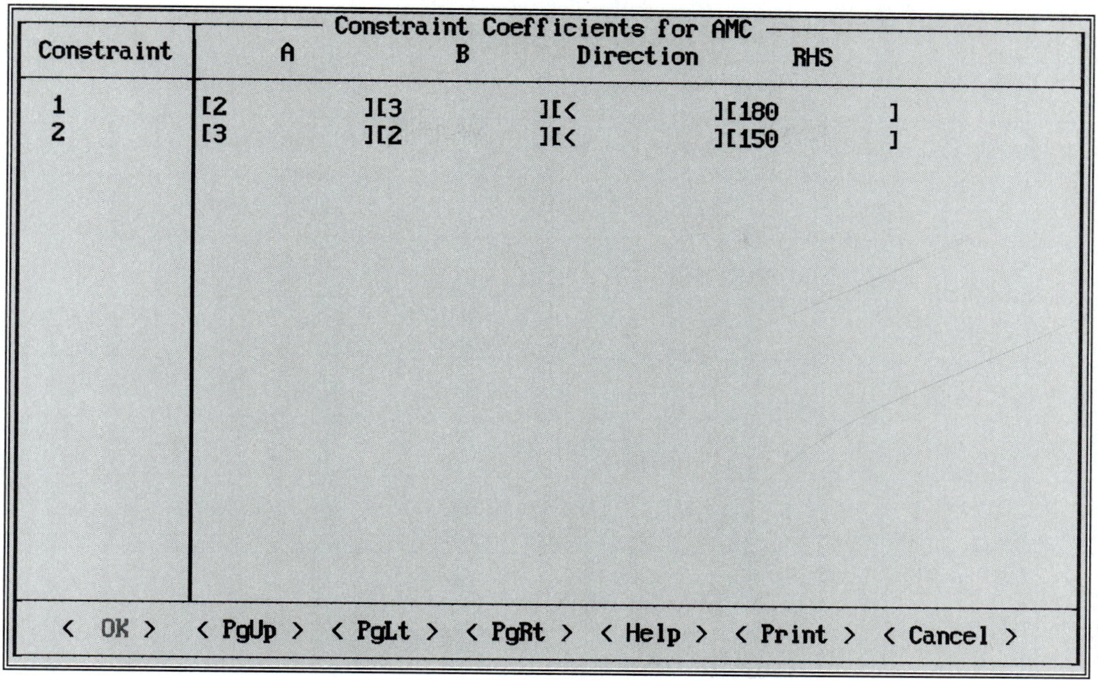

Figure 3-4. Constraints for AMC.

Solve the Problem

1. Select "Solve the Problem" from the "Solution" menu to solve the AMC problem. The message "Please standby . . ." will display for a short period while the problem is being solved.
2. You may also choose "Solve and Display Tableau" from the "Solution" menu to display the simplex tableaus. Figs. 3-5 to 3-8 show the simplex iterations. Note that you may choose the < Skip > option to skip the next tableaus or the < Hardcopy > option to print or save the current tableau.
3. After the problem is solved, select "Show the Solution" from the "Solution" menu to display the solution and sensitivity analysis. Fig. 3-9 shows the dialog to specify displaying all or nonzero solution and Figs. 3-10 and 3-11 show the results. The minimum and maximum "Obj. Coef." in Fig. 3-10 represent the range of the objective function coefficients for which the current basis holds. Similarly, the minimum and maximum "R. H. S." in Fig. 3-11 represent the range of the right-hand sides for which the current basis holds.
4. If the problem has a wide range of data, you may want to let the program scale the data in order to reduce the rounded errors. Fig. 3-12 shows the dialog if you choose "Specify Scaling" from the "Solution" menu. Click "YES" to confirm or click "NO" to use the original data.

Initial Tableau

		A	B	S1	S2		
Basis	c(j)	50	60	0	0	RHS	Ratio
S1	0	2	3	1	0	180	
S2	0	3	2	0	1	150	
c(j)-Z(j)		50	60	0	0	0	
* Big M		0	0	0	0	0	

Current OBJ (Max.) = 0

< Next > < Skip > < HardCopy > < Cancel >

Figure 3-5. Initial tableau for AMC.

Iteration 1

		A	B	S1	S2		
Basis	c(j)	50	60	0	0	RHS	Ratio
S1	0	2	3	1	0	180	60
S2	0	3	2	0	1	150	75
c(j)-Z(j)		50	60	0	0	0	
* Big M		0	0	0	0	0	

Current OBJ (Max.) = 0 IN: B OUT: S1

< Next > < Skip > < HardCopy > < Cancel >

Figure 3-6. Iteration 1 for AMC.

Iteration 2

		A	B	S1	S2		
Basis	c(j)	50	60	0	0	RHS	Ratio
B	60	.6666667	1	.3333333	0	60	90
S2	0	1.666667	0	-.666666	1	30	18
c(j)-Z(j)		10	0	-20	0	3600	
* Big M		0	0	0	0	0	

Current OBJ (Max.) = 3600 IN: A OUT: S2

< Next > < Skip > < HardCopy > < Cancel >

Figure 3-7. Iteration 2 for AMC.

Final Tableau (Total Iterations = 2)

		A	B	S1	S2		
Basis	c(j)	50	60	0	0	RHS	Ratio
B	60	4.768E-8	.9999999	.6	-.4	48	
A	50	1	-4.76E-8	-.4	.6	18	
c(j)-Z(j)		0	0	-16	-6	3780	
* Big M		0	0	0	0	0	

(Max.) Optimal OBJ value = 3780

< Next > < Skip > < HardCopy > < Cancel >

Figure 3-8. Final tableau for AMC.

All solution or non-zero solution only?

< All >   < Non-zero only >   < Cancel >

Figure 3-9. Options to specify displaying all or nonzero solution.

Solution Summary for AMC

08-23-1993 08:51:46   Page: 1 of 1

Variable Number	Variable Name	Solution	Opportunity Cost	Minimum Obj. Coef.	Current Obj. Coef.	Maximum Obj. Coef.
1	A	18	0	40	50	90
2	B	48	0	33.33334	60	75

Maximized OBJ = 3780   Iteration = 2   Elapsed CPU seconds = 0

< PageDown >   < PageUp >   < Hardcopy >   < Cancel >

Figure 3-10. Solution summary for AMC.

Constraint Summary for AMC

08-23-1993 08:52:24   Page: 1 of 1

Constraint Number	Constraint Status	Shadow Price	Surplus	Minimum R. H. S.	Current R. H. S.	Maximum R. H. S.
1	Tight (≤)	16	0	100	180	225
2	Tight (≤)	6	0	120	150	270

Maximized OBJ = 3780   Iteration = 2   Elapsed CPU seconds = 0

< PageDown >   < PageUp >   < Hardcopy >   < Cancel >

Figure 3-11. Constraint summary for AMC.

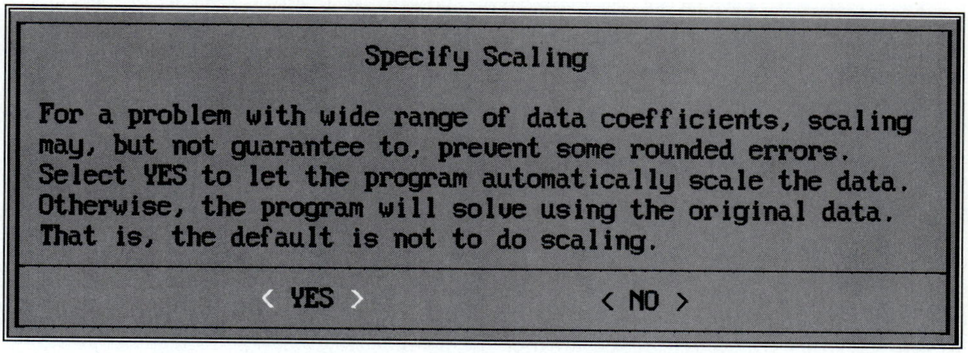

Figure 3-12. Specify scaling.

GRAPHIC METHOD

LP provides a function to solve and perform sensitivity analysis by using the graphic method if the problem has only two variables and your computer has a color and graphics adapter. Let us demonstrate the graphic method for the AMC problem. After you choose the option "Solve with Graphic Method" from the "Solution" menu, the program will ask you to define the scales of the two axes. You could let the LP automatically define the scale for you. Fig. 3-13 shows the dialog of defining the scales for the horizontal and vertical axes. In this case, each unit of horizontal axis represents two units of A, and each unit of vertical axis represents three units of B. After defining the scales, the graphic solution will be shown in Fig. 3-14. Note that multiple colors will be used to display the different constraints and the feasible region in the color screen.

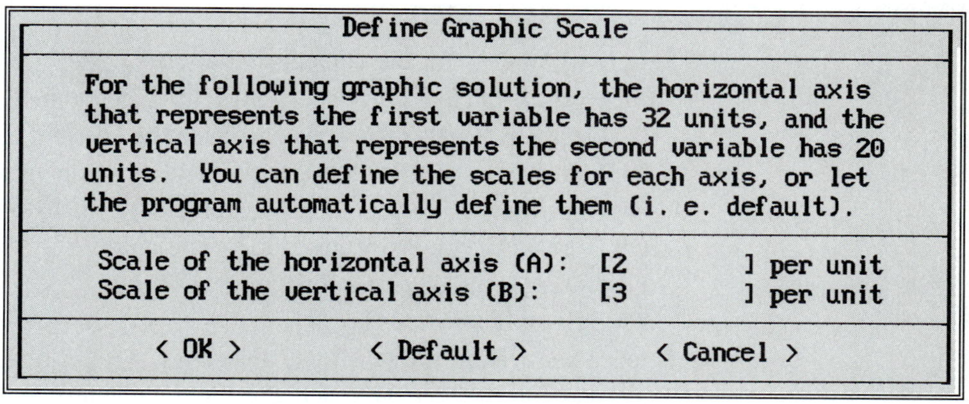

Figure 3-13. Example of defining graphic scale.

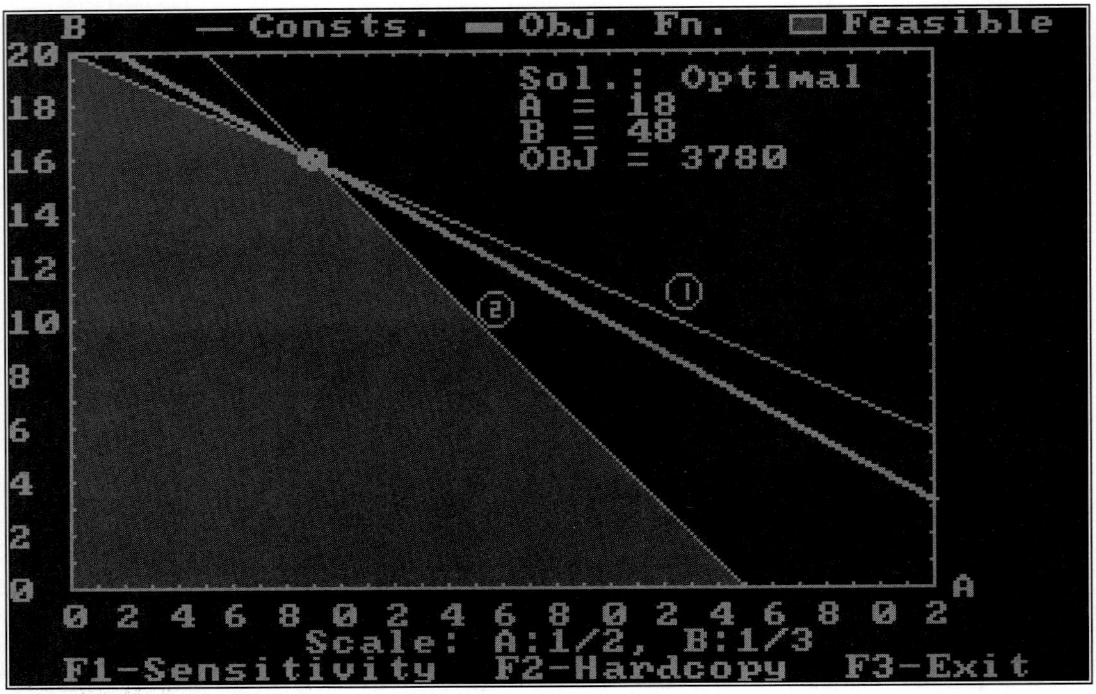

Figure 3-14. Graphic solution of AMC.

After the graphic solution is shown, you could use function keys to perform a sensitivity analysis or to hardcopy the graphic solution. If you are going to hardcopy the graphic solution ("F2" key) to the printer, make sure you have set up the right type of printer from the option "Printer Selection" of the "Options" menu. Otherwise, the output will not be satisfactory. In the following, we describe the function keys which hierarchically perform different functions for the graphic sensitivity analysis. Try a few function key sequences to see how the graphic sensitivity is performed.

- F1: Perform a sensitivity analysis
  - F1: Sensitivity analysis for the objective function
    - F1: Increase the first objective coefficient by one unit
    - F2: Decrease the first objective coefficient by one unit
    - F3: Increase the second objective coefficient by one unit
    - F4: Decrease the second objective coefficient by one unit
    - F5: Increase the objective function by one unit
    - F6: Decrease the objective function by one unit
    - F7: Exit to the previous level
  - F2: Select a constraint for a sensitivity analysis
    - F1: Increase the first variable coefficient by one unit
    - F2: Decrease the first variable coefficient by one unit

        - F3: Increase the second variable coefficient by one unit
        - F4: Decrease the second variable coefficient by one unit
        - F5: Increase the right-hand side by one unit
        - F6: Decrease the right-hand side by one unit
        - F7: Exit to the previous level
    - F3: Exit the sensitivity analysis
- F2: Hardcopy the graphic solution
- F3: Exit the graphic method

THE BIG M METHOD

If the problem contains "equality" (=) or "greater than or equal to" (≥) constraints, the LP program uses the Big M method to solve the problem. (An artificial variable is generated for each "=" or "≥" constraint, and a corresponding M coefficient is added to the objective function.) The following example (named BIGM) contains two "≥" constraints. Fig. 3-15 shows the simplex tableau of the first iteration for this problem. The artificial variables, which start with "A", and the coefficients of M are shown in the figure. M represents a non-Archimedean large number.

$$
\begin{array}{llllllll}
\text{Minimize:} & 2.5 & X_1 & + & 2 & X_2 & & \\
\text{Subject to:} & 6 & X_1 & + & 3 & X_2 & \geq & 100 \\
 & 3 & X_1 & + & 5 & X_2 & \geq & 120 \\
 & & X_1, X_2 \geq 0 & & & & &
\end{array}
$$

Iteration 1

		X1	X2	S1	A1	S2	A2
Basis	c(j)	2.5	2	0	0	0	0
A1	M	6	3	-1	1	0	0
A2	M	3	5	0	0	-1	1
c(j)-Z(j)		2.5	2	0	0	0	0
* Big M		-9	-8	1	0	1	0

Current OBJ (Min.) = 0 + (220 M)   IN: X1 OUT: A1

< Next > < Skip > < PgLt > < PgRt > < HardCopy > < Cancel >

Figure 3-15. Artificial variables and Big M values.

FREE-FORMAT MODEL ENTRY

The LP formulation can be entered or modified in free format. In this section, we will show you the free-format model entry by entering the following problem:

$$
\begin{array}{lrlrlrlll}
\text{Maximize:} & 3 & \text{AirCool} & + 2.5 & \text{WaterCool} & + 5 & \text{OilCool} & & \\
\text{Subject to:} & & \text{AirCool} & + & \text{WaterCool} & + & \text{OilCool} & \geq & 50000 \\
 & 2 & \text{AirCool} & + 3 & \text{WaterCool} & + 5 & \text{OilCool} & \leq & 180000 \\
 & 1.215 & \text{AirCool} & + 5.85 & \text{WaterCool} & + 3.03 & \text{OilCool} & \leq & 200000 \\
 & & & & & & \text{AirCool} & \geq & 10000 \\
 & & & & & 10000 \leq & \text{WaterCool} & \leq & 50000 \\
 & & & & & & \text{OilCool} & \geq & 15000
\end{array}
$$

and AirCool, WaterCool, and OilCool are nonnegative.

1. After selecting "Data Entry" from the "Input Data" menu, Fig. 3-16 shows the problem specification entry. Note that the free-format data entry is specified in Fig. 3-16. Then the variable names are entered in Fig. 3-17.
2. After the variable names are entered, the program will let you use commands to enter the LP model. You may enter the "H" or "Help" command to display the available commands. Fig. 3-18 shows the commands. Note that you can enter any command at the prompt "?=", and you can enter the data such as objective, constraints, or bounds at the prompt ">>". If you just hit the "RETURN" key after the prompt ">>", the program will return to the prompt "?=" and you may enter another command. The available commands are described below.

Bm:	Enter the bounds of variable *m* and specify its integrity.
Cn:	Enter the constraint *n*.
CnVm:	Enter the coefficient of constraint *n* variable *m*.
Dn:	Enter the direction of constraint *n*. Use to change direction.
H:	Recall the command information.
M:	Recall the modification menu.
Q:	Quit the free-format entry.
Rn:	Enter the right-hand side of constraint *n*. Use to change RHS.
S:	Show the whole model.

Note that the objective function is considered to be constraint "0". When you want to change the number of constraints or variables, use the modification menu to add or delete a constraint or variable. The free-format entry is not case sensitive. That is to say, the commands "b1" and "B1" are the same, and the variables "AirCool" and "airCOOL" are identical.

3. Fig. 3-19 shows the entry of the objective function (note that "c0" is used to specify the objective function). Fig. 3-20 shows the sequence of entering the three constraints, and Fig. 3-21 shows the sequence of entering the bounds for the three variables. After the model entry is done, use the command "S" to

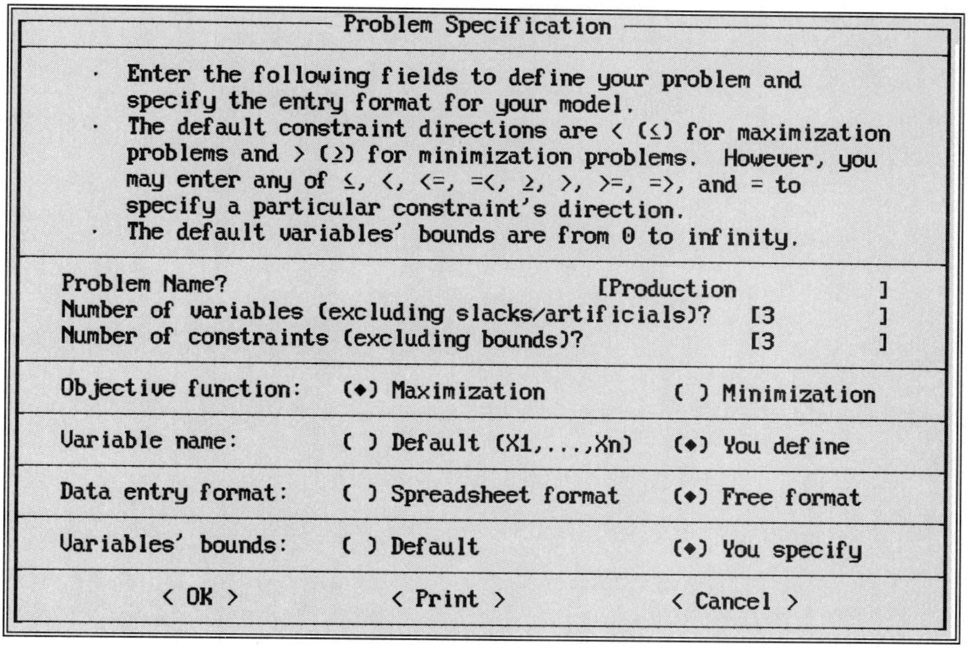

Figure 3-16. Problem specification for free-format entry.

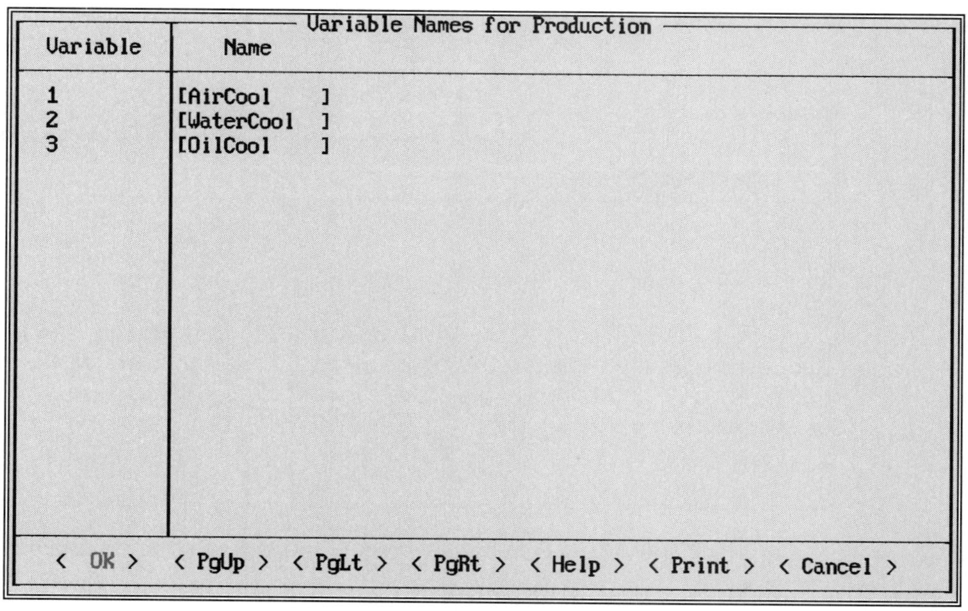

Figure 3-17. Variable names for Production.

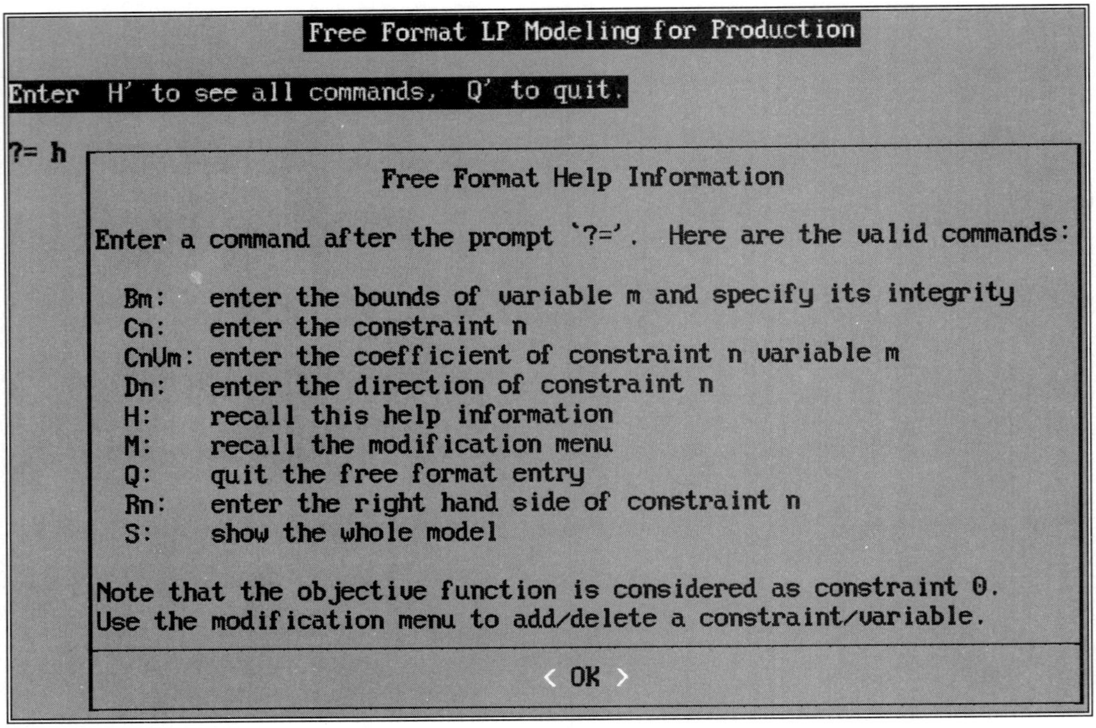

Figure 3-18. Available commands for free-format entry.

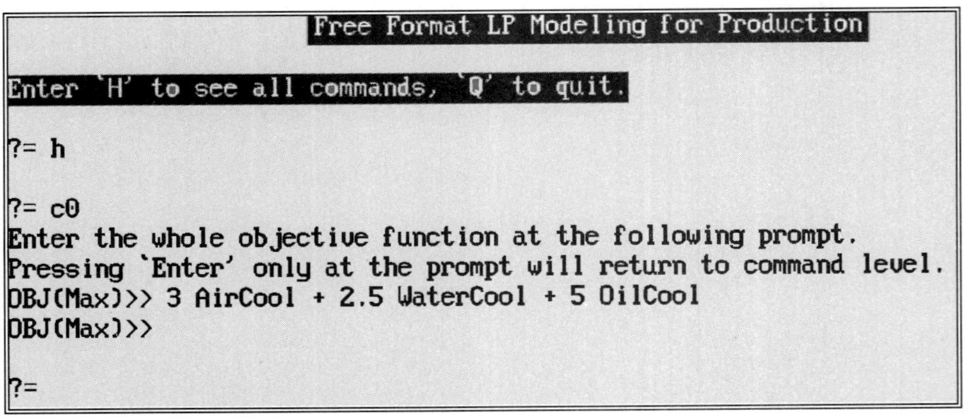

Figure 3-19. Free-format objective function entry for Production.

```
                    Free Format LP Modeling for Production

Enter `H' to see all commands, `Q' to quit.
?= c1
Enter the whole constraint at the following prompt.
Pressing `Enter' only at the prompt will return to command level.
Constraint 1>> AirCool + WaterCool + OilCool >= 50000
Constraint 1>>

?= c2
Enter the whole constraint at the following prompt.
Pressing `Enter' only at the prompt will return to command level.
Constraint 2>> 2 AirCool + 3 WaterCool + 5 OilCool <= 180000
Constraint 2>>

?= c3
Enter the whole constraint at the following prompt.
Pressing `Enter' only at the prompt will return to command level.
Constraint 3>> 1.215 AirCool + 5.85 WaterCool + 3.03 OilCool <= 200000
Constraint 3>>

?=
```

Figure 3-20. Free-format constraint entry for Production.

```
                    Free Format LP Modeling for Production

Enter `H' to see all commands, `Q' to quit.
?= b1
  The lower bound of AirCool (default=0) ? 10000
  The upper bound of AirCool (default=infinity) ?

?= b2
  The lower bound of WaterCool (default=0) ? 10000
  The upper bound of WaterCool (default=infinity) ? 50000

?= b3
  The lower bound of OilCool (default=0) ? 15000
  The upper bound of OilCool (default=infinity) ?

?=
```

Figure 3-21. Free-format bound entry for Production.

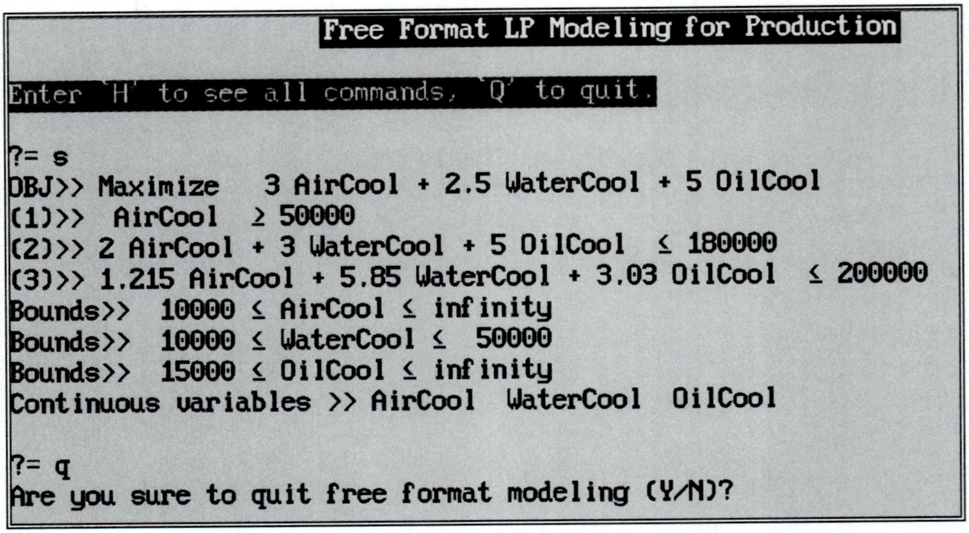

Figure 3-22. Show the whole model for Production and quit the free-format entry.

show the whole model and the command "Q" to quit the free-format entry. Fig. 3-22 demonstrates the action.

EXERCISES

1. Consider the following LP problem:

$$\begin{aligned}\text{Maximize:}\quad & 8X_1 + 12X_2\\ \text{Subject to:}\quad & 2X_1 + 5X_2 \le 250\\ & 11X_1 + 9X_2 \le 710\\ & X_1, X_2 \ge 0\end{aligned}$$

a. Find the optimal solution.

b. What are the ranges of optimality for the coefficients of the objective function and the right-hand sides?

2. Consider the following LP model:

$$\begin{aligned}\text{Maximize:}\quad & A + 3B - 4C\\ \text{Subject to:}\quad & A + B \le 150\\ & 3A + 2B - C \ge 210\\ & 5A - 2B + 4C \ge 315\\ & A,\ B,\ \text{and } C \ge 0\end{aligned}$$

a. Find the optimal solution.

b. What is the opportunity cost for each constraint?

3. Find the optimal solution for the following LP problem:

$$\begin{array}{llllllll}
\text{Maximize:} & 7X_1 + 9X_2 - 3X_3 + 11X_4 - X_5 + 2X_6 \\
\text{Subject to:} & X_1 + X_2 + X_3 + X_4 + X_5 + X_6 \le 200 \\
& 2X_1 + X_2 + 6X_3 - X_4 + 2X_5 + 7X_6 \ge 271 \\
& 4X_1 + 2X_3 + 3X_5 - X_6 \le 350 \\
& 7X_2 + 11X_3 - 4X_4 + 6X_5 \le 429 \\
& X_1 + 4X_3 + 7X_5 \le 310 \\
& X_1, X_2, X_3, X_4, X_5, \text{ and } X_6 \ge 0
\end{array}$$

4. Full Speed, Inc., produces three industrial parts from raw materials A and B. One unit of part X requires four units of A and three units of B; one unit of part Y requires seven units of A and two units of B; and one unit of Z requires three units of A and eight units of B. Transportation problems have restricted the company to, at most, 1700 units of material A and 1500 units of material B each month. The company has contracts on hand to supply at least 50 units of part X, 50 units of part Y, and 70 units of part Z. Industries can consume as much as the company produces. If the unit profits for parts X, Y, and Z are $15, $20, and $21, respectively, what is the best production plan for Full Speed to obtain maximum profit?

5. Midwestern Airline has its headquarters in a northwestern city. During the summer, the company's business increases substantially because of vacation travelers. Currently, Midwestern has an on-line reservation system. The following table lists the requirements for reservation clerks by two-hour periods during the day:

Period	Time	Clerks required
1	6 a.m. to 8 a.m.	3
2	8 a.m. to 10 a.m.	12
3	10 a.m. to Noon	13
4	Noon to 2 p.m.	10
5	2 p.m. to 4 p.m.	12
6	4 p.m. to 6 p.m.	10
7	6 p.m. to 8 p.m.	6
8	8 p.m. to 10 p.m.	5
9	10 p.m. to Midnight	4
10	Midnight to 2 a.m.	3

The company plans to use six work shifts, including two split shifts, as follows:

Shift	Times
1	6 a.m. to 2 p.m.
2	8 a.m. to 4 p.m.
3	10 a.m. to 6 p.m.
4	6 p.m. to 2 a.m.
5	10 a.m. to 1 p.m. 4 p.m. to 8 p.m.
6	8 a.m. to 11 a.m. 5 p.m. to 9 p.m.

Formulate an LP problem to determine the minimal number of reservation clerks required. Use QSB+ 3.0 to solve it.

6. Sesame Oil Company produces three grades of motor oil: regular, high power, and super power. They are blended from three types of crude oil. Each type of crude oil contains three important ingredients. The percentages of ingredients in each type of crude oil are:

	Ingredient		
Crude oil	I	II	III
A	80%	10%	5%
B	45%	30%	20%
C	30%	40%	25%

The specifications of the three types of motor oil are:

	Ingredient		
Motor oil	I	II	III
Super power	≥60%	≤25%	≤10%
High power	≥50%	≤30%	≤15%
Regular	≤40%	≥35%	≥20%

The costs per gallon for crude oil A, B, and C are \$0.65, \$0.50, and \$0.45, respectively. Daily demands for super power, high power, and regular are at least 50,000 gallons, 70,000 gallons, and 40,000 gallons. Establish a good blending plan for Sesame Oil. In other words, determine how many gallons of each type of crude oil should be used in each type of motor oil.

4

INTEGER LINEAR PROGRAMMING (ILP)

OVERVIEW OF THE ILP DECISION SUPPORT SYSTEM

This program solves mixed integer linear programming problems. You may prepare the problem using the following format for data entry:

Maximize:	3.2	GID1	+	4.0	GID2	−	5.0	GID3		
Subject to:	4.0	GID1	+	2.5	GID2	+	3.0	GID3	≤	50.0
	3.6	GID1	+	7.0	GID2	−	2.5	GID3	≤	86.9
	15	GID1				+	9.0	GID3	=	20.0

All variables are assumed to be nonnegative and GID1 and GID2 are integer.

You may specify free or spreadsheet format to enter your formulation and bounds. You can define variables with up to ten characters. Defaults are $X_1, X_2, \ldots,$ X_n. Problems can be saved on or read from a disk(ette). You can also display or print your problem and modify it as necessary. Furthermore, you can choose to display the detailed steps of the branch-and-bound method as the problem is being solved. Either the best or the newest bound rule can be used for branch selection. You may choose to print out the final solution.

TECHNICAL NOTES ON THE ILP PROGRAM

1. The ILP program uses the branch-and-bound procedure to solve mixed integer linear programming problems.
2. The ILP program uses the revised simplex with upper-bounding method to solve each individual branching node.
3. "Big M" will be used when you have "equality" or "greater than or equal to" constraints in the problem. ILP does not give M a specific value but treats it as a false number and keeps updating the coefficients of M in the objective function.
4. The integer solution is obtained when all the integer variables have the values close to the nearest integer within a specified tolerance. You may specify the tolerance in the solution menu. The default tolerance is 0.01.

5. You may choose the newest problem (bound) or best bound rule to perform the branch selection during the branch-and-bound procedure. The newest problem rule selects the most recently created node to be solved next, while the best bound rule chooses the most potential node, which has the best upper bound for the maximization problem or has the least lower bound for the minimization problem, to be solved next. The default is the newest problem rule.
6. Variables may have upper and lower bounds that can be entered as constraints or pure bounded values. The default bounds for each variable are 0 to infinity, which is represented by "M" in ILP.
7. All variables are assumed to be nonnegative. If you have some variables with only nonpositive values in your problem, you should transform them to nonnegative variables. Bounds can be negative. In the case of a negative lower bound, the correspondent variable will be shifted left before the model is solved.
8. The LP and ILP programs use the same data file format to store or retrieve data. The LP program will skip the identification of the integer variables.
9. The size of problems that can be solved by QSB+ 3.0 depends on the memory in your computer and the percentage of nonzero in the problem. For example, a 100 by 100 problem with 20% nonzero can be solved by QSB+ 3.0.
10. ILP keeps, at most, 2000 active nodes (branches) during the branch-and-bound process.
11. Besides the spreadsheet for data entry, ILP also provides a free format to enter the model by commands. Help information is available. Select the spreadsheet or free-format data entry at the problem specification.
12. Some notations are used in displaying the intermediate steps and final results. They are:

    ZL: Lower bound of the objective function

    ZU: Upper bound of the objective function

    #Node: Number of active nodes in the branch-and-bound procedure.

MENU STRUCTURE

The functions and options in each of the pull-down menus are hierarchically listed as follows:

Modules
- Linear Programming (LP)
- Integer Linear Programming (ILP)
- Goal Programming (GP)
- Quadratic Programming (QP)
- Nonlinear Programming (NLP)

- Dynamic Programming (DP)
- Transportation and Transshipment (TRP)
- Assignment and Traveling Salesman (ASTS)
- Specialized Network Modeling (SNET)
- Capacitated Network Flow Modeling (CNET)
- Project Scheduling: CPM/PERT
- Inventory Theory (INVT)
- Inventory Theory 2 (INVT2)
- Queuing Theory (QUEUE)
- Queuing System Simulation (QSIM)
- Decision Analysis (DA)
- Markov Process (MKV)
- Time Series Forecasting (TSFC)
- Financial Analysis (FA)
- Exit from QSB

Input Data
- Data Entry
- Read a File
- Show Data
- Print Data
- Modify Data
  - Modify the problem coefficients
  - Delete variable
  - Delete constraint
- Save
- Save As
- Exit from QSB

Solution
- Solve the Problem
- Solve and Display Steps
- Solve Continuous Value Only
- Specify Integer Tolerance
- Specify Branch Selection Rule
- Show the Solution
- Print the Solution
- Save the Solution

Options
- Color
- Monochrome
- Printer Selection

Help - ILP
- About ILP
- About the User Interface
- About the Edit Keys

SOLVING PROBLEMS WITH ILP

In the following sections, we will use an example problem to show how to enter and solve the problem. The general procedure and menu options are described in detail in the tutorial sections of Chapter 2.

Example

To demonstrate the use of ILP, consider the following problem. A nutrition plan requires at least 200 units of protein and 180 units of fat. Chemical analyses have shown that 1 unit of food A contains 6 units of protein and 3 units of fat, and 1 unit of food B contains 3 units of protein and 5 units of fat. The sales of these two types of food are in whole units with unit prices of \$2.50 for A and \$2 for B. What combination will satisfy the required nutrition levels and at the same time minimize the total cost?

The problem is modeled as follows.

Let X_a = number of units of food A used
X_b = number of units of food B used

The LP model is:

$$
\begin{array}{lrlrlll}
\text{Minimize:} & 2.5 & X_a & + & 2 & X_b & \\
\text{Subject to:} & 6.0 & X_a & + & 3 & X_b & \geq 200 \\
 & 3.0 & X_a & + & 5 & X_b & \geq 180 \\
 & \multicolumn{6}{l}{X_a, X_b \geq 0 \text{ and are integer}}
\end{array}
$$

Enter the Problem

Select "Data Entry" from the "Input Data" menu (refer to Chapter 2 for selecting a menu item). Figs. 4-1 to 4-5 show the data entry of this problem. Note that "Minimization" is selected for the objective function, "You define" is selected for the variable names, and "You specify" is selected for bounds and integrity in the problem specification of Fig. 4-1. The spreadsheet format is chosen for model entry. When you enter the direction for a constraint such as in Fig. 4-4, ">", ">=", and "≥" all represent "greater than or equal to", and "<", "<=", and "≤" all represent "less than or equal to". Three types of variables can be specified in Fig. 4-5. They are I for integer values, C for continuous values, and B for binary values (0 or 1).

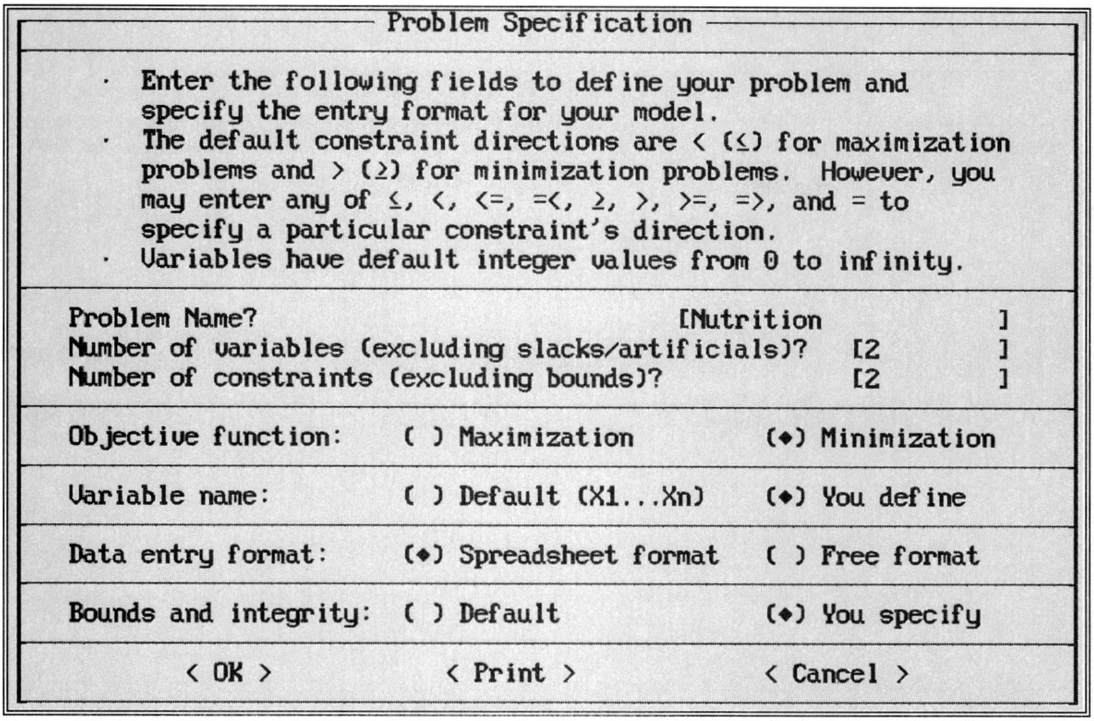

Figure 4-1. Problem specification for Nutrition.

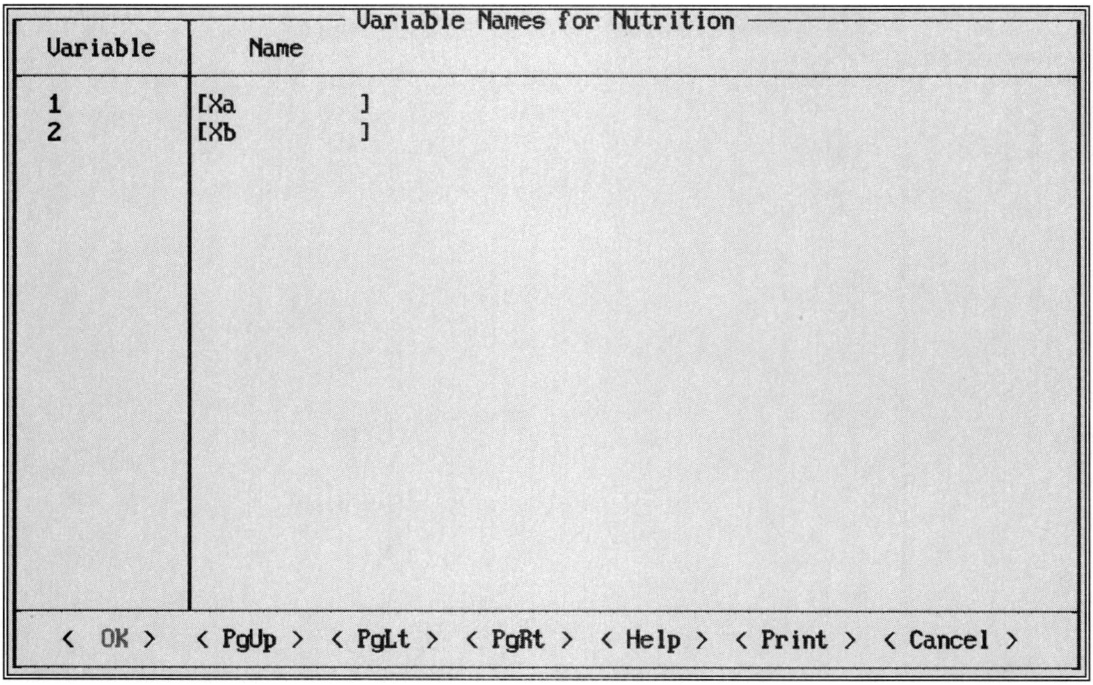

Figure 4-2. Variable names for Nutrition.

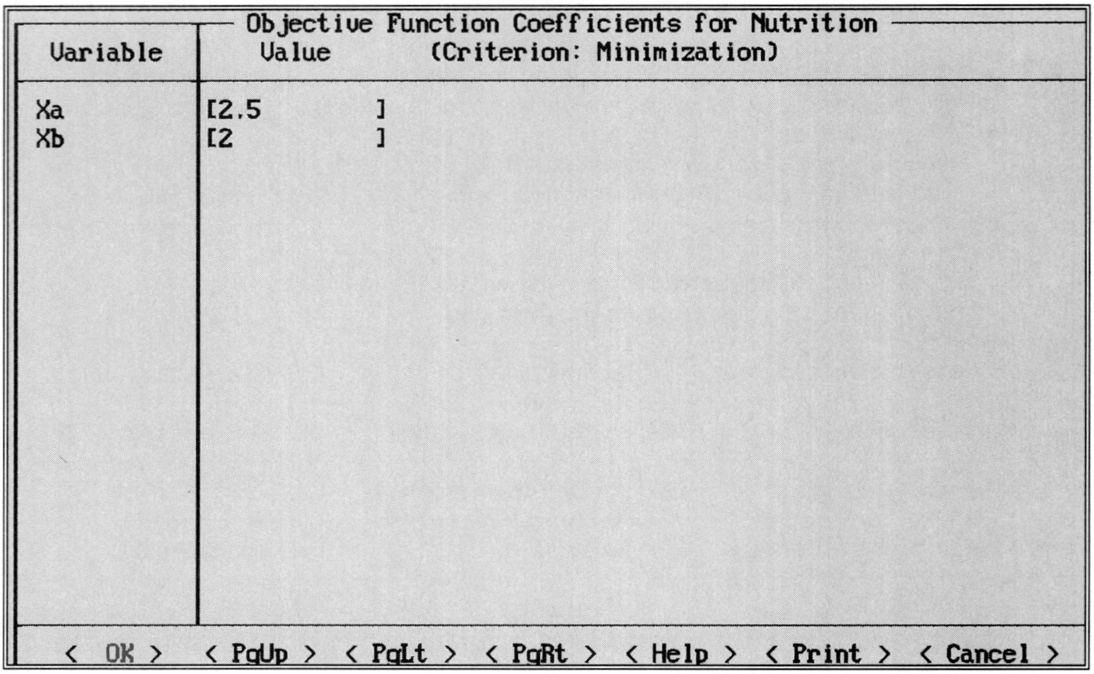

Figure 4-3. Objective function coefficients for Nutrition.

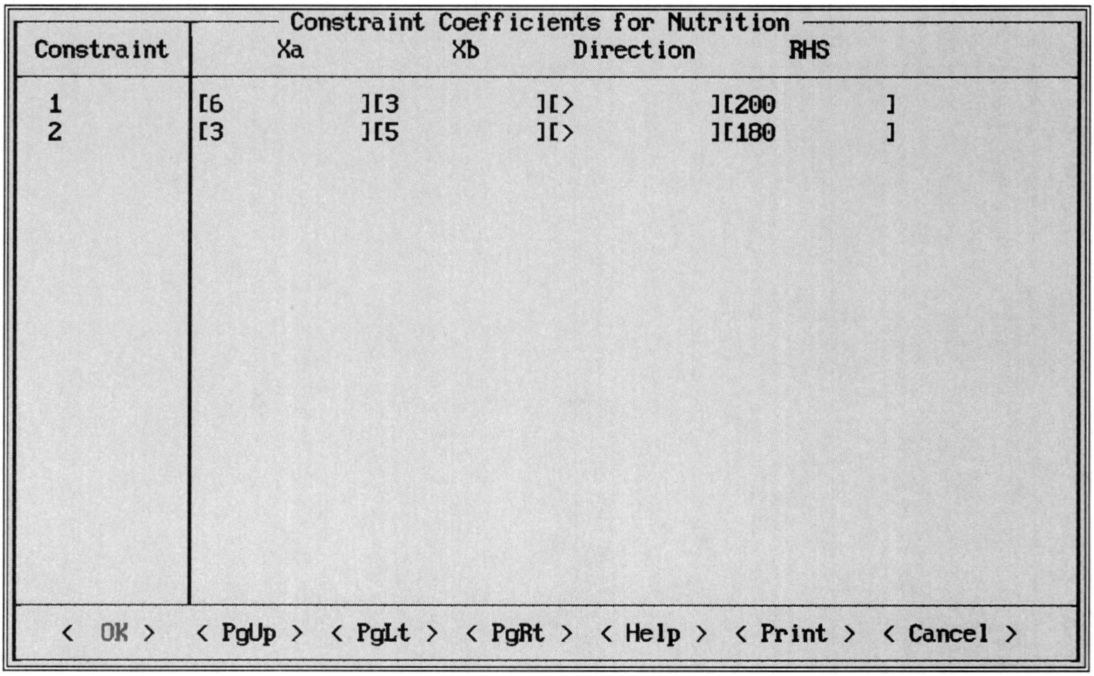

Figure 4-4. Constraints for Nutrition.

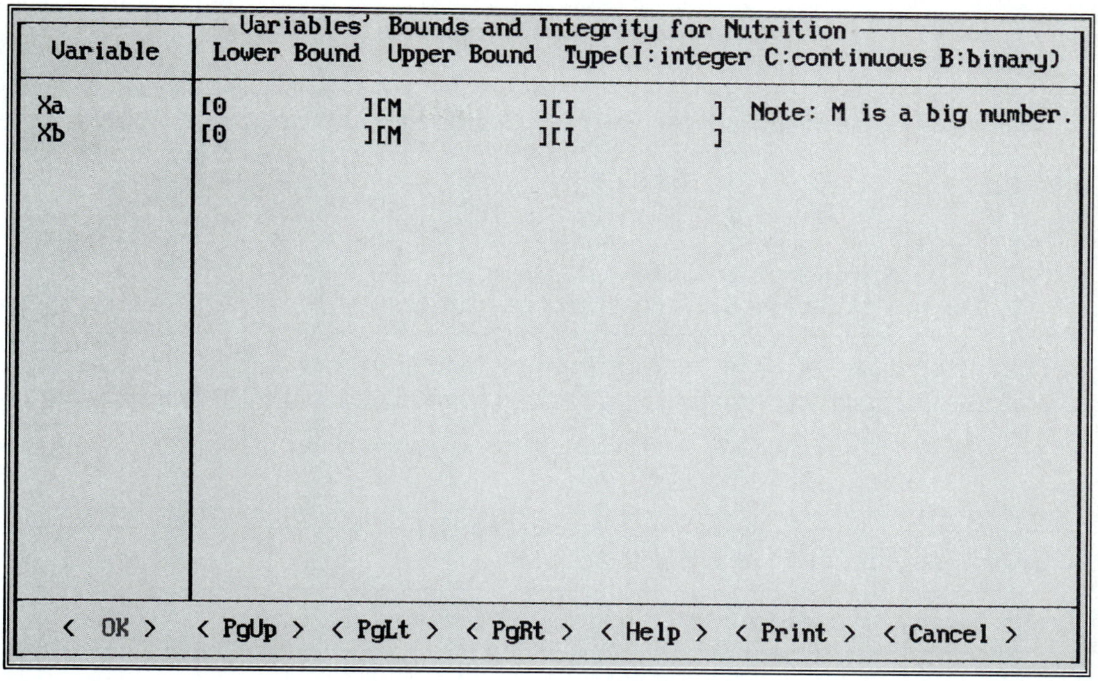

Figure 4-5. Bounds and integrity for Nutrition.

Solve the Problem

1. Select "Solve the Problem" from the "Solution" menu to solve the Nutrition problem. The message "Please standby . . ." will display for a short period while the problem is being solved.
2. You may also choose "Solve and Display Steps" from the "Solution" menu to display the branch-and-bound process. Figs. 4-6 to 4-10 show the iterations.

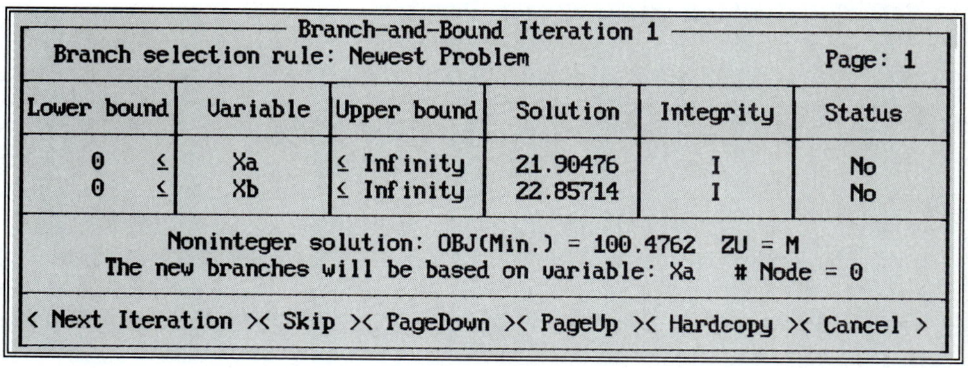

Figure 4-6. Iteration 1 by the newest problem rule.

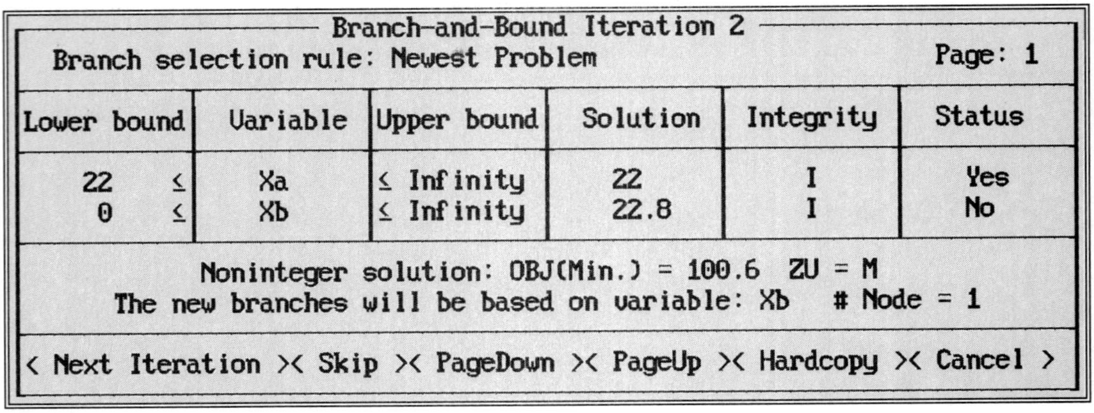

Branch-and-Bound Iteration 2

Branch selection rule: Newest Problem — Page: 1

Lower bound		Variable	Upper bound	Solution	Integrity	Status
22	≤	Xa	≤ Infinity	22	I	Yes
0	≤	Xb	≤ Infinity	22.8	I	No

Noninteger solution: OBJ(Min.) = 100.6 ZU = M

The new branches will be based on variable: Xb # Node = 1

< Next Iteration >< Skip >< PageDown >< PageUp >< Hardcopy >< Cancel >

Figure 4-7. Iteration 2 by the newest problem rule.

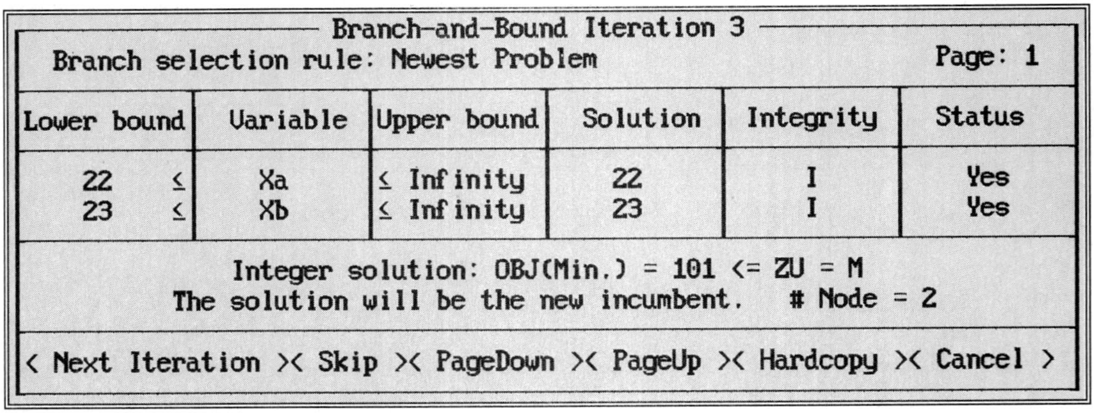

Branch-and-Bound Iteration 3

Branch selection rule: Newest Problem — Page: 1

Lower bound		Variable	Upper bound	Solution	Integrity	Status
22	≤	Xa	≤ Infinity	22	I	Yes
23	≤	Xb	≤ Infinity	23	I	Yes

Integer solution: OBJ(Min.) = 101 <= ZU = M

The solution will be the new incumbent. # Node = 2

< Next Iteration >< Skip >< PageDown >< PageUp >< Hardcopy >< Cancel >

Figure 4-8. Iteration 3 by the newest problem rule.

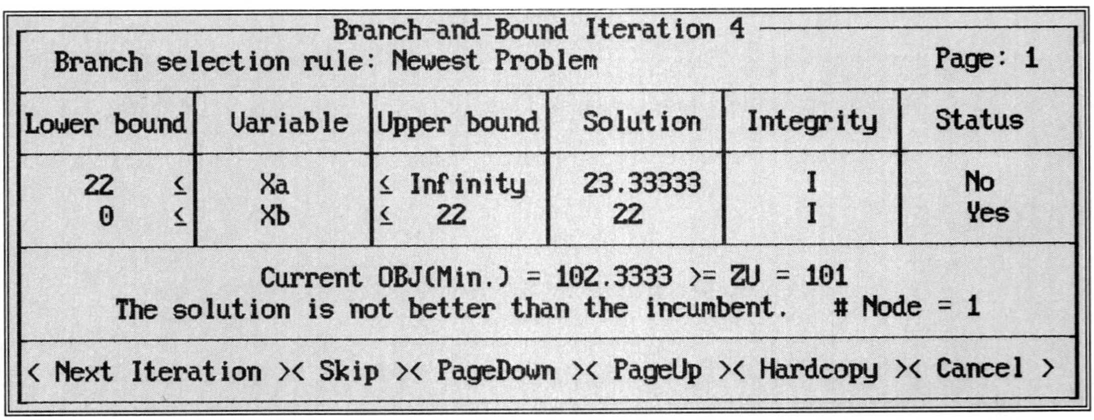

Branch-and-Bound Iteration 4

Branch selection rule: Newest Problem — Page: 1

Lower bound		Variable	Upper bound	Solution	Integrity	Status
22	≤	Xa	≤ Infinity	23.33333	I	No
0	≤	Xb	≤ 22	22	I	Yes

Current OBJ(Min.) = 102.3333 >= ZU = 101

The solution is not better than the incumbent. # Node = 1

< Next Iteration >< Skip >< PageDown >< PageUp >< Hardcopy >< Cancel >

Figure 4-9. Iteration 4 by the newest problem rule.

Note that you may choose the < Skip > option to skip the later iterations or the < Hardcopy > option to print or save the current iteration.

3. After the problem is solved, select "Show the Solution" from the "Solution" menu to display the solution. Fig. 4-11 shows the dialog to specify displaying all or nonzero solution, and Fig. 4-12 shows the solution.

Branch-and-Bound Iteration 5

Branch selection rule: Newest Problem Page: 1

Lower bound		Variable	Upper bound	Solution	Integrity	Status
0	≤	Xa	≤ 21	21	I	Yes
0	≤	Xb	≤ Infinity	24.66667	I	No

Current OBJ(Min.) = 101.8333 >= ZU = 101

The solution is not better than the incumbent. # Node = 0

< Next Iteration >< Skip >< PageDown >< PageUp >< Hardcopy >< Cancel >

Figure 4-10. Iteration 5 by the newest problem rule.

All solution or non-zero solution only?

< All > < Non-zero only > < Cancel >

Figure 4-11. Options to specify displaying all or nonzero solution.

Solution Summary for Nutrition

08-23-1993 10:09:33 Page: 1 of 1

Variable	Solution	Objective Coefficient	Variable	Solution	Objective Coefficient
Xa	22	2.5	Xb	23	2

Minimized OBJ = 101 Iteration = 5 Elapsed CPU seconds = .0625

Branch selection: Newest problem Integer tolerance = .01 Max. #node = 3

< PageDown > < PageUp > < Hardcopy > < Cancel >

Figure 4-12 Solution for Nutrition.

4. You may want to specify different integer tolerance to solve the problem. Choose "Specify Integer Tolerance" from the "Solution" menu. Fig. 4-13 illustrates entering an integer tolerance of 0.05.
5. You may want to select a different branching rule to solve the problem. Choose "Specify Branch Selection Rule" from the "Solution" menu. Fig. 4-14 shows the branch selection rules.

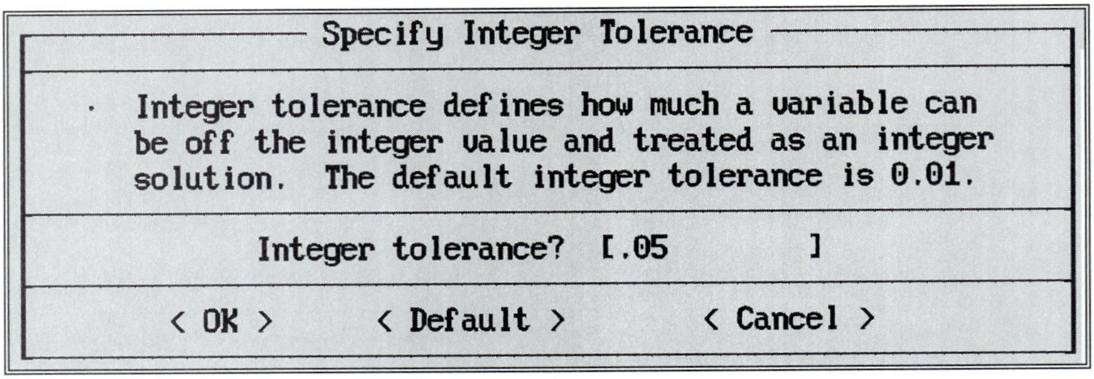

Figure 4-13. Specify the integer tolerance.

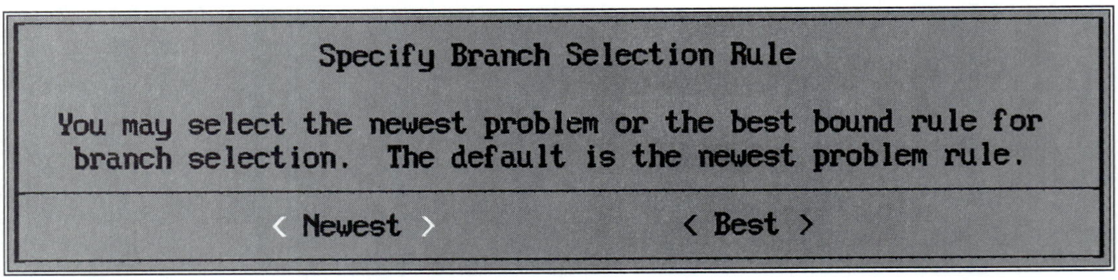

Figure 4-14. Specify the branch selection rule.

FREE-FORMAT MODEL ENTRY

The ILP formulation can be entered or modified in free format. In this section, we will show you the free-format model entry by entering the following problem:

$$
\begin{array}{llllllll}
\text{Maximize:} & 35\,X_1 & +\ 21\,X_2 & +\ 55\,X_3 & +\ 39\,X_4 & +\ 60\,X_5 & & \\
\text{Subject to:} & X_1 & +\ X_2 & +\ X_3 & +\ X_4 & +\ X_5 & \leq & 30 \\
 & 10\,X_1 & +\ 8\,X_2 & +\ 17\,X_3 & +\ 20\,X_4 & +\ 16\,X_5 & \leq & 200 \\
 & 15\,X_1 & +\ 3\,X_2 & +\ 6\,X_3 & +\ 32\,X_4 & +\ 19\,X_5 & \geq & 50
\end{array}
$$

$X_1 \leq 20,\ 3 \leq X_5 \leq 10$

X_1, X_2 are integer, and X_3, X_4 are binary (i.e., 0 or 1).

1. After selecting “Data Entry” from the “Input Data” menu, Fig. 4-15 shows the problem specification entry. Note that the free-format data entry is specified in Fig. 4-15. The variable names are defaulted.

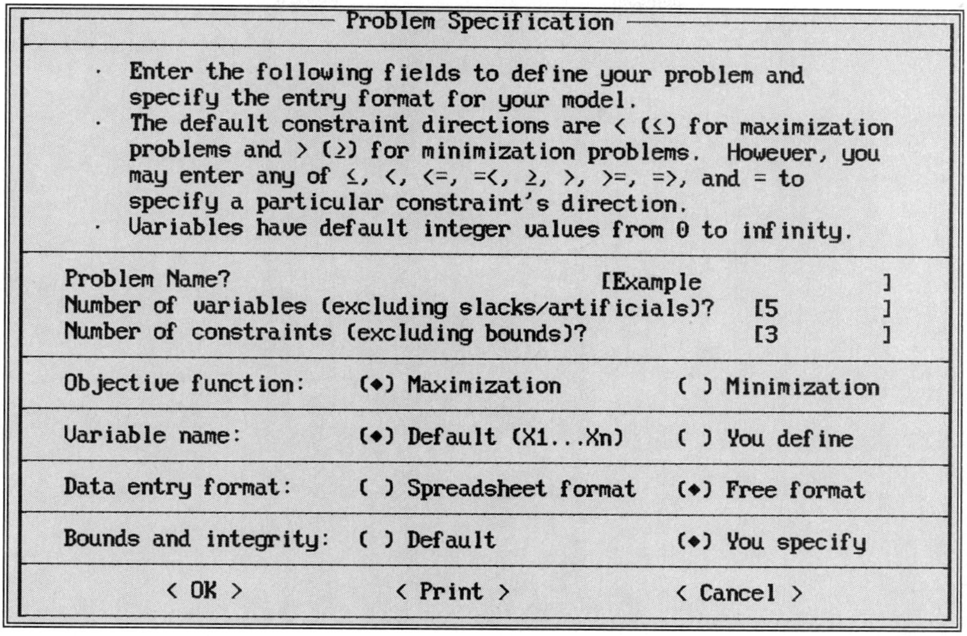

Figure 4-15. Problem specification for free-format entry.

2. After the problem specification is entered, the program will let you use commands to enter the ILP model. You may enter the “H” or “Help” command to display the available commands. Fig. 4-16 shows the commands. Note that you can enter any command at the prompt “?=”, and you can enter the data such as objective, constraints, or bounds at the prompt “>>”. If you just hit the “RETURN” key after the prompt “>>”, the program will return to the prompt “?=” and you may enter another command. The available commands are described below.

Bm:	Enter the bounds of variable *m* and specify its integrity.
Cn:	Enter the constraint *n*.
CnVm:	Enter the coefficient of constraint *n* variable *m*.
Dn:	Enter the direction of constraint *n*. Use to change direction.
H:	Recall the command information.
M:	Recall the modification menu.
Q:	Quit the free-format entry.
Rn:	Enter the right-hand side of constraint *n*. Use to change RHS.
S:	Show the whole model.

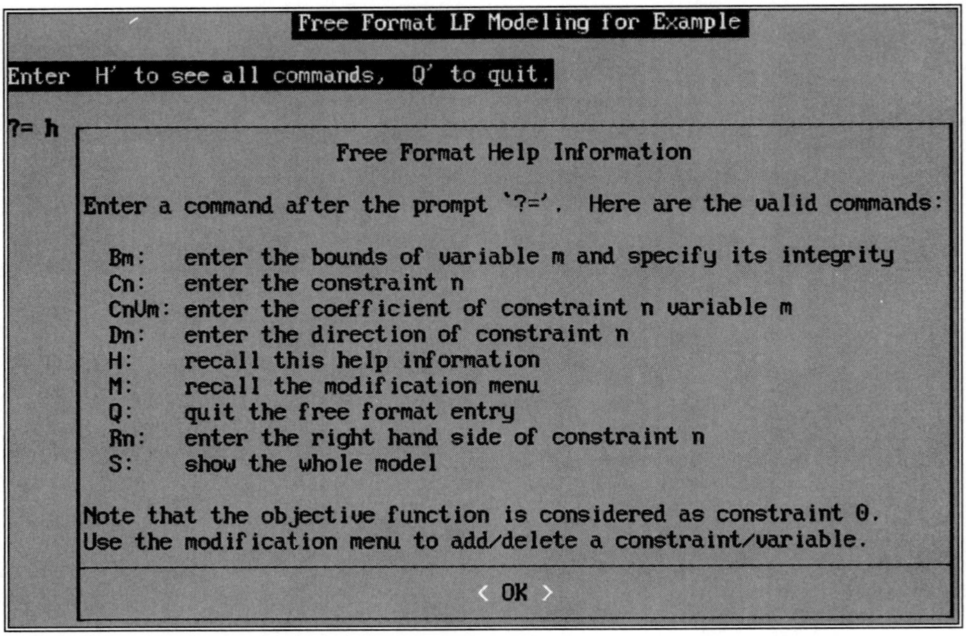

Figure 4-16. Available commands for free-format entry.

Note that the objective function is considered as constraint "0". When you want to change the number of constraints or variables, use the modification menu to add or delete a constraint or variable. The free-format entry is not case sensitive. That is to say, the commands "b1" and "B1" are the same, and the variables "X2" and "x2" are identical.

3. Fig. 4-17 shows the entry of the objective function (note that "c0" is used to specify the objective function). Fig. 4-18 shows the sequence of entering the three constraints, and Fig. 4-19 shows the sequence of entering the bounds and integrity for the five variables. After the model entry is done, use the command "S" to show the whole model and the command "Q" to quit the free-format entry. Fig. 4-20 demonstrates the action.

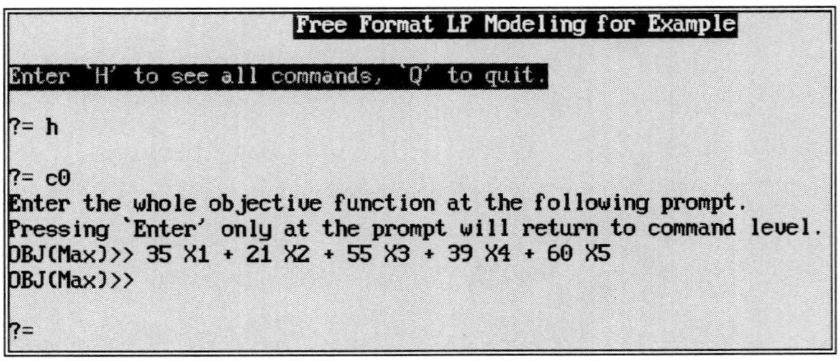

Figure 4-17. Free-format objective function entry.

```
                         Free Format LP Modeling for Example

Enter `H' to see all commands, `Q' to quit.
?= C1
Enter the whole constraint at the following prompt.
Pressing `Enter' only at the prompt will return to command level.
Constraint 1>> X1 + X2 + X3 + X4 + X5 <= 30
Constraint 1>>

?= C2
Enter the whole constraint at the following prompt.
Pressing `Enter' only at the prompt will return to command level.
Constraint 2>> 10 X1 + 8 X2 + 17 X3 + 20 X4 + 16 X5 <= 200
Constraint 2>>

?= C3
Enter the whole constraint at the following prompt.
Pressing `Enter' only at the prompt will return to command level.
Constraint 3>> 15 X1 + 3 X2 + 6 X3 + 32 X4 + 19 X5 >= 50
Constraint 3>>

?=
```

Figure 4-18. Free-format constraint entry.

```
                    Free Format LP Modeling for Example

Enter `H' to see all commands, `Q' to quit.
?= B1
  The lower bound of X1 (default=0) ?
  The upper bound of X1 (default=infinity) ? 20
  The integrity of X1: C(ontinuous) B(inary) I(nteger) ? I

?= B2
  The lower bound of X2 (default=0) ?
  The upper bound of X2 (default=infinity) ?
  The integrity of X2: C(ontinuous) B(inary) I(nteger) ? I

?= B3
  The lower bound of X3 (default=0) ?
  The upper bound of X3 (default=infinity) ?
  The integrity of X3: C(ontinuous) B(inary) I(nteger) ? B

?= B4
  The lower bound of X4 (default=0) ?
  The upper bound of X4 (default=infinity) ?
  The integrity of X4: C(ontinuous) B(inary) I(nteger) ? B

?=
```

Figure 4-19. Free-format bound and integrity entry.

```
                                  Free Format LP Modeling for Example

Enter 'H' to see all commands, 'Q' to quit.

?= S
OBJ>> Maximize   35 X1 + 21 X2 + 55 X3 + 39 X4 + 60 X5
(1)>>  X1  ≤ 30
(2)>> 10 X1 + 8 X2 + 17 X3 + 20 X4 + 16 X5  ≤ 200
(3)>> 15 X1 + 3 X2 + 6 X3 + 32 X4 + 19 X5  ≥ 50
Bounds>>  0 ≤ X1 ≤  20
Bounds>>  0 ≤ X3 ≤  1
Bounds>>  0 ≤ X4 ≤  1
Bounds>>  3 ≤ X5 ≤  10
Continuous variables >> X5
Integer variables >> X1  X2
Binary variables >> X3  X4

?= Q
Are you sure to quit free format modeling (Y/N)?
```

Figure 4-20. Show the whole model and quit the free format entry.

EXERCISES

1. Assume that X_1 and X_2 are integer with the upper-bound 40 and lower-bound 30 for exercise 1 in Chapter 3. Solve the problem by the ILP program, and observe each branch.
2. Assume that all variables for exercise 3 in Chapter 3 are integer with no bounds. Solve the problem by the ILP program.
3. Solve the following problem by ILP. Observe each iteration and draw a branch-and-bound tree.

$$
\begin{array}{llll}
\text{Maximize:} & 2X_1 + X_2 & & \\
\text{Subject to:} & 2X_1 + 2X_2 & \le & 8 \\
 & 4X_1 + X_2 & \le & 8 \\
 & X_1, X_2 \ge 0 \text{ and are integer.} & &
\end{array}
$$

4. Consider a capital budgeting problem in which five possible projects are being considered for implementation over the next three years. The expected returns for each project, the annual expenditures, and the budgets (all in thousands of dollars) are shown in the table. Assume that each approved project will continue over the entire three-year period.

Project	Expenditures Year 1	Year 2	Year 3	Expected return
1	5	1	8	22
2	4	7	10	40
3	3	9	2	25
4	7	4	1	16
5	8	6	10	28
Budget	22	25	30	

a. Formulate a zero-one integer linear programming model to maximize the total expected returns. Assume that unused funds cannot be carried forward. Use the ILP program to find the best solution.

b. When project 5 is selected, either project 1 or project 2 may be selected, but not both. Add this constraint and resolve it.

5. Midwestern Public Utility (MPU) must expand its electrical generation capacity by at least 1500 million kilowatts. It can do so in one or more of the following ways:

a. A conventional coal-fire plant could be built but must be located adjacent to a railroad right-of-way to facilitate the delivery of coal. Because of the desirability of land near existing railroad tracks, a suitable plant site will cost $2 million. The cost of building a conventional plant (exclusive of site costs) is estimated to be $0.5 million per million kilowatts of generating capacity.

b. A nuclear plant could be built but must be located in a remote area for safety. A suitable site can be obtained for $1 million. The cost of constructing the nuclear plant, exclusive of the site cost, is estimated to be $0.8 million per million kilowatts of generating capacity.

c. Due to recently passed legislation, a dam on a nearby river could be built. The dam will cost $4 million, but an attendant hydroelectric plant can be built at a cost of $0.1 million per million kilowatts of generating capacity. Unfortunately, the maximum capacity for such a plant is only 400 million kilowatts; moreover, if a dam is built, MPU must also agree to build a nuclear power plant.

Formulate an integer linear programming model to decide the least expensive means to expand the generating capacity by at least 1500 million kilowatts. Use the ILP program to solve it. Do you find any unreasonable conditions from the solution?

6. The CMC Company is opening a major research center at Austin, Texas, and it must purchase 400 desks for its offices. Three vendors in the area sell large volumes of desks. Vendor I can supply any number of desks for $500 each, plus a fixed order cost of $100. Vendor II can supply up to 350 desks. The first 100 desks will cost $550 each, while any additional desks over 100 will cost $490 each. There is no fixed ordering cost. Vendor III has a minimum order quantity of 50 desks and a maximum order quantity of 200 desks. If vendor III is used but fewer than 100 desks are purchased, then a fixed ordering cost of $300 is incurred. The price of a desk is $495. The company has decided to order from not more than two vendors.

a. Formulate an ILP model and use the ILP program to find the solution.

b. If fewer than 80 desks are ordered from vendor III, then vendor I must be used. Add this constraint and resolve the problem.

7. A metropolitan health planning agency is trying to locate several Health Maintenance Clubs (HMCs) that will provide prepaid health care. There are three potential site locations and four communities to be served by these sites. The table that follows shows the number of subscribers in thousands that can be assigned to a site if a HMC is opened there. The ability to capture subscribers depends upon how close the site is to the community and its resident population. It is possible to locate HMCs at more than one site.

	Community			
Site	1	2	3	4
1	50	10	25	20
2	20	15	20	40
3	25	20	10	25

Formulate a zero-one integer linear programming model to maximize total number of subscribers, using the variables:

X_{ij} = 1 if subscribers from *j* are assigned to site *i*, 0 otherwise

Y_i = 1 if site *i* is selected for HMC, 0 otherwise

Assume the HMCs will satisfy the following conditions:

a. Each HMC will have a minimum enrollment of 50,000 subscribers.

b. A community will be assigned to only one HMC.

c. If site 1 is selected, then either site 2 or site 3 may be selected, but not both.

Solve the problem by the ILP program.

8. A company manufactures gear boxes at three plants and ships them to three company-owned distribution centers. The variable production and distribution costs per unit shipped between plants and distribution centers, as well as the monthly production capacities of the plants, the monthly demand at the distribution centers, and the monthly fixed operating costs of plants and distribution centers are:

	Distribution center				
Plant	A	B	C	Capacity	Fixed cost
1	$25	30	27	600	$1700
2	27	25	29	600	2000
3	30	27	26	600	1900
Demand	500	500	500		
Fixed cost	$500	400	600		

The company has been hit by a recession. Management has decided to close one plant and one distribution center. Of course, demand at the closed distribution center will be lost (not satisfied). When a distribution center is closed, nothing will be shipped to it, and the fixed operating costs will become negligible. When a plant is closed, nothing will be manufactured or shipped from it. However, one half of the monthly fixed operating costs of the closed plant will still be incurred.

a. Formulate an integer programming model to help in deciding which plant and distribution center to close. Solve the model by the ILP program.

b. Assume that management has decided to close either plant 1 or plant 3 if either distribution center A or B is closed. Add this constraint and solve the problem.

9. The WAC Corporation has been awarded a contract to produce 800 radar units. The delivery schedule is as follows: April 30, 300 units; May 30, 500 units. Deviations from this schedule are not permitted. Also, radar units produced in April for delivery on May 30 can be stored in WAC's warehouse at a cost of $15 per unit. Each radar unit requires 20 hours of assembly labor. On April 1, the start of the contract, WAC has a total of 80 trained workers on its payroll. In addition, new workers can be hired on April 1 or May 1, as necessary. Each trained worker produces 120 regular hours of assembly labor per month. Each new worker requires 30 hours of initial training and therefore will produce only 90 hours during his or her first month of employment and 120 hours during the subsequent months. All workers receive fixed wages of $1200 per month and may be required to do overtime. However, the maximum overtime is restricted to 25 hours per month for any individual. Overtime is paid, in addition to regular wages, at $20 per hour. The cost of hiring new workers is $150 per worker, and all hiring is done on the first of the month. WAC wishes to restrict its entire work force to a maximum of 100 workers at any time. Further, it is WAC's policy not to lay off any worker. Assuming that exactly two trained workers will leave the company at the end of each month, WAC wishes to determine a minimum cost manpower plan for this contract. Solve the problem for WAC.

5

GOAL PROGRAMMING (GP)

OVERVIEW OF THE GP DECISION SUPPORT SYSTEM

This program solves linear goal programming problems. You may set up the problem using the following format for data entry.

Priority level 1:	Maximize:	3.2	GID1 +	4.0	GID2 −	5.0	GID3		
Priority level 2:	Minimize:	1.0	GID1 +	1.0	GID2 +	1.0	GID3		
	Subject to:	4.0	GID1 +	2.5	GID2 +	3.0	GID3	≤	50.0
		3.6	GID1 +	7.0	GID2 −	2.5	GID3	≤	86.9
		15.7	GID1		+	9.0	GID3	=	20.0
		GID1, GID2, and GID3 are nonnegative.							

The variables can be bounded; otherwise, they are assumed to be nonnegative. You may specify free or spreadsheet format to enter your formulation and bounds. You can define variables with up to ten characters. Defaults are $X_1, X_2, \ldots, Xn$. Problems can be saved on or read from a disk(ette). You can also display or print your problem and modify it as necessary. Based on the prioritized objective functions (goals), the program uses a multiphase simplex method to solve the problem lexicographically. When solving a problem, you have the option to let the program automatically scale the data in order to reduce rounded errors. You may choose to print out the final solution and the sensitivity analysis.

TECHNICAL NOTES ON THE GP PROGRAM

1. The data entry for a GP problem by the fixed or spreadsheet format is similar to the method described in the LP module (Chapter 3), except that the GP program allows multiple objective functions (goals).
2. The GP program uses a multiphase simplex method to solve any linear system with multiple prioritized objective functions. The program solves the problem in a way that satisfies the highest priority goal first and then sequentially optimizes the lower priority goals.
3. If the data in your problem have very wide-range values (e.g., 0.0001 and 10000),

you may normalize some of the data. Otherwise, round-off errors may occur. GP does allow you to scale the model data in order to avoid round-off errors. However, the results including the final solution and sensitivity analysis are based on the original data.

4. Variables may have upper and lower bounds that can be entered as constraints or pure bounded values. The default bounds for each variable are 0 to infinity, which is represented by "M" in GP.
5. All variables are assumed to be nonnegative. If you have some variables with nonpositive values only in your problem, you should transform them to nonnegative variables. Lower bounds can be negative. In the case of a negative lower bound, the correspondent variable will be shifted left before the model is solved.
6. The size of problems that can be solved by QSB+ 3.0 depends on the memory in your computer and the percentage of nonzero in the problem. One typical example is that a 100 by 100 problem with 20% nonzero can be solved by QSB+ 3.0.

MENU STRUCTURE

The functions and options in each of the pull-down menus are hierarchically listed as follows:

- Modules
  - Linear Programming (LP)
  - Integer Linear Programming (ILP)
  - Goal Programming (GP)
  - Quadratic Programming (QP)
  - Nonlinear Programming (NLP)
  - Dynamic Programming (DP)
  - Transportation and Transshipment (TRP)
  - Assignment and Traveling Salesman (ASTS)
  - Specialized Network Modeling (SNET)
  - Capacitated Network Flow Modeling (CNET)
  - Project Scheduling: CPM/PERT
  - Inventory Theory (INVT)
  - Inventory Theory 2 (INVT2)
  - Queuing Theory (QUEUE)
  - Queuing System Simulation (QSIM)
  - Decision Analysis (DA)
  - Markov Process (MKV)
  - Time Series Forecasting (TSFC)
  - Financial Analysis (FA)
  - Exit from QSB
- Input Data
  - Data Entry

- Read a File
- Show Data
- Print Data
- Modify Data
  - Modify the problem coefficients
  - Delete variable
  - Delete constraint
  - Delete goal
- Save
- Save As
- Exit from QSB

Solution
- Solve the Problem
- Specify Scaling
- Show the Solution
- Print the Solution
- Save the Solution
- Print Final Tableau

Options
- Color
- Monochrome
- Printer Selection

Help - GP
- About GP
- About the User Interface
- About the Edit Keys

SOLVING PROBLEMS WITH GP

In the following sections, we will use an example problem to show how to enter and solve the problem. The general procedure and menu options are described in detail in the tutorial sections of Chapter 2.

Example

To demonstrate the use of GP, consider the following problem having two prioritized goals. Note that priority levels represent the sequence of importance of the objective functions.

$$
\begin{array}{lll}
\text{Priority level 1:} & \text{Minimize:} & 3B + 2C \\
\text{Priority level 2:} & \text{Maximize:} & 10A + 9B + 8C \\
 & \text{Subject to:} & A + B \geq 30 \\
 & & B + C \geq 50 \\
 & & A + B + C \leq 80 \\
 & & 3A + 2C \leq 120 \\
 & & \text{All variables are nonnegative.}
\end{array}
$$

Enter the Problem

Select “Data Entry” from the “Input Data” menu (refer to Chapter 2 for selecting a menu item). Figs. 5-1 to 5-4 show the data entry of this problem. Note that “You define” is selected for the variable names, and “Default” is selected for bounds in the problem specification of Fig. 5-1. The spreadsheet format is chosen for model entry. When you enter the direction for a constraint such as in Fig. 5-4, “>”, “>=”, and “≥” all represent “greater than or equal to”, and “<”, “<=”, and “≤” all represent “less than or equal to”.

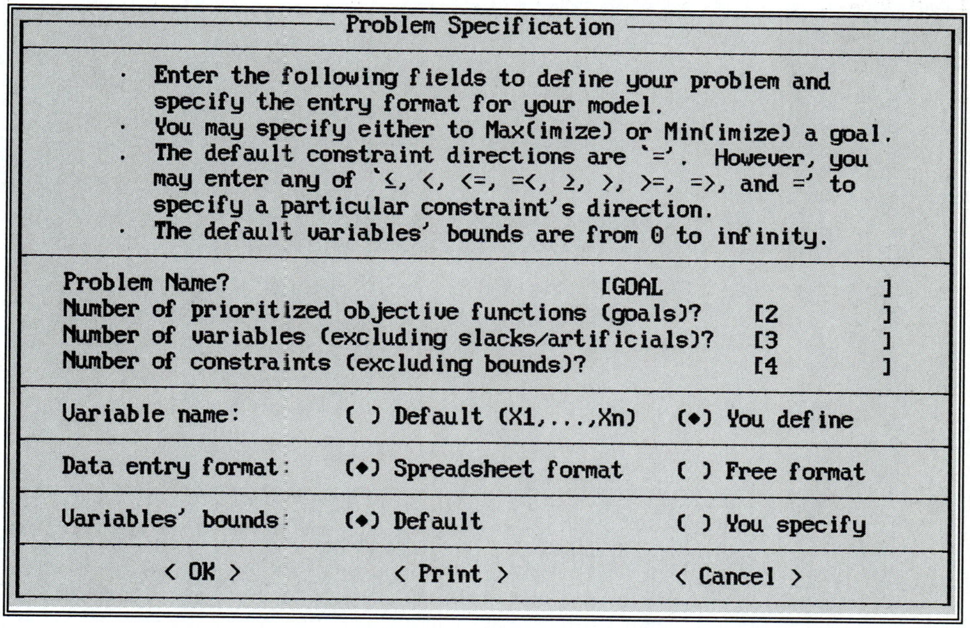

Figure 5-1. Problem specification for GOAL.

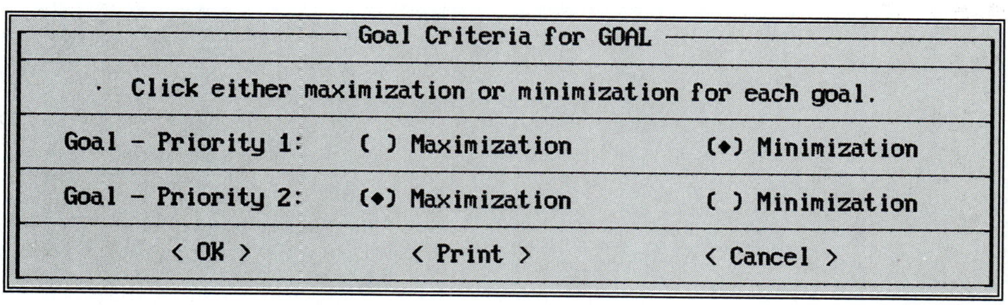

Figure 5-2. Objective criteria for GOAL.

Variable Names for GOAL

Variable	Name
1	[A]
2	[B]
3	[C]

< OK > < PgUp > < PgLt > < PgRt > < Help > < Print > < Cancel >

Figure 5-3. Variable names for GOAL.

GP Model Coefficients for GOAL

Constraint	A	B	C	Direction	RHS
Goal 1:Min.	[	][3	][2	][	][
Goal 2:Max.	[10	][9	][8	][	][
1	[1	][1	][	][>	][30
2	[	][1	][1	][>	][50
3	[1	][1	][1	][<	][80
4	[3	][	][2	][<	][120

< OK > < PgUp > < PgLt > < PgRt > < Help > < Print > < Cancel >

Figure 5-4. Model entry for GOAL.

Solve the Problem

1. Select "Solve the Problem" from the "Solution" menu to solve the problem.The message "Please standby..." will display for a short period while the problem is being solved.
2. After the problem is solved, select "Show the Solution" from the "Solution" menu to display the solution and sensitivity analysis. Figs. 5-5 to 5-7 show the solution and analyses of objective functions and constraints. Note that in Fig. 5-5 opportunity costs are listed only for the first four priority levels. The minimum and maximum "Goal Coef." in Fig. 5-6 represent the range of the objective function coefficients for which the current basis holds. Similarly, the minimum and maximum "R. H. S." in Fig. 5-7 represent the range of the right-hand sides for which the current basis holds.
3. If the problem has a wide range of data, you may want to let the program scale the data in order to reduce the rounded errors. Fig. 5-8 shows the dialog if you choose "Specify Scaling" from the "Solution" menu. Click "YES" to confirm or click "NO" to use the original data.

Solution Summary for GOAL

08-23-1993 10:28:04 Page: 1 of 1

Number	Variable	Solution	Opportunity Cost-Goal 1	Opportunity Cost-Goal 2	Opportunity Cost-Goal 3	Opportunity Cost-Goal 4
1	A	16	0	0		
2	B	14	0	0		
3	C	36	0	0		

Priority Goal 1: Minimized OBJ = 114
Priority Goal 2: Maximized OBJ = 574
Number of Iterations = 9 Elapsed CPU seconds = 0

< PageDown > < PageUp > < Hardcopy > < Cancel >

Figure 5-5. Solution summary for GOAL.

Analysis of Goal Coefficients for GOAL

08-23-1993 10:28:35 Page: 1 of 1

Variable Number	Variable Name	Priority Goal Level	Opportunity Cost	Minimum Goal Coef.	Current Goal Coef.	Maximum Goal Coef.
1	A	1	0	-1.5	0	1
2	B	1	0	2	3	M
3	C	1	0	-2	2	3
4	A	2	0	-M	10	M
5	B	2	0	-M	9	M
6	C	2	0	-M	8	M

< PageDown > < PageUp > < Hardcopy > < Cancel >

Figure 5-6. Analysis of the objective function coefficients for GOAL.

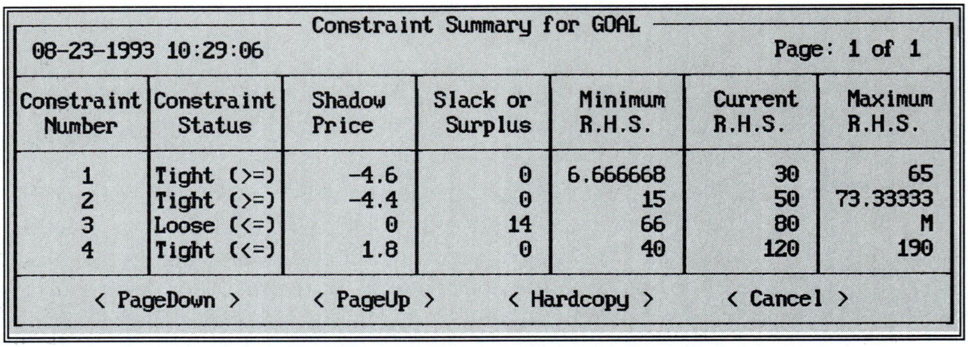

Constraint Summary for GOAL

08-23-1993 10:29:06 Page: 1 of 1

Constraint Number	Constraint Status	Shadow Price	Slack or Surplus	Minimum R.H.S.	Current R.H.S.	Maximum R.H.S.
1	Tight (>=)	-4.6	0	6.666668	30	65
2	Tight (>=)	-4.4	0	15	50	73.33333
3	Loose (<=)	0	14	66	80	M
4	Tight (<=)	1.8	0	40	120	190

< PageDown > < PageUp > < Hardcopy > < Cancel >

Figure 5-7. Analysis of the constraints for GOAL.

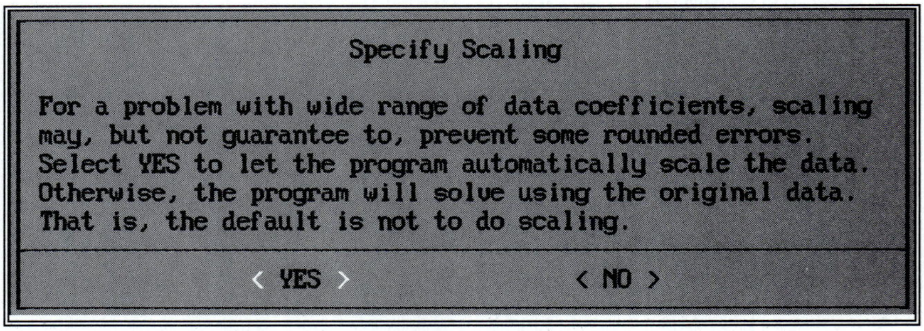

Figure 5-8. Specify scaling.

FREE-FORMAT MODEL ENTRY

The GP formulation can be entered or modified in free-format. In this section, we will show you the free-format model entry by entering the example problem "GOAL".

1. After selecting "Data Entry" from the "Input Data" menu, Fig. 5-9 shows the problem specification entry. Note that the free-format data entry is specified in Fig. 5-9. After the problem specification is entered, you then specify the goal criteria (Fig. 5-2) and enter the variable names (Fig. 5-3).

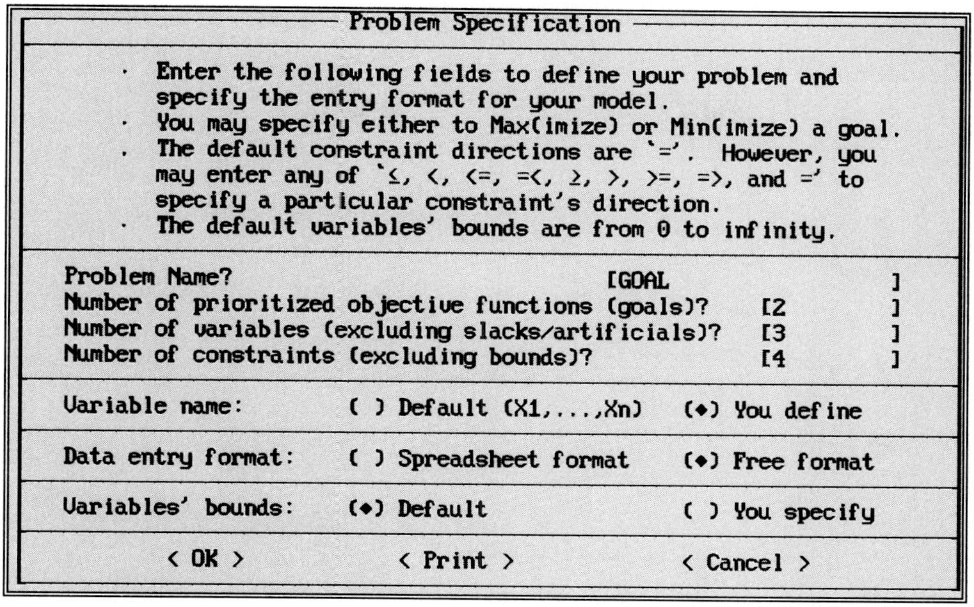

Figure 5-9. Problem specification for free-format entry.

2. The program will then let you use commands to enter the GP model. You may enter the "H" or "Help" command to display the available commands. Fig. 5-10 shows the commands. Note that you can enter any command at the prompt "?=", and you can enter the data such as objective, constraints, or bounds at the prompt ">>". If you just hit the "RETURN" key after the prompt ">>", the program will return to the prompt "?=" and you may enter another command. The available commands are described below.

Bm:	Enter the bounds of variable m.
Cn:	Enter the constraint n.
CnVm:	Enter the coefficient of constraint n variable m.
Dn:	Enter the direction of constraint n. Use to change direction.
Gn:	Enter the goal n.
GnVm:	Enter the coefficient of goal n variable m.
H:	Recall the command information.
M:	Recall the modification menu.
Q:	Quit the free-format entry.
Rn:	Enter the right-hand side of constraint n. Use to change RHS.
S:	Show the whole model.

When you want to change the number of constraints or variables, use the modification menu to add or delete a constraint or variable. The free-format entry is not case sensitive. That is to say, the commands “b1” and “B1” are the same, and the variables “A” and “a” are identical.

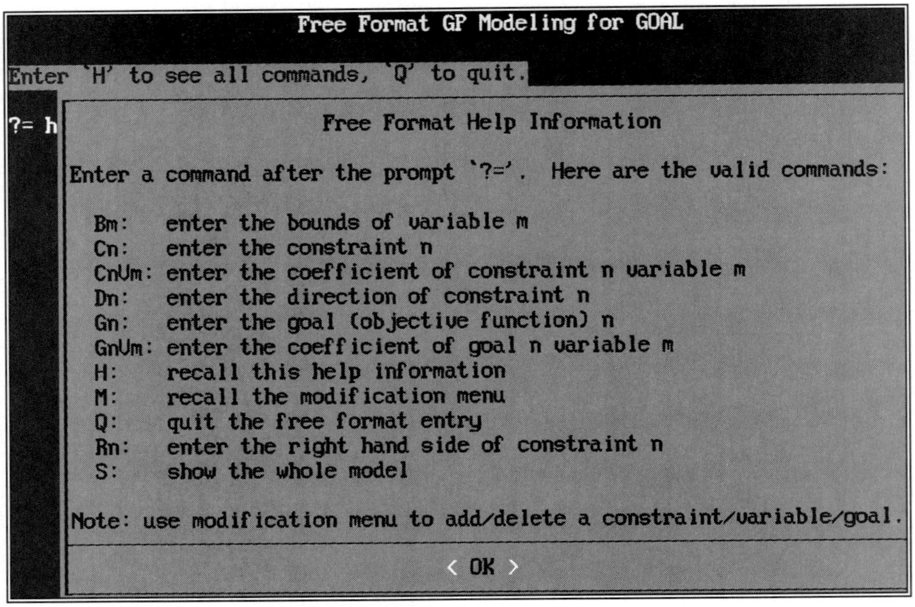

Figure 5-10. Available commands for free-format entry.

3. Fig. 5-11 shows the entry of the objective functions. Fig. 5-12 shows the sequence of entering the constraints. After the model entry is done, use the command “S” to show the whole model and the command “Q” to quit the free-format entry. Fig. 5-13 demonstrates the action.

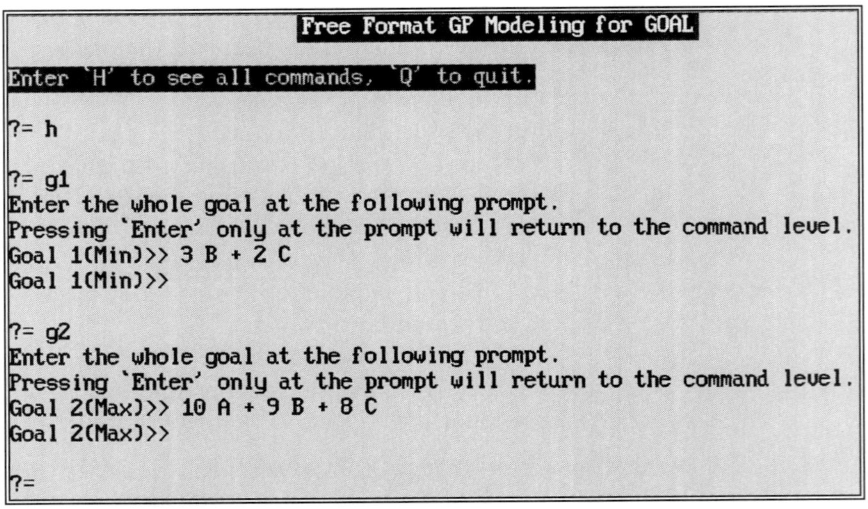

Figure 5-11. Free-format objective function entry.

```
Free Format GP Modeling for GOAL

Enter 'H' to see all commands, 'Q' to quit.
?= c1
Enter the whole constraint at the following prompt.
Pressing 'Enter' only at the prompt will return to the command level.
Constraint 1>> A + B >= 30
Constraint 1>>

?= C2
Enter the whole constraint at the following prompt.
Pressing 'Enter' only at the prompt will return to the command level.
Constraint 2>> B + C >= 50
Constraint 2>>

?= C3
Enter the whole constraint at the following prompt.
Pressing 'Enter' only at the prompt will return to the command level.
Constraint 3>> A + B + C <= 80
Constraint 3>>
?= C4
Enter the whole constraint at the following prompt.
Pressing 'Enter' only at the prompt will return to the command level.
Constraint 4>> 3 A + 2 c <= 120
Constraint 4>>

?=
```

Figure 5-12. Free-format constraint entry.

```
?= S
Goal 1>> Minimize    3 B + 2 C
Goal 2>> Maximize    10 A + 9 B + 8 C
(1)>>  A  ≥ 30
(2)>>  B  ≥ 50
(3)>>  A  ≤ 80
(4)>> 3 A + 2 C  ≤ 120

?= Q
Are you sure to quit free format modeling (Y/N)?
```

Figure 5-13. Show the whole model and quit the free-format entry.

EXERCISES

1. Consider the following GP model with two levels of goals:

Level 1: Minimize: P + N

Level 2: Maximize: A + 3 B − 4 C

$$\begin{aligned} \text{Subject to:} \quad & A + B && \leq 150 \\ & 3A + 2B - C && \geq 210 \\ & 5A - 2B + 4C + P - N && = 315 \end{aligned}$$

Assume all variables are nonnegative. Find the optimal solution.

2. Find the optimal solution for the following GP problem with two prioritized goals.

Goal 1: Maximize:
$$9X_1 + X_2 + 2X_3 + 19X_4 + X_5 + 8X_6$$

Goal 2: Maximize:
$$7X_1 + 9X_2 - 3X_3 + 11X_4 - X_5 + 2X_6$$

Subject to:

$$\begin{aligned} X_1 + X_2 + X_3 + X_4 + X_5 + X_6 &\leq 200 \\ 2X_1 + X_2 + 6X_3 - X_4 + 2X_5 + 7X_6 &\geq 271 \\ 4X_1 + 2X_3 + 3X_5 - X_6 &\leq 350 \\ 7X_2 + 11X_3 - 4X_4 + 6X_5 &\leq 429 \\ X_1 + 4X_3 + 7X_5 &\leq 310 \end{aligned}$$

X_1, X_2, X_3, X_4, X_5, and $X_6 \geq 0$

3. Sesame Oil Company produces three grades of motor oil: regular, high power, and super power. They are blended from three types of crude oil. Each type of crude oil contains three important ingredients. The percentages of ingredients in each type of crude oil are:

	Ingredient		
Crude oil	I	II	III
A	80%	10%	5%
B	45%	30%	20%
C	30%	40%	25%

The specifications of the three types of motor oil are:

	Ingredient		
Motor oil	I	II	III
Super power	≥60%	≤25%	≤10%
High power	≥50%	≤30%	≤15%
Regular	≤40%	≥35%	≥20%

The costs per gallon for crude oil A, B, and C are \$0.65, \$0.50, and \$0.45, respectively. Daily demands for super power, high power, and regular are at least 50,000 gallons, 70,000 gallons, and 40,000 gallons. However, Sesame Oil can purchase crude oil A at most 60,000 gallons, crude oil B at most 40,000 gallons, and crude oil C at most 50,000 gallons from OPEC countries each day. The management has the following goals in priority.

a. Maximize the profit if the market prices for the three motor oils per gallon are \$1.05, \$1.19, and \$1.35, respectively.

b. Satisfy the demands as much as possible.

Based on these goals, how many gallons of each type of crude oil should be used in each type of motor oil and at what levels are the goals achieved?

6

QUADRATIC PROGRAMMING (QP)

OVERVIEW OF THE QP DECISION SUPPORT SYSTEM

This program solves quadratic programming problems. You may set up the problem using the following format for data entry.

Maximize:	3.2	GID1	+	4.0	GID2	−	5.0	GID3	+	3	GID1**2
									−	5	GID2 * GID3
Subject to:	4.0	GID1	+	2.5	GID2	+	3.0	GID3	≤	50.0	
	3.6	GID1	+	7.0	GID2	−	2.5	GID3	≤	86.9	
	15.7	GID1				+	9.0	GID3	=	20.0	

GID1, GID2, and GID3 are nonnegative and ** represents exponentiation.

The variables can be bounded; otherwise, they are assumed to be nonnegative. You may specify free or spreadsheet format to enter your formulation and bounds. You can define variables with up to ten characters. Defaults are $X_1, X_2, \ldots, X_n$. Problems can be saved on or read from a disk(ette). You can also display or print your problem and modify it as necessary. A modified simplex method is used to solve the problem. It guarantees a global optimal solution when the objective function has a definite matrix. Otherwise, it may end up with a local optimal solution. When solving a problem, you have the option to let the program automatically scale the data in order to reduce rounded errors.

TECHNICAL NOTES ON THE QP PROGRAM

1. The QP program converts the quadratic programming problem to the linear system by using the Kuhn-Tucker conditions and then solves the problem by using the revised simplex with upper-bounding method.
2. The QP program also determines the characteristics of the quadratic objective function, which may be definite, semidefinite, or indefinite. In the case of maximization (minimization), the QP program will find the optimal solution if the objective function is convex (concave); that is, when the coefficients of quad-

ratic terms form a negative (positive) semidefinite or definite matrix. Otherwise, the solution may not be global optimal.

3. When entering your problem by free-format, enter the quadratic terms by the format, for example, of X**2, 3*X*Y, or 5X*X (X and Y are variables; ** represents to the power of). Note that X**2 and X*X are treated the same in this program.
4. Variables may have upper and lower bounds that can be entered as constraints or pure bounded values. The default bounds for each variable are 0 to infinity, which is represented by "M" in QP.
5. All variables are assumed to be nonnegative. If you have some variables with nonpositive values only in your problem, you should transform them to nonnegative variables. Bounds can be negative. In the case of a negative lower bound, the correspondent variable will be shifted left before the model is solved.
6. The size of problems that can be solved by QSB+ 3.0 depends on the memory in your computer and the percentage of nonzero in the problem. One typical example is that a 30 by 30 problem with 10% nonzero can be solved by QSB+ 3.0.

MENU STRUCTURE

The functions and options in each of the pull-down menus are hierarchically listed as follows:

Modules
- Linear Programming (LP)
- Integer Linear Programming (ILP)
- Goal Programming (GP)
- Quadratic Programming (QP)
- Nonlinear Programming (NLP)
- Dynamic Programming (DP)
- Transportation and Transshipment (TRP)
- Assignment and Traveling Salesman (ASTS)
- Specialized Network Modeling (SNET)
- Capacitated Network Flow Modeling (CNET)
- Project Scheduling: CPM/PERT
- Inventory Theory (INVT)
- Inventory Theory 2 (INVT2)
- Queuing Theory (QUEUE)
- Queuing System Simulation (QSIM)
- Decision Analysis (DA)
- Markov Process (MKV)
- Time Series Forecasting (TSFC)
- Financial Analysis (FA)
- Exit from QSB

- Input Data
  - Data Entry
  - Read a File
  - Show Data
  - Print Data
  - Modify Data
    - Modify the problem coefficients
    - Delete variable
    - Delete constraint
  - Save
  - Save As
  - Exit from QSB
- Solution
  - Solve the Problem
  - Check Quadratic Matrix
  - Show the Solution
  - Print the Solution
  - Save the Solution
- Options
  - Color
  - Monochrome
  - Printer Selection
- Help - QP
  - About QP
  - About the User Interface
  - About the Edit Keys

SOLVING PROBLEMS WITH QP

In the following sections, we will use an example problem to show how to enter and solve the problem. The general procedure and menu options are described in detail in the tutorial sections of Chapter 2.

Example

To demonstrate the use of QP, consider the following problem.

Maximize:	3.2GID1	+	5.0GID2	+	5.0GID3	−	GID1**2
						−	2GID2**2
						−	5GID3**2
Subject to:	4.0GID1	+	2.5GID2	+	3.0GID3	≥	50.0
	3.6GID1	+	7.0GID2	−	2.5GID3	=	86.9
	GID1, GID2, and GID3 are nonnegative.						

Enter the Problem

Select “Data Entry” from the “Input Data” menu (refer to Chapter 2 for selecting a menu item). Figs. 6-1 to 6-4 show the data entry of this problem. Note that “You define” is selected for the variable names, and “Default” is selected for bounds in the problem specification of Fig. 6-1. The spreadsheet format is chosen for model entry. When you enter the direction for a constraint such as in Fig. 6-4, “>”, “>=”, and “≥” all represent “greater than or equal to”, and “<”, “<=”, and “≤” all represent “less than or equal to”.

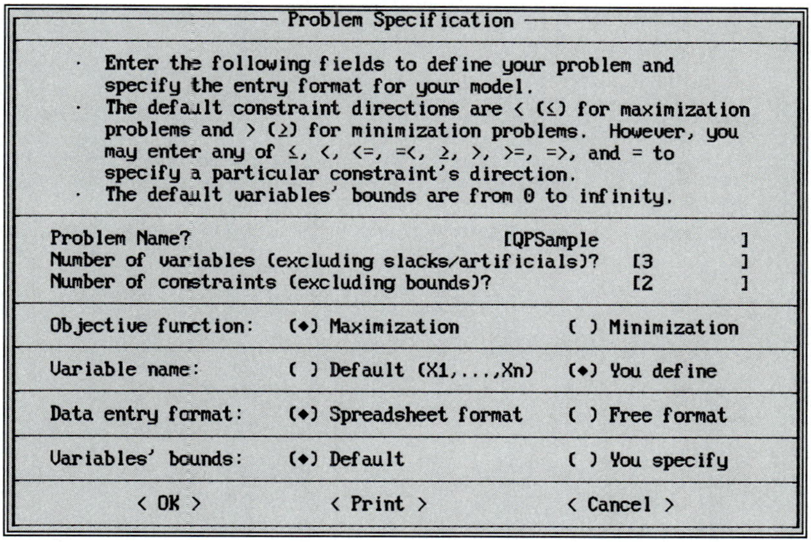

Figure 6-1. Problem specification for QPSample.

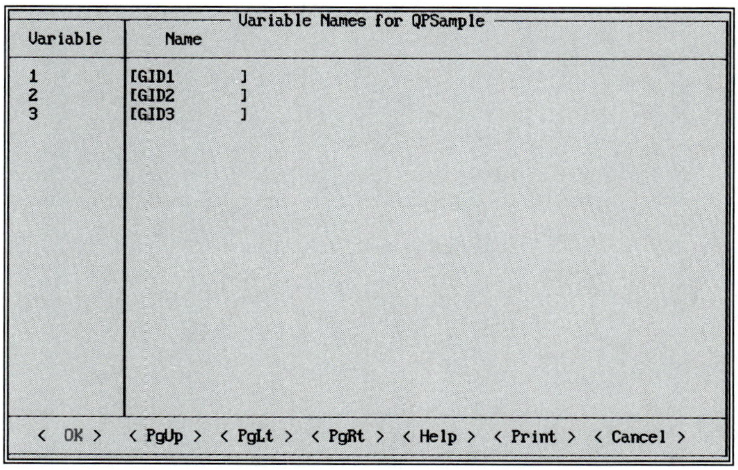

Figure 6-2. Variable names for QPSample.

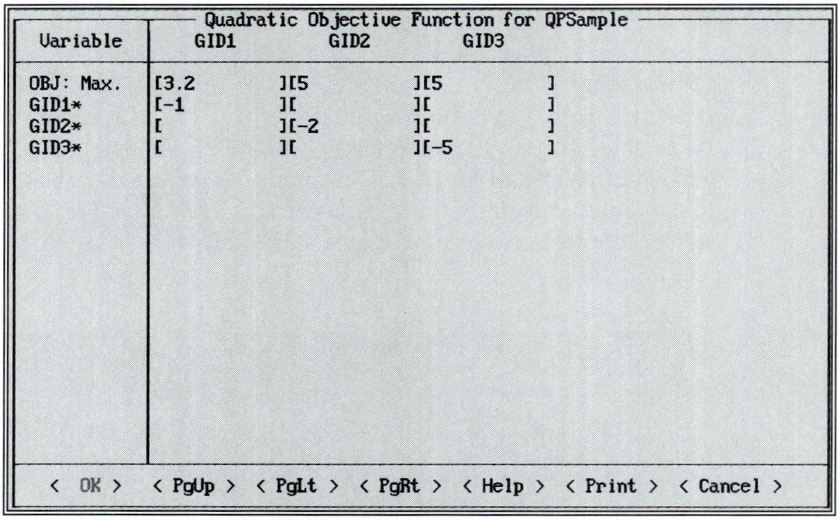

Figure 6-3. Objective function for QPSample.

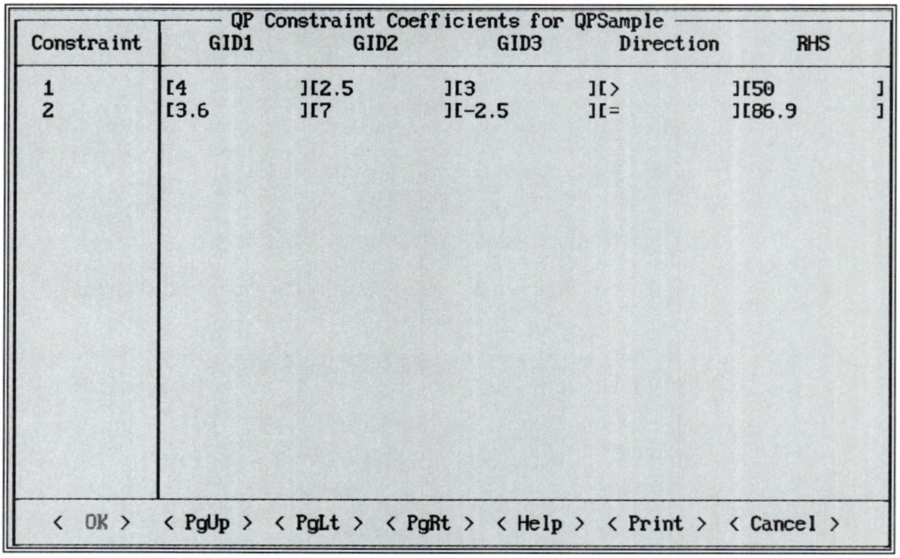

Figure 6-4. Constraint entry for QPSample.

Solve the Problem

1. Select "Solve the Problem" from the "Solution" menu to solve the problem. The message "Please standby . . ." will display for a short period while the problem is being solved.

2. After the problem is solved, select "Show the Solution" from the "Solution" menu to display the solution. Fig. 6-5 and Fig. 6-6 show the solution and analyses of constraints. The slack or surplus in Fig. 6-6 represents the range that the right-hand side will be reached.
3. If you just want to know the property of the matrix of the quadratic terms in the objective function, choose "Check Quadratic Matrix" from the "Solution" menu. Fig. 6-7 shows the property of the quadratic matrix of this example problem.

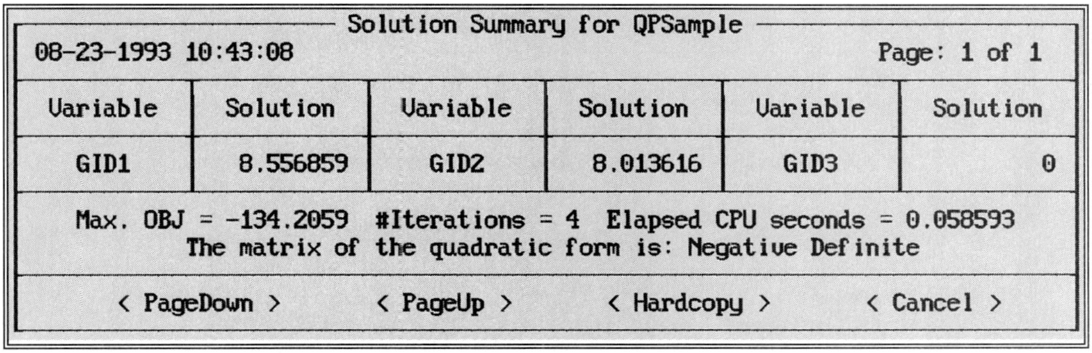

Solution Summary for QPSample
08-23-1993 10:43:08 Page: 1 of 1

Variable	Solution	Variable	Solution	Variable	Solution
GID1	8.556859	GID2	8.013616	GID3	0

Max. OBJ = -134.2059 #Iterations = 4 Elapsed CPU seconds = 0.058593
The matrix of the quadratic form is: Negative Definite

< PageDown > < PageUp > < Hardcopy > < Cancel >

Figure 6-5. Solution summary for QPSample.

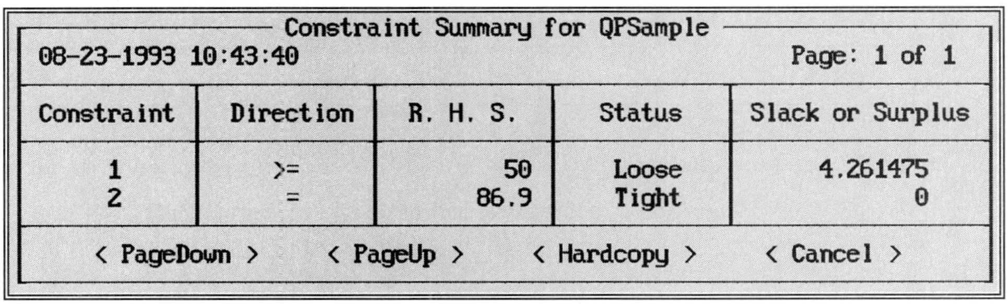

Constraint Summary for QPSample
08-23-1993 10:43:40 Page: 1 of 1

Constraint	Direction	R. H. S.	Status	Slack or Surplus
1	>=	50	Loose	4.261475
2	=	86.9	Tight	0

< PageDown > < PageUp > < Hardcopy > < Cancel >

Figure 6-6. Analysis of the constraints for QPSample.

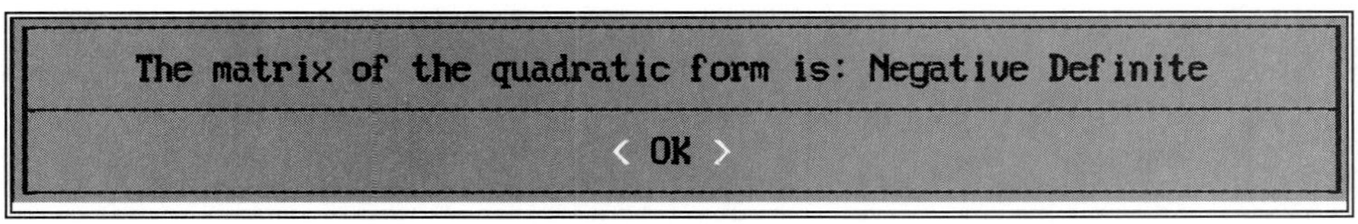

Figure 6-7. Check the property of the quadratic form.

FREE-FORMAT MODEL ENTRY

The QP formulation can be entered or modified in free format. In this section, we will show you the free-format model entry by entering the above example problem "QPSample".

1. After selecting "Data Entry" from the "Input Data" menu, Fig. 6-8 shows the problem specification entry. Note that the free-format data entry is specified in Fig. 6-8. After the problem specification is entered, you then enter the variable names (Fig. 6-2).

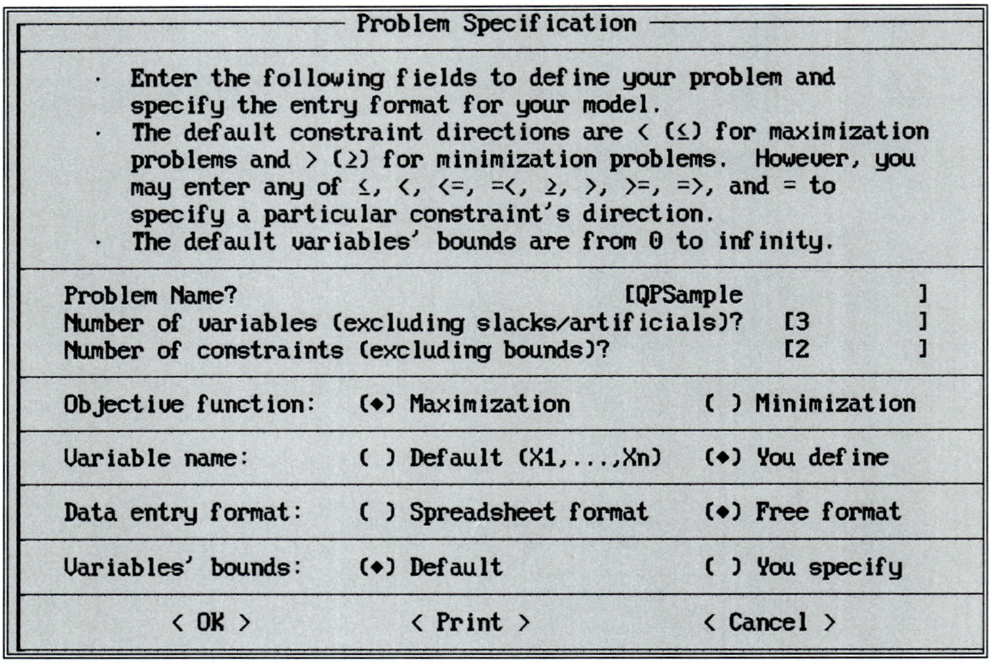

Figure 6-8. Problem specification for free-format entry.

2. The program will then let you use commands to enter the model. You may enter the "H" or "Help" command to display the available commands. Fig. 6-9 shows the commands. Note that you can enter any command at the prompt "?=", and you can enter the data such as objective, constraints, or bounds at the prompt ">>". If you just hit the "RETURN" key after the prompt ">>", the program will return to the prompt "?=" and you may enter another command. The available commands are described below.

Bm:	Enter the bounds of variable *m*.
Cn:	Enter the constraint *n*.
CnVm:	Enter the coefficient of constraint *n* variable *m*.

Dn: Enter the direction of constraint *n*. Use to change direction.
H: Recall the command information.
M: Recall the modification menu.
O: Enter the objective function.
Q: Quit the free-format entry.
Rn: Enter the right-hand side of constraint *n*. Use to change RHS.
S: Show the whole model.
VnVm: Enter the coefficient of the objective function quadratic term Vn*Vm.

When you want to change the number of constraints or variables, use the modification menu to add or delete a constraint or variable. The free-format entry is not case sensitive. That is to say, the commands “b1” and “B1” are the same, and the variables “GID1” and “gid1” are identical.

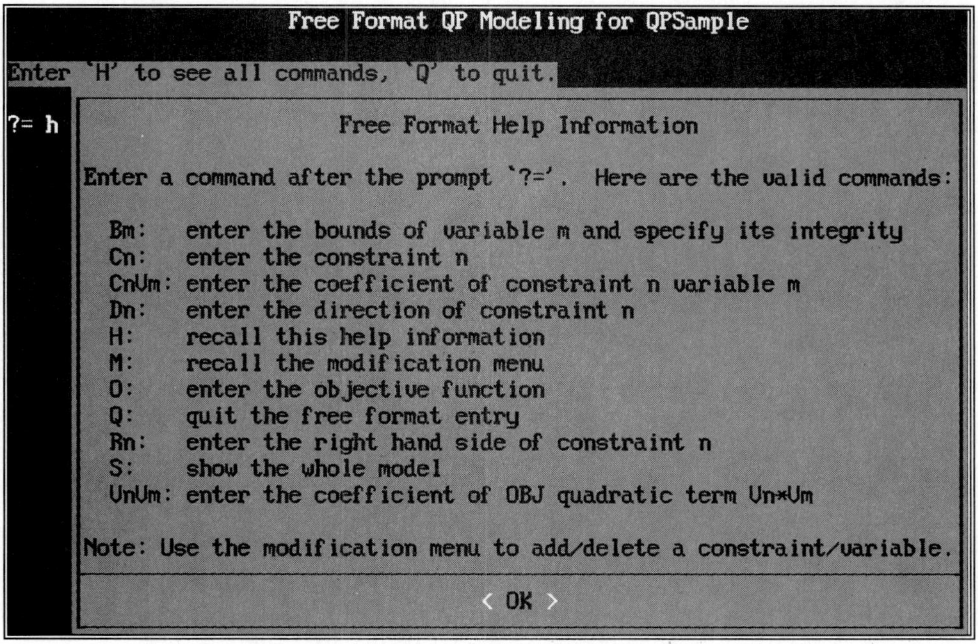

Figure 6-9. Available commands for free-format entry.

3. Fig. 6-10 shows the entry of the objective function and constraints. After the model entry is done, use the command “S” to show the whole model and the command “Q” to quit the free-format entry. Fig. 6-11 demonstrates the action.

```
                        Free Format QP Modeling for QPSample

Enter `H' to see all commands, `Q' to quit.
?= O
Enter the whole objective function at the following prompt.
Pressing `Enter' only at the prompt will return to command level.
OBJ(Max)>> 3.2 GID1 + 5 GID2 + 5 GID3 - GID1**2 - 2 GID2**2 - 5 GID3**2
OBJ(Max)>>

?= C1
Enter the whole constraint at the following prompt.
Pressing `Enter' only at the prompt will return to command level.
Constraint 1>> 4 GID1 + 2.5 GID2 + 3 GID3 >= 50
Constraint 1>>

?= C2
Enter the whole constraint at the following prompt.
Pressing `Enter' only at the prompt will return to command level.
Constraint 2>> 3.6 GID1 + 7 GID2 - 2.5 GID3 = 86.9
Constraint 2>>

?=
```

Figure 6-10. Free-format model entry.

```
?= S
OBJ>> Maximize    3.2GID1 + 5GID2 + 5GID3-2GID2*GID2-5GID3*GID3
(1)>> 4 GID1 + 2.5 GID2 + 3 GID3  ≥ 50
(2)>> 3.6 GID1 + 7 GID2 - 2.5 GID3  = 86.9

?= Q
Are you sure to quit free format modeling (Y/N)?
```

Figure 6-11. Show the whole model and quit the free-format entry.

EXERCISES

1. Find the optimal solution for the following QP problem:

Maximize: $8X_1 + 12X_2 - 2X_1^2 - 3X_2^2$

Subject to:

$2X_1 + 5X_2 \leq 250$

$11X_1 + 9X_2 \leq 710$

$X_1, X_2 \geq 0$

2. Solve the following QP model:

Maximize: $A + 3B - 4C - 2A_2 + 2AB - 2B_2 - C_2$

Subject to: $A + B \leq 150$

$$
\begin{aligned}
3A + 2B - C &\geq 210 \\
5A - 2B + 4C &\geq 315 \\
A, B, \text{ and } C &\geq 0
\end{aligned}
$$

3. Find the optimal solution for the following QP problem:

Maximize:

$$
\begin{aligned}
&7X_1 + 9X_2 - 3X_3 + 11X_4 - X_5 + 2X_6 \\
&- X_1^2 - X_2^2 - 0.5X_3^2 - 0.5X_4^2 - 5X_5^2 - 5X_6^2 \\
&- 2X_1X_2 - X_3X_4 - 10X_5X_6
\end{aligned}
$$

Subject to:

$$
\begin{aligned}
X_1 + X_2 + X_3 + X_4 + X_5 + X_6 &\leq 200 \\
2X_1 + X_2 + 6X_3 - X_4 + 2X_5 + 7X_6 &\geq 271 \\
4X_1 + 2X_3 + 3X_5 - X_6 &\leq 350 \\
7X_2 + 11X_3 - 4X_4 + 6X_5 &\leq 429 \\
X_1 + 4X_3 + 7X_5 &\leq 310 \\
X_1, X_2, X_3, X_4, X_5, \text{ and } X_6 &\geq 0
\end{aligned}
$$

7

NONLINEAR PROGRAMMING (NLP)

OVERVIEW OF THE NLP DECISION SUPPORT SYSTEM

This program solves nonlinear programming problems. Typical nonlinear problems are formulated as follows.

Maximize/Minimize:	$f(X_1, \ldots, X_n)$
Subject to	$g_i(X_1, \ldots, X_n) \leq a_i$
	$h_j(X_1, \ldots, X_n) \geq b_j$
	$e_k(X_1, \ldots, X_n) = c_k$

where f, g, h, e are functions of variables X_1 to X_n, and a, b, c are right-hand-side constants. A possible function can be a combination of polynomial terms and ABS, ATN, CINT, COS, EXP, FIX, INT, LOG, SGN, SIN, SQR and TAN functions. These functions will be described shortly.

A line search methodology is used to solve unconstrained problems. A sequential unconstrained minimization technique (SUMT) with penalty function methodology is used to solve constrained problems. You may set solution domain and parameters for the solution process.

The variables can be bounded; otherwise, they are assumed to be nonnegative. The free format is used to enter the problem formulation. You can define variables with up to ten characters. Defaults are $X_1, X_2, \ldots, X_n$. Problems can be saved on or read from a disk(ette). You can also display or print your problem and modify it as necessary.

TECHNICAL NOTES ON THE NLP PROGRAM

1. The function in an NLP program is an expression which consists of constants, variables, arithmetic operations, scientific functions, and polynomial terms. The arithmetic operations and their order of precedence are listed in Table 7-1 and the available scientific functions are listed in Table 7-2.

Table 7-1. Arithmetic operations.

Hierarchy or precedence	Operator symbol	Operations
1	^	Exponentiation
2	−	Negation
3	*, /	Multiplication and division
4	\	Integer division
5	MOD	Modulo arithmetic
6	+, −	Addition and subtraction

Table 7-2. Scientific functions.

Function symbol	Action
ABS	Absolute value
ATN	Arctangent function
CINT	Rounding to an integer
COS	Cosine function
EXP	Exponential function
FIX	Truncating to an integer
INT	Floor function
LOG	Natural logarithm
SGN	Sign value (1, 0, −1)
SIN	Sine function
SQR	Square root
TAN	Tangent function

Sample functions that are acceptable to the NLP program are illustrated as follows. Assume that X, Y, Z, A, B, and C are variable names.

```
COS(X+Y/Z)−TAN(A*B^2)
X*Y^3.5+(C^2/(LOG(A−Y*Z)−5)
X^2+Y^2+Z^2−1.5Y*Z+1.05X*Z
```

2. NLP classifies the nonlinear problems into unconstrained and constrained problems. An unconstrained problem has only the objective function and no constraint. Variable bounds are not considered as constraints.
3. In NLP, unconstrained problems are solved by line search methods. Golden Section Method and Dichotomous Search Method are employed sequentially to solve a single-variable unconstrained problem and retain the best solution. Hooke and Jeeves Line Search Method, which includes cyclic exploratory search and pattern direction move, is used to solve a multi-variable unconstrained problem. A small tolerance value may be assigned to help stop the search. When the consecutive search value is within the tolerance value, the

search will stop. The default tolerance is 0.0001. You can also specify the boundary and starting point for the search and specify the CPU seconds to stop the search. If you are not satisfied with the solution, you may try to solve the problem with different tolerance value, starting point, boundary, and/or CPU seconds.

4. For the unconstrained problems, the quality of the solution depends very much on the property of the objective function. The line search usually stops very close to global optimal if the objective function is convex for minimization and concave for maximization. However, as mentioned above, tolerance value, starting point, boundary, and running CPU time may also affect the solution quality.

5. In NLP, the constrained problems are solved by Sequential Unconstrained Minimization Technique (SUMT). The basic idea of SUMT is, at each sequential stage, to convert the constrained problem into an unconstrained problem by using penalty parameters when constraints are violated. For any nonlinear constrained problem, it can be represented by the following general form:

Minimize: $f(x)$
Subject to: $g_i(x) = 0$, where $i = 1$ to m

Where x is the variable vector, f is the objective function, g_i is the constraint i, and m is the number of constraints. Any inequality constraint can be converted to equality by adding or subtracting a slack or surplus to the left-hand side. A nonzero right-hand side can be removed by subtracting to the left-hand side.

Let	$E(x) = \Sigma_i \lvert g_i \rvert p$	Sum of all the constraint violation to the power p
	p	A positive integer power
	ε	Stopping tolerance value
	β	Scalar constant
	k	Stage
	μ_k	Penalty parameter at stage k
	x_k	Optimal solution of x at stage k

SUMT works as follows:

Step 0. Set values for p, ε, β, and let $k=1$.
Set μ_1, and initial solution x_1.

Step 1. Solve the unconstrained problem:
Minimize: $f(x) + \mu_k E(x)$
Let x_{k+1} be the optimal.

Step 2. If $E(x_{k+1}) < \varepsilon$ or $\mu_k E(x_{k+1}) < \varepsilon$ or all $\lvert g_i(x_{k+1}) \rvert < \varepsilon$ then
x_{k+1} is the best solution, stop.
else
Let $\mu_k = \beta \mu_k$, $k = k+1$, and go to Step 1.

6. The default setting for the SUMT method is $p = 2, \varepsilon = 0.0001, \beta = 10, \mu_1 = 100$. Again, for the constrained problems, the quality of the solution depends very much on the property of the objective function and the above parameter setting. The starting point (x_1), boundary, and running CPU time may also affect the solution quality.
7. Since nonlinear functions can vary so much, NLP only allows problem formulation by free format. Variables may have upper and lower bounds that can be entered as constraints or as pure bounded values; however, bounds are recommended.

MENU STRUCTURE

The functions and options in each of the pull-down menus are hierarchically listed as follows:

- Modules
  - Linear Programming (LP)
  - Integer Linear Programming (ILP)
  - Goal Programming (GP)
  - Quadratic Programming (QP)
  - Nonlinear Programming (NLP)
  - Dynamic Programming (DP)
  - Transportation and Transshipment (TRP)
  - Assignment and Traveling Salesman (ASTS)
  - Specialized Network Modeling (SNET)
  - Capacitated Network Flow Modeling (CNET)
  - Project Scheduling: CPM/PERT
  - Inventory Theory (INVT)
  - Inventory Theory 2 (INVT2)
  - Queuing Theory (QUEUE)
  - Queuing System Simulation (QSIM)
  - Decision Analysis (DA)
  - Markov Process (MKV)
  - Time Series Forecasting (TSFC)
  - Financial Analysis (FA)
  - Exit from QSB
- Input Data
  - Data Entry
  - Read a File
  - Show Data
  - Print Data
  - Modify Data
  - Save

Save As
Exit from QSB

Solution
Solve the Problem
Specify Bounds and Starting Point
Specify Algorithm Parameters
Show the Solution
Print the Solution
Save the Solution

Options
Color
Monochrome
Printer Selection

Help - NLP
About NLP
About the User Interface
About the Edit Keys

SOLVING PROBLEMS WITH NLP

In the following sections, we will use example problems to show how to enter and solve the problem. The general procedure and menu options are described in detail in the tutorial sections of Chapter 2.

Example - Single-Variable Unconstrained Problem

It is estimated that the labor cost of a paper manufacturer can be calculated by the following function:

$$\text{Labor Cost} = 2\,(\text{Workforce} - 1000)^2 + 500\ \text{Workforce} + 460000$$

where Workforce represents the employment level. The first term of the cost function is the deviation costs (firing and hiring) to the current workforce level (1000), the second term is the direct salary, and the third term is the constant one-time charge. What is the best workforce level for the paper firm?

Enter the Problem

1. Select "Data Entry" from the "Input Data" menu (refer to Chapter 2 for selecting a menu item). Fig. 7-1 shows the problem specification of this problem. Note that "You define" is selected for the variable name, and "You specify" is selected for bounds. Fig. 7-2 shows the entry of the variable name and its boundary.

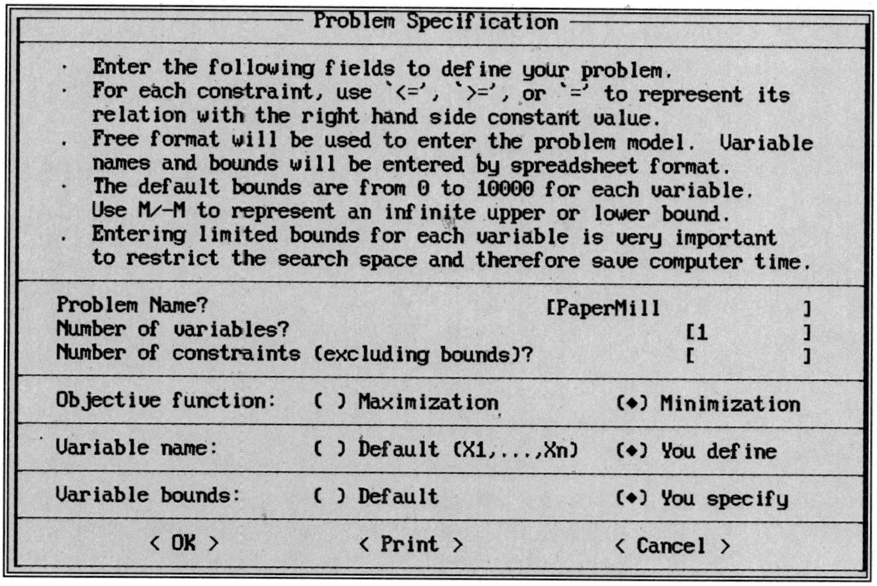

Figure 7-1. Problem specification for PaperMill.

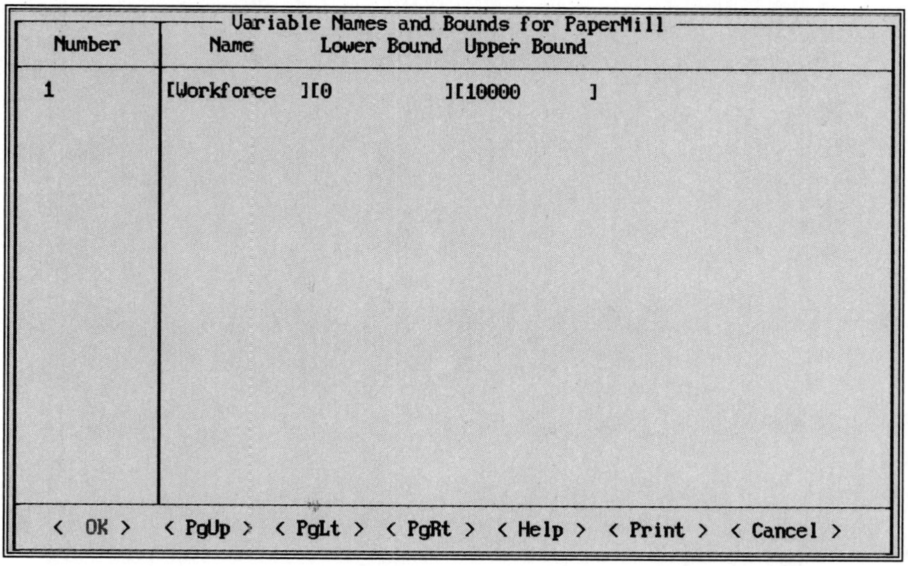

Figure 7-2. Variable name and its bounds for PaperMill.

2. The NLP formulation can be entered or modified only by free-format. The program will let you use commands to enter the model. You may enter the "H" or "Help" command to display the available commands. Fig. 7-3 shows the command information after you enter "H" command. Note that you can enter any command at the prompt "?=", and you can enter the data such as objective,

constraints, or bounds at the prompt ">>". The available commands are described below.

Bm:	Enter the bounds of variable m.
Cn:	Enter the constraint n.
Dn:	Enter the direction of constraint n. Use to change direction.
H:	Recall the command information.
OBJ:	Enter the objective function.
Q:	Quit the free-format entry.
Rn:	Enter the right-hand side of constraint n. Use to change RHS.
SCn:	Show the constraint n only.
SM:	Show the whole model.
SO:	Show the objective function only.
SV:	Show all variables.

When you want to change the number of constraints or variables, reenter the problem from the "Data Entry" option of the "Input Data" menu. The free-format entry is not case sensitive. That is to say, the commands "b1" and "B1" are the same, and the variables "WORKFORCE" and "workforce" are identical.

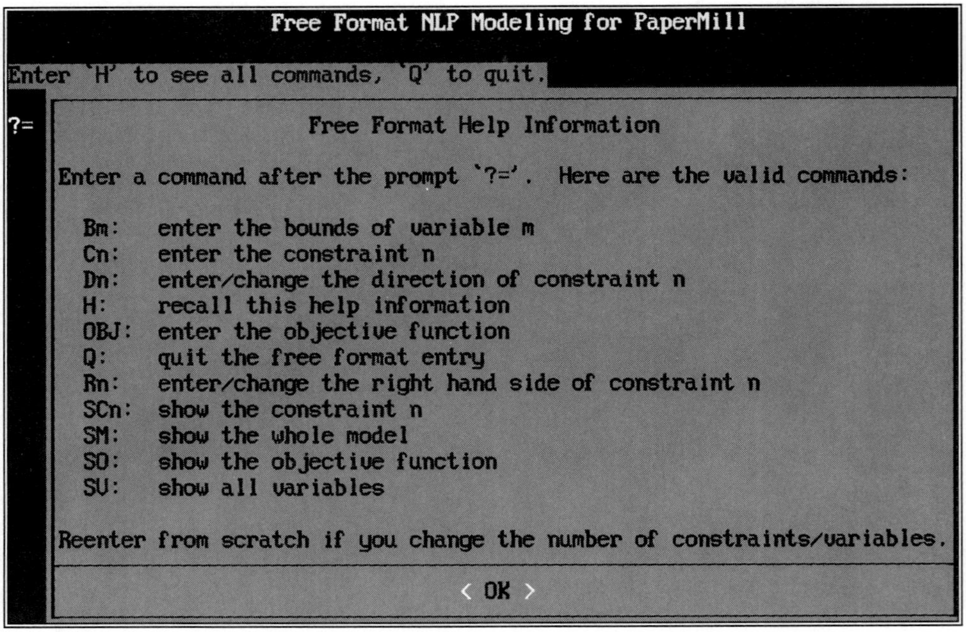

Figure 7-3. Available commands for free-format entry.

3. Fig. 7-4 shows the entry of the objective function of PaperMill (note that there is no constraint). After the model entry is done, use the command "SM" to show the whole model and the command "Q" to quit the free-format entry. Fig. 7-4 also demonstrates the action.

```
                          Free Format NLP Modeling for PaperMill

Enter `H' to see all commands, `Q' to quit.

?= h

?= obj
Enter the whole objective function at the following prompt.
Press `Enter' when finish typing.
Minimize>> 2(Workforce-1000)^2 + 500 Workforce + 460000

?= sm
Minimize>>  2(Workforce-1000)^2 + 500 Workforce + 460000
Bounds>>  0 ≤ Workforce ≤  10000

?= q
Are you sure to quit free format modeling (Y/N)?
```

Figure 7-4. Free-format model entry for PaperMill.

Solve the Problem

1. Select "Solve the Problem" from the "Solution" menu to solve the problem. The message "Please standby . . ." will display for a short period while the problem is being solved.
2. After the problem is solved, select "Show the Solution" from the "Solution" menu to display the solution. Fig. 7-5 shows the solution.
3. If the solution is not satisfactory, you may want to try other solution search domain and parameters. Select "Specify Bounds and Starting Point" from the "Solution" menu to try another search domain (Fig. 7-6), and select "Specify Algorithm Parameters" to try another set of stopping parameters (Fig. 7-7).

Solution Summary for PaperMill

08-23-1993 10:56:47 Page: 1 of 1

Variable	Solution	Variable	Solution	Variable	Solution
Workforce	874.8605				

Minimized OBJ = 928750.1 Elapsed CPU seconds = .1601563

< PageDown > < PageUp > < Hardcopy > < Cancel >

Figure 7-5. Solution for PaperMill.

Specify Solution Domain for PaperMill

Variable	Lower Bound	Upper Bound	Initial Solution
Workforce	[500]	[1500]	[1000]

< OK > < PgUp > < PgLt > < PgRt > < Help > < Print > < Cancel >

Figure 7-6. Specify initial solution and boundary for PaperMill.

Specifiy Solution Parameter

- Refer to the manual for parameters used for solution algorithm.
- You may click 'Default' for default parameter values.
- Default run time is 3600 seconds. The program will solve the problem up to specified run time and keep the best solution.
- Default stopping tolerance (delta) is 0.0001.

Maximum run time in seconds? [3600]
Stopping tolerance (delta)? [.0001]

< OK > < Default > < Print > < Cancel >

Figure 7-7. Specify solution parameter for PaperMill.

Example - Multi-Variable Unconstrained Problem

Minimize the following function with the specified boundary.

$$X_1^2 + 2X_1X_2 + 2X_2^2 + X_3^2 - X_2X_3 + X_1 + 3X_2 - X_3$$

where $0 \le X_1 \le 100$, $0 \le X_2 \le 200$, $0 \le X_3 \le 300$.

Enter the Problem

Select "Data Entry" from the "Input Data" menu. Fig. 7-8 shows the problem specification of this problem. Fig. 7-9 shows the variable names and bounds, and Fig. 7-10 shows the function entry.

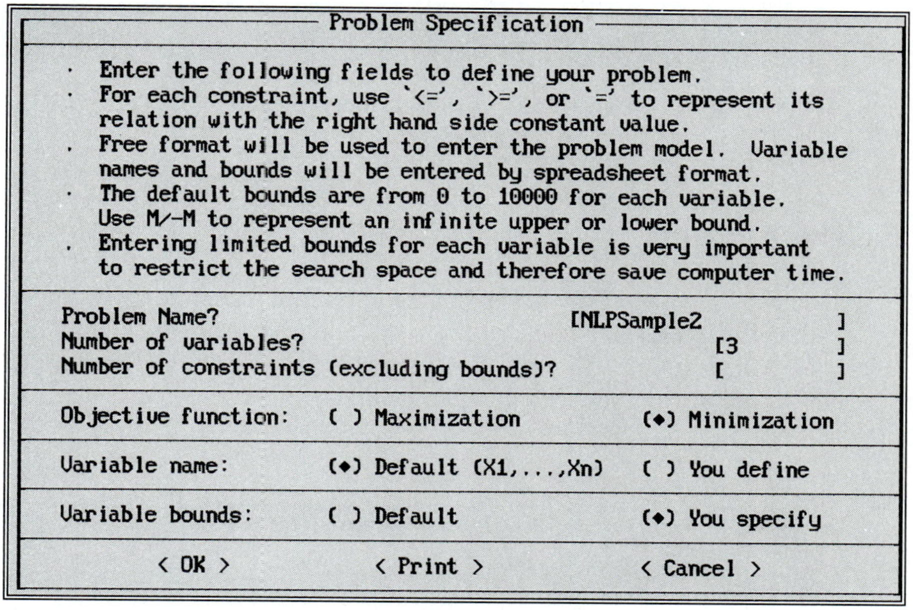

Figure 7-8. Problem specification for NLPSample2.

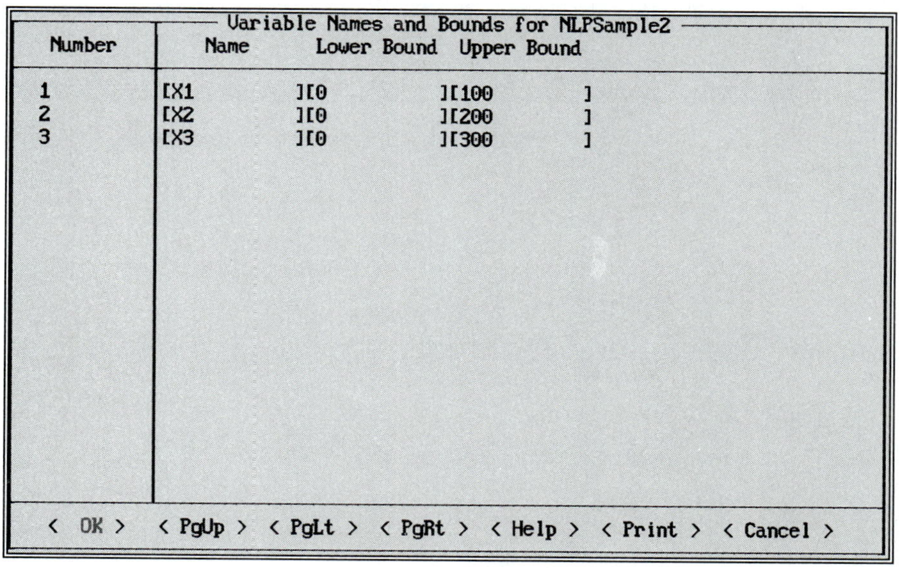

Figure 7-9. Variable names and bounds for NLPSample2.

```
                    Free Format NLP Modeling for NLPSample2

Enter 'H' to see all commands, 'Q' to quit.

?= o
Enter the whole objective function at the following prompt.
Press 'Enter' when finish typing.
Minimize>> X1^2 + 2 X1 * X2 + 2 X2^2 + X3^2 - X2 * X3 + X1 + 3 X2 - X3

?= Q
```

Figure 7-10. Free-format model entry for NLPSample2.

Solve the Problem

Select "Solve the Problem" from the "Solution" menu to solve the problem. After the problem is solved, select "Show the Solution" from the "Solution" menu to display the solution. Fig. 7-11 shows the solution. Again, you may solve the problem with other search domain and parameters.

Solution Summary for NLPSample2

08-23-1993 11:02:55 — Page: 1 of 1

Variable	Solution	Variable	Solution	Variable	Solution
X1	0	X2	0	X3	.4981911

Minimized OBJ = -.2499967 — Elapsed CPU seconds = .328125

< PageDown > < PageUp > < Hardcopy > < Cancel >

Figure 7-11. Solution for NLPSample2.

Example - Constrained Problem

Solve the following constrained problem:

Maximize: $-X_1^2 + 2X_1X_2 + X_2^2 - \mathrm{EXP}(-X_1 - X_2)$

Subject to:

$$X_1^2 + X_2^2 = 4$$
$$X_1 + X_2 \le 1$$

where $-5 \le X_1 \le 5$, $-5 \le X_2 \le 5$.

Enter the Problem

Select "Data Entry" from the "Input Data" menu. Fig. 7-12 shows the problem specification of this problem. Fig. 7-13 shows the variable names and bounds, and Fig. 7-14 shows the function entry.

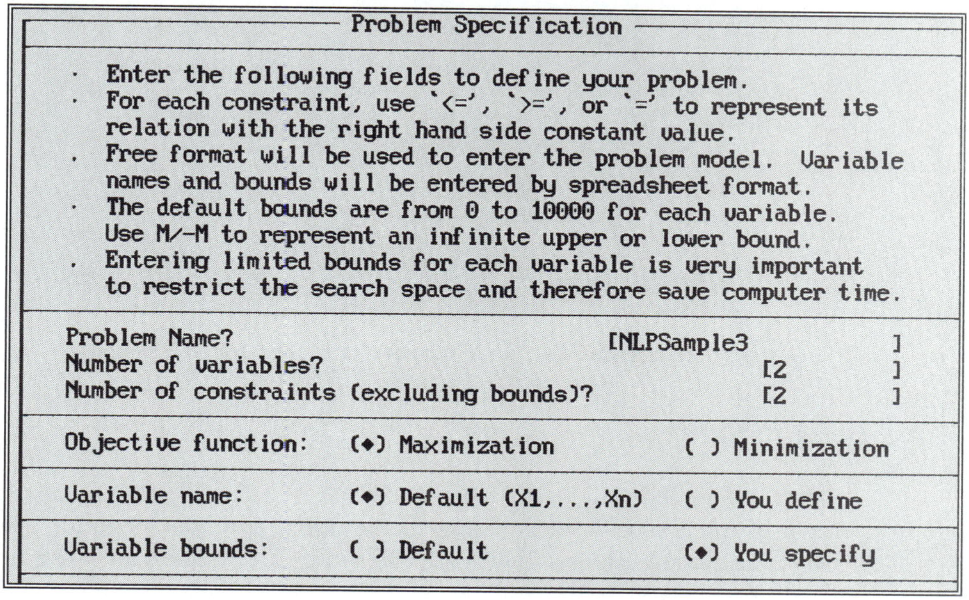

Figure 7-12. Problem specification for NLPSample3.

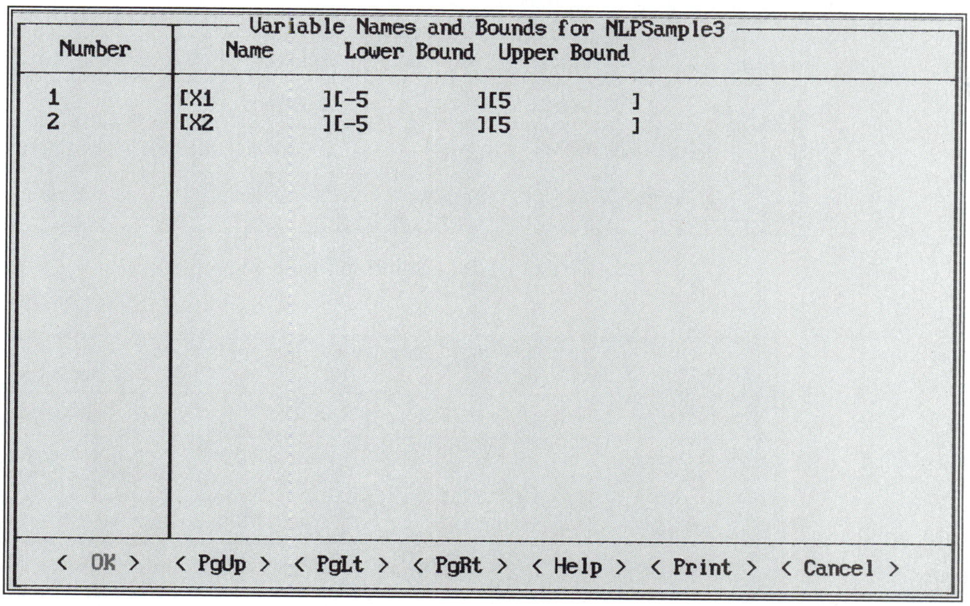

Figure 7-13. Variable names and bounds for NLPSample3.

```
Free Format NLP Modeling for NLPSample3

Enter 'H' to see all commands, 'Q' to quit.

?= o
Enter the whole objective function at the following prompt.
Press 'Enter' when finish typing.
Maximize>> - X1^2 + 2 X1 * X2 + X2^2 - EXP(-X1-X2)

?= C1
Enter the whole constraint at the following prompt.
Press 'Enter' when finish typing.
C1>> X1^2 + X2^2 = 4

?= C2
Enter the whole constraint at the following prompt.
Press 'Enter' when finish typing.
C2>> X1 + X2 <= 1

?= Q
```

Figure 7-14. Free-format model entry for NLPSample4.

Solve the Problem

Select "Solve the Problem" from the "Solution" menu to solve the problem. After the problem is solved, select "Show the Solution" from the "Solution" menu to display the solution. Fig. 7-15 and Fig. 7-16 show the solution and constraint analysis. Again, you may solve the problem with other search domain and parameters.

Solution Summary for NLPSample3

08-23-1993 11:07:10 Page: 1 of 1

Variable	Solution	Variable	Solution	Variable	Solution
X1	-.8062807	X2	1.829445		

Maximized OBJ = -.6127676 Elapsed CPU seconds = 4.621094

< PageDown > < PageUp > < Hardcopy > < Cancel >

Figure 7-15. Solution for NLPSample3.

Constraint Summary for NLPSample3

08-23-1993 11:07:49 Page: 1 of 1

Constraint	Direction	RHS Value	Status	Slack	RHSViolation
1	=	4	Under	0	0.00304198
2	<=	1	Over	0	0.02316439

Maximized OBJ = -.6127676 Elapsed CPU seconds = 4.621094

< PageDown > < PageUp > < Hardcopy > < Cancel >

Figure 7-16. Constraint summary for NLPSample3.

EXERCISES

1. Find the optimal solution for the following NLP problem:

Maximize: $\text{SIN}(X) + \text{COS}(X)$ for $0 \le X \le 1.5708$

2. Find the optimal solution for the following NLP problem:

Minimize: $X_1^2 + 2X_2^2 - 2X_1 X_2 - 2 X_2$

$0 \le X_1, X_2 \le 10$

3. Solve the following NLP problem:

Maximize: $10000\,X - 4000\,X^2 + 400\,X^3 - 10\,X^4$

Subject to: $X^2 + X \le 500$

$0 \le X \le 100$

4. Solve the following NLP model:

Maximize: $A + 3\,B - 4\,C + 2\,A^2 - 2\,A\,B + 2\,B^2 + C^2$

Subject to:

$A + B \le 150$

$3\,A + 2\,B - C \ge 210$

$5\,A - 2\,B + 4\,C \ge 315$

$0 \le A, B, \text{ and } C \le 100$

5. Solve the following NLP model:

Maximize: $\text{SIN}(2A) + \text{COS}(3B) + \text{SIN}(A+B) + \text{LOG}(1/(A+1))$

Subject to:

$-A^2 + 10B \le 1$

$10A + B^2 \le 100$

$0 \le A, B \le 10$

8

DYNAMIC PROGRAMMING (DP)

OVERVIEW OF THE DP DECISION SUPPORT SYSTEM

This program contains three well-known dynamic programming algorithms: the stagecoach problem, the knapsack problem, and a production and inventory control problem. DP solves multi-stage multi-state problems. The solution procedure uses backward recursion from the last stage (that is, the stage closest to the destination) to the first stage.

The data required for the stagecoach problem are the number of stages, the number of states for each stage, and the distances or returns between states on successive stages. For the knapsack problem, the space requirements and return values for each stage are required. The data required for the production and inventory control problem are demand; storage capacity with associated unit cost; production capacity with associated unit cost; and setup, holding, and/or shortage costs for each stage. The stage transformation function and return function used in this program are assumed to be linear. The problem can be saved on or read from a disk(ette). After the data has been entered, you may choose options to solve the problems and display, print, or save the results.

TECHNICAL NOTES ON THE DP PROGRAM

1. The DP program is designed to solve three types of popular dynamic programming problems with multiple stages and each stage with multiple states: the stagecoach problem, the knapsack problem, and a production and inventory control problem. The size of the problems solved by the DP program depends on the memory size of your computer.
2. For the stagecoach problem, a single starting node and a single ending node are assumed. If your problem has multiple starting or ending nodes, add a dummy starting or ending node to link the original starting nodes or ending nodes with zero distances (costs or returns).
3. For the production and inventory control problem, any initial inventory should be used to satisfy the demands from the beginning of the planning horizon as

much as possible. In other words, reduce the demands from the beginning with the initial inventory quantity. If shortage is not allowed, enter "M" (infinity) for the shortage costs.

4. The DP program can display a detailed decision and return table for each stage. The tables will contain enough information for you to inspect the dynamic programming solution process.

MENU STRUCTURE

The functions and options in each of the pull-down menus are hierarchically listed as follows:

- Modules
  - Linear Programming (LP)
  - Integer Linear Programming (ILP)
  - Goal Programming (GP)
  - Quadratic Programming (QP)
  - Nonlinear Programming (NLP)
  - Dynamic Programming (DP)
  - Transportation and Transshipment (TRP)
  - Assignment and Traveling Salesman (ASTS)
  - Specialized Network Modeling (SNET)
  - Capacitated Network Flow Modeling (CNET)
  - Project Scheduling: CPM/PERT
  - Inventory Theory (INVT)
  - Inventory Theory 2 (INVT2)
  - Queuing Theory (QUEUE)
  - Queuing System Simulation (QSIM)
  - Decision Analysis (DA)
  - Markov Process (MKV)
  - Time Series Forecasting (TSFC)
  - Financial Analysis (FA)
  - Exit from QSB
- Input Data
  - Data Entry
  - Read a File
  - Show Data
  - Print Data
  - Modify Data
    - Modify the problem data
    - Delete one stage
  - Save
  - Save As
  - Exit from QSB

Solution
- Solve the Problem
- Solve and Display Steps
- Show the Solution
- Print the Solution
- Save the Solution

Options
- Color
- Monochrome
- Printer Selection

Help - DP
- About DP
- About the User Interface
- About the Edit Keys

SOLVING PROBLEMS WITH DP

In the following sections, we will use example problems to show how to enter and solve the DP problems. The general procedure and menu options are described in detail in the tutorial sections of Chapter 2.

Example - Stagecoach Problem

To demonstrate the use of DP, consider a typical stagecoach problem in Fig. 8-1. The number on each branch (arc) represents the distance between nodes. What is the shortest route from node 1 to node 10?

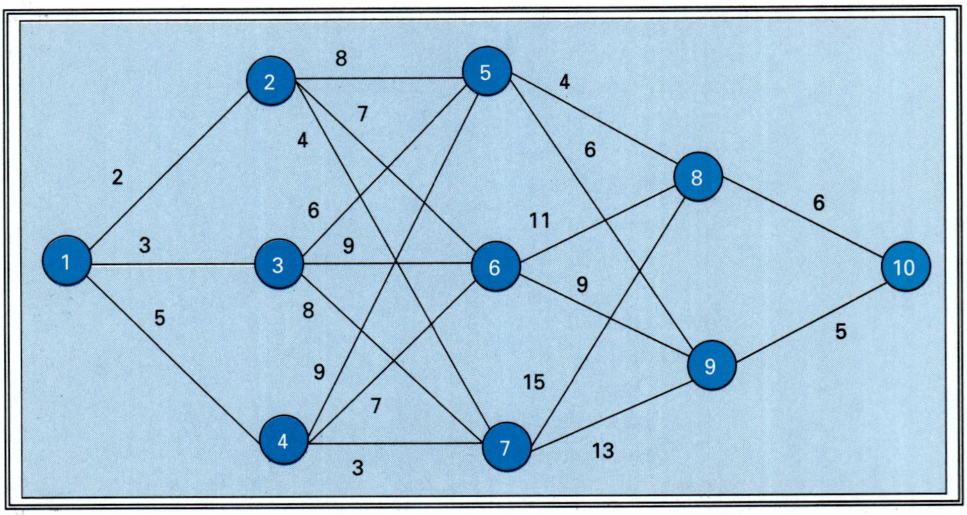

Figure 8-1. A sample stagecoach problem.

Enter the Problem

Select "Data Entry" from the "Input Data" menu (refer to Chapter 2 for selecting a menu item). Figs. 8-2 to 8-12 show the data entry of this problem. Note that Fig. 8-4

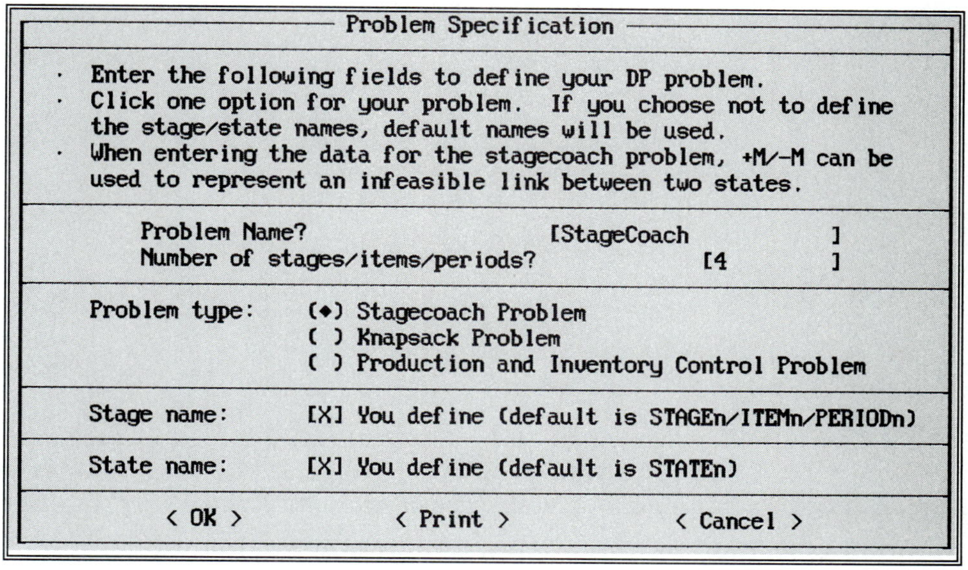

Figure 8-2. Problem specification for Stagecoach.

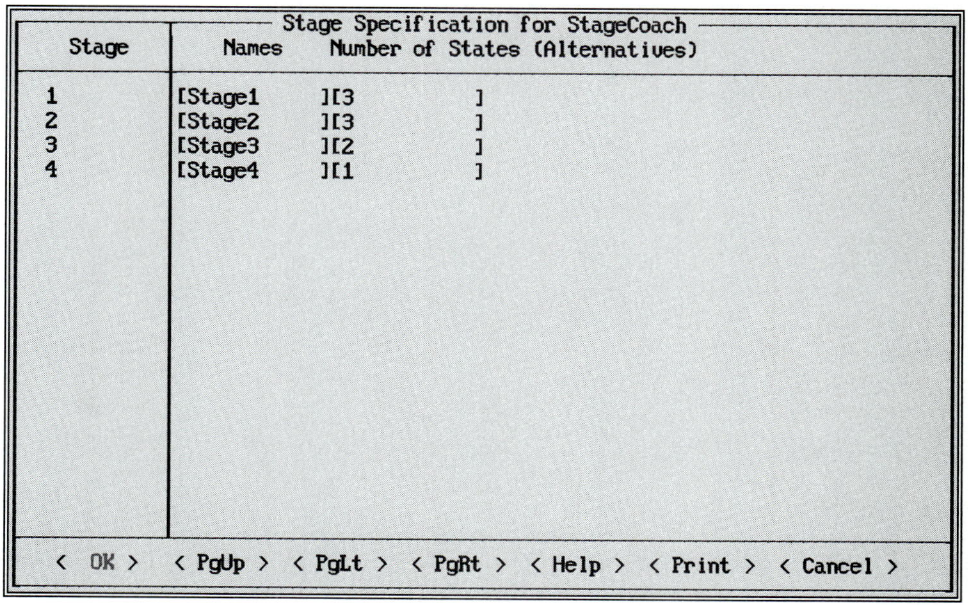

Figure 8-3. Stage specification for Stagecoach.

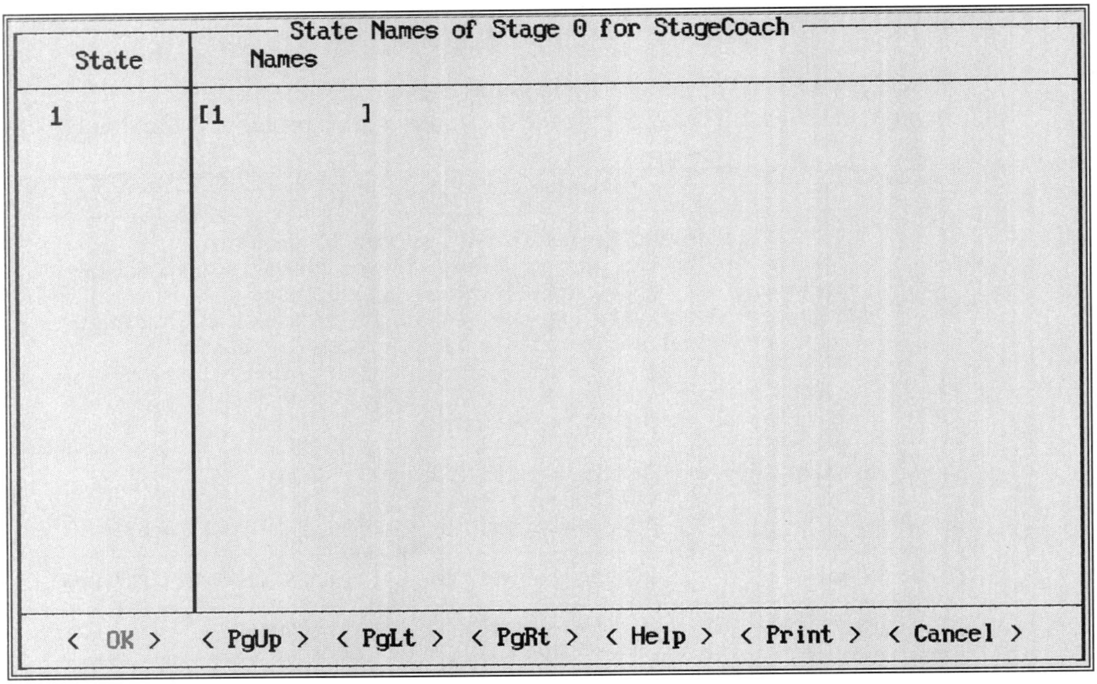

Figure 8-4. State name of stage 0 (starting point) for Stagecoach.

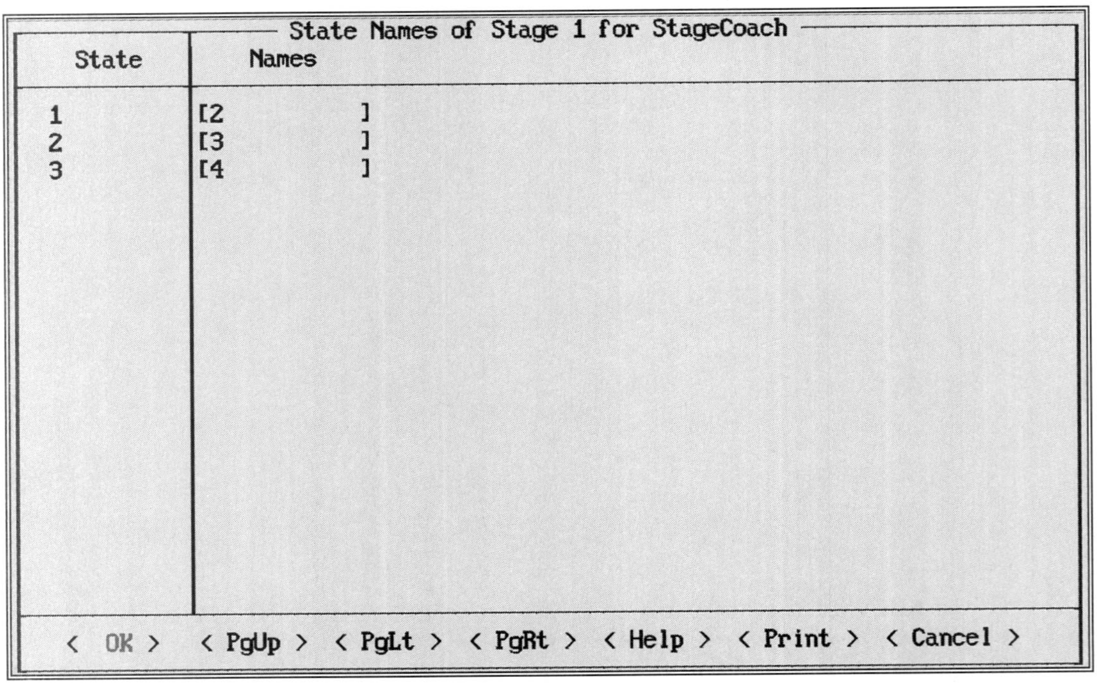

Figure 8-5. State names for stage 1.

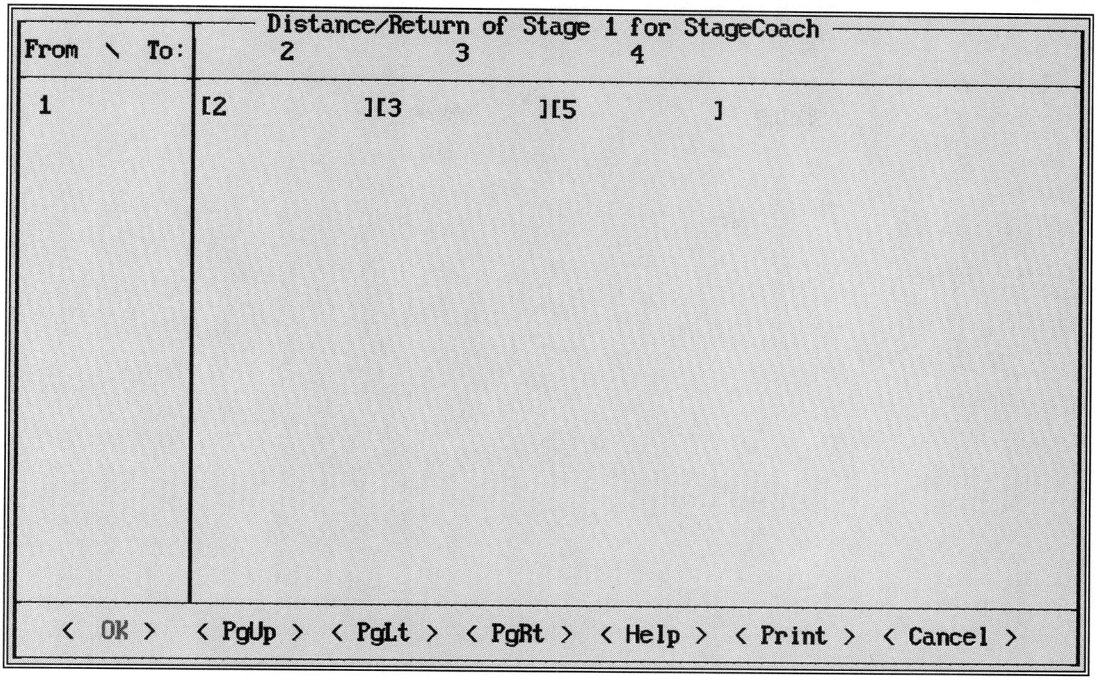

Figure 8-6. Distances for stage 1.

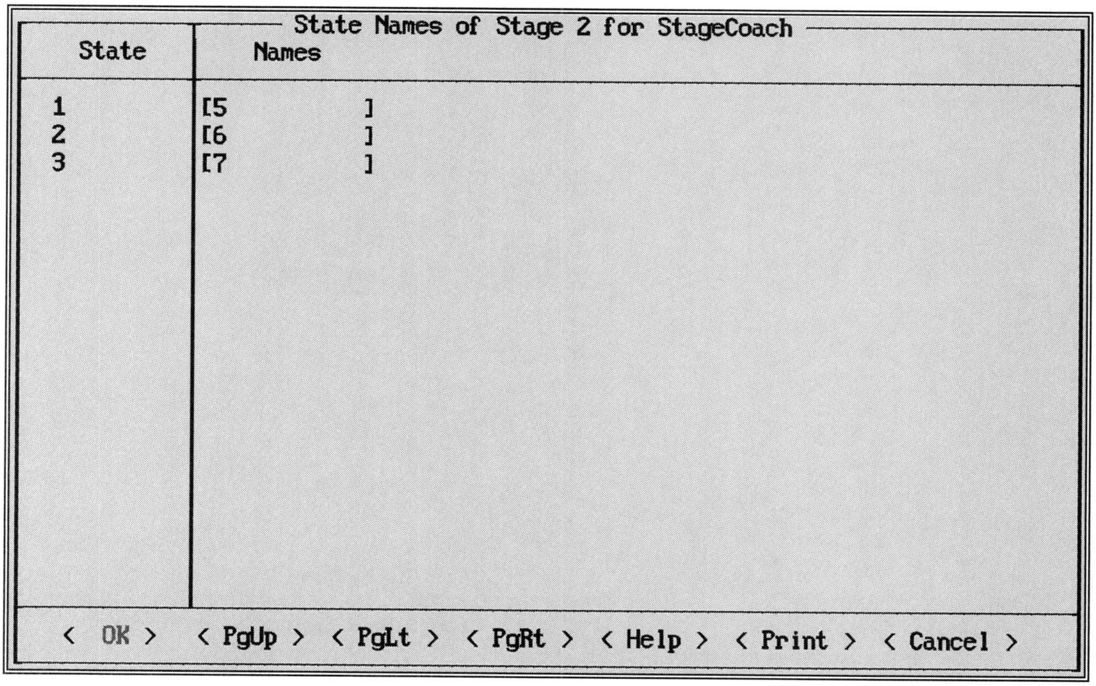

Figure 8-7. State names for stage 2.

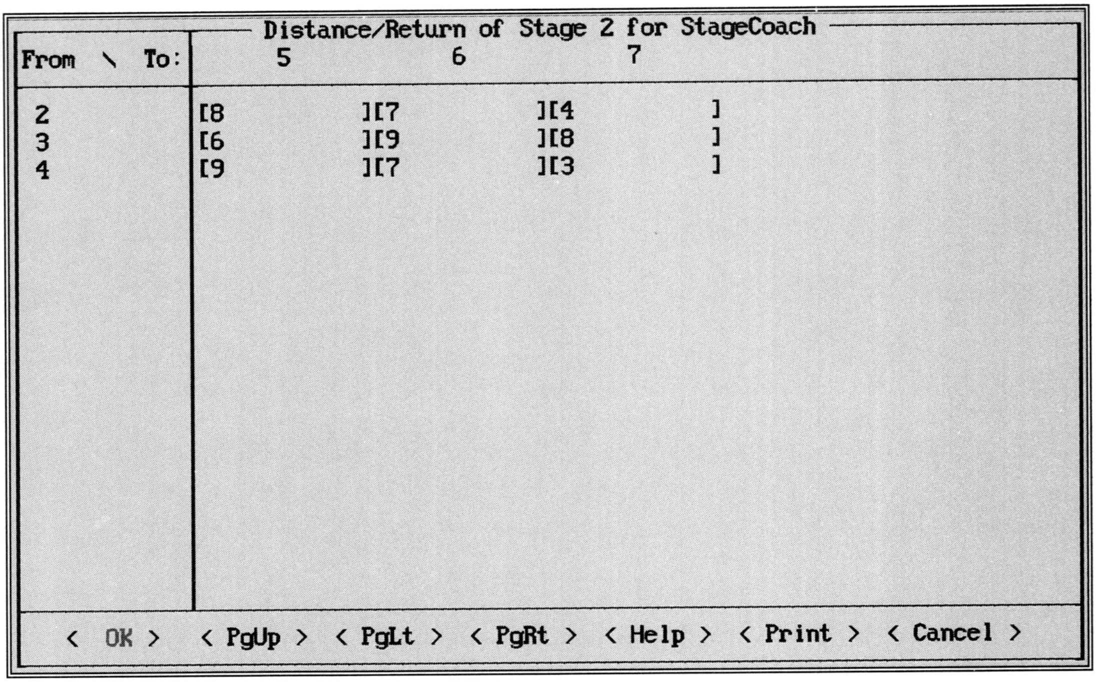

Figure 8-8. Distances for stage 2.

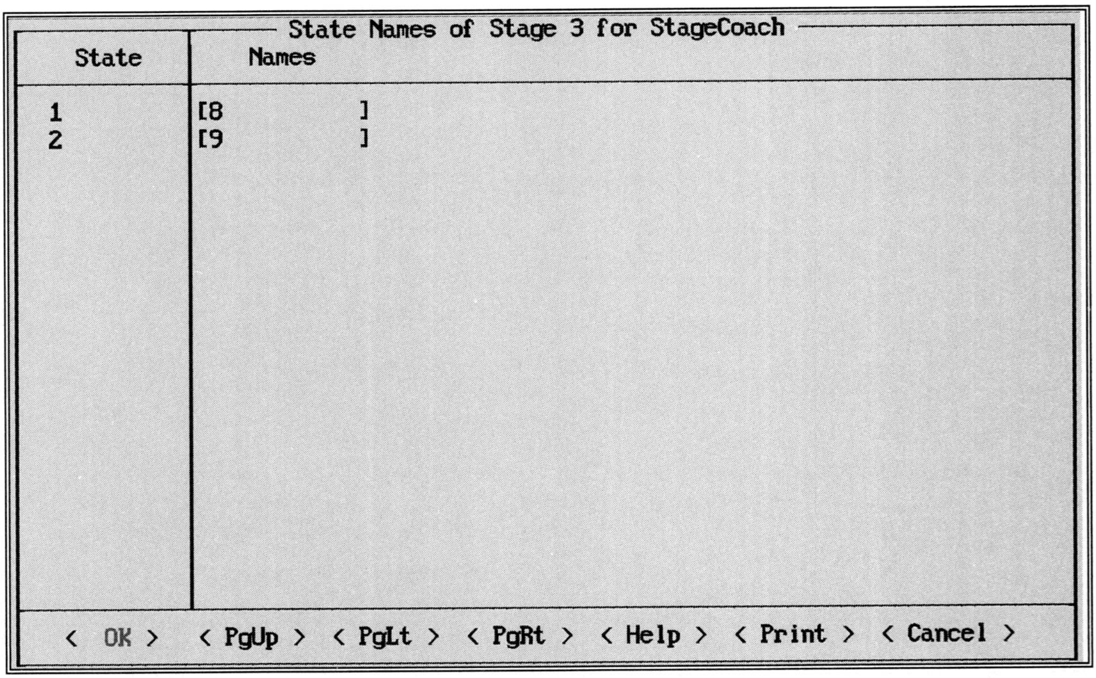

Figure 8-9. State names for stage 3.

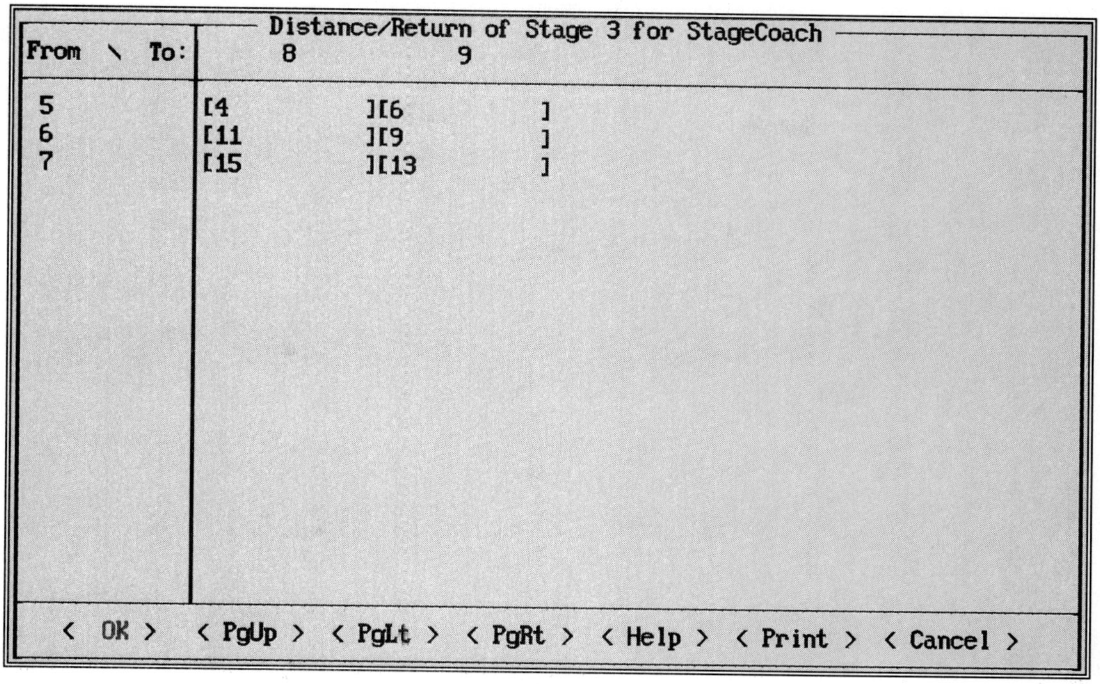

Figure 8-10. Distances for stage 3.

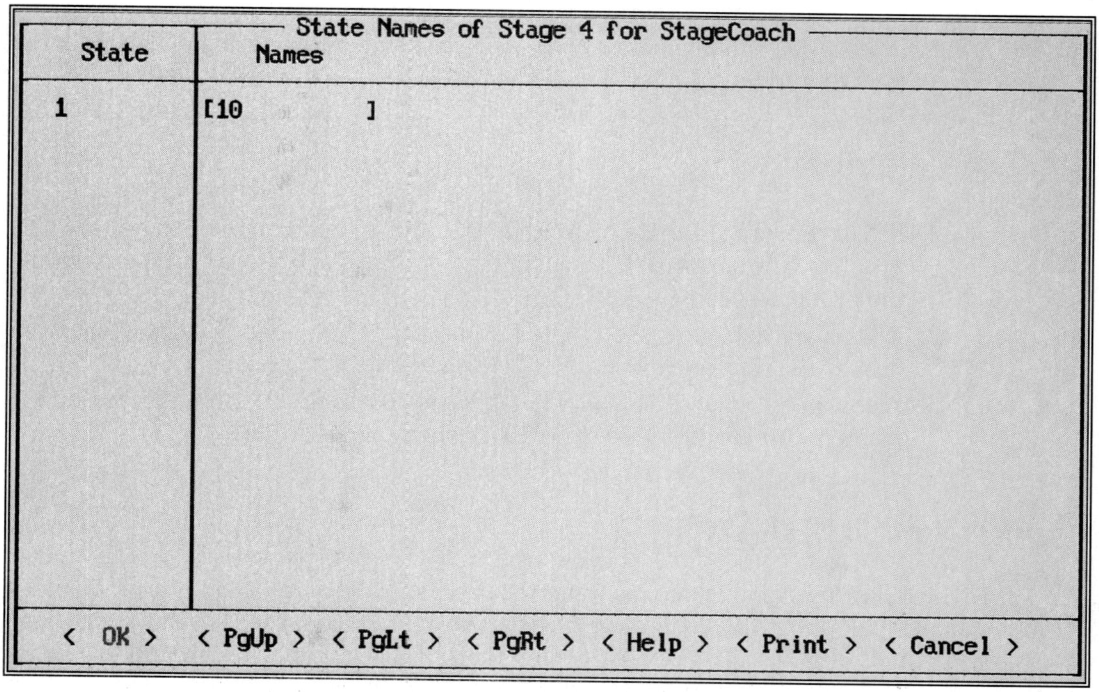

Figure 8-11. State names for stage 4.

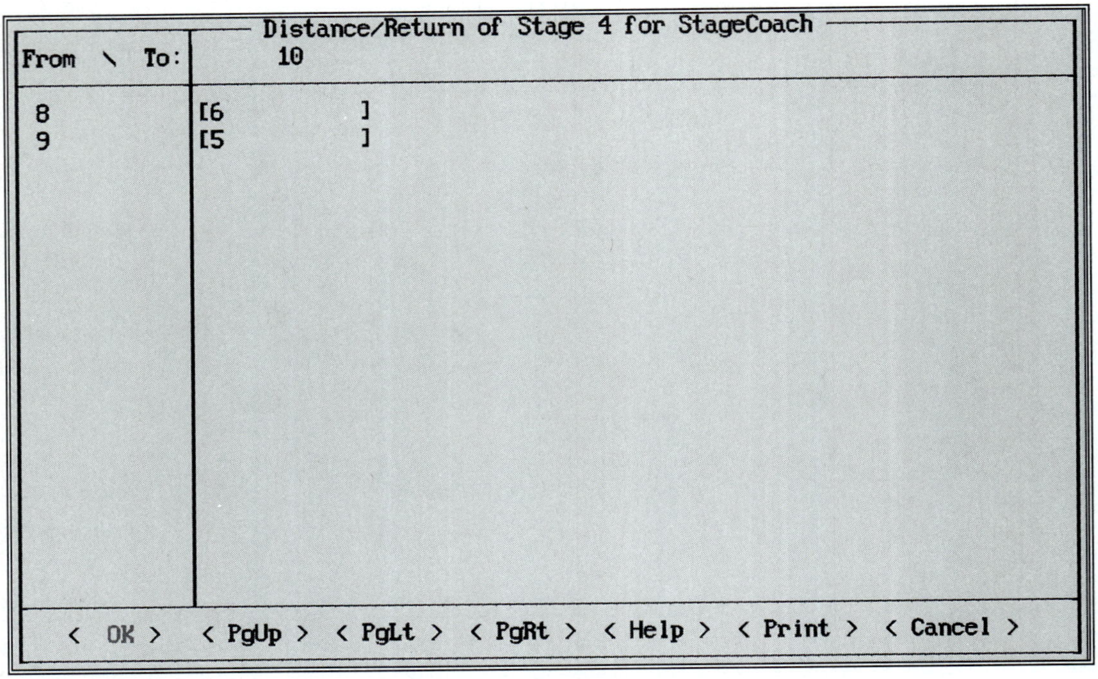

Figure 8-12. Distances for stage 4.

defines the initial point name. At each stage, we define the state names and enter the distances from states to states (Figs. 8-5 to 8-12).

Solve the Problem

1. Select "Solve the Problem" from the "Solution" menu to solve the stagecoach problem. The message "Please standby. . ." will display for a short period while the problem is being solved.
2. You may also choose "Solve and Display Steps" from the "Solution" menu to display the solution process. Fig. 8-13 shows the detail.
3. After the problem is solved, select "Show the Solution" from the "Solution" menu to display the solution. Fig. 8-14 shows the solution.

Example - Knapsack Problem

The following example demonstrates the procedure to solve a knapsack problem using the DP program. A salesman travels around the country in his van to sell different kinds of goods. The van has twenty units of space. For a specific trip, the salesman has four different types of goods to carry. Each type of goods has limited available units, requires different units of space, and provides a different profit for the sales-

Stagecoach Solution Steps for StageCoach

08-23-1993 11:24:57 Page: 1 of 1

Period Stage	Input State	Connection Decision	Output State	Distance/Value to Destination
Stage1	1	1 - 3	3	19
Stage2	2	2 - 5	5	18
Stage2	3	3 - 5	5	16
Stage2	4	4 - 5	5	19
Stage3	5	5 - 8	8	10
Stage3	6	6 - 9	9	14
Stage3	7	7 - 9	9	18
Stage4	8	8 - 10	10	6
Stage4	9	9 - 10	10	5

< PageDown > < PageUp > < Hardcopy > < Cancel >

Figure 8-13. Solution steps for Stagecoach.

Stagecoach Problem Solution for StageCoach

08-23-1993 11:25:27 Page: 1 of 1

Stage	From State	To State	Distance to Destination
Stage1	1	3	19
Stage2	3	5	16
Stage3	5	8	10
Stage4	8	10	6

Distance/Value from 1 to 10 = 19 Elapsed CPU seconds = 0

< PageDown > < PageUp > < Hardcopy > < Cancel >

Figure 8-14. The final solution for Stagecoach.

man. Table 8-1 displays this information. Suppose that the salesman can sell what he carries. Suggest how the salesman can maximize his profit for this trip.

Table 8-1. Related information for the salesman's next trip.

Types of goods	Units available	Space required per unit	Profit per unit
A	5	10	8
B	3	6	10
C	4	3	4
D	2	5	7

Enter the Problem

Select "Data Entry" from the "Input Data" menu. Figs. 8-15 to 8-18 show the data entry of this problem.

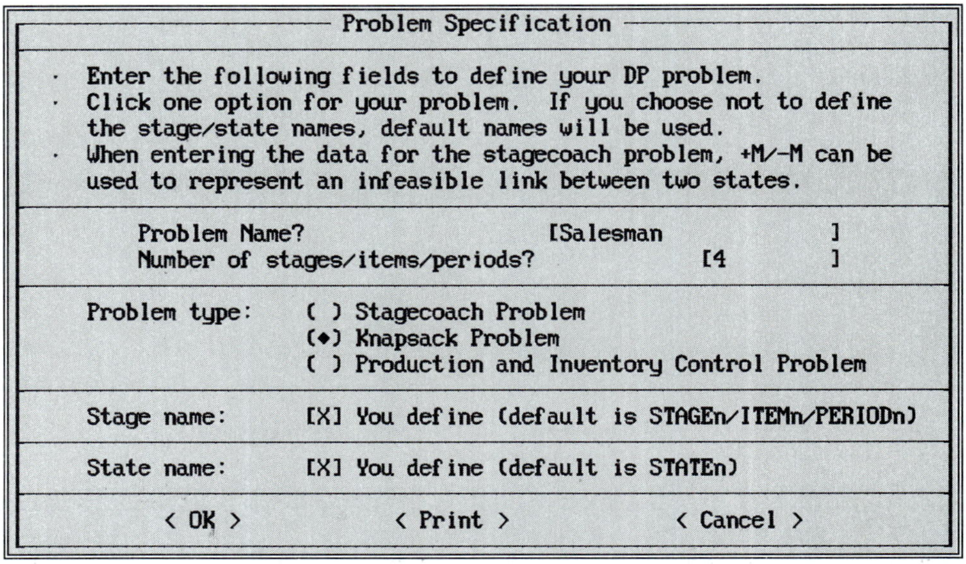

Figure 8-15. Specification for the knapsack problem.

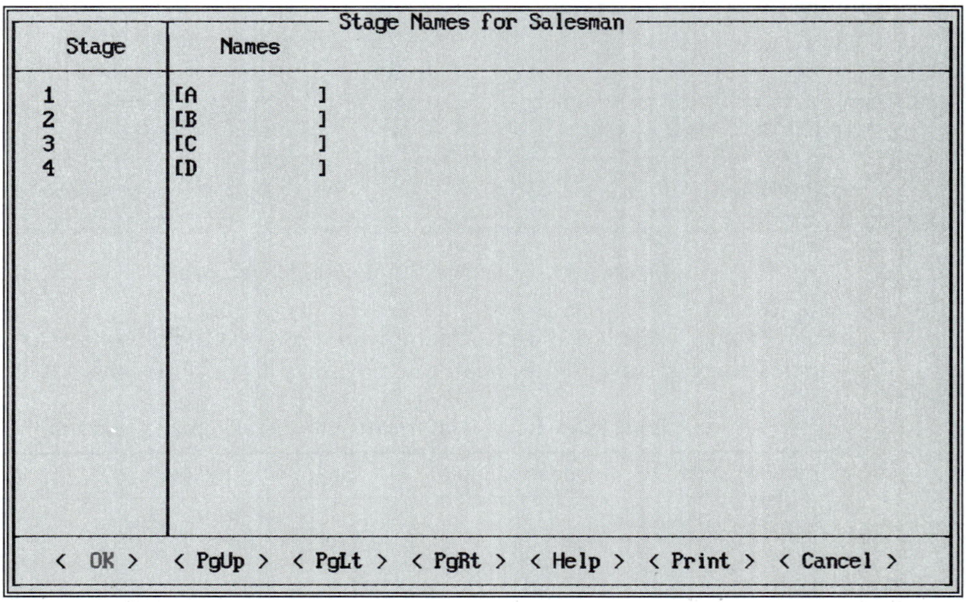

Figure 8-16. Stage names for Salesman.

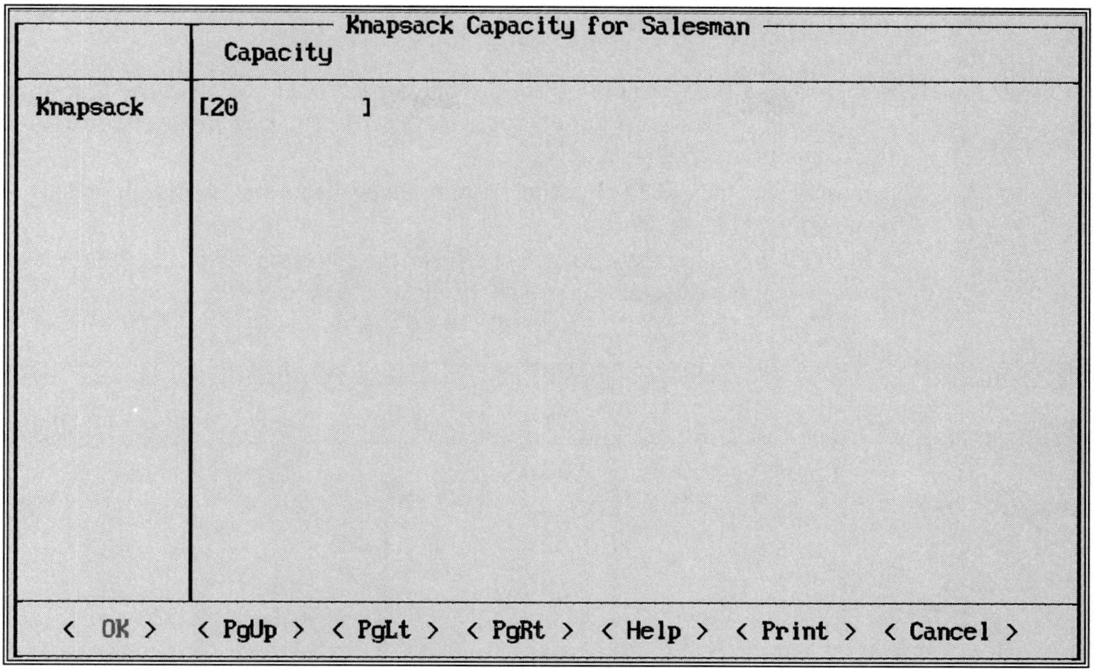

Figure 8-17. Knapsack capacity for Salesman.

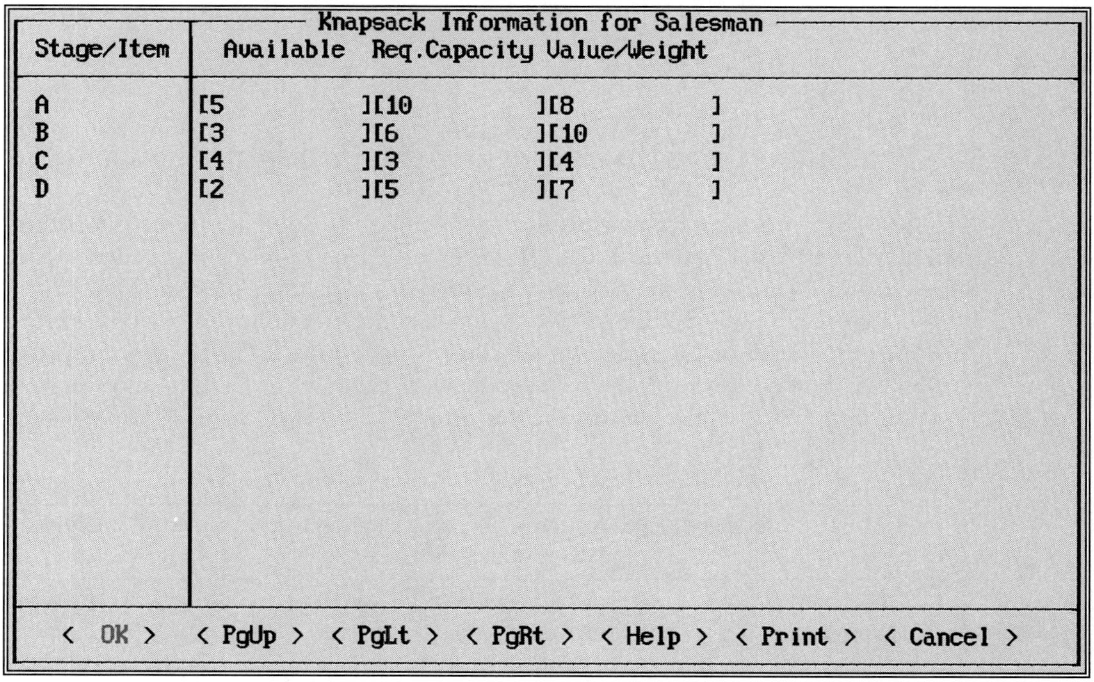

Figure 8-18. Knapsack data for Salesman.

Solve the Problem

1. Select "Solve the Problem" from the "Solution" menu to solve the Salesman problem. The message "Please standby. . ." will display for a short period while the problem is being solved.
2. You may also choose "Solve and Display Steps" from the "Solution" menu to display the solution process.
3. After the problem is solved, select "Show the Solution" from the "Solution" menu to display the solution. Fig. 8-19 shows the solution.

Knapsack Problem Solution for Salesman

08-23-1993 11:28:21 Page: 1 of 1

Item	Carry Quantity	Return/Value	Capacity Left
A	0	0	20
B	2	20	8
C	1	4	5
D	1	7	0

Total Return Value = 31 Elapsed CPU seconds = 0

< PageDown > < PageUp > < Hardcopy > < Cancel >

Figure 8-19. The final solution for Salesman.

Example - Production and Inventory Control Problem

The following example demonstrates the procedure to solve a production and inventory control problem using the DP program. BBC produces tailor-made space shuttle components. For the next four months, BBC has to deliver one kind of special component. Table 8-2 shows the related production and inventory information for the next four months. Note that shortage is not allowed. If BBC does not have inventory right now, what is the best production schedule for BBC to implement to minimize total cost while meeting the demand?

Table 8-2. Production and inventory information for BBC.

Month	Demand	Production capacity	Storage capacity	Production setup cost	Unit cost	Holding cost
January	4	6	4	$500	$300	$100
February	5	4	3	450	320	100
March	3	7	2	500	250	120
April	4	5	4	600	350	140

Enter the Problem

Select "Data Entry" from the "Input Data" menu. Figs. 8-20 to 8-23 show the data entry of this problem. Note that after you finish entering the data in Fig. 8-22, click

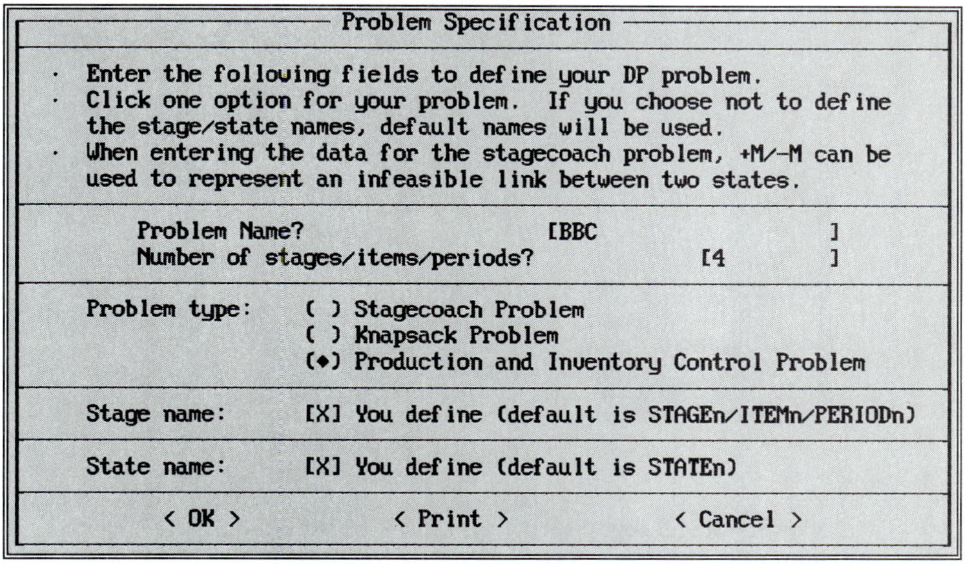

Figure 8-20. Specification of the production and inventory control problem BBC.

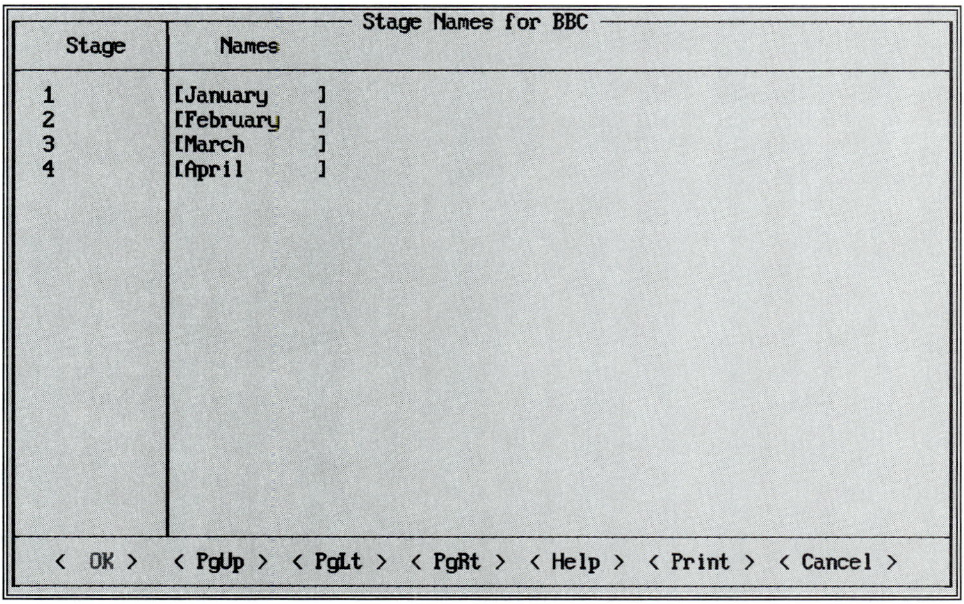

Figure 8-21. Stage names for BBC.

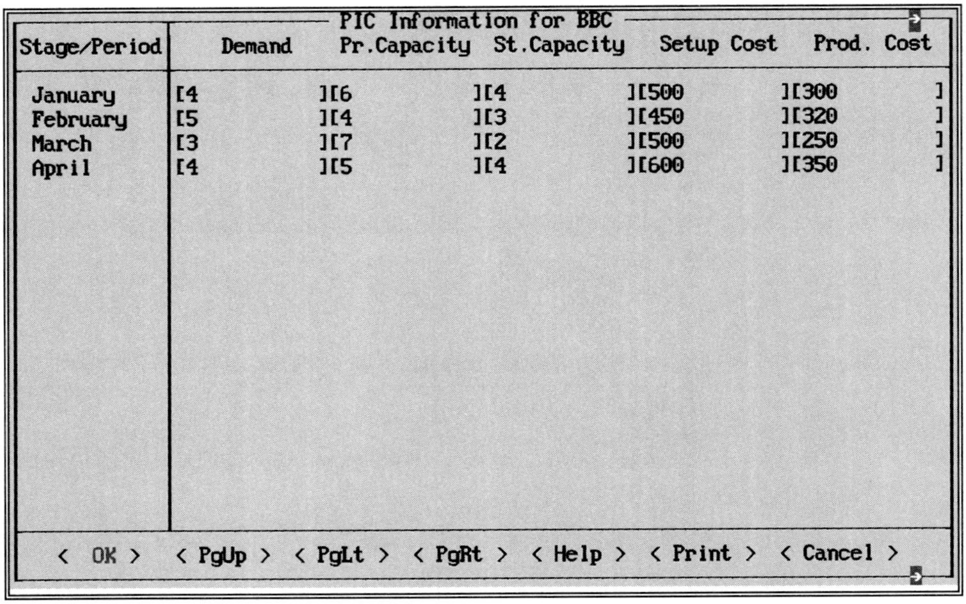

Figure 8-22. PIC data for BBC.

or select the button "PgRt" (right page) to enter the data in Fig. 8-23. "M" has been entered for shortage costs in Fig. 8-23 for not allowing shortage. Here are some abbreviations in Fig. 8-22 and Fig. 8-23.

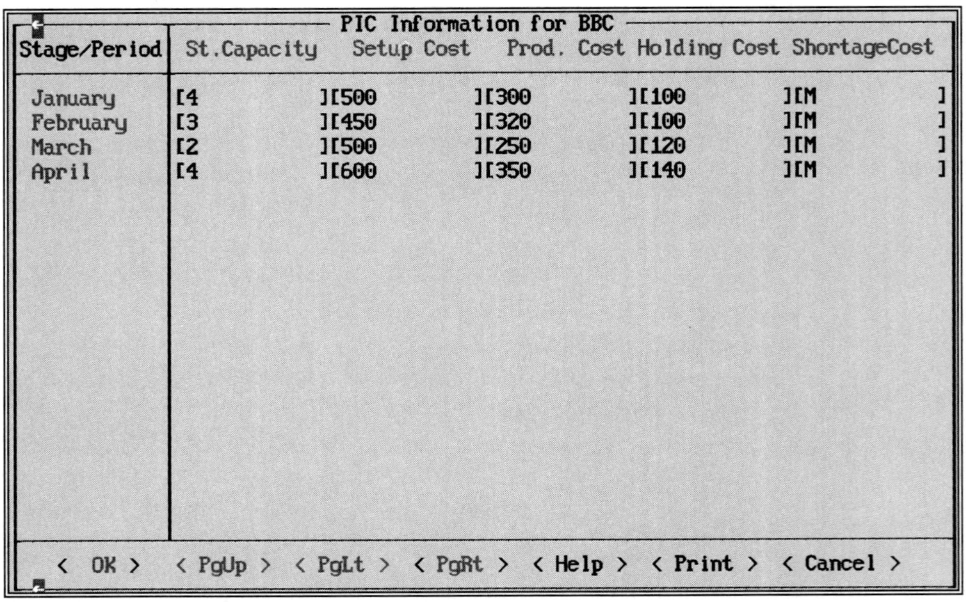

Figure 8-23. PIC data for BBC (continued).

— Pr. Capacity: Production capacity
— St. Capacity: Storage capacity
— Prod. Cost: Production cost

Solve the Problem

1. Select "Solve the Problem" from the "Solution" menu to solve the BBC problem. The message "Please standby . . ." will display for a short period while the problem is being solved.
2. You may also choose "Solve and Display Steps" from the "Solution" menu to display the solution process.
3. After the problem is solved, select "Show the Solution" from the "Solution" menu to display the solution. Fig. 8-24 shows the solution.

PIC Problem Solution for BBC

08-23-1993 11:32:54 Page: 1 of 1

Period (Stage)	Start Invtry.	Prodtn. Qty.	End Invtry.	Setup Cost	Prodtn. Cost	Holding Cost	Shortage Cost	Total Cost
January	0	5	1	500	1500	100	0	2100
February	1	4	0	450	1280	0	0	1730
March	0	3	0	500	750	0	0	1250
April	0	4	0	600	1400	0	0	2000

Total Cost = 7080 Elapsed CPU seconds = 0.058593

< PageDown > < PageUp > < Hardcopy > < Cancel >

Figure 8-24. The final solution for BBC.

EXERCISES

1. Consider the network shown in Fig. 8-25. The numbers on the arcs are distances in miles. Infinite distance is assumed if there is no direct linkage between two nodes. What is the shortest route from node 1 to node 16?
2. Consider the network shown in Fig. 8-26. The number on each arc is the travel time in minutes. Infinite distance is assumed if there is no direct linkage between two nodes. What is the shortest time to travel from city 1 to city 25?
3. A local retail shop has available a 6 ft x 3 ft x 2 ft display area for cosmetics products. The shop must determine which of its top 10 target products to place in the display area. The unit profits and unit space requirements follow. The space requirements are expressed in cubic feet, which include the surrounding space for an attractive visual effect. Recommend a solution for this display decision.

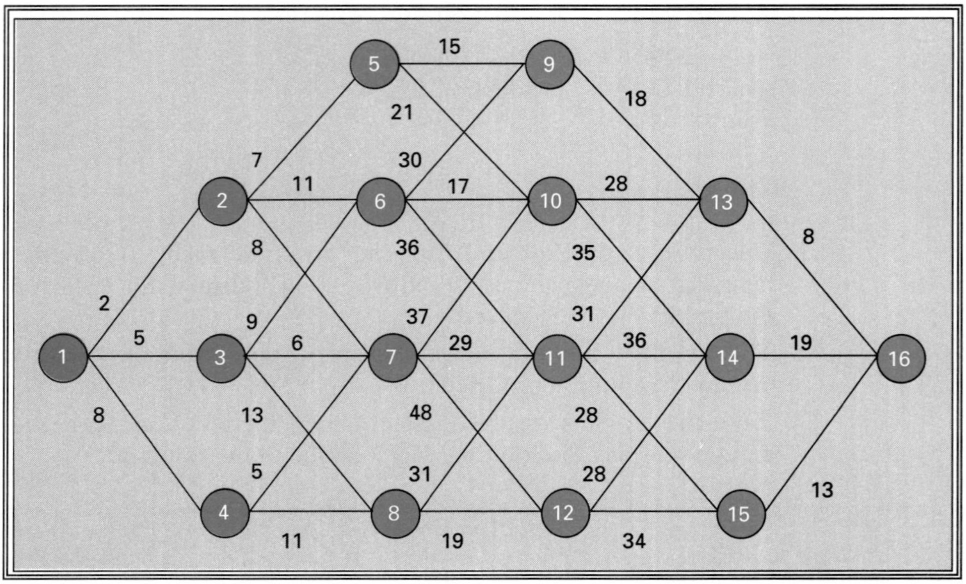

Figure 8-25. The network for exercise 1.

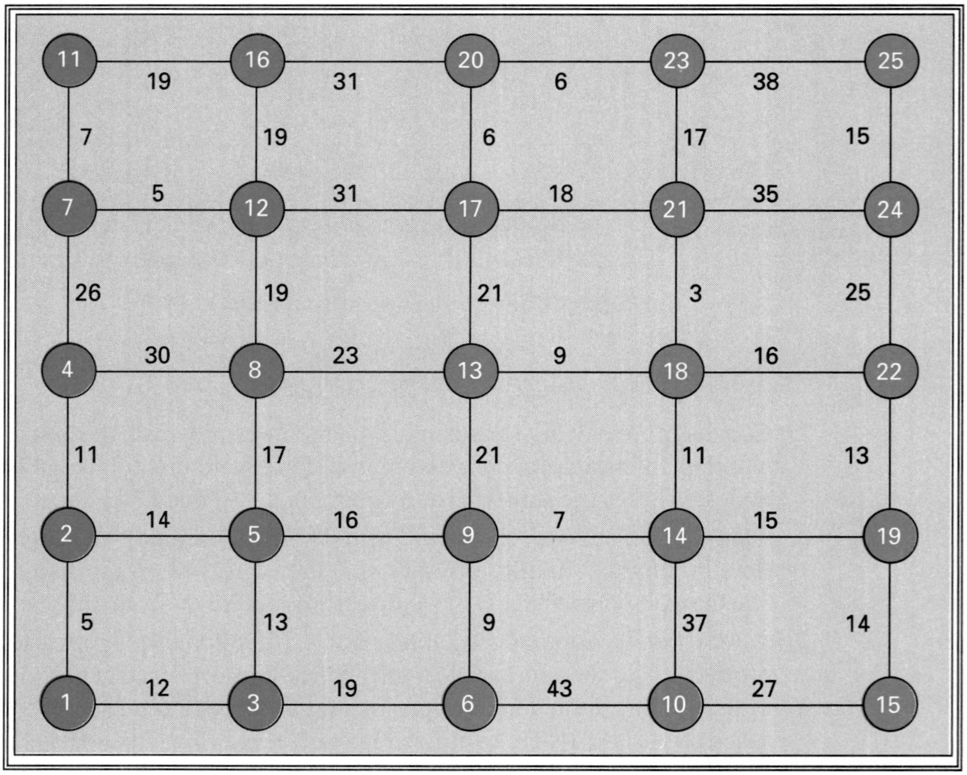

Figure 8-26. The network for exercise 2.

Product	1	2	3	4	5	6	7	8	9	10
Profit	$3	2	1	5	9	7	4	6	4	8
Space	5	6	3	7	13	15	7	9	6	8

4. You have $30,000 to take advantage of an investment opportunity. The following table lists the stock alternatives and related information. How would you allocate your $30,000? Assume the purchase of stocks is in units of a thousand.

Alternative	Cost per unit	Available in thousands	Expected profit per unit
Stock 1	$2	5	$1
2	4	6	1.8
3	3	2	1.9
4	5	7	2
5	8	4	2.1

5. The following table lists information related to a production and inventory control situation. If the initial inventory is two units, determine a production plan to minimize the total cost (where PC: production cost, SC: storage cost; PSC: production setup cost; UPC: unit production cost, UHC: unit holding cost). Assume that shortage is not allowed.

Month	Demand	PC	SC	PSC	UPC	UHC
1	10	12	5	$1000	$200	$80
2	12	14	5	1100	210	100
3	15	13	5	1100	220	90
4	6	14	10	1200	210	80
5	7	13	8	1500	250	100
6	8	10	5	1400	240	110

6. Jeming Industries, Inc., produces high-power transformers for industries. For the next 10 months, the company has the following demands: 1, 2, 7, 6, 5, 3, 4, 5, 6, and 2 units. Because of the unstable labor market, the company can produce at most 4, 5, 6, 7, 8, 7, 4, 6, 4, and 3 units, respectively. The company has a stockroom that can hold 5 units of the finished product. The current stock is 2 units. The production setup cost is $500 per setup and the variable production cost is $200 per unit. The carrying cost is $40 per unit per month. Assume that Jeming plans the production schedule month by month. Decide on a plan for the company that will meet demand while minimizing the total cost. No shortage is allowed.

9

TRANSPORTATION AND TRANSSHIPMENT PROBLEMS (TRP)

OVERVIEW OF THE TRP DECISION SUPPORT SYSTEM

This program solves transportation and transshipment problems. A source or supply point is defined as having only outgoing flows, a destination or sink point is defined as having only incoming flows, while a transshipment point is defined as having both. The capacities or demands are assumed to be of real value, as are the cost or profit coefficients. TRP provides capabilities to enter, save, and retrieve problems and to solve, display, and print solutions.

After entering a problem, TRP automatically converts the problem to a transportation problem and solves it using the transportation simplex method. TRP provides many alternatives to find the initial feasible solution. You have the option of displaying solution tableaus. TRP allows you to define names of sources, destinations, and transshipment points with up to ten characters. The capacity or demand on each point, and the transportation costs or profits between each point are the required data.

TECHNICAL NOTES ON THE TRP PROGRAM

1. For a source or a destination, the net supply or demand must be a positive real number. For a transshipment point, the net supply is entered as a positive number, while the net demand is entered as a negative number.
2. To enter the transportation cost/profit coefficients, a very large positive/negative number or +M/−M could be entered to represent no direct linkage (flow) between two nodes when the spreadsheet format is used.
3. In terms of the free-format data entry, enter a pair of starting and ending nodes to represent a possible shipment. The node names can be in upper case or lower case. A huge cost/profit, which is "M or −M", is assumed if the linkage between two nodes is not specified.
4. The shipment (linkage) from a node to itself is not allowed.

5. When the total demand is not equal to the total supply, the program will automatically add a dummy supply or demand.
6. The TRP program uses the MOdified DIstribution (MODI) method (or Transportation Simplex method) to solve transshipment and transportation problems. The size of problems that can be solved by TRP is dependent on the memory in your computer. For example, a transshipment problem with 50 sources, 50 destinations, and 50 transshipment points, or a transportation problem with 100 sources and 100 destinations can be solved by a PC with 640K memory.
7. Degeneracy is handled by a basis with 0 value.
8. When solving a problem, you can display every iteration of the MODI method tableau. The stepping-stone path will be marked by "*", and the incoming basis (recipient cell) will be marked by "**".
9. You can select one of the eight methods to find the initial solution. The default is Row Minimum (RM) method. The eight initial solution methods are:
   - **a.** Row Minimum (RM)
   - **b.** Modified Row Minimum (MRM)
   - **c.** Vogel's Approximation Method (VAM)
   - **d.** Column Minimum (CM)
   - **e.** Modified Column Minimum (MCM)
   - **f.** Matrix Minimum (MM)
   - **g.** NorthWest Corner Method (NWC)
   - **h.** Russell's Approximation Method (RAM)
10. Some notations are used during the solution process:

U(i):	Dual value for source *i*
V(j):	Dual value for destination *j*
e(i, j):	Net change in total cost/profit resulting from shipping one unit from source *i* to destination *j*
@ Cost/Profit:	Unit cost or profit
Opport. Cost:	Opportunity cost
M:	A non-Archimedean large number

MENU STRUCTURE

The functions and options in each of the pull-down menus are hierarchically listed as follows:

Modules
- Linear Programming (LP)
- Integer Linear Programming (ILP)
- Goal Programming (GP)
- Quadratic Programming (QP)

    - Nonlinear Programming (NLP)
    - Dynamic Programming (DP)
    - Transportation and Transshipment (TRP)
    - Assignment and Traveling Salesman (ASTS)
    - Specialized Network Modeling (SNET)
    - Capacitated Network Flow Modeling (CNET)
    - Project Scheduling: CPM/PERT
    - Inventory Theory (INVT)
    - Inventory Theory 2 (INVT2)
    - Queuing Theory (QUEUE)
    - Queuing System Simulation (QSIM)
    - Decision Analysis (DA)
    - Markov Process (MKV)
    - Time Series Forecasting (TSFC)
    - Financial Analysis (FA)
    - Exit from QSB
- Input Data
    - Data Entry
    - Read a File
    - Show Data
    - Print Data
    - Modify Data
        - Modify the problem coefficients
        - Delete one source
        - Delete one destination
        - Delete one transshipment point
    - Save
    - Save As
    - Exit from QSB
- Solution
    - Solve the Problem
    - Solve and Display Tableau
    - Solve Initial Solution Only
    - Select Initial Solution Method
        - Row Minimum (RM)
        - Modified Row Minimum (MRM)
        - Vogel's Approximation Method (VAM)
        - Column Minimum (CM)
        - Modified Column Minimum (MCM)
        - Matrix Minimum (MM)
        - NorthWest Corner Method (NWC)
        - Russell's Approximation Method (RAM)
    - Show the Solution
    - Print the Solution
    - Save the Solution

Options
  Color
  Monochrome
  Printer Selection
Help - TRP
  About TRP
  About the User Interface
  About the Edit Keys

SOLVING PROBLEMS WITH TRP

In the following sections, we will use example problems to show how to enter and solve the problems. The general procedure and menu options are described in detail in the tutorial sections of Chapter 2.

Example

To demonstrate the use of TRP, consider the following problem. ABC Oil Company has three oil storage points and four oil demand points. The company needs a shipping schedule that minimizes the total transportation cost and does not exceed the storage capacities. The demands, supplies, and cost information are shown in Table 9-1. What is the best schedule for distributing oil from storage to demand points while minimizing the total transportation cost?

Table 9-1. Capacities and unit costs for ABC Company.

	Demand point				
Storage	Dallas	Kansas	Tampa	Miami	Supply
Boston	5	4	5	6	100
Denver	3	3	6	6	200
Austin	2	5	7	8	400
Demand	200	100	150	250	

Enter the Problem

Select "Data Entry" from the "Input Data" menu (refer to Chapter 2 for selecting a menu item). Figs. 9-1 to 9-5 show the data entry of this problem. Note that "Minimization" is selected for the objective function, and "You define" is selected for the source and destination names. After the source and destination data are entered, select either spreadsheet format or free format (Fig. 9-4) for cost data entry. Fig. 9-5 shows the spreadsheet cost entry.

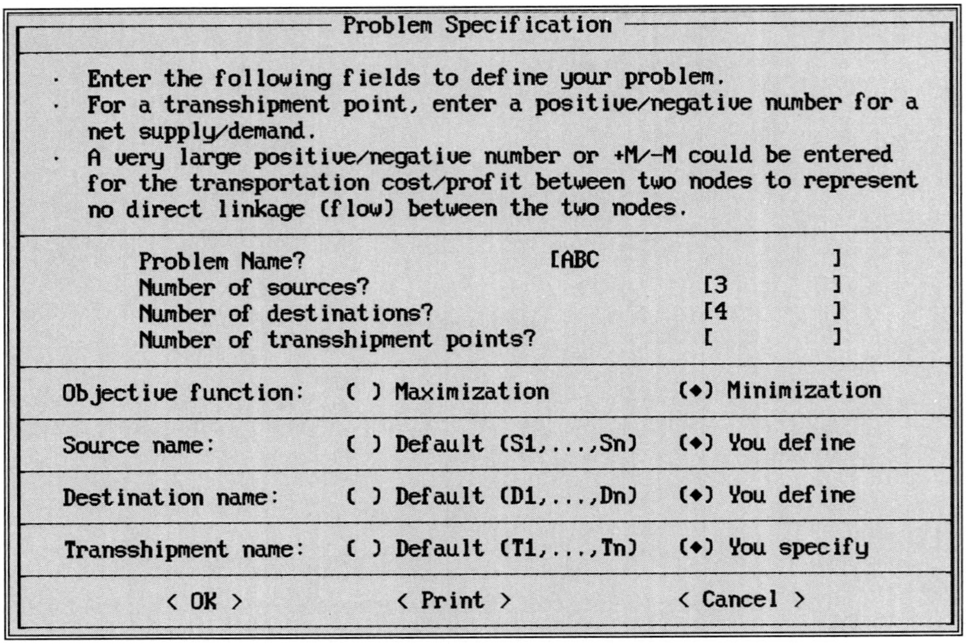

Figure 9-1. Problem specification for ABC.

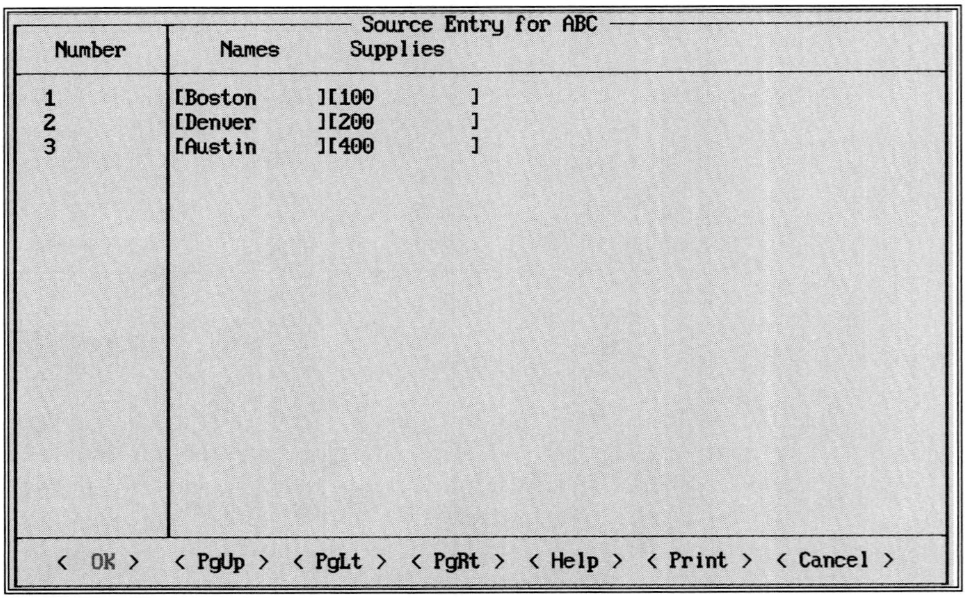

Figure 9-2. Sources for ABC.

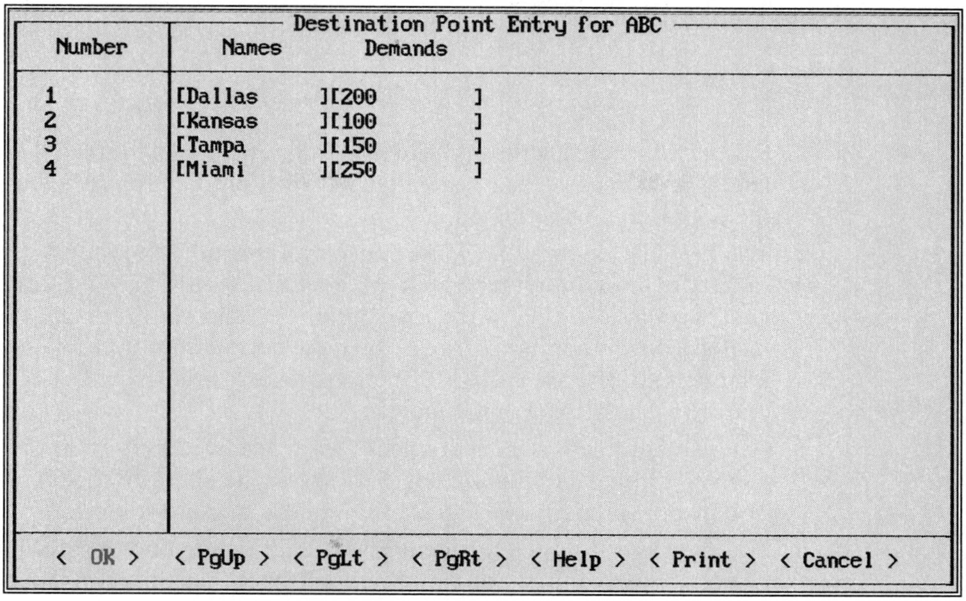

Figure 9-3. Destinations for ABC.

Figure 9-4. Select spreadsheet format for ABC.

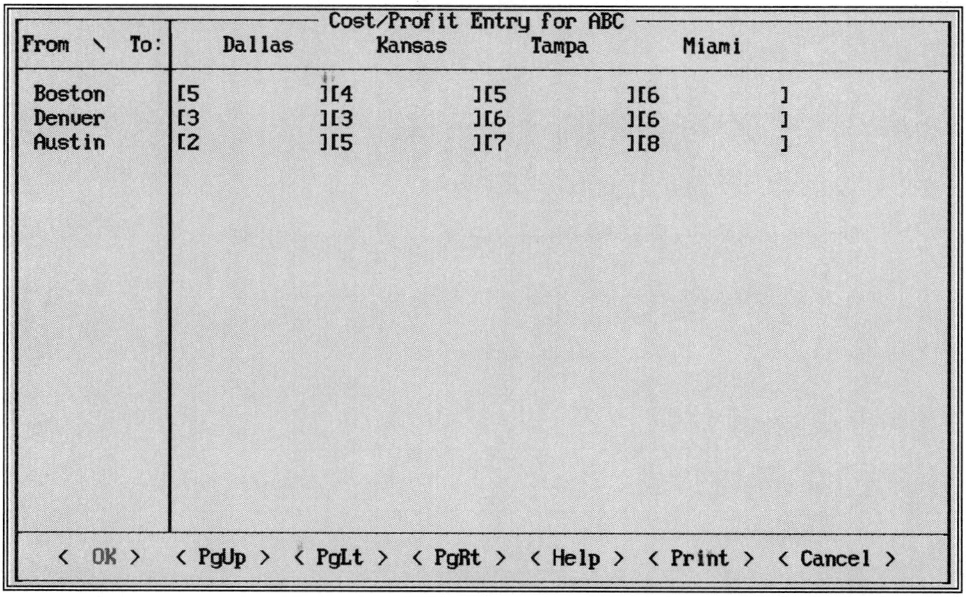

Figure 9-5. Cost entry for ABC.

Solve the Problem

1. Select "Solve the Problem" from the "Solution" menu to solve the ABC problem. The message "Please standby . . ." will display for a short period while the problem is being solved.
2. You may also choose "Solve and Display Tableau" from the "Solution" menu to display the solution tableau. Figs. 9-6 to 9-11 show the iterations. Note that you may choose the < Skip > option to skip the later iterations or the < Hardcopy > option to print or save the current iteration. When the tableau is larger than one screen, use the options "PgDn", "PgUp", "PgLt", and "PgRt" to control the display of the tableau.
3. After the problem is solved, select "Show the Solution" from the "Solution" menu to display the solution. Fig. 9-12 shows the dialog to specify displaying all or nonzero solution, and Fig. 9-13 shows the nonzero solution.
4. You may want to use a different initial solution method to solve the problem. Choose "Select Initial Solution Method" from the "Solution" menu. Fig. 9-14 shows the options. As mentioned in Chapter 2, you may use a mouse to click an item in the list box or use the "Tab" and up/down arrow keys to choose an item from the box. The default initial solution method is Row Minimum (RM).

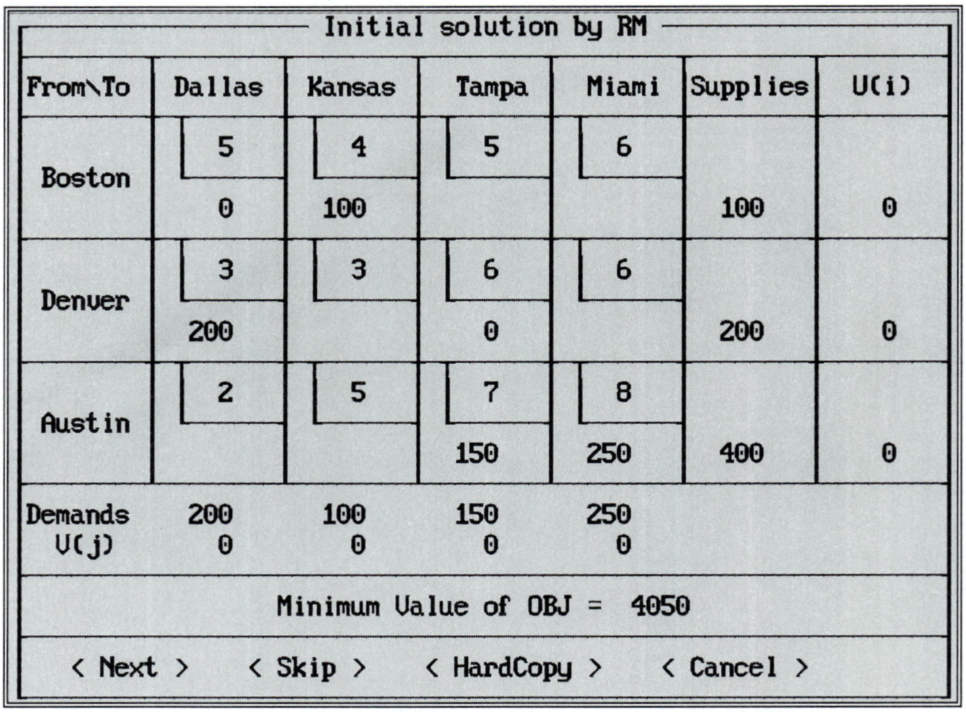

Initial solution by RM

From\To	Dallas	Kansas	Tampa	Miami	Supplies	U(i)
Boston	[5] 0	[4] 100	[5]	[6]	100	0
Denver	[3] 200	[3]	[6] 0	[6]	200	0
Austin	[2]	[5]	[7] 150	[8] 250	400	0
Demands	200	100	150	250		
V(j)	0	0	0	0		

Minimum Value of OBJ = 4050

< Next > < Skip > < HardCopy > < Cancel >

Figure 9-6. Initial solution by Row Minimum (RM) for ABC.

Iteration 1

From\To	Dallas	Kansas	Tampa	Miami	Supplies	U(i)
Boston	* 5 / 0	4 / 100	5 / **	6	100	0
Denver	* 3 / 200	3	* 6 / 0	6	200	-2
Austin	2	5	7 / 150	8 / 250	400	-1
Demands	200	100	150	250	*represents donor or recipient cell	
U(j)	5	4	8	9		

Current Minimum Value of OBJ = 4050 with e(1, 3) =-3

< Next > < Skip > < HardCopy > < Cancel >

Figure 9-7. Iteration 1 for ABC.

Iteration 2

From\To	Dallas	Kansas	Tampa	Miami	Supplies	U(i)
Boston	* 5 / 0	4 / 100	* 5 / 0	6	100	0
Denver	3 / 200	3	6	6	200	-2
Austin	2 / **	5	* 7 / 150	8 / 250	400	2
Demands	200	100	150	250	*represents donor or recipient cell	
U(j)	5	4	5	6		

Current Minimum Value of OBJ = 4050 with e(3, 1) =-5

< Next > < Skip > < HardCopy > < Cancel >

Figure 9-8. Iteration 2 for ABC.

Iteration 3

From\To	Dallas	Kansas	Tampa	Miami	Supplies	U(i)
Boston	[5]	[4] * 100	[5] * 0	[6]	100	0
Denver	[3] * 200	[3] **	[6]	[6]	200	3
Austin	[2] * 0	[5]	[7] * 150	[8] 250	400	2
Demands	200	100	150	250	*represents donor	
V(j)	0	4	5	6	or recipient cell	

Current Minimum Value of OBJ = 4050 with e(2, 2) =-4

< Next > < Skip > < HardCopy > < Cancel >

Figure 9-9. Iteration 3 for ABC.

Iteration 4

From\To	Dallas	Kansas	Tampa	Miami	Supplies	U(i)
Boston	[5]	[4]	[5] 100	[6]	100	0
Denver	[3] * 100	[3] 100	[6]	[6] **	200	3
Austin	[2] * 100	[5]	[7] 50	[8] * 250	400	2
Demands	200	100	150	250	*represents donor	
V(j)	0	0	5	6	or recipient cell	

Current Minimum Value of OBJ = 3650 with e(2, 4) =-3

< Next > < Skip > < HardCopy > < Cancel >

Figure 9-10. Iteration 4 for ABC.

Final tableau (Total iterations = 4)

From\To	Dallas	Kansas	Tampa	Miami	Supplies	U(i)
Boston	5	4	5 100	6	100	0
Denver	3	3 100	6	6 100	200	0
Austin	2 200	5	7 50	8 150	400	2
Demands	200	100	150	250		
V(j)	0	3	5	6		

Minimum Value of OBJ = 3350 with multiple optimals.

< Next > < Skip > < HardCopy > < Cancel >

Figure 9-11. Final tableau for ABC.

All solution or non-zero solution only?

< All > < Non-zero only > < Cancel >

Figure 9-12. Options to specify displaying all or nonzero solution.

Solution for ABC

08-23-1993 11:54:34 Page: 1 of 1

From	To	Shipment	@ Cost/Profit	Opport. Cost
Boston	Tampa	100	5	0
Denver	Kansas	100	3	0
Denver	Miami	100	6	0
Austin	Dallas	200	2	0
Austin	Tampa	50	7	0
Austin	Miami	150	8	0

Minimized OBJ = 3350 Iteration = 4 Elapsed CPU seconds = 0

< PageDown > < PageUp > < Hardcopy > < Cancel >

Figure 9-13. Solution for ABC.

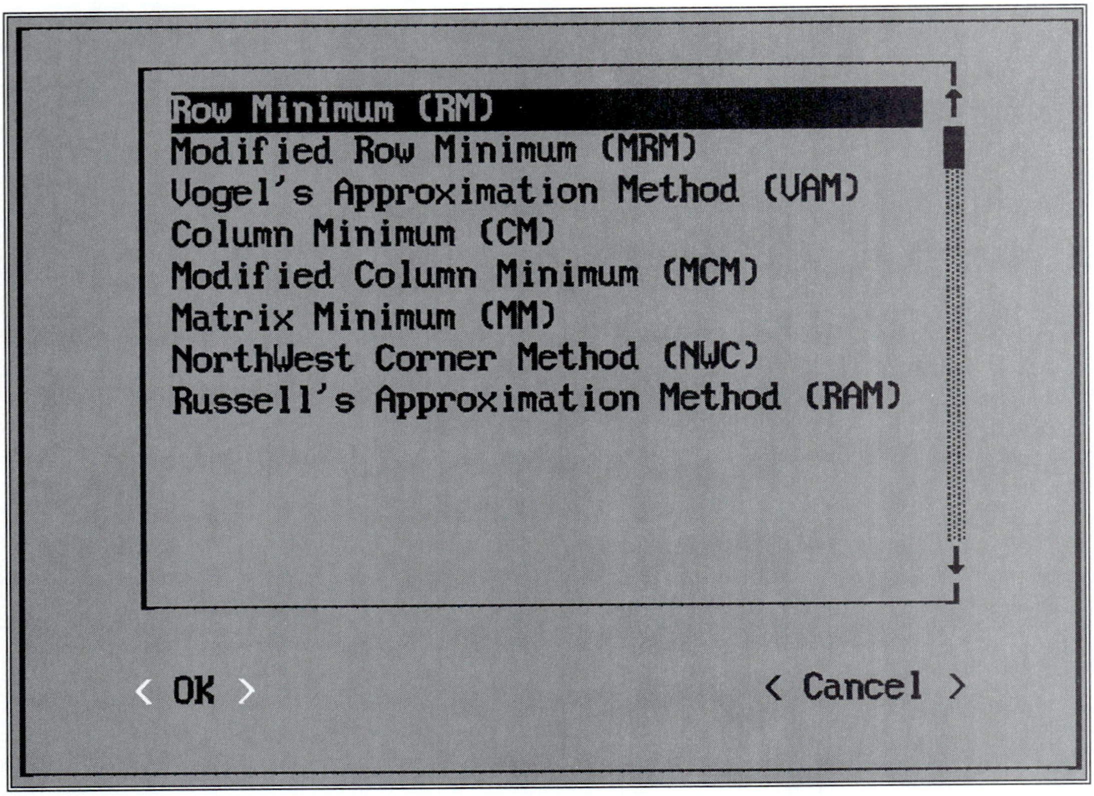

Figure 9-14. Choice of the initial solution methods.

5. You may want to solve the problem by the initial solution heuristic only to save computer time with a little sacrifice of the solution quality. Choose "Solve Initial Solution Only" from the "Solution" menu.

Transshipment Problem and Free-Format Data Entry

We will use the transshipment problem shown in Fig. 9-15 to demonstrate how to use the free format to enter this problem. The numbers on each arc represent the unit shipping costs. S1 and S2 are sources with capacities of 600 and 800, respectively. D1, D2, and D3 are destinations with demands of 500, 350, and 900, respectively. T1 and T4 are transshipment points with net demands of 200 and 100, respectively, while T2 and T3 are transshipment points with net supplies of 350 and 200, respectively. Note that the negative capacity for a transshipment point represents a net demand, and the positive one represents a net supply.

Enter the Problem

Select "Data Entry" from the "Input Data" menu. Figs. 9-16 to 9-22 show the data entry of this problem. Note that "Minimization" is selected for the objective function, and "Default" is selected for the source, destination, and transshipment point names. Select the free format in Fig. 9-20 for cost data entry. Fig. 9-21 and Fig. 9-22 show the free-format interactive session to enter the unit costs of possible shipments between nodes. Note that if there is no arc connecting a pair of nodes, it is assumed that there is no shipment between them, and the unit cost will be assumed to be infinity.

Solve the Problem

Select "Solve the Problem" from the "Solution" menu to solve the Transshipment problem. Fig. 9-23 shows the nonzero solution of Transshipment.

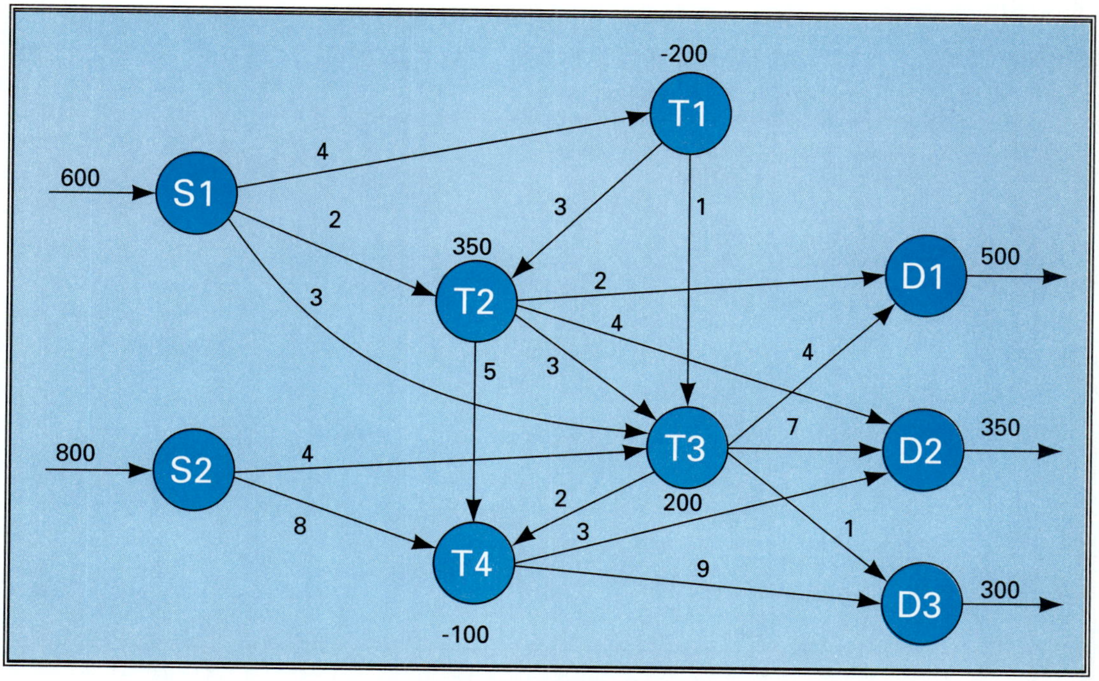

Figure 9-15. A transshipment problem.

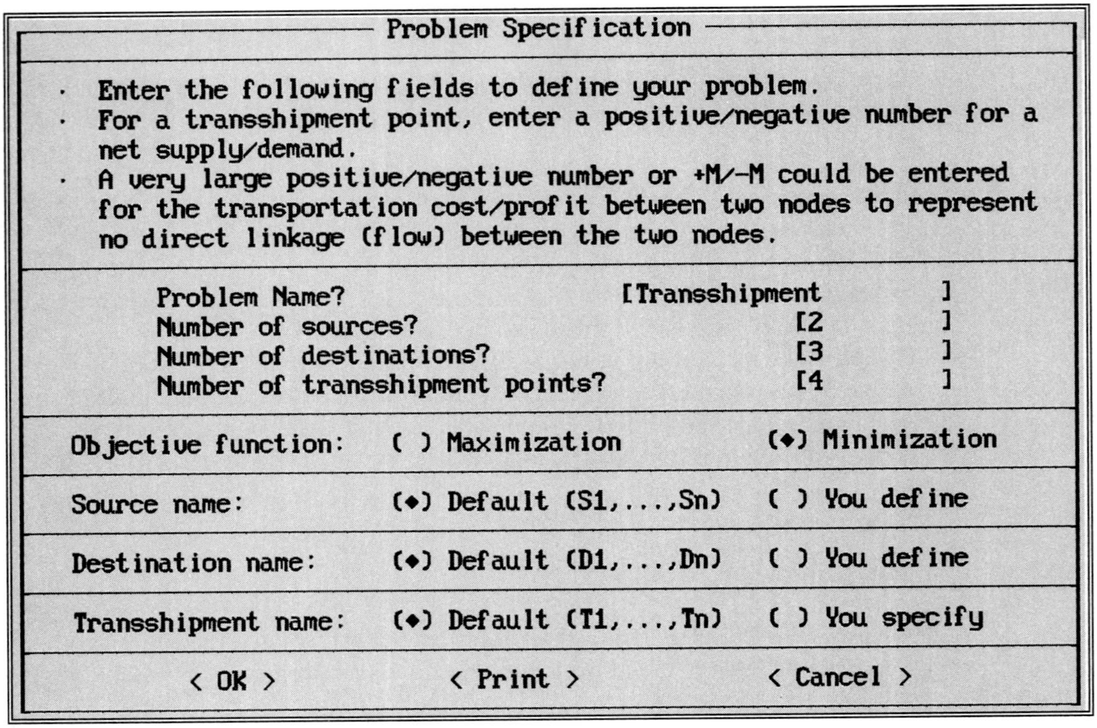

Problem Specification

- Enter the following fields to define your problem.
- For a transshipment point, enter a positive/negative number for a net supply/demand.
- A very large positive/negative number or +M/-M could be entered for the transportation cost/profit between two nodes to represent no direct linkage (flow) between the two nodes.

Problem Name? [Transshipment]
Number of sources? [2]
Number of destinations? [3]
Number of transshipment points? [4]

Objective function: ( ) Maximization (◆) Minimization

Source name: (◆) Default (S1,...,Sn) ( ) You define

Destination name: (◆) Default (D1,...,Dn) ( ) You define

Transshipment name: (◆) Default (T1,...,Tn) ( ) You specify

< OK > < Print > < Cancel >

Figure 9-16. Problem specification for Transshipment.

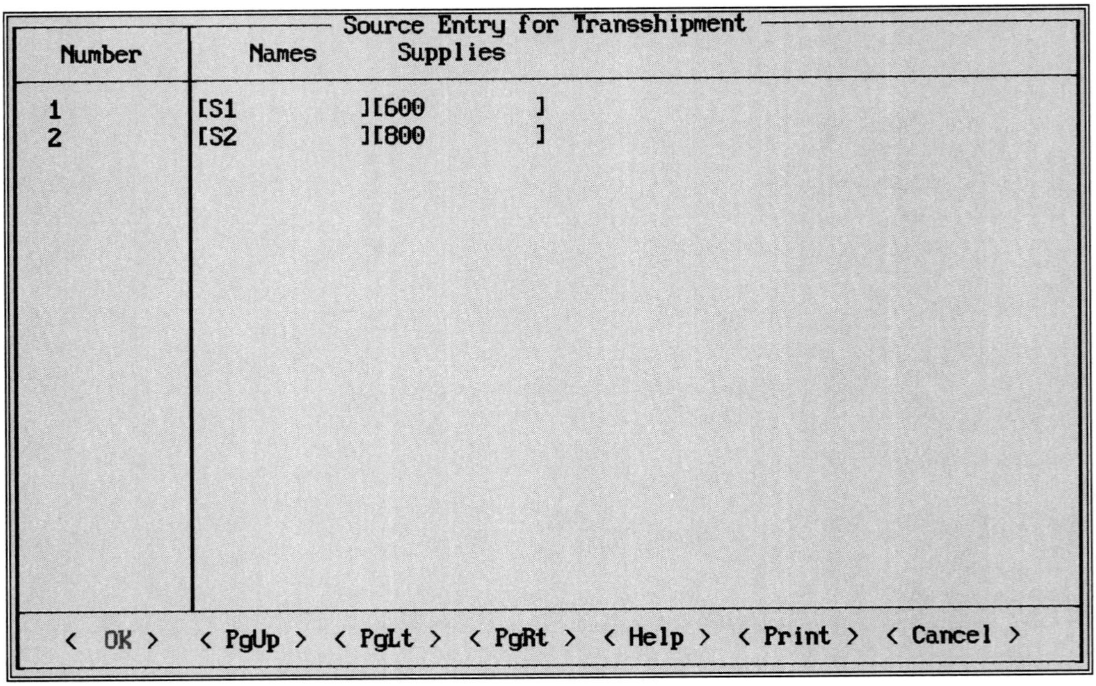

Source Entry for Transshipment

Number	Names	Supplies
1	[S1]	[600]
2	[S2]	[800]

< OK > < PgUp > < PgLt > < PgRt > < Help > < Print > < Cancel >

Figure 9-17. Sources for Transshipment.

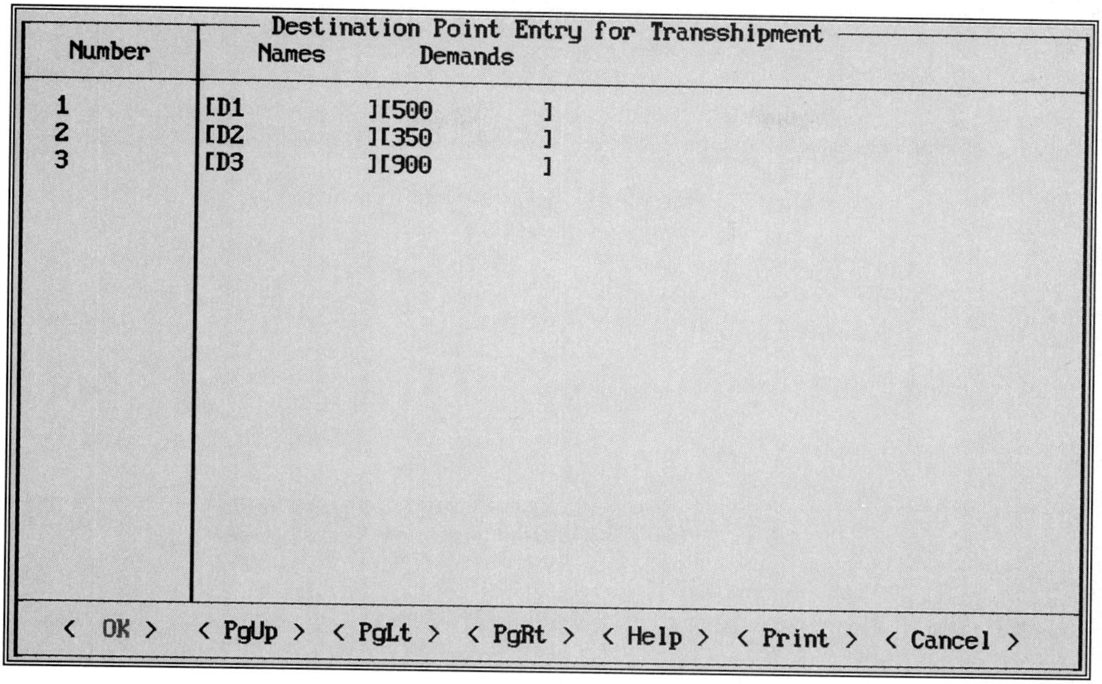

Figure 9-18. Destinations for Transshipment.

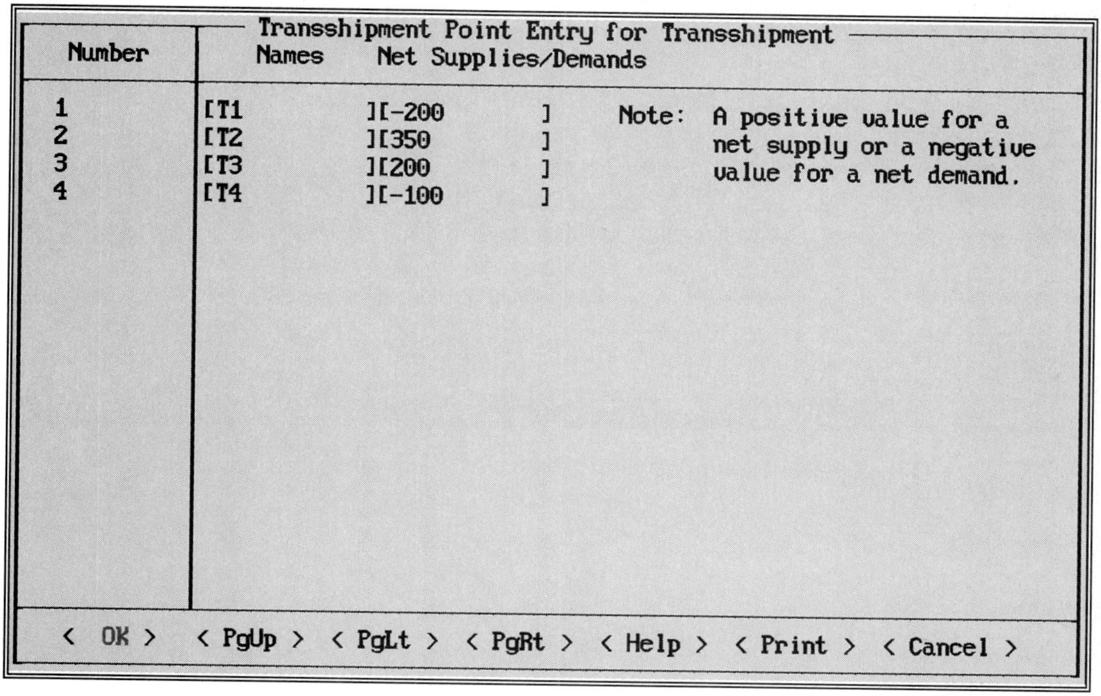

Figure 9-19. Transshipment points for Transshipment.

Figure 9-20. Select the free-format entry.

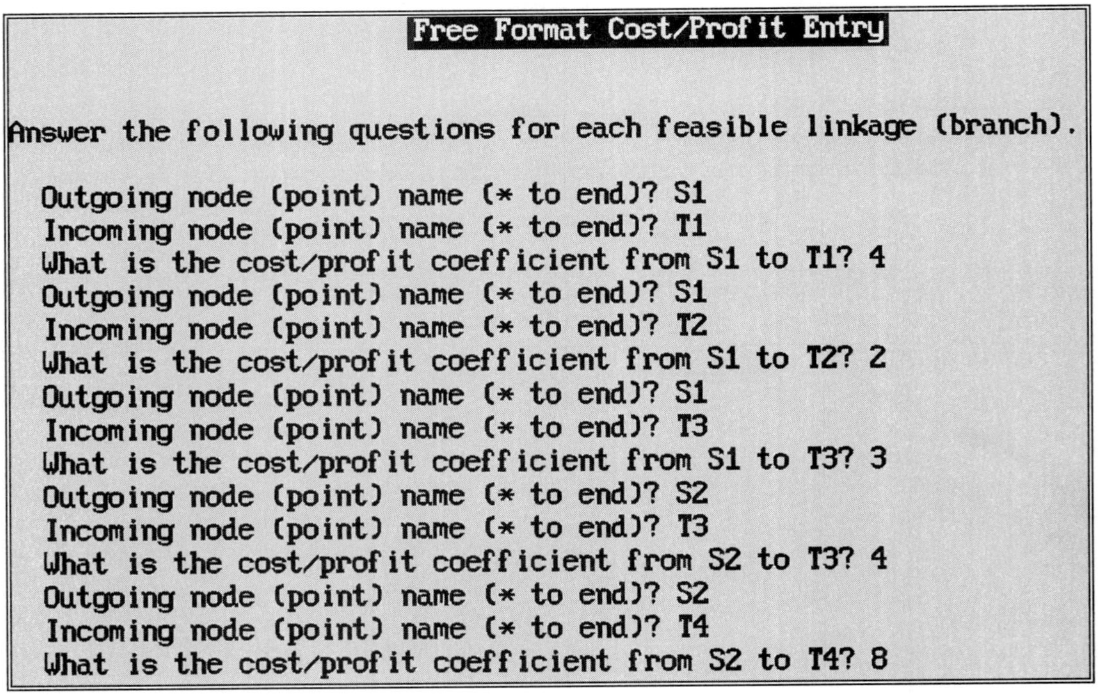

Figure 9-21. Free-format entry of cost coefficients for Transshipment.

```
Outgoing node (point) name (* to end)? T1
Incoming node (point) name (* to end)? T2
What is the cost/profit coefficient from T1 to T2?
Outgoing node (point) name (* to end)? T1
Incoming node (point) name (* to end)? T3
What is the cost/profit coefficient from T1 to T3?
Outgoing node (point) name (* to end)? T2
Incoming node (point) name (* to end)? T3
What is the cost/profit coefficient from T2 to T3?
Outgoing node (point) name (* to end)? T2
Incoming node (point) name (* to end)? T4
What is the cost/profit coefficient from T2 to T4?
Outgoing node (point) name (* to end)? T2
Incoming node (point) name (* to end)? D1
What is the cost/profit coefficient from T2 to D1?
Outgoing node (point) name (* to end)? T2
Incoming node (point) name (* to end)? D2
What is the cost/profit coefficient from T2 to D2?
Outgoing node (point) name (* to end)? T3
Incoming node (point) name (* to end)? T4
```

```
Outgoing node (point) name (* to end)? T3
Incoming node (point) name (* to end)? D1
What is the cost/profit coefficient from T3 to D1?
Outgoing node (point) name (* to end)? T3
Incoming node (point) name (* to end)? D2
What is the cost/profit coefficient from T3 to D2?
Outgoing node (point) name (* to end)? T3
Incoming node (point) name (* to end)? D3
What is the cost/profit coefficient from T3 to D3?
Outgoing node (point) name (* to end)? T4
Incoming node (point) name (* to end)? D2
What is the cost/profit coefficient from T4 to D2?
Outgoing node (point) name (* to end)? T4
Incoming node (point) name (* to end)? D3
What is the cost/profit coefficient from T4 to D3?
```

Figure 9-22. Free-format entry of cost coefficients for Transshipment (cont.).

Solution for Transshipment

08-23-1993 12:06:53 Page: 1 of 1

From	To	Shipment	@ Cost/Profit	Opport. Cost
S1	T1	200	4	0
S1	T2	400	2	0
S2	T3	800	4	0
T2	D1	500	2	0
T2	D2	250	4	0
T3	D3	900	1	0
T3	T4	100	2	0
Dummy	D2	100	0	0

Minimized OBJ = 7900 Iteration = 4 Elapsed CPU seconds = 0

< PageDown > < PageUp > < Hardcopy > < Cancel >

Figure 9-23. Solution for Transshipment.

EXERCISES

1. Consider the transportation problem with the following unit costs and capacities. Find the optimal solution by using the TRP program.

	Destination			
Source	A	B	C	Supply
1	5	1	6	200
2	8	4	3	350
3	7	9	5	170
Demand	220	300	200	

2. Consider a distribution problem for which the unit transportation costs, demands, and supplies are listed as follows. Find the optimal solution. Compare the iteration numbers to solve the problem by using the NorthWest Corner method or the Vogel's method as the initial solution method.

Source	Austin	Columbus	Dallas	Boston	Los Angeles	Supply
	Destination					
New York	100	50	90	30	130	30,000
Chicago	90	30	70	50	110	20,000
Pittsburgh	95	30	75	40	120	20,000
Demand	10,000	12,000	15,000	17,000	25,000	

3. Nine jobs are available for ten individuals. According to the skill levels, each person will have different earnings per hour for different jobs. The following table shows these earnings per hour. Use the TRP to find the best assignment in order to maximize the total earnings per hour for the ten individuals.

	Person									
Job	1	2	3	4	5	6	7	8	9	10
1	3	1	8	4	3	2	7	4	2	5
2	6	1	3	5	6	6	3	8	9	10
3	9	4	3	1	5	6	9	3	1	2
4	7	9	3	4	8	4	6	9	3	1
5	2	5	7	4	2	1	2	2	6	8
6	5	4	3	4	3	7	8	6	5	9
7	8	7	6	3	9	4	3	5	6	1
8	5	4	2	8	7	6	3	7	8	9
9	5	9	1	3	6	7	4	2	1	5

4. Diho Dairy has two farms that supply milk for three local supermarkets. Demands for each supermarket during a delivery period are 6000, 4000, and 3800 gallons, respectively. Diho's two farms have the capacity to produce 8500 gallons and 6500 gallons of milk, respectively, per delivery period. The distances from each farm to each supermarket are listed in the table. The company needs to find a shipping schedule that minimizes the total transportation cost. Assume that the unit transportation cost is proportional to the travel distance.

Farm	Kenwood	Submatrix	King Vegetable	Supply
	Supermarket			
Happy	5 miles	10	7	8500
Jucy	13	5	11	6500
Demand	6000	4000	3000	

5. A company presently operates four manufacturing plants that distribute a product to three warehouses. Currently, the capacity of the plants and the demands of the warehouses are stable. These are listed with the unit shipping costs in the following table. Find the optimal distribution plan for the company.

	Warehouse			
Plant	A	B	C	Capacity
1	20	19	21	12,200
2	19	22	18	2,800
3	20	20	20	2,500
4	21	20	19	2,200
Demand	7,300	3,500	5,600	

6. A company has a six-month demand for its product broken down per month as follows: 1000, 1200, 1500, 2000, 1800, and 1500 units. The company has two ways to produce its product: regular time and overtime. The unit costs for regular time and overtime production are \$10 and \$14, respectively. Regular time can produce 1000 units per month; overtime can produce 800 units per month. The company can also hold the demands and satisfy them in the following months by giving customers a \$2 discount per unit per one-month delay. Maximum delay allowed is two months. Extra production will be carried to the next month. The carrying cost for each finished product is \$3 per month. Formulate a transportation problem to represent this production planning problem to minimize

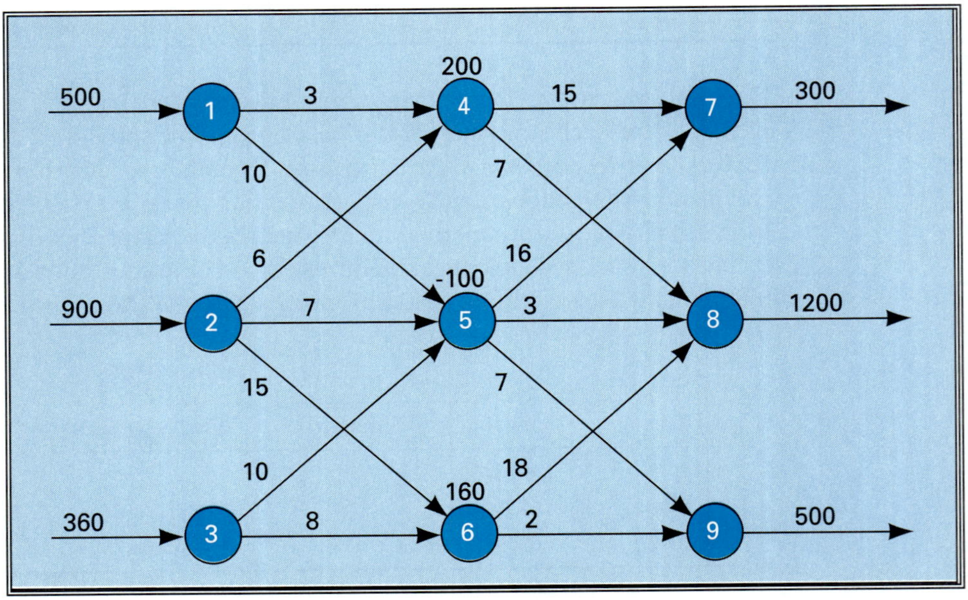

Figure 9-24. The transshipment problem for exercise 7.

the total production cost while meeting the demands. Use the TRP program to solve it.

7. Solve the transshipment problem in Fig. 9-24 to minimize the total cost. The numbers on each arc between nodes represent the unit shipping costs.
8. Solve the transshipment problem in Fig. 9-25 to minimize the total cost. The numbers on each arc between nodes represent the unit shipping costs.

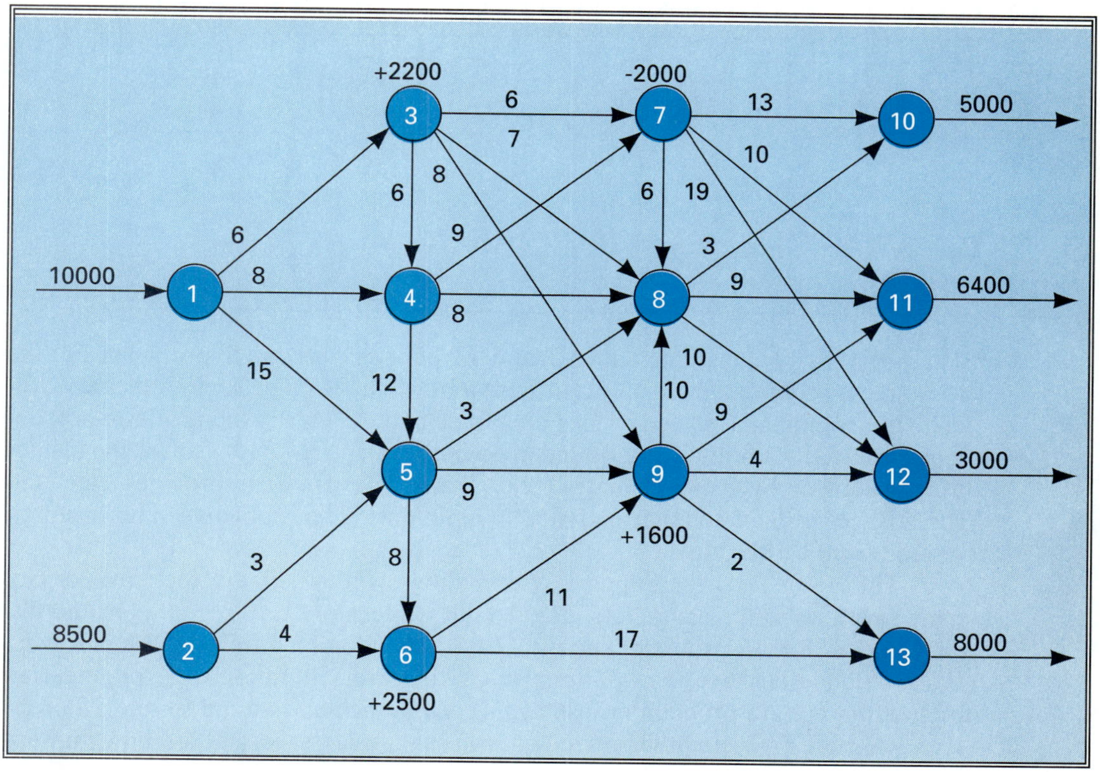

Figure 9-25. The transshipment problem for exercise 8.

10

ASSIGNMENT AND TRAVELING SALESMAN PROBLEMS (ASTS)

OVERVIEW OF THE ASTS DECISION SUPPORT SYSTEM

This program solves assignment (AS) and traveling salesman (TS) problems. For the assignment problems, tasks may represent jobs while the objects may indicate workers. The assignment is solved by the Hungarian method. The traveling salesman problem is solved by a branch-and-bound procedure which repeatedly solves the assignment problem by assigning city-to-city links. The program provides free and spreadsheet formats to enter and modify input data. The problem can be saved on or read from a disk(ette).

The ASTS Decision Support System allows you to define object, task, or city names with up to ten characters. The default names are O1, O2, . . . , On and T1, T2, . . . , Tn for AS problems and C1, C2, . . . , Cn for TS problems. When solving the problem, you have the option of displaying every iteration of the Hungarian method for the AS problem or displaying each branch-and-bound for the TS problem. After the problem has been solved, you can display, save, and print the final solution.

TECHNICAL NOTES ON THE ASTS PROGRAM

1. To enter the cost/profit/distance coefficients, a very large positive/negative number or +M/−M can be entered to represent no direct assignment or linkage between two nodes when the spreadsheet format is used. A node represents an object, a task, or a city.
2. In terms of the free-format data entry, enter a pair of connecting nodes to represent a possible assignment or linkage. A huge cost or a negative profit, which is "M" or "−M" depending on a maximization or minimization objective, is assumed if the linkage between two nodes is not specified.
3. The assignment (linkage) from a node to itself is not allowed.

4. The ASTS program uses a labeling algorithm (Hungarian method) to solve assignment problems that are assumed to make one-to-one assignments. If the number of objects and the number of tasks are not the same, ASTS will automatically add the appropriate number of dummy tasks or objects.
5. ASTS can display the Hungarian method tableau, where zeros are crossed by arrows.
6. If the problem is to maximize the objective, ASTS will convert it to a minimization problem in the tableau by finding the appropriate opportunity loss for each potential assignment.
7. For the traveling salesman problem, ASTS employs a branch-and-bound procedure to solve assignment problems sequentially. Each individual assignment problem contains different restrictions of the city linkages. The best-bound rule is used to select the next problem to be solved. The program keeps 10,000 active nodes at most during the branch-and-bound procedure. A heuristic method which links a city to the closest unvisited city is also available in ASTS to quick-solve the traveling salesman problem.
8. The typical size of the assignment problem that can be solved by ASTS is 150 objects and 150 tasks. The size of the traveling salesman problem that can be solved may be 100 cities if the PC has 640K memory. The branch-and-bound for the traveling salesman may take a long time if the number of cities is large. When the number of cities is large, it is recommended to solve the problem by the heuristic method and check if the solution is satisfactory.

MENU STRUCTURE

The functions and options in each of the pull-down menus are hierarchically listed as follows:

- Modules
  - Linear Programming (LP)
  - Integer Linear Programming (ILP)
  - Goal Programming (GP)
  - Quadratic Programming (QP)
  - Nonlinear Programming (NLP)
  - Dynamic Programming (DP)
  - Transportation and Transshipment (TRP)
  - Assignment and Traveling Salesman (ASTS)
  - Specialized Network Modeling (SNET)
  - Capacitated Network Flow Modeling (CNET)
  - Project Scheduling: CPM/PERT
  - Inventory Theory (INVT)
  - Inventory Theory 2 (INVT2)
  - Queuing Theory (QUEUE)
  - Queuing System Simulation (QSIM)
  - Decision Analysis (DA)

  - Markov Process (MKV)
  - Time Series Forecasting (TSFC)
  - Financial Analysis (FA)
  - Exit from QSB
- Input Data
  - Data Entry
  - Read a File
  - Show Data
  - Print Data
  - Modify Data
    - Modify the problem configuration
    - Delete one object
    - Delete one task
    - Delete one city
  - Save
  - Save As
  - Exit from QSB
- Solution
  - Solve the Problem
  - Solve and Display Steps
  - Solve by Heuristic Method
  - Show the Solution
  - Print the Solution
  - Save the Solution
- Options
  - Color
  - Monochrome
  - Printer Selection
- Help - ASTS
  - About ASTS
  - About the User Interface
  - About the Edit Keys

SOLVING PROBLEMS WITH ASTS

In the following sections, we will use example problems to show how to enter and solve the problems. The general procedure and menu options are described in detail in the tutorial sections of Chapter 2.

Example - Assignment Problem

To demonstrate the use of ASTS, consider the following example. Austin Computer Service Company (ACSC) has four customers who require service for their computer facilities. The customers are designated A, B, C, and D, respectively. ACSC has four technicians capable of providing these services. Because of the different specialties of these technicians, their service times vary according to the specific customer. These possible service times are shown in Table 10-1. The manager of ACSC wants to determine an assignment schedule that will minimize the total service time for the four customers.

Table 10-1. Service times in hours.

	Customer			
Technician	A	B	C	D
John	3	6	7	10
Peter	5	6	3	8
Toshi	2	8	4	16
Rudy	8	6	5	9

Enter the Problem

Select "Data Entry" from the "Input Data" menu (refer to Chapter 2 for selecting a menu item). Figs. 10-1 to 10-5 show the data entry of this problem. Note that "Assignment" is selected for the problem type, "Minimization" is selected for the objective function, and "You define" is selected for the object and task names. After

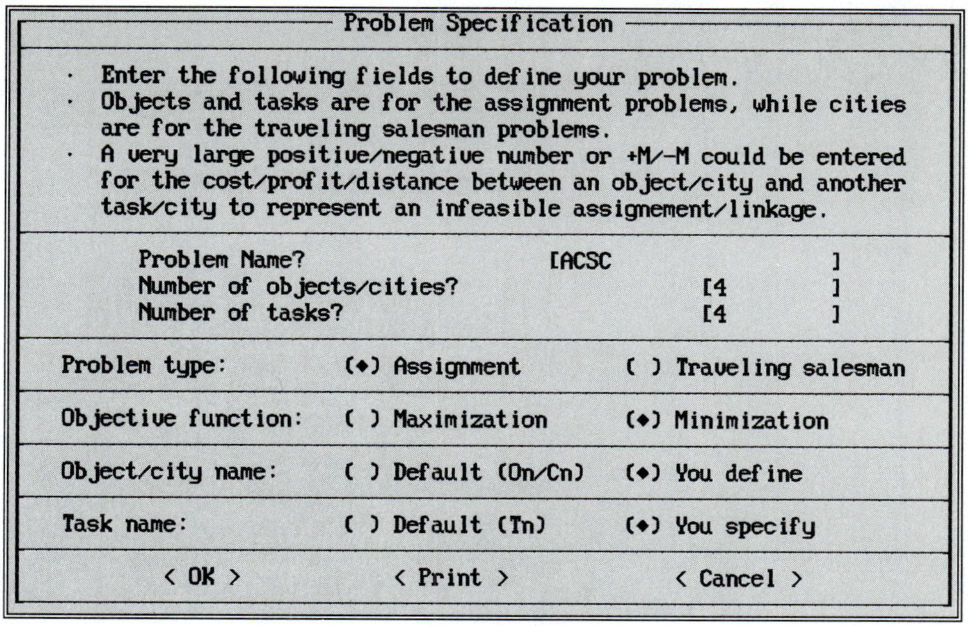

Figure 10-1. Problem specification for ACSC.

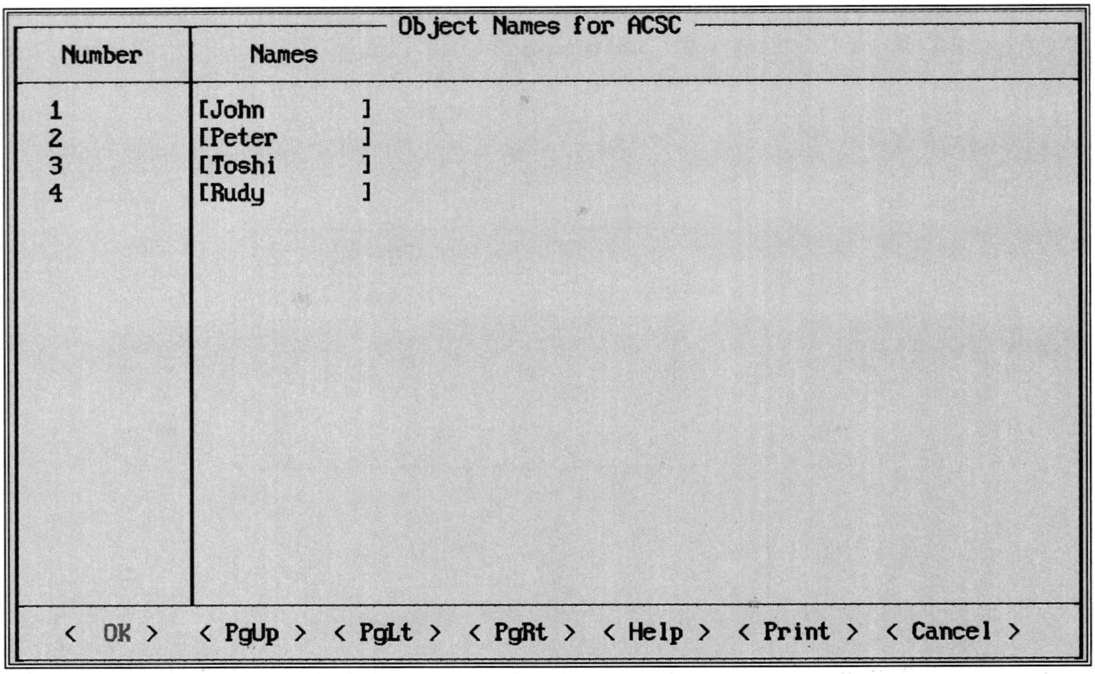

Figure 10-2. Object names for ACSC.

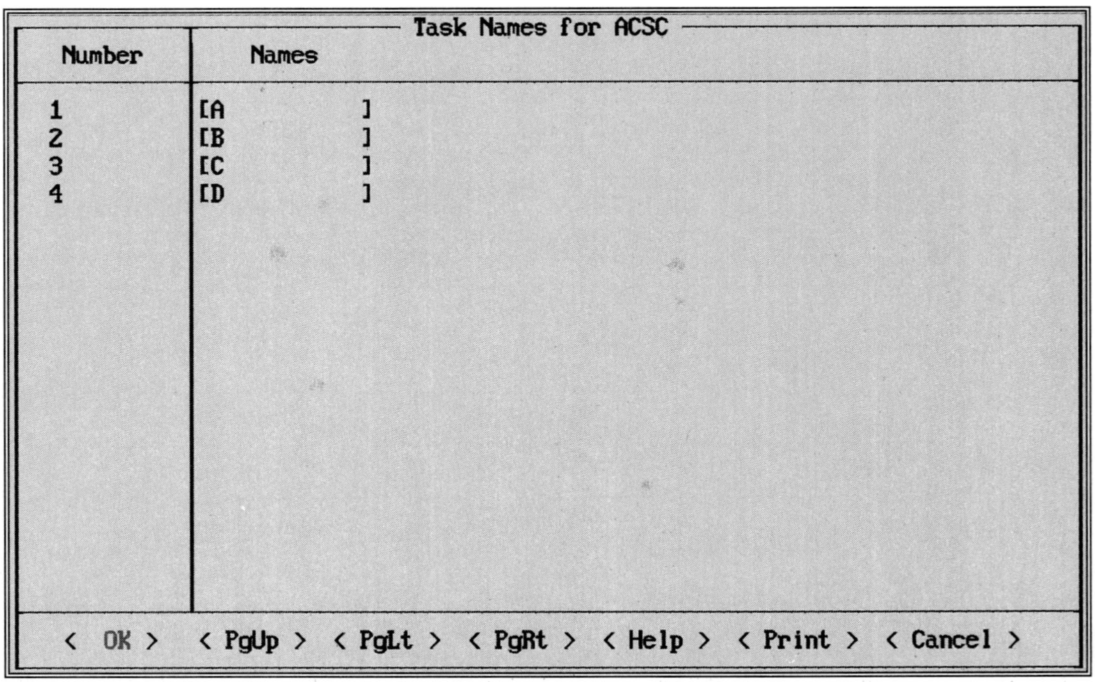

Figure 10-3. Task names for ACSC.

Figure 10-4. Select spreadsheet format for ACSC.

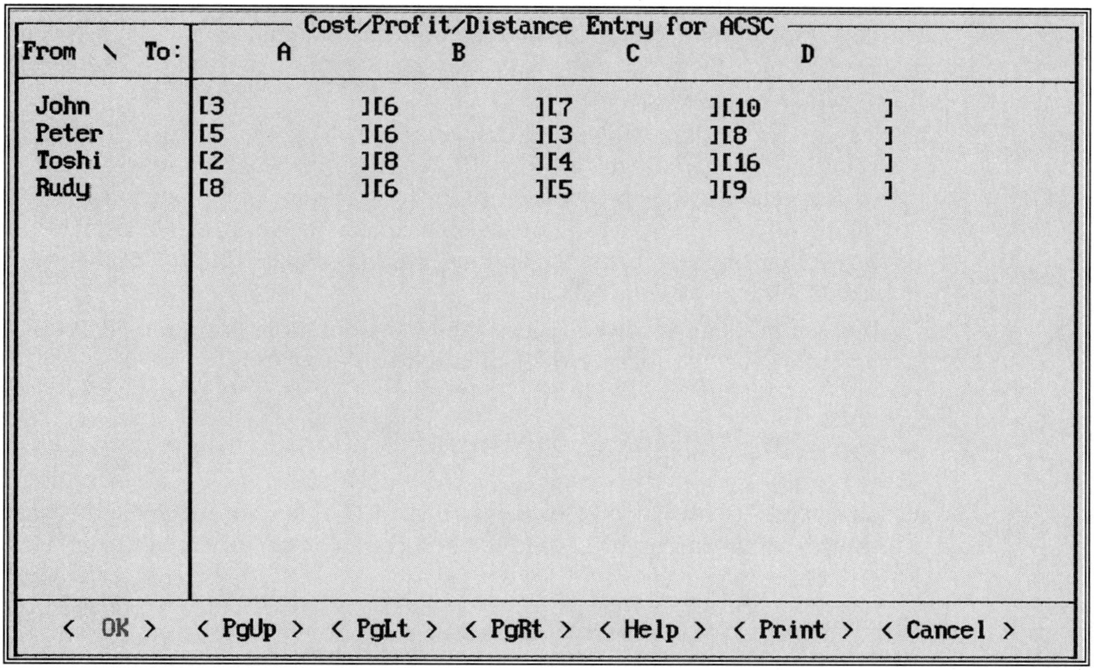

Figure 10-5. Service time entry for ACSC.

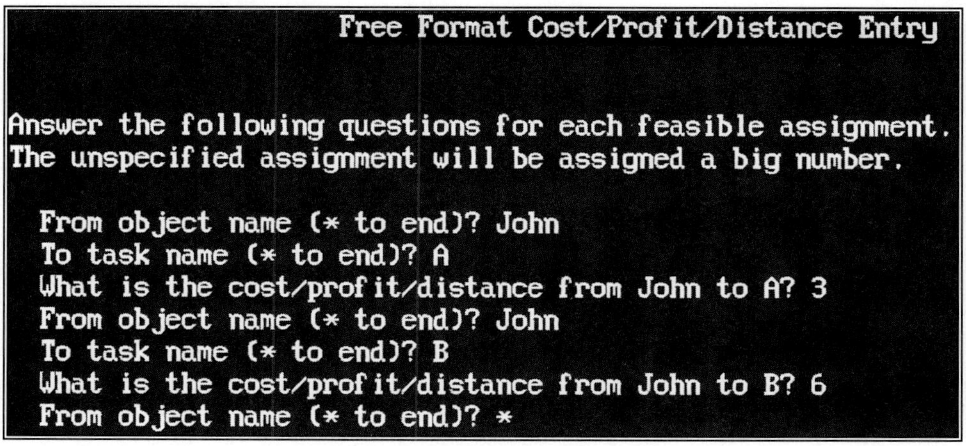

Figure 10-6. Sample free-format entry for ACSC.

the object and task names are entered, select either spreadsheet format or free format (Fig. 10-4) for service time entry. Fig. 10-5 shows the spreadsheet entry. If you choose to enter the service time by the free format in Fig. 10-4, Fig. 10-6 illustrates the free-format data entry (incomplete). Note that "*" is entered to end the sequence.

Solve the Problem

1. Select "Solve the Problem" from the "Solution" menu to solve the problem. The message "Please standby . . ." will display for a short period while the problem is being solved.
2. You may also choose "Solve and Display Steps" from the "Solution" menu to display the Hungarian tableau. Figs. 10-7 to 10-9 show the iterations. Note that you may choose the < Skip > option to skip the later iterations or the < Hardcopy > option to print or save the current iteration. When the tableau is larger than one screen, use the options "PgDn", "PgUp", "PgLt", and "PgRt" to control the display of tableau.
3. After the problem is solved, select "Show the Solution" from the "Solution" menu to display the solution. Fig. 10-10 shows the solution.

Example — Traveling Salesman Problem

A salesman needs to travel to all the cities in Fig. 10-11 at least once. Given the traveling distances shown in Fig. 10-11, find the best route for the salesman to minimize

Initial Tableau

Object\Task	A	B	C	D	Cover Line
John	3	6	7	10	
Peter	5	6	3	8	
Toshi	2	8	4	16	
Rudy	8	6	5	9	
Cover Line					

< Next >   < Skip >   < HardCopy >   < Cancel >

Figure 10-7. Initial tableau for ACSC.

Iteration 1

Object\Task	A	B	C	D	Cover Line
John	0	2	4	3	
Peter	2	2	0	1	←
Toshi	0	5	2	10	
Rudy	3	0	0	0	←
Cover Line	↑				

< Next >   < Skip >   < HardCopy >   < Cancel >

Figure 10-8. Iteration 1 for ACSC.

Final Tableau (Total Iterations = 2)

Object\Task	A	B	C	D	Cover Line
John	0	0	2	1	
Peter	4	2	0	1	
Toshi	0	3	0	8	
Rudy	5	0	0	0	
Cover Line	↑	↑	↑	↑	

< Next >   < Skip >   < HardCopy >   < Cancel >

Figure 10-9. Final tableau for ACSC.

Assignment Solution for ACSC

08-23-1993 12:16:34 Page: 1

Object	Task	Cost/Profit	Object	Task	Cost/Profit
John	B	6	Toshi	A	2
Peter	C	3	Rudy	D	9

Minimized OBJ = 20 # Iterations = 2 CPU seconds = 0

< PageDown > < PageUp > < Hardcopy > < Cancel >

Figure 10-10. Solution summary for ACSC.

his total travel distance. Note that if there is no arc to connect a pair of cities, it means there is no direct travel between them, and the direct distance will be assumed to be infinity. If the linkage between cities is two-way, you need to enter the distances of both ways since in a traveling situation, the traveling distances may be different each way. For example, enter 100 for both LA to DEV and DEV to LA.

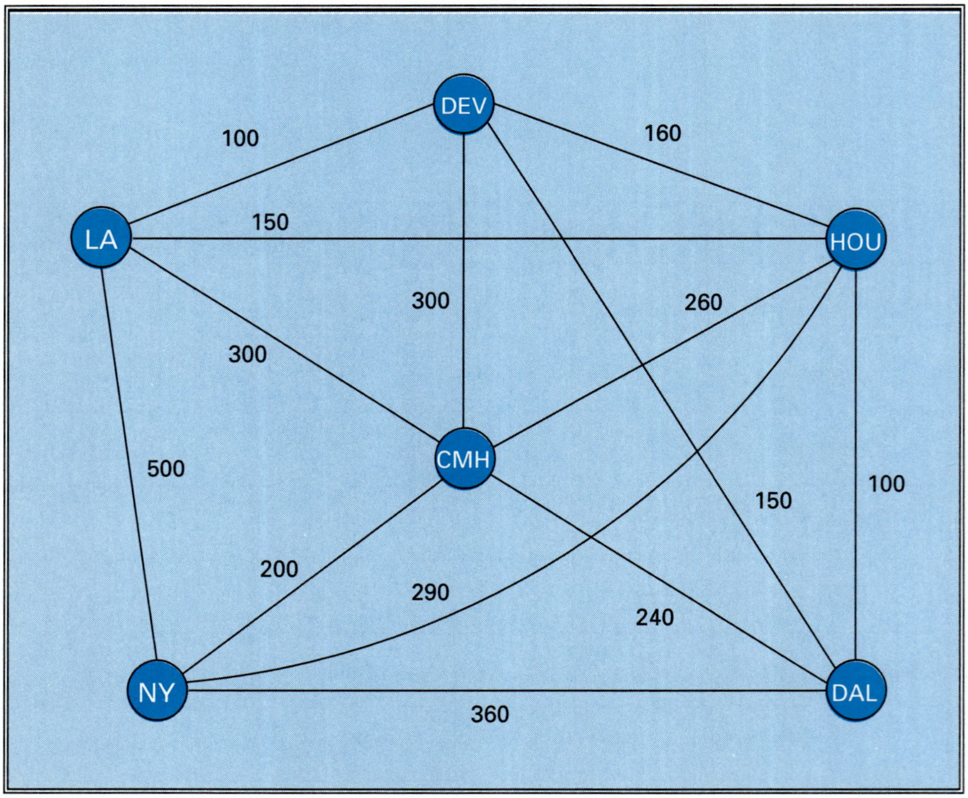

Figure 10-11. A traveling salesman problem.

Enter the Problem

Select "Data Entry" from the "Input Data" menu. Fig. 10-12 defines the problem. Note that "Traveling salesman" is selected for the problem type, "Minimization" is selected for the objective function, and "You define" is selected for the city names. After the city names are entered (Fig. 10-13), select either spreadsheet format or free format (Fig. 10-4) for distance entry. Fig. 10-14 and Fig. 10-15 show the spreadsheet entry. Note that Fig. 10-15 is the right page of Fig. 10-14 by pressing the "PgRt" button. If you choose to enter the distance by the free format, Fig. 10-16 illustrates the free-format data entry (incomplete). Note that "*" is entered to end the sequence.

Solve the Problem

1. Select "Solve the Problem" from the "Solution" menu to solve the problem. The message "Please standby . . ." will display for a short period while the problem is being solved.
2. You may also choose "Solve and Display Steps" from the "Solution" menu to display the branch-and-bound process. Figs. 10-17 to 10-23 show the iterations. Note that you may choose the < Non-stop > option to skip the later iterations or the < Hardcopy > option to print or save the current iteration. To demonstrate the route from each solution, let us use Iteration 1 (Fig. 10-17) as an example. The routes from this solution are LA-DEV-LA, HOU-DAL-HOU, and

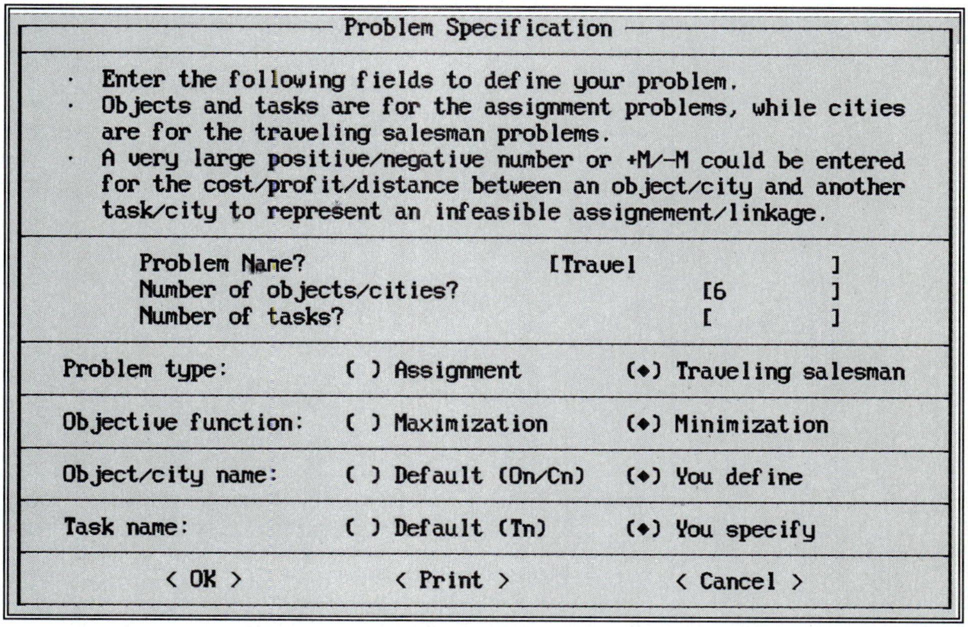

Figure 10-12. Problem definition for Travel.

City Names for Travel

Number	Names
1	[LA]
2	[DEV]
3	[HOU]
4	[CMH]
5	[NY]
6	[DAL]

< OK > < PgUp > < PgLt > < PgRt > < Help > < Print > < Cancel >

Figure 10-13. City names for Travel.

Cost/Profit/Distance Entry for Travel

From \ To:	LA	DEV	HOU	CMH	NY
LA	[M]	[100]	[150]	[300]	[500]
DEV	[100]	[M]	[160]	[300]	[M]
HOU	[150]	[160]	[M]	[260]	[290]
CMH	[300]	[300]	[260]	[M]	[200]
NY	[500]	[M]	[290]	[200]	[M]
DAL	[M]	[150]	[100]	[240]	[360]

< OK > < PgUp > < PgLt > < PgRt > < Help > < Print > < Cancel >

Figure 10-14. Distance entry for Travel.

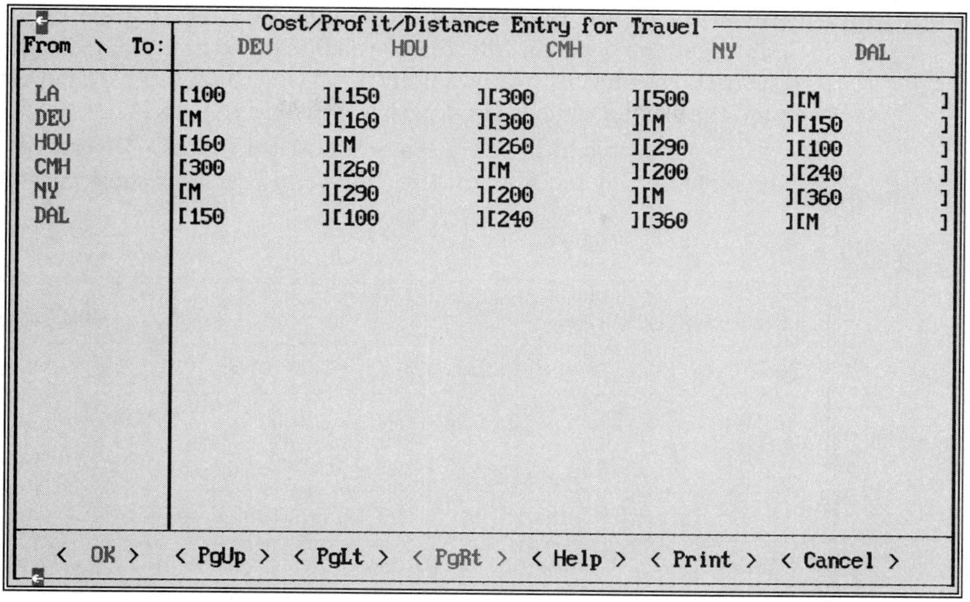

Figure 10-15. Distance entry for Travel (continued).

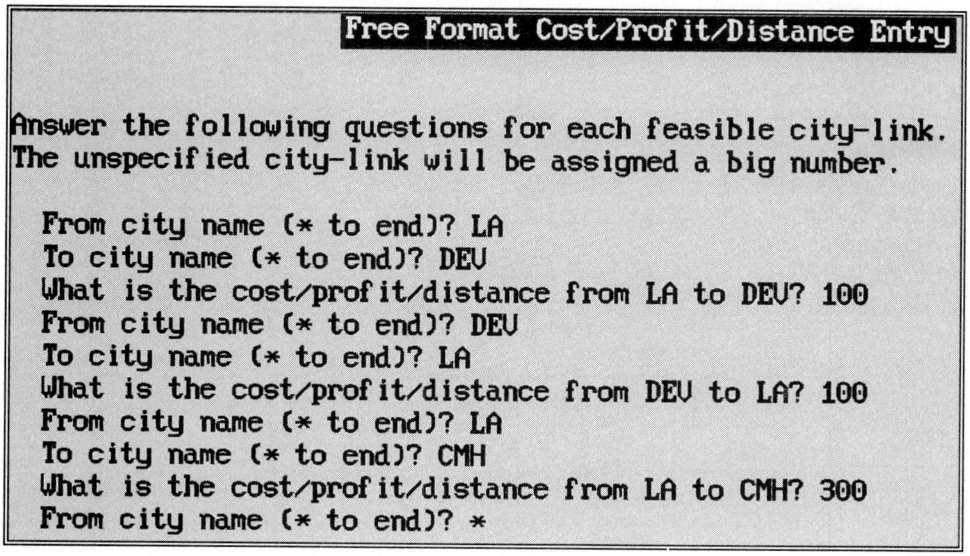

Figure 10-16. Sample free-format distance entry for Travel.

CMH-NY-CMH. They do not form a single route so that the solution is infeasible, and the program will create branches based on this infeasible solution by restricting some city linkages. Iteration 4 (Fig. 10-20) forms a feasible solution, and the unique route is LA-CMH-NY-HOU-DAL-DEV-LA.

3. After the problem is solved, select "Show the Solution" from the "Solution" menu to display the solution. Fig. 10-24 and Fig. 10-25 show the solution.

Branch-and-bound Iteration 1 for Travel

08-23-1993 12:23:29 Page: 1

From City	To City	Cost/Dist.	From City	To City	Cost/Dist.
LA	DEV	100	CMH	NY	200
DEV	LA	100	NY	CMH	200
HOU	DAL	100	DAL	HOU	100

Current Minimized OBJ = 800 (infeasible route) ZU = 1210

< PageDown > < PageUp > < Hardcopy > < Cancel > < Non-stop >

Figure 10-17. Iteration 1 for Travel.

Branch-and-bound Iteration 2 for Travel

08-23-1993 12:23:56 Page: 1

From City	To City	Cost/Dist.	From City	To City	Cost/Dist.
LA	DEV	100	CMH	NY	200
DEV	DAL	150	NY	CMH	200
HOU	LA	150	DAL	HOU	100

Current Minimized OBJ = 900 (infeasible route) ZU = 1210

< PageDown > < PageUp > < Hardcopy > < Cancel > < Non-stop >

Figure 10-18. Iteration 2 for Travel.

Branch-and-bound Iteration 3 for Travel

08-23-1993 12:24:22 Page: 1

From City	To City	Cost/Dist.	From City	To City	Cost/Dist.
LA	HOU	150	CMH	NY	200
DEV	LA	100	NY	CMH	200
HOU	DAL	100	DAL	DEV	150

Current Minimized OBJ = 900 (infeasible route) ZU = 1210

< PageDown > < PageUp > < Hardcopy > < Cancel > < Non-stop >

Figure 10-19. Iteration 3 for Travel.

Branch-and-bound Iteration 4 for Travel

08-23-1993 12:24:46 Page: 1

From City	To City	Cost/Dist.	From City	To City	Cost/Dist.
LA	CMH	300	CMH	NY	200
DEV	LA	100	NY	HOU	290
HOU	DAL	100	DAL	DEV	150

Current Minimized OBJ = 1140 (feasible route) ZU = 1210

< PageDown > < PageUp > < Hardcopy > < Cancel > < Non-stop >

Figure 10-20. Iteration 4 for Travel.

Branch-and-bound Iteration 5 for Travel

08-23-1993 12:25:08 Page: 1

From City	To City	Cost/Dist.	From City	To City	Cost/Dist.
LA	HOU	150	CMH	DAL	240
DEV	LA	100	NY	CMH	200
HOU	NY	290	DAL	DEV	150

Current Minimized OBJ = 1130 (feasible route) ZU = 1140

< PageDown > < PageUp > < Hardcopy > < Cancel > < Non-stop >

Figure 10-21. Iteration 5 for Travel.

Branch-and-bound Iteration 6 for Travel

08-23-1993 12:25:35 Page: 1

From City	To City	Cost/Dist.	From City	To City	Cost/Dist.
LA	DEV	100	CMH	NY	200
DEV	DAL	150	NY	HOU	290
HOU	LA	150	DAL	CMH	240

Current Minimized OBJ = 1130 (feasible route) ZU = 1130

< PageDown > < PageUp > < Hardcopy > < Cancel > < Non-stop >

Figure 10-22. Iteration 6 for Travel.

4. You may also choose "Solve by Heuristic Method" from the "Solution" menu to quick-solve the problem. It does not guarantee the optimal solution if you choose to solve by the heuristic method. However, the heuristic method solves quickly and, in general, results in a good solution.

Branch-and-bound Iteration 7 for Travel

08-23-1993 12:25:57 Page: 1

From City	To City	Cost/Dist.	From City	To City	Cost/Dist.
LA	DEV	100	CMH	LA	300
DEV	DAL	150	NY	CMH	200
HOU	NY	290	DAL	HOU	100

Current Minimized OBJ = 1140 (feasible route) ZU = 1130

< PageDown > < PageUp > < Hardcopy > < Cancel > < Non-stop >

Figure 10-23. Iteration 7 for Travel.

Traveling Salesman Solution for Travel

08-23-1993 12:26:28 Page: 1

From City	To City	Cost/Dist.	From City	To City	Cost/Dist.
LA	HOU	150	CMH	DAL	240
DEV	LA	100	NY	CMH	200
HOU	NY	290	DAL	DEV	150

Minimized OBJ = 1130 # Iterations = 7 CPU seconds = .0625

< PageDown > < PageUp > < Hardcopy > < Cancel >

Figure 10-24. Final solution for Travel.

Final Route for Travel

08-23-1993 12:26:54 Page: 1

LA ==> HOU ==> NY ==> CMH ==> DAL ==> DEV ==> LA

Minimized OBJ = 1130 # Iterations = 7 CPU seconds = .0625

< OK > < Hardcopy > < Cancel >

Figure 10-25. Final traveling route for Travel.

EXERCISES

1. The following assignment table shows the costs of finishing three jobs by three different persons. Assume each person is allowed to take one job. Use the ASTS program to solve this problem and show each step of the Hungarian method.

	Job		
Worker	1	2	3
A	10	12	25
B	19	20	22
C	15	26	17

2. Solve the following unbalanced assignment problem. M represents a huge penalty to make the assignment. All the numbers in the table represent costs.

	Object				
Task	A	B	C	D	E
1	11	19	M	19	20
2	38	M	15	14	10
3	23	17	21	M	M
4	31	37	28	35	46
5	27	43	23	18	M
6	15	21	33	17	28

3. Solve exercise 3 in Chapter 9 using the ASTS program.
4. On Monday morning, Super Garage has five cars coming in for service. Each of the five mechanics can service any of the cars. The number of hours required for each mechanic to repair each car is summarized here. What is the minimum total time assignment?

	Mechanic				
Car	Teddy	Bill	Simpson	Malon	Smith
Olds	6	5	4.5	5.5	6
Chev	4	3.5	5	4.5	3
Toyo	2	3.5	3.5	4	3
Maz	5	4.5	3.5	4	5
Cadi	4	6	5.5	4.5	6

5. A United Nations organization has five agricultural consultants to help underdeveloped countries increase their food supplies. Many African countries have famine problems because of bad weather. Each consultant can help different countries increase their food supplies to different levels. The expected food increases per capita from each consultant follow. Assume that each country has

about the same population. Recommend a consultant to country assignment that will maximize the food supply increase.

	Country				
Consultant	A	B	C	D	E
1	12	15	13	14	17
2	11	17	14	16	19
3	14	15	11	18	18
4	15	13	12	17	16
5	13	15	12	15	14

6. A neighbor of yours won a game and received seven different toys as prizes. He has five children and doesn't know how to allocate these toys. You suggest that he use a management science technique to solve his problem. After a short discussion, both of you agree that because of the children's different ages, they may have different satisfaction or utility levels for each toy. Also, the father thinks that his two youngest children could each have a second toy. You remind him that if a child receives two toys, the utility of the second toy will be only 60% of the original utility level. The satisfaction or utility level for each child for each toy is shown here. Assume children 1 and 2 are the youngest. Formulate an assignment problem and use the ASTS program to find a solution that maximizes total satisfaction.

	Child				
Toy	1	2	3	4	5
A	5	6	7	8	9
B	4	3	5	7	6
C	3	8	6	7	5
D	7	5	4	3	5
E	6	4	7	5	4
F	8	7	6	6	5
G	7	7	8	6	7

7. Solve the following traveling salesman problem to minimize the total travel distance.

From	To city					
city	1	2	3	4	5	6
1	-	35	18	60	15	35
2	35	-	28	50	39	26
3	18	28	-	25	45	54
4	60	50	25	-	12	31
5	15	39	45	12	-	29
6	35	26	54	31	29	-

8. Solve the following traveling salesman problem to minimize the total travel distance.

From city	To city							
	LA	Houston	SL	NY	Seattle	SF	DC	Boston
LA	-	1500	1800	3000	2000	500	2900	3500
Houston	1500	-	1200	1800	2500	2000	1500	2500
SL	1800	1200	-	1500	1500	1200	1500	2000
NY	3000	1800	1500	-	3000	3200	250	600
Seattle	2000	2500	1500	3000	-	1000	3000	3500
SF	500	2000	1200	3200	1000	-	3000	3500
DC	2900	1500	1500	250	3000	3000	-	900
Boston	3500	2500	2000	600	3500	3500	900	-

11

SPECIALIZED NETWORK MODELING (SNET)

OVERVIEW OF THE SNET DECISION SUPPORT SYSTEM

This program contains three specialized network algorithms: the shortest route (path), the maximal flow, and the minimal spanning tree problems. The shortest route finds the shortest distance from a start node to any other nodes on the network; the maximal flow determines the most quantity that flows from a source node to a sink node; and the minimal spanning tree solves the minimum total length of branches that link all the nodes.

When entering the problem, you may name each node with up to ten characters. The start or source node should be the number 1 node, and the end or sink node should be the last node. A spreadsheet matrix is provided for entering the distances or flow capacities from one node to the others. Options such as save, read, modify, and print are standard for the input data. You may choose to display detailed steps when solving the problem. After the solution has been obtained, you may display, print, or save it.

TECHNICAL NOTES ON THE SNET PROGRAM

1. A network is defined to contain a set of nodes and a set of arcs (branches or edges) that link the nodes. In SNET, the arcs are assumed to be not directed. Each arc in the shortest route and the minimal spanning tree problems has a distance measure, while each arc in the maximal flow problem has flow capacities on both directions.
2. When entering the distance for the shortest route and minimal spanning tree problems by the spreadsheet format, a blank, a huge value, or "M" can be used to represent an infeasible link. For the maximal flow problem, enter a blank or 0 to represent zero flow capacity.
3. For the shortest route problem, you need to identify a start node and an end node. The first node defined in the data entry process is assumed to be the start node, and the last node is assumed to be the end node.

4. In SNET, the shortest route problem is solved by a labeling procedure; the maximal flow problem is solved by the flow augmenting procedure; and the minimal spanning tree problem is solved by a greedy algorithm which directly connects the best choice at each step.

MENU STRUCTURE

The functions and options in each of the pull-down menus are hierarchically listed as follows:

- Modules
  - Linear Programming (LP)
  - Integer Linear Programming (ILP)
  - Goal Programming (GP)
  - Quadratic Programming (QP)
  - Nonlinear Programming (NLP)
  - Dynamic Programming (DP)
  - Transportation and Transshipment (TRP)
  - Assignment and Traveling Salesman (ASTS)
  - Specialized Network Modeling (SNET)
  - Capacitated Network Flow Modeling (CNET)
  - Project Scheduling: CPM/PERT
  - Inventory Theory (INVT)
  - Inventory Theory 2 (INVT2)
  - Queuing Theory (QUEUE)
  - Queuing System Simulation (QSIM)
  - Decision Analysis (DA)
  - Markov Process (MKV)
  - Time Series Forecasting (TSFC)
  - Financial Analysis (FA)
  - Exit from QSB
- Input Data
  - Data Entry
  - Read a File
  - Show Data
  - Print Data
  - Modify Data
    - Modify the problem configuration
    - Delete one node
  - Save
  - Save As
  - Exit from QSB
- Solution
  - Solve the Problem
  - Solve and Display Steps

Show the Solution
Print the Solution
Save the Solution

Options
Color
Monochrome
Printer Selection

Help - SNET
About SNET
About the User Interface
About the Edit Keys

SOLVING PROBLEMS WITH SNET

In the following sections, we will use example problems to show how to enter and solve the problems. The general procedure and menu options are described in detail in the tutorial sections of Chapter 2.

Example - The Shortest Route Problem

A network is shown in Fig. 11-1. The number on each branch represents the distance between the two nodes. What is the shortest route from node 1 to node 10?

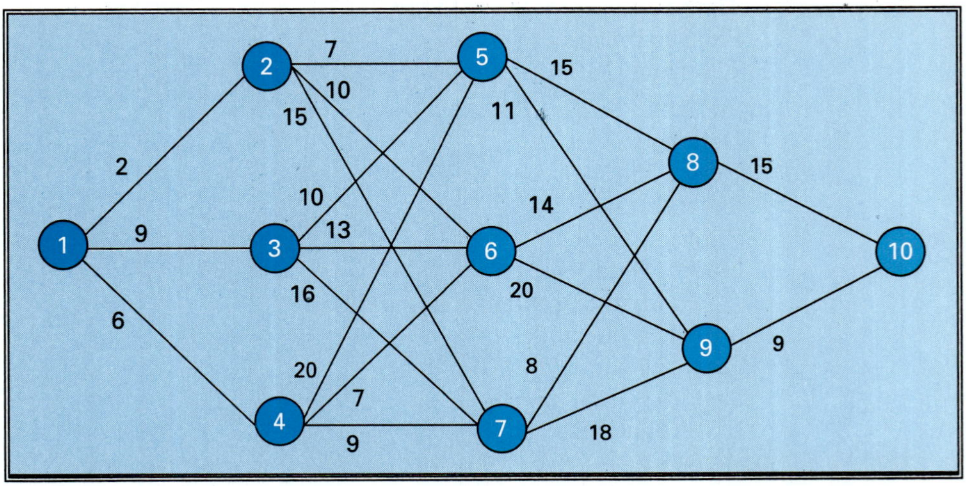

Figure 11-1. A network.

Enter the Problem

Select "Data Entry" from the "Input Data" menu (refer to Chapter 2 for selecting a menu item). Figs. 11-2 to 11-6 show the data entry of this problem. Note that "Shortest

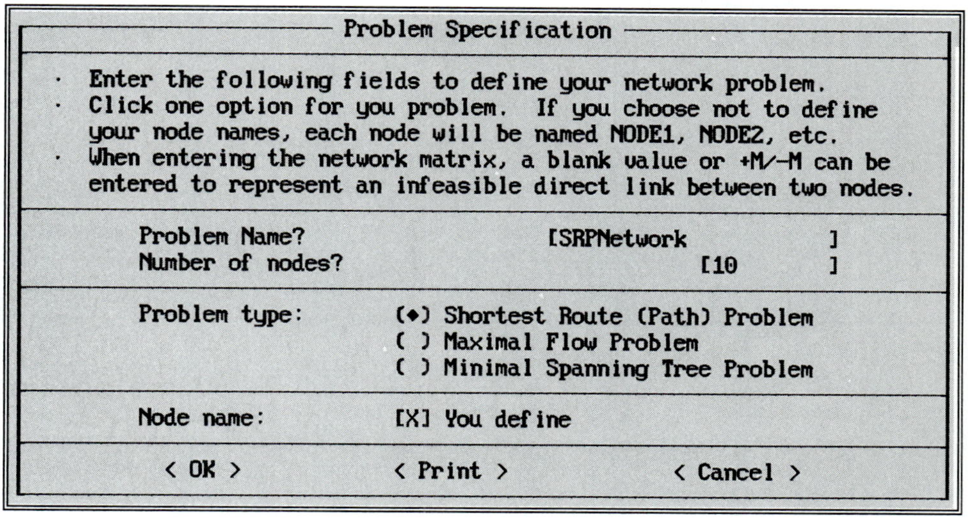

Figure 11-2. Problem specification for SRPNetwork.

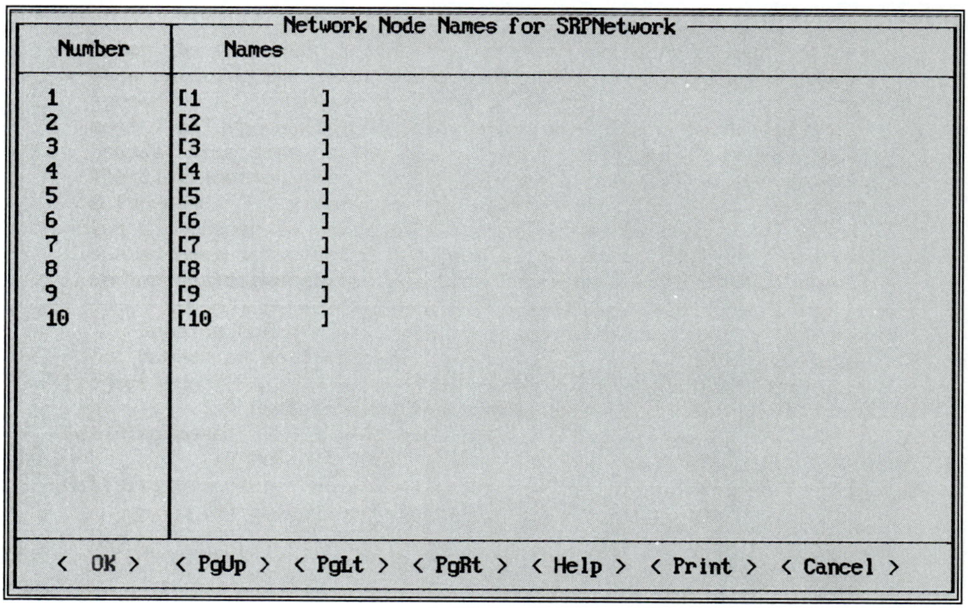

Figure 11-3. Node names for SRPNetwork.

Route" is selected for the problem type, and "You define" is specified for the node names. After the node names are entered, select either spreadsheet format or free format (Fig. 11-4) for distance entry. Fig. 11-5 and Fig. 11-6 show the spreadsheet entry. Note that Fig. 11-6 is the right page of Fig. 11-5 by pressing the "PgRt" button. If you choose to enter the distances by the free format in Fig. 11-4, Fig. 11-7 illustrates the free-format data entry (incomplete). Note that "*" is entered to end the sequence.

Figure 11-4. Select spreadsheet format for SRPNetwork.

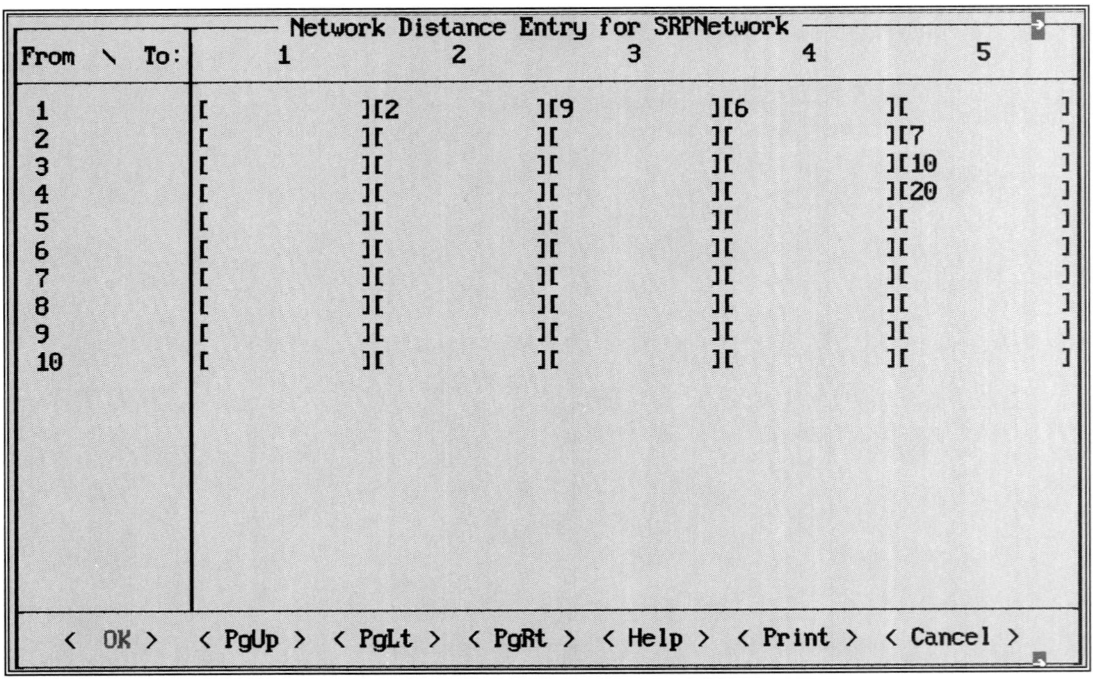

Figure 11-5. Distance entries for SRPNetwork.

```
              Network Distance Entry for SRPNetwork
From \ To:      6          7          8          9          10

 1          [         ][         ][         ][         ][         ]
 2          [10       ][15       ][         ][         ][         ]
 3          [13       ][16       ][         ][         ][         ]
 4          [7        ][9        ][         ][         ][         ]
 5          [         ][         ][15       ][11       ][         ]
 6          [         ][         ][14       ][20       ][         ]
 7          [         ][         ][8        ][18       ][         ]
 8          [         ][         ][         ][         ][15       ]
 9          [         ][         ][         ][         ][9        ]
 10         [         ][         ][         ][         ][         ]

  < OK >  < PgUp >  < PgLt >  < PgRt >  < Help >  < Print >  < Cancel >
```

Figure 11-6. Distance entries for SRPNetwork (continued).

```
                    Free Format Distance Entry

Answer the following questions for each feasible direct link.

  From node name (* to end)? 1
  To node name (* to end)? 2
  What is the distance from 1 to 2? 2
  From node name (* to end)? 1
  To node name (* to end)? 3
  What is the distance from 1 to 3? 9
  From node name (* to end)? *
```

Figure 11-7. Sample free-format entry for SRPNetwork .

Solve the Problem

1. Select "Solve the Problem" from the "Solution" menu to solve the problem. The message "Please standby . . ." will display for a short period while the problem is being solved.

2. You may also choose "Solve and Display Steps" from the "Solution" menu to display the labeling process. Fig. 11-8 shows the iterations. Note that you need to press any key for the next iteration or press the "G" key to skip the later iterations.

```
                 Labeling Steps for the Shortest Route Problem

Step 1 : Permanently label node 1
    Update the following nodes and labels (i.e., distance and predecessor):
        Node 2: ( 2 ; 1 )
        Node 3: ( 9 ; 1 )
        Node 4: ( 6 ; 1 )

Step 2 : Permanently label node 2
    Update the following nodes and labels (i.e., distance and predecessor):
        Node 5: ( 9 ; 2 )
        Node 6: ( 12 ; 2 )
        Node 7: ( 17 ; 2 )

Step 3 : Permanently label node 4
    Update the following nodes and labels (i.e., distance and predecessor):
        Node 7: ( 15 ; 4 )

Step 4 : Permanently label node 3
    Update the following nodes and labels (i.e., distance and predecessor):
         None

Step 5 : Permanently label node 5
    Update the following nodes and labels (i.e., distance and predecessor):
        Node 8: ( 24 ; 5 )
        Node 9: ( 20 ; 5 )

Step 6 : Permanently label node 6
    Update the following nodes and labels (i.e., distance and predecessor):
         None

Step 7 : Permanently label node 7
    Update the following nodes and labels (i.e., distance and predecessor):
        Node 8: ( 23 ; 7 )

Step 8 : Permanently label node 9
    Update the following nodes and labels (i.e., distance and predecessor):
        Node 10: ( 29 ; 9 )

Step 9 : Permanently label node 8
    Update the following nodes and labels (i.e., distance and predecessor):
         None

Step 10 : Permanently label node 10
    Update the following nodes and labels (i.e., distance and predecessor):
         None
```

Figure 11-8. Solution steps for SRPNetwork.

3. After the problem is solved, select "Show the Solution" from the "Solution" menu to display the solution. Fig. 11-9 shows the solution. It shows, for example, the shortest distance from node 1 to node 10 is 29, and, by using the predecessor information, the shortest route is 1-2-5-9-10.

Example - A Minimal Spanning Tree

Suppose you want to find a tree that links all the nodes in Fig. 11-1 and minimizes the total distance of the tree. The procedure for entering the data for this problem is the same as for the shortest route problem except for choosing "minimal spanning tree" for the problem type in Fig. 11-2. Assume the problem name "MSTNetwork" is entered. Fig. 11-10 shows the connecting steps if "Solve and Display Steps" is selected, and Fig. 11-11 shows the connection of the minimal spanning tree.

Shortest Distance From 1 for SRPNetwork

08-23-1993 12:39:27 Page: 1 of 1

Node	Predecessor	Distance	Node	Predecessor	Distance
2	1	2	7	4	15
3	1	9	8	7	23
4	1	6	9	5	20
5	2	9	10	9	29
6	2	12			

Overall shortest distance = 29 Elapsed CPU seconds = 0

< PageDown > < PageUp > < Hardcopy > < Cancel >

Figure 11-9. Solution summary for SRPNetwork.

Example — The Maximal Flow Problem

A communication network (Fig. 11-12) transfers information among different locations. The numbers on each branch represent the information inflow and outflow capacities for that branch. For example, the flow capacity from node 1 to node 2 is 10, and from node 2 to node 1 is 6. What is the possible maximum information flow from node 1 to node 7?

Enter the Problem

Select "Data Entry" from the "Input Data" menu. Figs. 11-13 to 11-16 show the data entry of this problem. Note that "Maximal Flow" is selected for the problem type, and "You define" is specified for the node names. After the node names are entered

```
                    Steps for the Minimal Spanning Tree Problem


Step 1 : Connect node 1
    The unconnected node closest to the connected nodes is: 2
    The shortest distance is from 1 to 2 with distance = 2

Step 2 : Connect node 2
    The unconnected node closest to the connected nodes is: 4
    The shortest distance is from 1 to 4 with distance = 6

Step 3 : Connect node 4
    The unconnected node closest to the connected nodes is: 5
    The shortest distance is from 2 to 5 with distance = 7

Step 4 : Connect node 5
    The unconnected node closest to the connected nodes is: 6
    The shortest distance is from 4 to 6 with distance = 7

Step 5 : Connect node 6
    The unconnected node closest to the connected nodes is: 3
    The shortest distance is from 1 to 3 with distance = 9
```

```
Step 6 : Connect node 3
    The unconnected node closest to the connected nodes is: 7
    The shortest distance is from 4 to 7 with distance = 9

Step 7 : Connect node 7
    The unconnected node closest to the connected nodes is: 8
    The shortest distance is from 7 to 8 with distance = 8

Step 8 : Connect node 8
    The unconnected node closest to the connected nodes is: 9
    The shortest distance is from 5 to 9 with distance = 11

Step 9 : Connect node 9
    The unconnected node closest to the connected nodes is: 10
    The shortest distance is from 9 to 10 with distance = 9

Step 10 : Connect node 10
    The unconnected node closest to the connected nodes is:  None
```

Figure 11-10. Solution steps for MSTNetwork.

Minimal Spanning Tree for MSTNetwork

08-23-1993 14:41:00 Page: 1 of 1

From Node	To Node	Distance	From Node	To Node	Distance
1	2	2	4	7	9
1	3	9	7	8	8
1	4	6	5	9	11
2	5	7	9	10	9
4	6	7			

Total connected distance = 68 Elapsed CPU seconds = 0.050781

< PageDown > < PageUp > < Hardcopy > < Cancel >

Figure 11-11. Final solution for MSTNetwork.

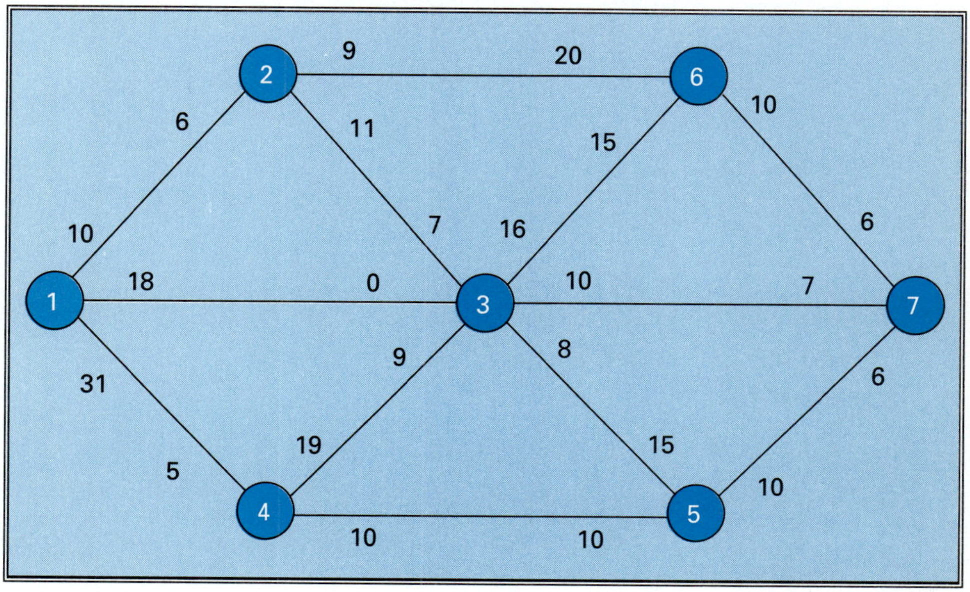

Figure 11-12. A communication network.

(Fig. 11-14), select either spreadsheet format or free-format (Fig. 11-4) for flow capacity entry. Fig. 11-14 and Fig. 11-15 show the spreadsheet entry. Note that Fig. 11-15 is the right page of Fig. 11-14 by pressing the "PgRt" button. If you choose to enter the distances by the free-format (Fig. 11-4), Fig. 11-17 illustrates the free-format data entry (incomplete). Note that "*" is entered to end the sequence.

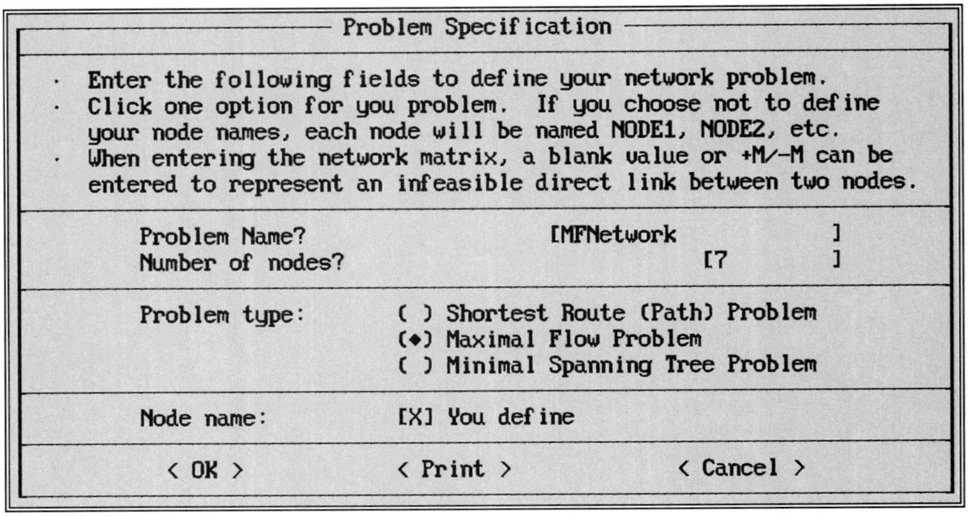

Figure 11-13. Specification of the maximal flow problem.

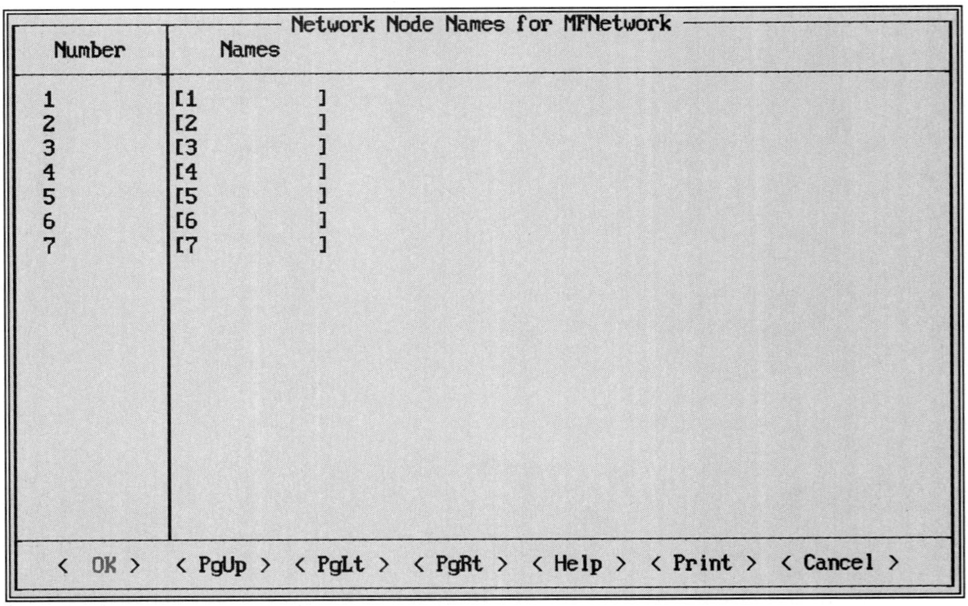

Figure 11-14. Node names for MFNetwork.

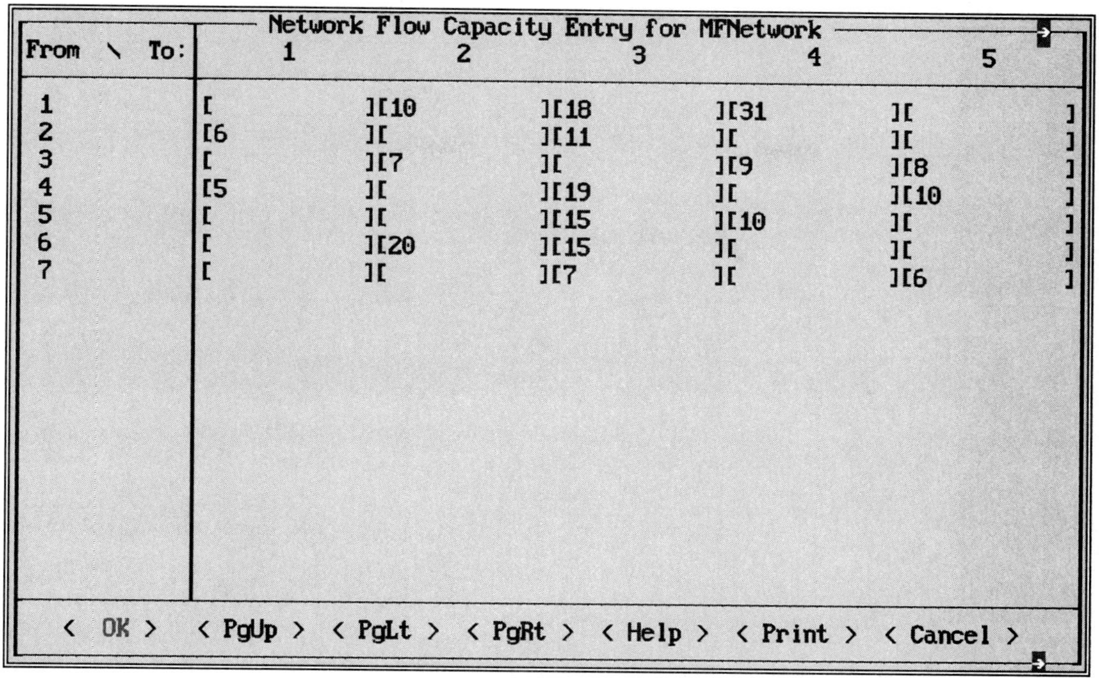

Figure 11-15. Flow capacities for MFNetwork.

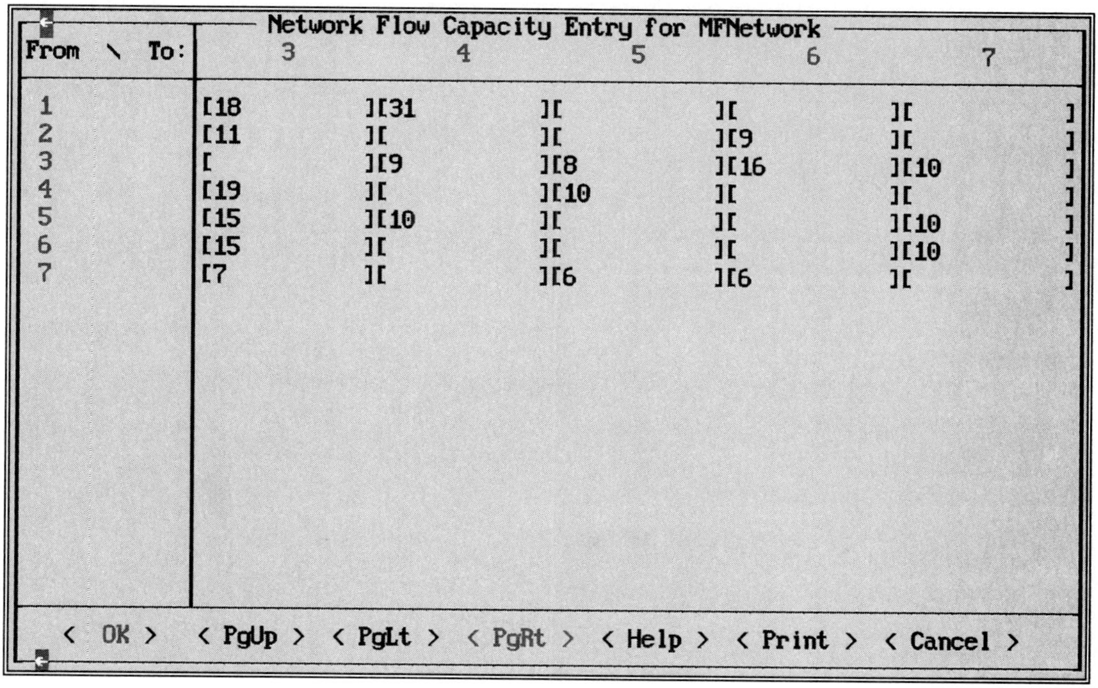

Figure 11-16. Flow capacities for MFNetwork (continued).

```
                    Free Format Flow Capacity Entry

Answer the following questions for each feasible direct link.

  From node name (* to end)? 1
  To node name (* to end)? 2
  What is the flow capacity from 1 to 2? 10
  From node name (* to end)? 2
  To node name (* to end)? 1
  What is the flow capacity from 2 to 1? 6
  From node name (* to end)? *
```

Figure 11-17. Sample free-format entry for MFNetwork.

Solve the Problem

1. Select "Solve the Problem" from the "Solution" menu to solve the problem. The message "Please standby . . ." will display for a short period while the problem is being solved.
2. You may also choose "Solve and Display Steps" from the "Solution" menu to display the flow augmenting process. Fig. 11-18 shows the iterations. Each it-

```
                    Steps for the Maximal Flow Problem


Step 1 : Flow = 9 , determined by branch from 3 to 4
    The path selected is: 1 - 2 - 3 - 4 - 5 - 7

Step 2 : Flow = 1 , determined by branch from 1 to 2
    The path selected is: 1 - 2 - 3 - 5 - 7

Step 3 : Flow = 9 , determined by branch from 2 to 6
    The path selected is: 1 - 3 - 2 - 6 - 7

Step 4 : Flow = 1 , determined by branch from 6 to 7
    The path selected is: 1 - 3 - 6 - 7

Step 5 : Flow = 8 , determined by branch from 1 to 3
    The path selected is: 1 - 3 - 7

Step 6 : Flow = 2 , determined by branch from 3 to 7
    The path selected is: 1 - 4 - 3 - 7
```

Figure 11-18. Solution steps for MFNetwork.

Maximal Flow From Source to Sink for MFNetwork

08-23-1993 14:52:36 Page: 1 of 1

From Node	To Node	Net Flow	From Node	To Node	Net Flow
1	2	10	3	5	1
1	3	18	3	6	1
1	4	2	3	7	10
2	3	1	4	5	9
2	6	9	5	7	10
3	4	7	6	7	10

Total maximal flow = 30 Elapsed CPU seconds = 0

< PageDown > < PageUp > < Hardcopy > < Cancel >

Figure 11-19. Final solution for MFNetwork.

eration augments net flow from node 1 to 7. Note that you need to press any key for the next iteration or press the "G" key to skip the later iterations.

3. After the problem is solved, select "Show the Solution" from the "Solution" menu to display the solution. Fig. 11-19 shows the solution.

EXERCISES

1. Find the shortest route from node 1 to 11 for the network shown in Fig. 11-20.
2. Consider the network in Fig. 11-20. Find the minimal spanning tree.
3. Find the shortest route from node 1 to every other node for the network shown in Fig. 11-21.

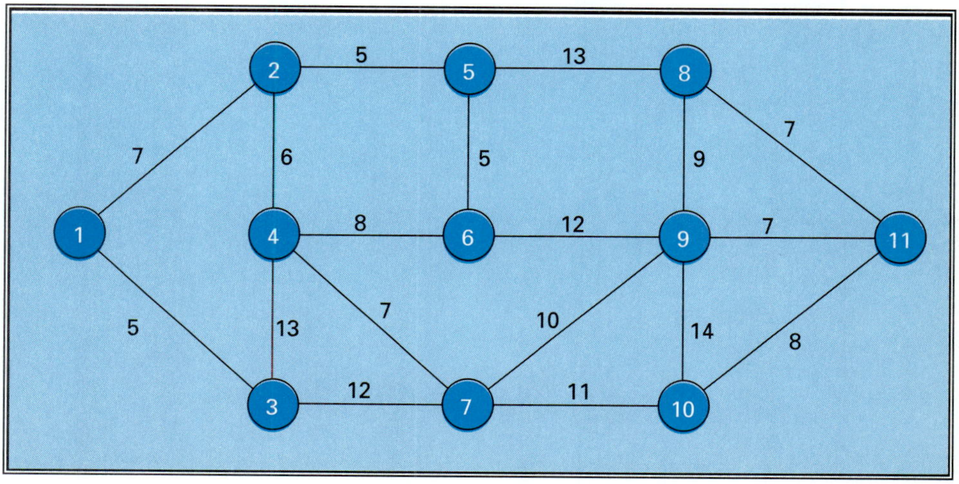

Figure 11-20. Network for exercises 1 and 2.

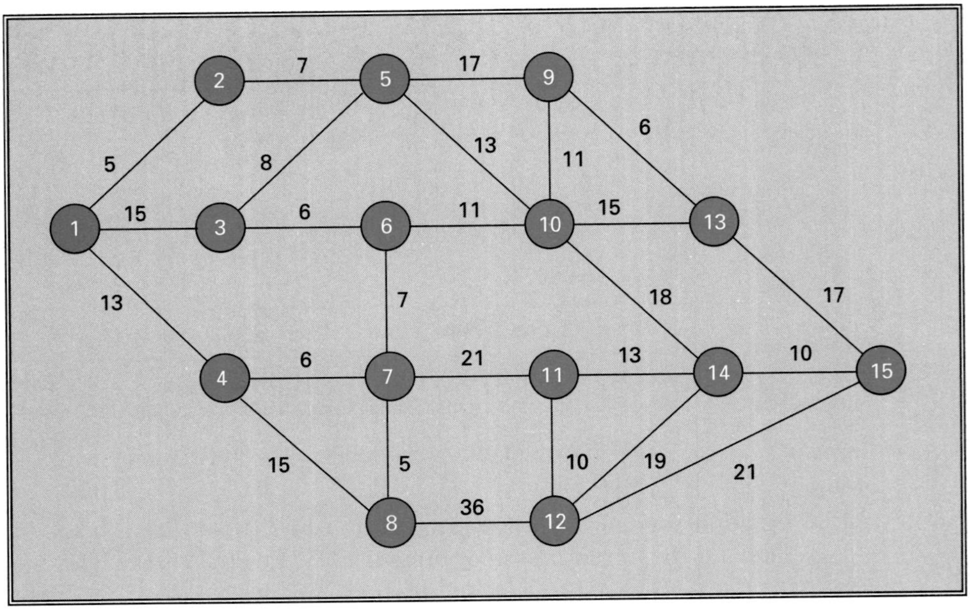

Figure 11-21. Network for exercises 3 and 4.

4. Consider the network in Fig. 11-21. Construct a minimal spanning tree.
5. The flow capacities between nodes are shown on the network in Fig. 11-22. The numbers on each arc represent flow capacities. For example, 15 is the flow capacity from node 1 to 2, and 16 is the flow capacity from node 2 to 1. Use the SNET program to find the maximal flow from node 1 to node 11.

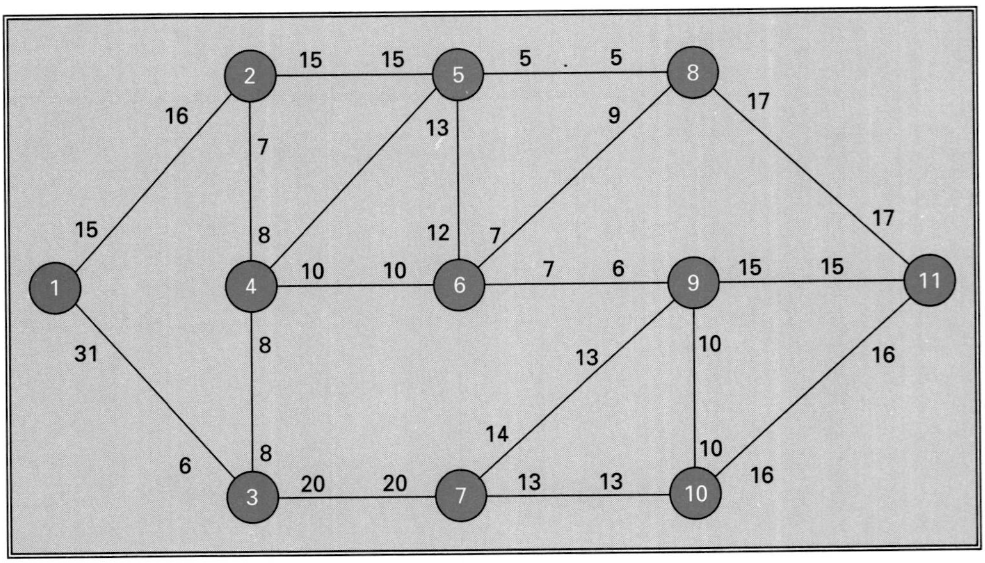

Figure 11-22. Network for exercise 5.

6. A new neighborhood is being built. The distances (in yards) between each house follow. A local telephone company is trying to build a communications network for this neighborhood. How should the company connect the cable to minimize the total length?

	To house						
From house	1	2	3	4	5	6	7
1	—	1500	1400	3500	3200	2500	3700
2	1500	—	4500	1700	2200	2300	2900
3	1400	4500	—	3100	2800	1900	1500
4	3500	1700	3100	—	1900	2500	1300
5	3200	2200	2800	1900	—	3500	1600
6	2500	2300	1900	2500	3500	—	5600
7	3700	2900	1500	1300	1600	5600	—

12

CAPACITATED NETWORK FLOW MODELING (CNET)

OVERVIEW OF THE CNET DECISION SUPPORT SYSTEM

This program solves capacitated network flow problems. A specialized network simplex is used to solve the problems. The size of the problems solvable by CNET depends on your computer's memory and the number of nodes and arcs/edges/linkages of your network. The transportation and transshipment, assignment, shortest route/path, maximal flow, and minimal spanning tree problems are special cases of the capacitated network flow problems. They can also be solved by this program. However, special algorithms have been developed in other modules (TRP, ASTS, SNET) to solve them more efficiently.

When entering the problem, you may name each node with up to ten characters, specify their net demands or supplies, and set flow capacities, that is, lower and upper bounds, between nodes. Use the spreadsheet matrix to enter the possible connections among nodes and then enter the information associated with each connection (arc or branch). Options such as to save, read, modify, and print are standard for the input data. You may display, print, or save the solution as it has been obtained.

TECHNICAL NOTES ON THE CNET PROGRAM

1. A network is defined as containing a set of nodes and a set of arcs (branches or edges) that link the nodes. In CNET, the arcs are assumed to be directed and all nodes are connected. Each arc is associated with a flow capacity, that is, lower and upper bounds, and cost or profit. Each node has either a net supply or a net demand.
2. The goal of a CNET problem is to find network flows which are within the capacities of each connection (arc) and optimize the specified objective function. The capacitated network flow problems are also called the minimum cost flow network problems. However, CNET allows you to maximize or minimize the objective function.

3. The network simplex method with upper-bound technique is used to solve the CNET problems. The general formulation of the CNET problem is described as follows.

   Let X_{ij}: Flow from node *i* to *j*.
   C_{ij}: Unit cost or profit associated with flow from node *i* to *j*.
   U_{ij}: Maximum flow allowed from node *i* to *j* (upper bound).
   L_{ij}: Minimum flow required from node *i* to *j* (lower bound).
   b_i: Supply or demand of node *i*, where $i = 1$ to *n*. $b_i > 0$ if node *i* has a net supply and $b_i < 0$ if node *i* has a net demand.
   n: The number of nodes in the network.

   The linear programming model is

   Maximize/minimize: $\Sigma_{i,j}\, C_{ij}\, X_{ij}$
   Subject to:
   $\Sigma_j X_{ij} - \Sigma_j X_{ji} = b_i$ for all $j = 1$ to *n*, $i = 1$ to *n*.
   and $L_{ij} \leq X_{ij} \leq U_{ij}$ for the arc from node *i* to node *j*, where $i = 1$ to *n* and $j = 1$ to *n*.

4. When the total net supply is not equal to the total net demand, CNET will automatically generate a dummy node with excess supply or demand to make the above equality constraints valid. However, if the flow capacities (bounds) make it impossible either to consume all supplies or to satisfy all demands, the problem is designated as infeasible.
5. The default flow bounds of each connection (arc) is from 0 to infinity, which is "M" in CNET.

MENU STRUCTURE

The functions and options in each of the pull-down menus are hierarchically listed as follows:

Modules
- Linear Programming (LP)
- Integer Linear Programming (ILP)
- Goal Programming (GP)
- Quadratic Programming (QP)
- Nonlinear Programming (NLP)
- Dynamic Programming (DP)
- Transportation and Transshipment (TRP)
- Assignment and Traveling Salesman (ASTS)
- Specialized Network Modeling (SNET)
- Capacitated Network Flow Modeling (CNET)
- Project Scheduling: CPM/PERT
- Inventory Theory (INVT)
- Inventory Theory 2 (INVT2)

- Queuing Theory (QUEUE)
- Queuing System Simulation (QSIM)
- Decision Analysis (DA)
- Markov Process (MKV)
- Time Series Forecasting (TSFC)
- Financial Analysis (FA)
- Exit from QSB

Input Data
- Data Entry
- Read a File
- Show Data
- Print Data
- Modify Data
  - Modify the problem
  - Delete one node
- Save
- Save As
- Exit from QSB

Solution
- Solve the Problem
- Show the Solution
- Print the Solution
- Save the Solution

Options
- Color
- Monochrome
- Printer Selection

Help - CNET
- About CNET
- About the User Interface
- About the Edit Keys

SOLVING PROBLEMS WITH CNET

In the following sections, we will use an example problem to show how to enter and solve the problem. The general procedure and menu options are described in detail in the tutorial sections of Chapter 2.

Example

A network is shown in Fig. 12-1, where the number next to a node represents a net supply or demand, the number on each branch represents the unit flow cost, and the number in the brackets represents the maximum flow capacity. For example, 100 on top of node A shows net supply 100, -200 below the node H shows the net demand

200; 6 on arc A to D represents the unit flow cost and [50] below the arc represents the maximum flow from A to D. What is the minimum cost flow?

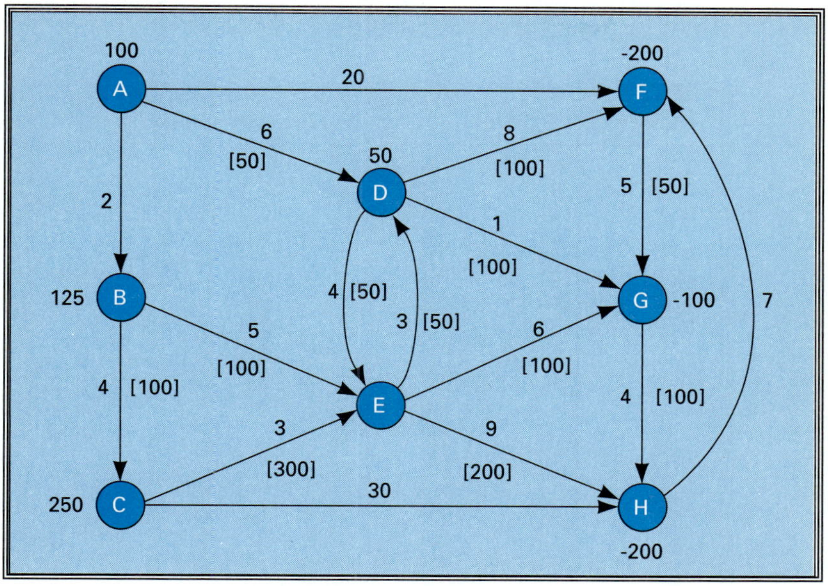

Figure 12-1. A network.

Enter the Problem

Select "Data Entry" from the "Input Data" menu (refer to Chapter 2 for selecting a menu item). Figs. 12-2 to 12-6 show the data entry of this problem. Note that "Minimization" is selected for the objective criterion, and "You define" is specified for the node names. Fig. 12-3 shows the entry of the node names, net supplies, and/or net demands. For example, 200 is entered as the net demand of the node F. Fig.

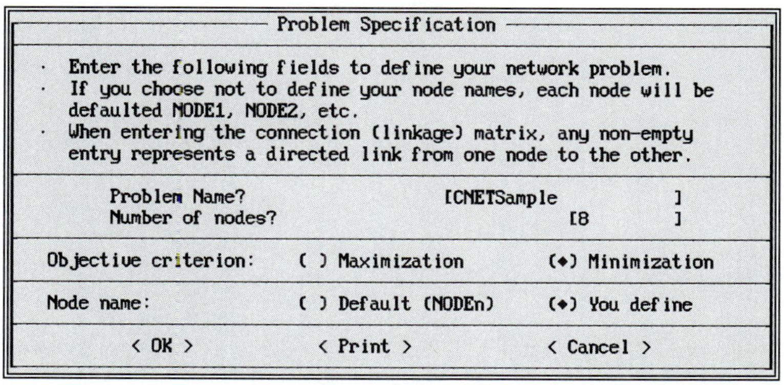
Problem Specification

· Enter the following fields to define your network problem.
· If you choose not to define your node names, each node will be defaulted NODE1, NODE2, etc.
· When entering the connection (linkage) matrix, any non-empty entry represents a directed link from one node to the other.

Problem Name? [CNETSample]
Number of nodes? [8]

Objective criterion: ( ) Maximization (•) Minimization

Node name: ( ) Default (NODEn) (•) You define

< OK > < Print > < Cancel >

Figure 12-2. Problem specification for CNETSample.

12-4 and Fig. 12-5 show the spreadsheet connection matrix. Note that Fig. 12-5 is the right page of Fig. 12-4 by pressing the "PgRt" button. Any non-empty entry will specify a connection from one node to the other. Fig. 12-6 shows the data associated with each connection, including unit costs and flow capacity bounds. M is infinity.

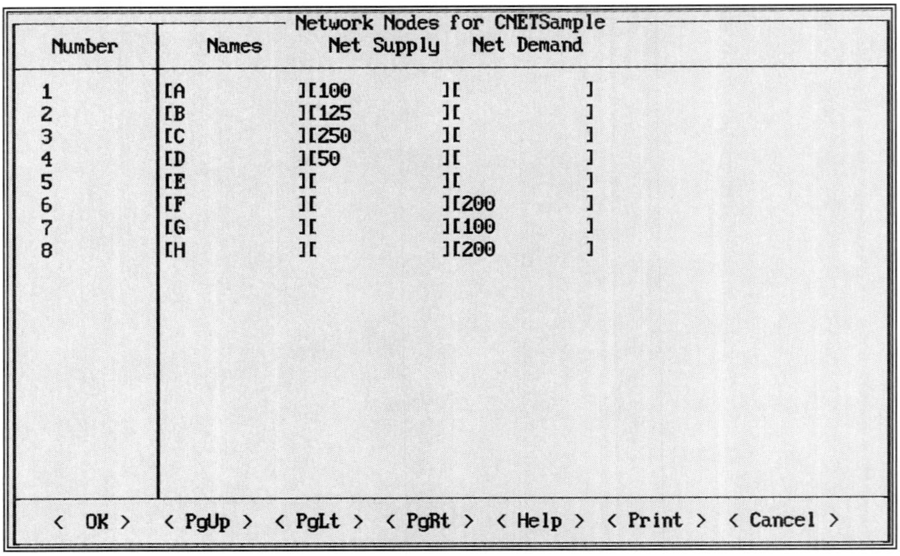

Figure 12-3. Node names and supplies/demands for CNETSample.

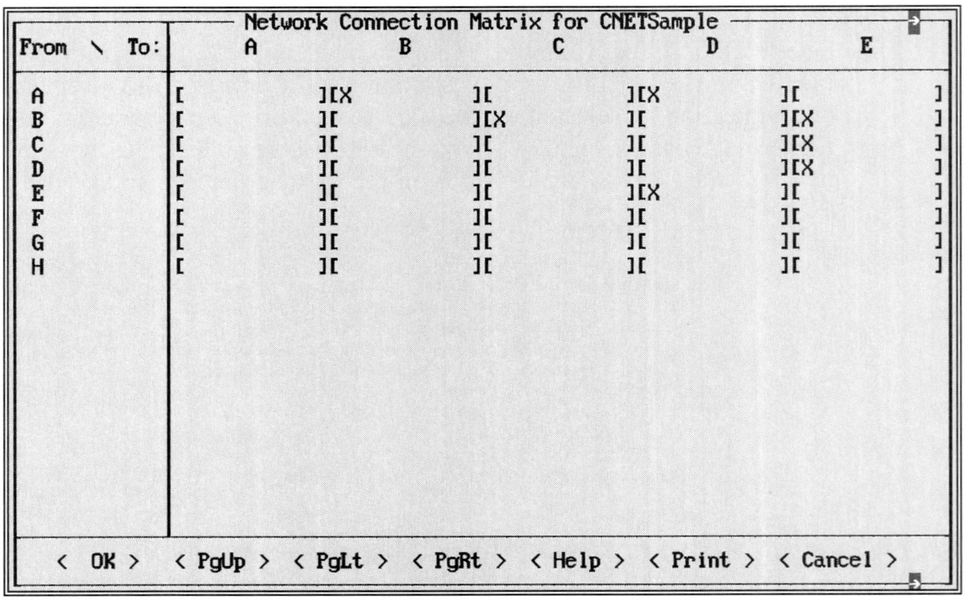

Figure 12-4. Node connections for CNETSample.

Network Connection Matrix for CNETSample

From \ To:	D	E	F	G	H
A	X		X		
B		X			
C		X			X
D		X	X	X	
E	X			X	X
F				X	
G					X
H			X		

< OK > < PgUp > < PgLt > < PgRt > < Help > < Print > < Cancel >

Figure 12-5. Node connections for CNETSample (continued).

Flow Costs and Capacities for CNETSample

Number	From	To	Cost/Profit	Min. Flow	Max. Flow
1	A	B	12		M
2	A	D	6		50
3	A	F	20		M
4	B	C	4		100
5	B	E	5		100
6	C	E	3		300
7	C	H	30		M
8	D	E	4		50
9	D	F	8		100
10	D	G	1		100
11	E	D	3		50
12	E	G	6		100
13	E	H	9		200
14	F	G	5		50
15	G	H	4		100
16	H	F	7		M

< OK > < PgUp > < PgLt > < PgRt > < Help > < Print > < Cancel >

Figure 12-6. Arc/branch information for CNETSample.

Solve the Problem

1. Select "Solve the Problem" from the "Solution" menu to solve the problem. The message "Please standby . . ." will display for a short period while the problem is being solved.
2. After the problem is solved, select "Show the Solution" from the "Solution" menu to display the solution. Fig. 12-7 and Fig. 12-8 show the solution. Note that there is an excess supply 25 units left at node B.

Network Flow for CNETSample

08-23-1993 15:16:05 Page: 1 of 2

From Node	To Node	Net Flow	Unit Cost	Min. Flow	Max. Flow
A	B	0	12	0	M
A	D	50	6	0	50
A	F	50	20	0	M
B	C	0	4	0	100
B	E	100	5	0	100
C	E	250	3	0	300
C	H	0	30	0	M
D	E	0	4	0	50
D	F	100	8	0	100
D	G	50	1	0	100
E	D	50	3	0	50
E	G	100	6	0	100

Objective Value = 6500 Elapsed CPU seconds = .046875
Unused Supply = 25

< PageDown > < PageUp > < Hardcopy > < Cancel >

Figure 12-7. Solution summary for CNETSample.

Network Flow for CNETSample

08-23-1993 15:16:33 Page: 2 of 2

From Node	To Node	Net Flow	Unit Cost	Min. Flow	Max. Flow
E	H	200	9	0	200
F	G	0	5	0	50
G	H	50	4	0	100
H	F	50	7	0	M

Objective Value = 6500 Elapsed CPU seconds = .046875
Unused Supply = 25

< PageDown > < PageUp > < Hardcopy > < Cancel >

Figure 12-8. Solution summary for CNETSample (continued).

EXERCISES

Note: In the following problems, the numbers next to the nodes are net supplies (positive) or demands (negative); the numbers associated with each arc are unit flow costs or profits; and the numbers in the brackets are upper bounds of the flows.

1. Fig. 12-9 shows a network flow problem.
   a. Solve the network flow to minimize the total flow cost.

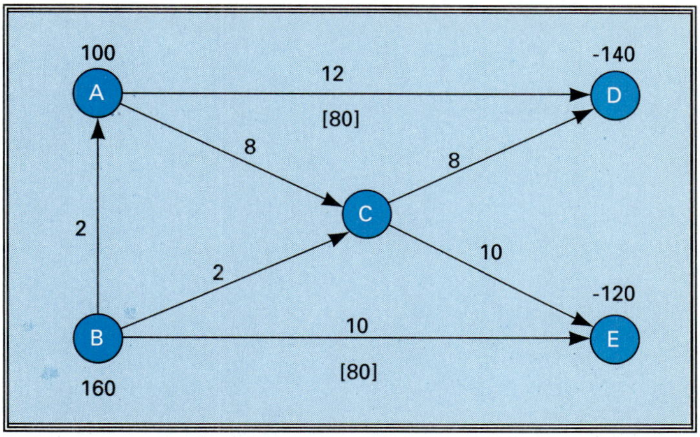

Figure 12-9. Network for exercise 1.

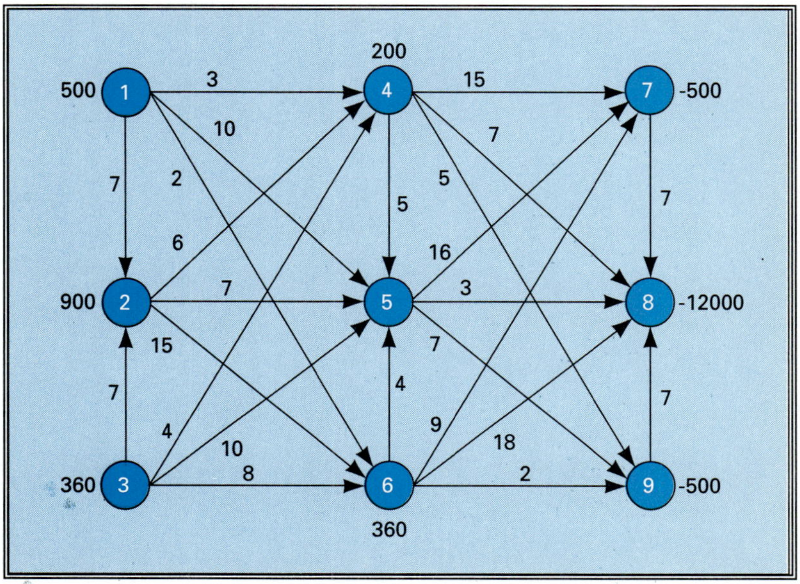

Figure 12-10. Network for exercise 2.

b. If the flow from node B to node C is limited to 60, what is the optimal solution?

c. If both the flows from node B to node C and node A to node C are limited to 40, is the network still feasible?

2. Fig. 12-10 shows a network flow problem. Find the optimal solution to minimize the total cost. Assume that the flow capacity at each branch is 300 units at most.

13

PROJECT SCHEDULING: CPM/PERT (CPM)

OVERVIEW OF THE CPM DECISION SUPPORT SYSTEM

This program solves project scheduling with certain (deterministic) or uncertain activity durations. For the project with certain or deterministic times and costs, the program will analyze the critical path and perform the crashing (expediting) analysis if the crashing times and costs are also entered. The marginal costs to expedite each activity are assumed to be linear. The crashing analysis is solved by the linear programming method. This method for analyzing projects with deterministic durations and costs is usually called Critical Path Method (CPM).

For the project with uncertain durations, you may enter the three time estimates or specify a distribution for each activity. The program will solve the critical path and perform the probability analysis. The activities are assumed to be independent and the number of activities on the critical path is large enough so that the project completion time is assumed to follow the normal distribution. This method for analyzing projects with uncertain durations is usually called Program Evaluation and Review Technique (PERT).

Activity names and durations are entered by spreadsheet format. You may name up to ten characters for each activity. The precedence relations among activities can be entered by either spreadsheet or free format. You can save, read, modify, and print the input data. After the solution has been obtained, you may display, print, or save it.

TECHNICAL NOTES ON THE CPM PROGRAM

1. You may draw the project network in AOA (activity-on-arc) or AON (activity-on-node) format. However, you do not need to draw the network in order to enter the project into the program, as long as the activity precedence relation is known.
2. CPM allows the project to have multiple starting points or multiple ending points. Therefore, you don't need to create a node for a dummy start or

a node for a dummy end such as in the conventional project network drawing.

3. In the case of multiple starting points, each starting point is assumed to have the same earliest start. In the case of multiple ending points, each ending point is assumed to have the same latest finish.
4. For the certain duration project (CPM), crash times and costs are required if you want to perform "crashing" analysis. Crash times usually represent how fast activities can be expedited. By doing crashing analysis, the program will try to find the least-cost way to reduce the activity durations in order to finish the project in a specified time.
5. When performing the crashing analysis, CPM will automatically form a linear programming model for each crashing situation and use the revised simplex method to find the optimal crashing strategy.
6. For the uncertain duration project (PERT), you may choose from five possible distributions for the activity durations. The distributions and their parameters are listed in Table 13-1. When you specify a distribution for an activity, enter at least the first three letters of the distribution. The default is the beta distribution with the three time estimates: optimistic, most likely, and pessimistic times.

Table 13-1. Possible probability distribution for activity duration.

Distribution	Parameter 1	Parameter 2	Parameter 3
Beta	Optimistic time	Most likely time	Pessimistic time
Exponential	Mean		
Normal	Mean	Variance	
Uniform	Lower limit	Upper limit	
Arbitrary	Mean	Variance	

7. The probability analysis assumes that activities are independent and all paths are also independent. It also assumes that your network has a large enough number of activities to assume the normality of the critical path. Therefore, when the activities are not independent or the number of activities is not large, the probability analysis may be highly biased.

MENU STRUCTURE

The functions and options in each of the pull-down menus are hierarchically listed as follows:

Modules
  Linear Programming (LP)
  Integer Linear Programming (ILP)
  Goal Programming (GP)
  Quadratic Programming (QP)

- Nonlinear Programming (NLP)
- Dynamic Programming (DP)
- Transportation and Transshipment (TRP)
- Assignment and Traveling Salesman (ASTS)
- Specialized Network Modeling (SNET)
- Capacitated Network Flow Modeling (CNET)
- Project Scheduling: CPM/PERT
- Inventory Theory (INVT)
- Inventory Theory 2 (INVT2)
- Queuing Theory (QUEUE)
- Queuing System Simulation (QSIM)
- Decision Analysis (DA)
- Markov Process (MKV)
- Time Series Forecasting (TSFC)
- Financial Analysis (FA)
- Exit from QSB

Input Data
- Data Entry
- Read a File
- Show Data
- Print Data
- Modify Data
  - Modify the problem configuration
  - Delete one activity
- Save
- Save As
- Exit from QSB

Solution
- CPM:
  - Solve with Normal Times
  - Solve with Crash Times
  - Crashing Analysis
- PERT:
  - Solve with Expected Times
  - Probability Analysis
- Show the Solution
- Print the Solution
- Save the Solution

Options
- Color
- Monochrome
- Printer Selection

Help - CPM
- About CPM
- About the User Interface
- About the Edit Keys

SOLVING PROBLEMS WITH CPM

In the following sections, we will use example problems to show how to enter and solve the problems. The general procedure and menu options are described in detail in the tutorial sections of Chapter 2.

Example - CPM

To demonstrate the use of CPM with certain duration activities, consider the following sample project. A construction project has 12 activities. Table 13-2 shows the completion times in days and the costs of activities. The predecessors of each activity are also shown in the table, as well as the crash times and crash costs of activities. What are the normal completion time and total cost for the entire project? What is the critical path? If management wants to speed up the project by two days, how can this be done? How about speeding up by five days?

Table 13-2. Times and costs for the construction project.

Activity		Normal	Crash	Normal	Crash	Immediate
No.	Name	time	time	cost	cost	predecessor
1	A	5	3	$2000	$2500	—
2	B	4	4	3000	3000	—
3	C	8	7	4000	5000	—
4	D	3	2	1200	1500	A
5	E	7	5	2000	3000	A
6	F	5	5	3000	3000	C
7	G	4	3	3000	3700	C
8	H	3	3	8000	8000	B, D
9	I	9	6	700	1600	F, H
10	J	11	7	1500	2000	F, H
11	K	8	6	600	1500	E, I
12	L	10	9	1000	1050	G, J

Enter the Problem

1. Select "Data Entry" from the "Input Data" menu (refer to Chapter 2 for selecting a menu item).
2. Fig. 13-1 shows the problem specification. Note that "Certain durations (CPM)" is selected for the project type, "You define" is specified for the activity names, and "Spreadsheet format" is selected for the activity precedence relations.
3. Fig. 13-2 shows the entry of the activity names, normal times, crash times, normal costs, and crash costs.
4. Figs. 13-3 to 13-5 show the activity precedence relation entry. For example, in Fig. 13-3, activities are from A to D and E. That is, A immediately precedes D

and E. Note that Fig. 13-4 is the right page of Fig. 13-3 by pressing the "PgRt" button, and similarly Fig. 13-5 is the right page of Fig. 13-4. Any non-empty entry will specify an immediate connection from one activity to the other.

5. If you specify "Free format" to enter the precedence relations in Fig. 13-1, use the format similar to Fig. 13-6 to enter the activity relations. Note that Fig. 13-6 is only a sample, not a complete entry for the problem.

```
. Enter the following fields for your project scheduling problem.
. When entering the uncertain activity durations on the following
  spreadsheet, columns 2 to 4 can be three time estimates (optimistic/
  most likely/pessimistic), mean and variance, or lower and upper
  bounds, depending on the distribution specified in column 5.
. The distribution codes are: 0 (default, beta), 1 (exponential),
  2 (normal), 3 (uniform) and 4 (arbitrary).
. You may choose to enter activity relations by free (Q/A) format.  If
  spreadsheet is selected, any non blank entry, e.g. `X', represents
  an immediate precedence relation from one activity to another.

    Problem Name?                        [Construction        ]
    Number of activities?                            [12      ]
 Project type:
         (•) Certain durations (CPM)     ( ) Uncertain durations (PERT)
 Activity name:
         ( ) Default (An)                (•) You define
 Activity precedence relation:
         (•) Spreadsheet format          ( ) Free format

       < OK >             < Print >             < Cancel >
```

Figure 13-1. Problem specification for Construction.

Project Activities for Construction

Number	Names	Normal Time	Crash Time	Normal Cost	Crash Cost
1	[A	][5	][3	][2000	][2500]
2	[B	][4	][4	][3000	][3000]
3	[C	][8	][7	][4000	][5000]
4	[D	][3	][2	][1200	][1500]
5	[E	][7	][5	][2000	][3000]
6	[F	][5	][5	][3000	][3000]
7	[G	][4	][3	][3000	][3700]
8	[H	][3	][3	][8000	][8000]
9	[I	][9	][6	][700	][1600]
10	[J	][11	][7	][1500	][2000]
11	[K	][8	][6	][600	][1500]
12	[L	][10	][9	][1000	][1050]

< OK > < PgUp > < PgLt > < PgRt > < Help > < Print > < Cancel >

Figure 13-2. Entry of activities for Construction.

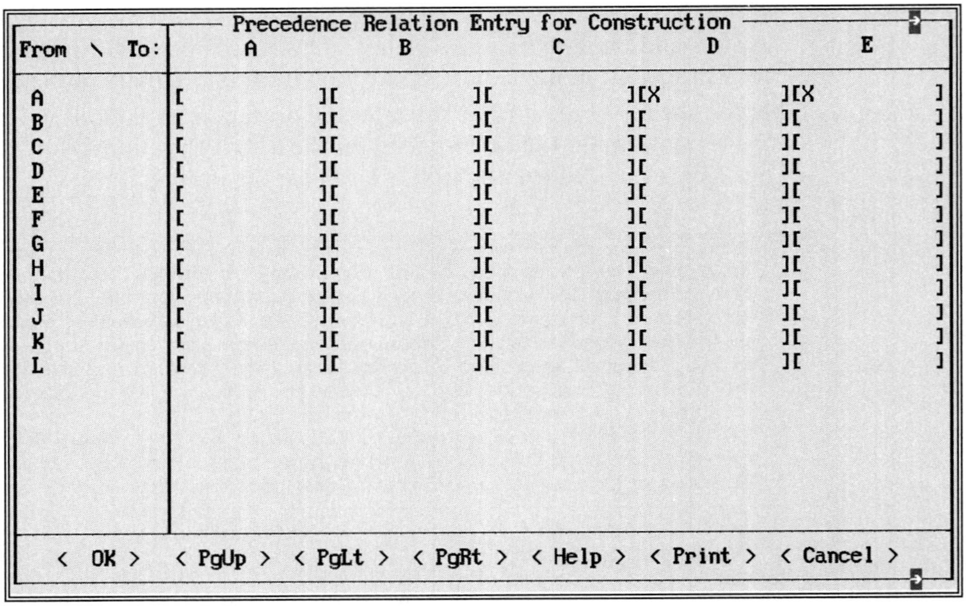

Precedence Relation Entry for Construction

From \ To:	A	B	C	D	E
A	[ ]	[ ]	[ ]	[X]	[X]
B	[ ]	[ ]	[ ]	[ ]	[ ]
C	[ ]	[ ]	[ ]	[ ]	[ ]
D	[ ]	[ ]	[ ]	[ ]	[ ]
E	[ ]	[ ]	[ ]	[ ]	[ ]
F	[ ]	[ ]	[ ]	[ ]	[ ]
G	[ ]	[ ]	[ ]	[ ]	[ ]
H	[ ]	[ ]	[ ]	[ ]	[ ]
I	[ ]	[ ]	[ ]	[ ]	[ ]
J	[ ]	[ ]	[ ]	[ ]	[ ]
K	[ ]	[ ]	[ ]	[ ]	[ ]
L	[ ]	[ ]	[ ]	[ ]	[ ]

< OK > < PgUp > < PgLt > < PgRt > < Help > < Print > < Cancel >

Figure 13-3. Activity precedence relations for Construction.

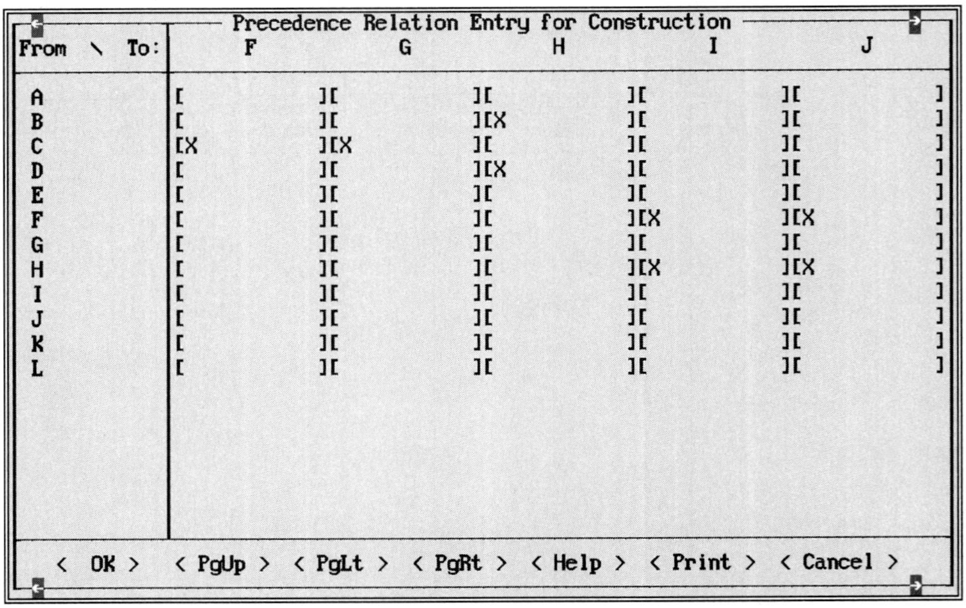

Precedence Relation Entry for Construction

From \ To:	F	G	H	I	J
A	[ ]	[ ]	[ ]	[ ]	[ ]
B	[ ]	[ ]	[X]	[ ]	[ ]
C	[X]	[X]	[ ]	[ ]	[ ]
D	[ ]	[ ]	[X]	[ ]	[ ]
E	[ ]	[ ]	[ ]	[ ]	[ ]
F	[ ]	[ ]	[ ]	[X]	[X]
G	[ ]	[ ]	[ ]	[ ]	[ ]
H	[ ]	[ ]	[ ]	[X]	[X]
I	[ ]	[ ]	[ ]	[ ]	[ ]
J	[ ]	[ ]	[ ]	[ ]	[ ]
K	[ ]	[ ]	[ ]	[ ]	[ ]
L	[ ]	[ ]	[ ]	[ ]	[ ]

< OK > < PgUp > < PgLt > < PgRt > < Help > < Print > < Cancel >

Figure 13-4. Activity precedence relations for Construction (continued).

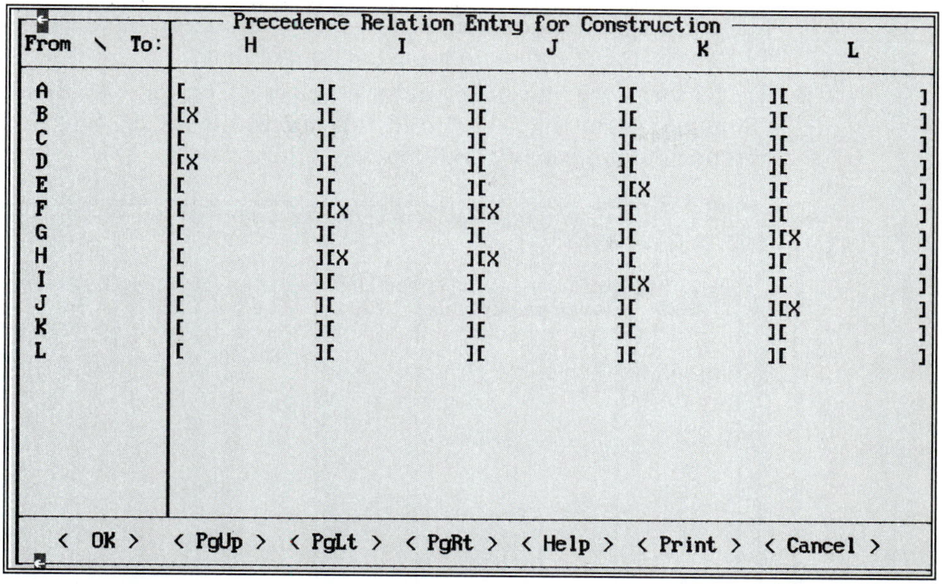

Figure 13-5. Activity precedence relations for Construction (continued).

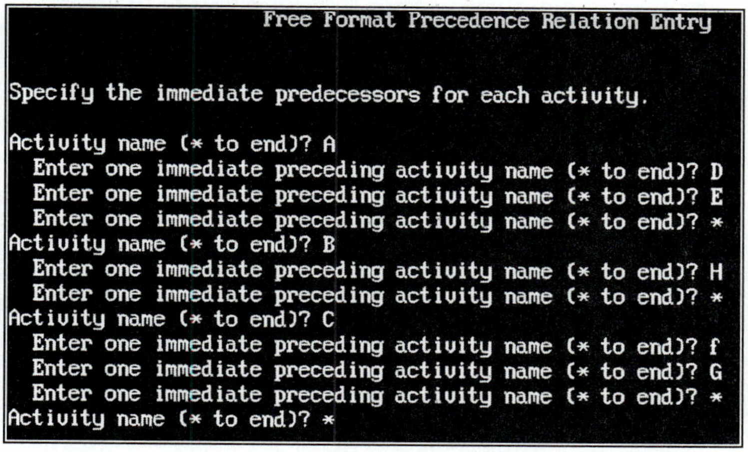

Figure 13-6. Sample free-format activity precedence relation entry for Construction.

Solve the Problem

1. Select "Solve with Normal Times" from the "Solution" menu to solve the problem. The message "Please standby . . ." will display for a short period while the problem is being solved for the critical path. You may also solve the critical path using the crash times by selecting "Solve with Crash Times" from the "Solution" menu.
2. After the problem is solved, select "Show the Solution" from the "Solution"

menu to display the solution. Fig. 13-7 shows the critical path analysis, and Fig. 13-8 shows the critical path using the normal times.

3. To perform the crashing analysis, select "Crashing Analysis" from the "Solution" menu. Figs. 13-9 to 13-14 demonstrate the crashing analyses of expediting the project by 2 and 5 days and their results.

Critical Path Analysis for Construction

08-23-1993 15:27:28 Page: 1 of 1

No.	Activity Name	Activity Duration	Activity Variance	Earliest Start	Latest Start	Earliest Finish	Earliest Start	Slack LS - ES
1	A	5	0	0	2	5	7	2
2	B	4	0	0	6	4	10	6
3	C	8	0	0	0	8	8	Critical
4	D	3	0	5	7	8	10	2
5	E	7	0	5	19	12	26	14
6	F	5	0	8	8	13	13	Critical
7	G	4	0	8	20	12	24	12
8	H	3	0	8	10	11	13	2
9	I	9	0	13	17	22	26	4
10	J	11	0	13	13	24	24	Critical
11	K	8	0	22	26	30	34	4
12	L	10	0	24	24	34	34	Critical

Completion Time = 34 (Using Normal Times) CPU seconds = 0
Total Cost = 30000 Total Cost on Critical Path = 9500

< PageDown > < PageUp > < Hardcopy > < Cancel >

Figure 13-7. Activity analysis for Construction.

```
                    Critical Path for Construction

Critical path: C ==> F ==> J ==> L.  Cost on this path = 9500

Done.
```

Figure 13-8. Critical path for Construction.

```
                    Crashing Analysis for Construction

Completion time with normal time = 34  with total cost = 30000
Completion time with crash time = 28  with total cost = 35850

By what time do you want to finish the project (0 to end)? 32

  Crash activity J    1 time units with additional cost = 125
  Crash activity L    1 time units with additional cost = 50

  To finish in 32 , the total cost = 30175

Do you want to show the critical path analysis (Y/N)? Y
```

Figure 13-9. The crash analysis of reducing two days.

Critical Path Analysis for Construction

08-23-1993 15:29:10 Page: 1 of 1

No.	Activity Name	Activity Duration	Activity Variance	Earliest Start	Latest Start	Earliest Finish	Earliest Start	Slack LS - ES
1	A	5	0	0	2	5	7	2
2	B	4	0	0	6	4	10	6
3	C	8	0	0	0	8	8	Critical
4	D	3	0	5	7	8	10	2
5	E	7	0	5	17	12	24	12
6	F	5	0	8	8	13	13	Critical
7	G	4	0	8	19	12	23	11
8	H	3	0	8	10	11	13	2
9	I	9	0	13	15	22	24	2
10	J	10	0	13	13	23	23	Critical
11	K	8	0	22	24	30	32	2
12	L	9	0	23	23	32	32	Critical

Completion Time = 32 (After Crashing Analysis) CPU seconds = .3789063
Total Cost = 30175 Total Cost on Critical Path = 9675

< PageDown > < PageUp > < Hardcopy > < Cancel >

Figure 13-10. Activity analysis after reducing two days for Construction.

```
                    Critical Path for Construction

Critical path: C ==> F ==> J ==> L.  Cost on this path = 9675

Done.
```

Figure 13-11. Critical path after reducing two days for Construction.

```
                    Crashing Analysis for Construction

Completion time with normal time = 34  with total cost = 30000
Completion time with crash time = 28  with total cost = 35850

By what time do you want to finish the project (0 to end)? 29

  Crash activity I   1 time units with additional cost = 300
  Crash activity J   4 time units with additional cost = 500
  Crash activity L   1 time units with additional cost = 50

  To finish in 29 , the total cost = 30850

Do you want to show the critical path analysis (Y/N)? Y
```

Figure 13-12. The crash analysis of reducing five days.

Critical Path Analysis for Construction

08-23-1993 15:30:47 Page: 1 of 1

No.	Activity Name	Activity Duration	Activity Variance	Earliest Start	Latest Start	Earliest Finish	Earliest Start	Slack LS - ES
1	A	5	0	0	2	5	7	2
2	B	4	0	0	6	4	10	6
3	C	8	0	0	0	8	8	Critical
4	D	3	0	5	7	8	10	2
5	E	7	0	5	14	12	21	9
6	F	5	0	8	8	13	13	Critical
7	G	4	0	8	16	12	20	8
8	H	3	0	8	10	11	13	2
9	I	8	0	13	13	21	21	Critical
10	J	7	0	13	13	20	20	Critical
11	K	8	0	21	21	29	29	Critical
12	L	9	0	20	20	29	29	Critical

Completion Time = 29 (After Crashing Analysis) CPU seconds = .3828125
Total Cost = 30850 Total Cost on Critical Path = 11650

< PageDown > < PageUp > < Hardcopy > < Cancel >

Figure 13-13. Activity analysis after reducing five days for Construction.

Critical Path for Construction

Critical path: C ==> F ==> I ==> K. Cost on this path = 8600

Critical path: C ==> F ==> J ==> L. Cost on this path = 10050

Done.

Figure 13-14. Critical path after reducing five days for Construction.

Example - PERT

Assume that the activities of the construction project involve uncertain factors and Table 13-3 shows the three time estimates for the activities. The optimistic times occur when everything goes smoothly, the most likely times occur in a normal situation, and the pessimistic times occur when the weather gets very bad. Management wants to know the expected completion time of the entire project and its critical path. Management also wants to estimate the probability of finishing the project within 30 days, 33 days, 35 days, or 38 days.

Table 13-3. Three time estimates (in days) for the construction project.

Activity		Optimistic time	Most likely time	Pessimistic time	Immediate predecessor
No.	Name				
1	A	3	5	7	—
2	B	4	4	5	—
3	C	5	8	10	—
4	D	2	3	4	A
5	E	5	7	9	A
6	F	4	5	6	C
7	G	3	4	8	C
8	H	3	3	3	B, D
9	I	9	9	12	F, H
10	J	10	11	12	F, H
11	K	6	8	11	E, I
12	L	8	10	12	G, J

Enter the Problem

1. Select "Data Entry" from the "Input Data" menu (refer to Chapter 2 for selecting a menu item).
2. Fig. 13-15 shows the problem specification. Note that "Uncertain durations (PERT)" is selected for the project type, "You define" is specified for the ac-

```
                     Problem Specification
 · Enter the following fields for your project scheduling problem.
 · When entering the uncertain activity durations on the following
   spreadsheet, columns 2 to 4 can be three time estimates (optimistic/
   most likely/pessimistic), mean and variance, or lower and upper
   bounds, depending on the distribution specified in column 5.
 · The distribution codes are: 0 (default, beta), 1 (exponential),
   2 (normal), 3 (uniform) and 4 (arbitrary).
 · You may choose to enter activity relations by free (Q/A) format.  If
   spreadsheet is selected, any non blank entry, e.g. `X', represents
   an immediate precedence relation from one activity to another.

      Problem Name?                         [Construction         ]
      Number of activities?                             [12       ]
 Project type:
            ( ) Certain durations (CPM)  (•) Uncertain durations (PERT)
 Activity name:
            ( ) Default (An)             (•) You define
 Activity precedence relation:
            (•) Spreadsheet format       ( ) Free format

        < OK >            < Print >            < Cancel >
```

Figure 13-15. Problem specification for Construction with uncertain times.

tivity names, and "Spreadsheet format" is selected for the activity precedence relations.

3. Fig. 13-16 shows the entry of the activity names and three time estimates. Note that the distribution is blank because the default beta distribution with three time estimates is assumed. If you use other distributions for the activity durations, refer to Table 13-1 in the Technical Notes section of this chapter for the associated parameters.
4. The activity precedence relation entry is the same as Figs. 13-3 to 13-5. You may also enter the precedence relations by free format as illustrated in Fig. 13-6.

Solve the Problem

1. Select "Solve with Expected Times" from the "Solution" menu to solve the problem. The message "Please standby. . ." will display for a short period while the problem is being solved for the critical path.
2. After the problem is solved, select "Show the Solution" from the "Solution" menu to display the solution. Fig. 13-17 shows the critical path analysis, and Fig. 13-18 shows the critical path using the expected times.
3. To perform the probability analysis, select "Probability Analysis" from the "Solution" menu. Fig. 13-19 demonstrates the probability analyses of finishing the project in 30, 33, 35, and 38 days and their results. Note that the normal distribution is assumed for the completion time of the critical path C-F-J-L.

Project Activities for Construction

Number	Names	Op.Tm./Par.1	ML.Tm./Par.2	Ps.Tm./Par.3	Distribution
1	A	3	5	7	
2	B	4	4	5	
3	C	5	8	10	
4	D	2	3	4	
5	E	5	7	9	
6	F	4	5	6	
7	G	3	4	8	
8	H	3	3	3	
9	I	9	9	12	
10	J	10	11	12	
11	K	6	8	11	
12	L	8	10	12	

< OK > < PgUp > < PgLt > < PgRt > < Help > < Print > < Cancel >

Figure 13-16. Entry of activities for Construction with uncertain times.

Critical Path Analysis for Construction

08-23-1993 15:36:14 Page: 1 of 1

No.	Activity Name	Activity Duration	Activity Variance	Earliest Start	Latest Start	Earliest Finish	Earliest Start	Slack LS - ES
1	A	5	.4444444	0	1.833336	5	6.833336	1.833336
2	B	4.166667	0.027777	0	5.666669	4.166667	9.833336	5.666669
3	C	7.833333	.6944444	0	0.000002	7.833333	7.833336	Critical
4	D	3	.1111111	5	6.833336	8	9.833336	1.833336
5	E	7	.4444444	5	18.66667	12	25.66667	13.66667
6	F	5	.1111111	7.833333	7.833336	12.83333	12.83334	Critical
7	G	4.5	.6944444	7.833333	19.33334	12.33333	23.83334	11.5
8	H	3	0	8	9.833336	11	12.83334	1.833336
9	I	9.5	.25	12.83333	16.16667	22.33333	25.66667	3.333334
10	J	11	.1111111	12.83333	12.83334	23.83333	23.83334	Critical
11	K	8.166667	.6944444	22.33333	25.66667	30.5	33.83334	3.333335
12	L	10	.4444444	23.83333	23.83334	33.83334	33.83334	Critical

Expected Completion Time = 33.83334 CPU seconds = .046875
Total Variance = 4.027778 Total Variance on Critical Path = 1.361111

< PageDown > < PageUp > < Hardcopy > < Cancel >

Figure 13-17. Activity analysis for Construction with uncertain times.

```
                    Critical Path for Construction

Critical path: C ==> F ==> J ==> L.  Variance on this path = 1.361111
Variance

Done.
```

Figure 13-18. Critical path for Construction with uncertain times.

EXERCISES

1. Consider the project network in Fig. 13-20 with the AOA convention, where node represents event and arc represents activity. Find the ES, LS, EF, LF, and criticality of each activity. Also find the critical path. Note that the letters on each arc represent the activity names and the numbers below or next to each arc represent the activity durations.

```
                   Probability Analysis for Construction

The following probability calculation assumes that activities are
independent and so are all paths.  It also assumes that your network
has a large enough number of activities to assume the normality.
Therefore, when the activities are not independent or the number of
activities is not large, the analysis may be biased.


Expected completion time (50% chance) =  33.83334

When do you expect to finish your project (0 to end) ? 30


Critical path: C ==> F ==> J ==> L.  Variance on this path = 1.361111
  The probability to finish in 30 is 0.051128%.

Do you want to enter another scheduled completion time (Y/N)? y
```

```
When do you expect to finish your project (0 to end) ? 33


Critical path: C ==> F ==> J ==> L.  Variance on this path = 1.361111
  The probability to finish in 33 is 23.75311%.

Do you want to enter another scheduled completion time (Y/N)? y

When do you expect to finish your project (0 to end) ? 35


Critical path: C ==> F ==> J ==> L.  Variance on this path = 1.361111
  The probability to finish in 35 is 84.13508%.

Do you want to enter another scheduled completion time (Y/N)? y
```

```
When do you expect to finish your project (0 to end) ? 38


Critical path: C ==> F ==> J ==> L.  Variance on this path = 1.361111
  The probability to finish in 38 is 99.98212%.

Do you want to enter another scheduled completion time (Y/N)? n
```

Figure 13-19. The probability analyses for Construction.

2. Perform the CPM analysis for the AON project network shown in Fig. 13-21, where node represents activity and arc represents the precedence relation. Note that the letters in each node represent the activity names and the numbers above each node represent the activity durations.
3. In planning a project to introduce a new product, the required activities are shown in Table 13-4.

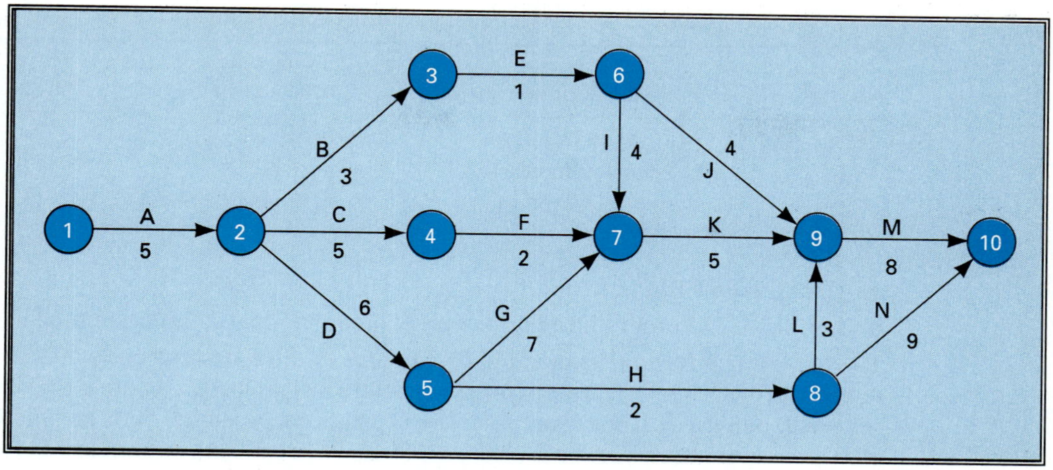

Figure 13-20. AOA network for exercise 1.

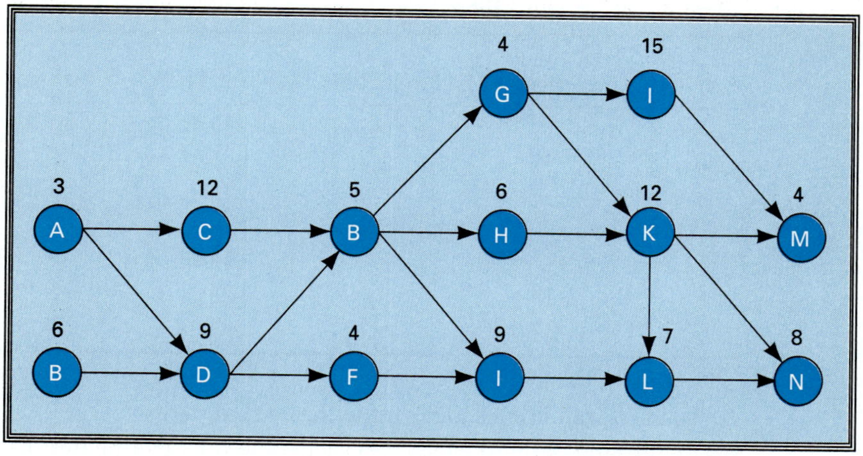

Figure 13-21. AON network for exercise 2.

Table 13-4. Project data for exercise 3.

Activity	Description	Immediate predecessor	Duration
A	Product design	—	5 months
B	Market research	—	1
C	Production analysis	A	2
D	Product model	A	3
E	Sales brochure	A	2
F	Cost analysis	C	3
G	Product testing	D	4

Table 13-4. Project data for exercise 3 (continued).

Activity	Description	Immediate predecessor	Duration
H	Sales training	B, E	2
I	Pricing & forecasting	H	1
J	Project report	F, G, I	1

a. Construct a CPM network.

b. Use the CPM program to find the critical path and its completion time.

4. The following information in Table 13-5 relates to the times and costs of activities in a project. The scheduled completion time is eight weeks. There is a $2500 per week penalty cost for each week the project is delayed beyond the scheduled completion time. There is also a $1000 per week incentive bonus paid for each week ahead of schedule for the project completion.

Table 13-5. Project data for exercise 4.

Activity	Immediate predecessor	Normal time	Normal cost	Crash time	Crash cost
A	—	3 weeks	$3000	2 weeks	$5000
B	—	4	4000	2	6000
C	—	5	5000	3	8000
D	A	0	0	0	0
E	A	8	5000	6	6000
F	B,D	3	3000	2	4000
G	C	5	4000	3	8000

a. Using normal times, determine the critical path.

b. Determine the best (least cost) schedule for carrying out the project.

5. The information in Table 13-6 relates to the activities necessary for completing a project.

Table 13-6. Project data for exercise 5.

Activity	Immediate predecessor	Normal time	Normal cost	Crash time	Crash cost
A	—	8 weeks	$4000	6 weeks	$6000
B	—	5	1500	4	2000
C	—	6	2500	4	3000
D	A	4	1800	3	2000
E	A,B	6	1000	5	1200
F	C	7	2000	5	3000
G	A	5	3000	3	6000
H	D,E,F	8	4500	5	9000

Table 13-6. Project data for exercise 5 (continued).

Activity	Immediate predecessor	Normal time	Normal cost	Crash time	Crash cost
I	C	9	6000	4	10000
J	D,E,F	6	6000	4	8000
K	G,H	4	2000	3	3200
L	D,E,F	6	3000	3	9000
M	I,J	4	8000	2	12000

The scheduled completion time of the project is 20 weeks. There is a $1500 penalty for each week the project is delayed beyond the scheduled completion time.

a. Construct an AON network to represent this project.

b. Use the normal time to find the critical path and its completion time.

c. Determine the optimal (least cost) schedule for this project.

6. Perform the PERT analysis for the project shown below. The three time estimates for each activity are listed in Table 13-7.

Table 13-7. Project data for exercise 6.

Activity	Optimistic time	Most likely time	Pessimistic time	Immediate predecessor
A	1	2	3	—
B	6	8	15	—
C	4	5	6	A
D	1	7	11	B
E	3	4	6	B
F	5	5	5	C
G	8	9	10	D
H	6	8	10	D
I	5	7	9	E
J	5	9	11	H,I
K	10	13	15	F,G,J
L	6	8	14	H,I

7. Perform the PERT analysis for the AON network shown in Fig. 13-21 of exercise 2 if the activity durations are uncertain and their three time estimates are shown in Table 13-8.

Table 13-8. Project data for exercise 7.

Activity	Optimistic time	Most likely time	Pessimistic time
A	1	2	3
B	4	6	8
C	9	12	12

Table 13-8. Project data for exercise 7 (continued).

Activity	Optimistic time	Most likely time	Pessimistic time
D	6	8	9
E	3	5	9
F	3	3	4
G	3	4	5
H	5	6	9
I	4	9	10
J	12	15	15
K	8	12	12
L	7	8	9
M	3	4	6
N	7	8	10

8. Consider the following project. Its three time estimates for each activity are shown in Table 13-9. Find the probability of finishing the project within 55 days.

Table 13-9. Project data for exercise 8.

Activity	Immediate predecessor	Optimistic time	Most likely time	Pessimistic time
A	-	5 days	6 days	8 days
B	A	1	7	11
C	A	3	3	3
D	B	4	4	6
E	C	1	2	3
F	C	6	8	9
G	D	4	5	6
H	D	3	4	5
I	H	6	6	7
J	E,G	7	8	9
K	E,G	11	12	13
L	F	5	5	5
M	F	3	3	5
N	M	10	12	13
O	K,L	9	11	14
P	J	4	6	8
Q	O	1	2	3
R	I,P,Q	2	3	4
S	O	6	7	8
T	O	9	9	10
U	N	11	11	11

Table 13-9. Project data for exercise 8. (continued)

Activity	Immediate predecessor	Optimistic time	Most likely time	Pessimistic time
V	R	5	6	9
W	T,U	4	6	8
X	S	3	4	4
Y	V	1	2	3
Z	X,W	5	7	8

9. The following project to develop an orbiting solar collector has been funded by NASA as its contribution to solve the nation's energy crisis. The time estimates are in months and are shown in Table 13-10.

a. Draw an AON network.

b. Find the critical path.

c. Determine the probability of finishing the project within 18 months.

Table 13-10. Project data for exercise 9.

Activity	Immediate predecessor	Optimistic time	Most likely time	Pessimistic time
A	—	4	6	8
B	—	1	2	3
C	A	4	4	4
D	A	4	5	6
E	B	7	10	16
F	B	8	9	10
G	C	2	2	2
H	D,E,G	2	3	7
I	F	1	3	11

10. Table 13-11 shows the project activities. The durations of activities are uncertain and are recorded by the sequence of optimistic, most likely, and pessimistic times. The durations are given in working days. The scheduled completion time of the project is 10 working days.

a. Find the critical path of the project.

b. Determine the probability of completing the project on or before the scheduled completion time.

c. If the project is delayed beyond its scheduled completion time, a fixed penalty cost of $1000 will be incurred. We can either keep the scheduled completion time of 10 days or extend the scheduled completion time to 12 days. The extension would require a renegotiated contract that would cost $200. Should the contract be renegotiated?

Table 13-11. Project data for exercise 10.

Activity	Predecessor	Optimistic time	Most likely time	Pessimistic time
A1	—	1	2	3
A2	—	3	4	5
A3	A1	2	4	6
A4	A1	1	3	4
A5	A3	0	0	0
A6	A2	2	4	6
A7	A2	1	1	1
A8	A6	0	0	0
A9	A6	1	1	1
A10	A4,A5,A7,A8	2	4	6

11. The project shown in Table 13-12 indicates the activities for completing a project. Activity durations are given in days.

a. Perform the PERT analysis and find the critical path.

b. Determine the probability of the project taking more than 16 days.

c. Assume that the scheduled project time is 16 days. If the project is late, a penalty of $5000 will be incurred. However, we have been offered the opportunity to extend the scheduled time to 18 days, but this will cost us $300 for renegotiating the contract. Should the contract be renegotiated?

d. Assume that we want to sign a contract that specifies the completion date of the project, and we want to be 95% certain of meeting or beating that date. What completion date should be specified in the contract?

Table 13-12. Project data for exercise 11.

Activity	Predecessor	Optimistic time	Most likely time	Pessimistic time
A	—	1	2	3
B	—	2	3	4
C	B	1	3	5
D	—	1	3	5
E	A,C	4	4	4
F	B	3	4	5
G	B	5	5	5
H	D	6	8	10
I	E	1	2	2
J	H	2	4	6

14

INVENTORY THEORY (INVT)

OVERVIEW OF THE INVT DECISION SUPPORT SYSTEM

This program contains three basic inventory models: uniform demand economic order quantity (EOQ), uniform demand quantity discount analysis, and single-period stochastic demand problem. EOQ analysis finds the optimal order quantity having the least costs including shortage and lost-sales costs. Quantity discount analysis solves the least cost order quantity using all-unit or incremental discount method. You may also assign an order quantity and let the program perform cost analysis. Graphic analyses are also available for both types of problems.

The single-period stochastic demand problem is also called the newsboy problem. The allowed demand distributions are normal, uniform, exponential, triangular, Poisson, binomial, geometric, discrete, and Laplace. The program solves the best order quantity to optimize the expected profit in a single period. You can also assign an order quantity or service level and let the program compute the expected profit.

A spreadsheet is used for entering the data. The program has options to save, read, modify, and print the input data. After the solution has been obtained, you may display, print, or save it.

TECHNICAL NOTES ON THE INVT PROGRAM

1. For the economic order quantity (EOQ), the program solves the EOQ, displays, or plots the inventory related costs, which include holding, ordering, shortage, and lost-sale costs. You can also assign an order quantity and let the INVT program calculate the inventory related costs. The data for the EOQ problem includes demand per period, order or setup cost per order, holding cost per unit per period, shortage cost per unit per period, lost-sale cost per unit, replenishment or production rate per period, lead time for a new order in period, and unit cost. Shortage defaults are not allowed, lost-sale costs zero, replenishment rate is infinite, and lead time is zero.
2. For discount analysis, the all-unit discount represents that all the order units are priced with the same discounted rate, while incremental discount represents that the order units are priced incrementally with different discount rates based

on the break quantities. You can also specify that the holding, shortage, or lost-sale cost remains constant or is discounted. The input data include demand per period, order or setup cost per order, holding cost per unit per period, shortage cost per unit per period, lost-sale cost per unit, replenishment or production rate per period, lead time for a new order in period, unit cost, discount breaks, and discount percentages. Default values are the same as for EOQ data.

3. For the single-period stochastic demand problem (newsboy problem), the input data includes unit acquisition cost, unit selling price, unit shortage cost, unit salvage value, order or setup cost, initial inventory, demand distribution and parameters. Demand is stochastic and uncertain and may follow any of the distributions in Table 14-1. When specifying a demand distribution in data entry, the first three letters are required. Based on the specified demand distribution and operational data, the program solves the order quantity to maximize the expected profit for the single period. In particular, the Laplace density function is given as follows:

$f(x) = e^{-|x-\mu|/b} /(2b)$
where x is the demand, μ is the mean, and variance $= 2b^2$.

Table 14-1. Possible demand distributions.

Distribution	Parameters 1, 2, and/or 3
Normal	Mean, standard deviation
Uniform	Lower bound, upper bound
Exponential	Mean
Triangular	Lower bound, mode, upper bound
Poisson	Mean
Binomial	n, p
Geometric	p
Discrete	Mean, number of discrete values
Laplace	Mean, b

MENU STRUCTURE

The functions and options in each of the pull-down menus are hierarchically listed as follows:

Modules
- Linear Programming (LP)
- Integer Linear Programming (ILP)
- Goal Programming (GP)
- Quadratic Programming (QP)
- Nonlinear Programming (NLP)
- Dynamic Programming (DP)

- Transportation and Transshipment (TRP)
- Assignment and Traveling Salesman (ASTS)
- Specialized Network Modeling (SNET)
- Capacitated Network Flow Modeling (CNET)
- Project Scheduling: CPM/PERT
- Inventory Theory (INVT)
- Inventory Theory 2 (INVT2)
- Queuing Theory (QUEUE)
- Queuing System Simulation (QSIM)
- Decision Analysis (DA)
- Markov Process (MKV)
- Time Series Forecasting (TSFC)
- Financial Analysis (FA)
- Exit from QSB

Input Data
- Data Entry
- Read a File
- Show Data
- Print Data
- Modify Data
- Save
- Save As
- Exit from QSB

Solution
- EOQ
  - Solve the EOQ
  - Assign an Order Quantity
  - Show Inventory Cost Curve
- Quantity Discounts
  - Solve the Quantity Discounts
  - Assign an Order Quantity
  - Show Inventory Cost Curve
- Newsboy Problem
  - Solve the Problem
  - Assign Order Quantity/Service Level
- Show the Solution
- Print the Solution
- Save the Solution

Options
- Color
- Monochrome
- Printer Selection

Help - INVT
- About INVT
- About the User Interface
- About the Edit Keys

SOLVING PROBLEMS WITH INVT

In the following sections, we will use example problems to show how to enter and solve the problems. The general procedure and menu options are described in detail in the tutorial sections of Chapter 2.

Example - Economic Order Quantity (EOQ)

TV Shack is a local television retailer. From experience, the company knows that the demand for televisions is very steady, with a mean of 600 sets per year, and that the ordering cost is \$50 per order. The annual holding cost, including capital cost and warehousing cost, is 20% of the purchasing price. The wholesaler offers a price of \$300 per set. What quantity should the retailer order each time so that the inventory cost is minimized?

Enter the Problem

1. Select "Data Entry" from the "Input Data" menu (refer to Chapter 2 for selecting a menu item).
2. Fig. 14-1 shows the problem specification. Note that "Uniform Demand EOQ Problem" is selected for the problem type since the demand is steady (uniform).
3. Fig. 14-2 shows the EOQ data entry. Note that the unit holding cost is equal to \$60, which is 20% of \$300.

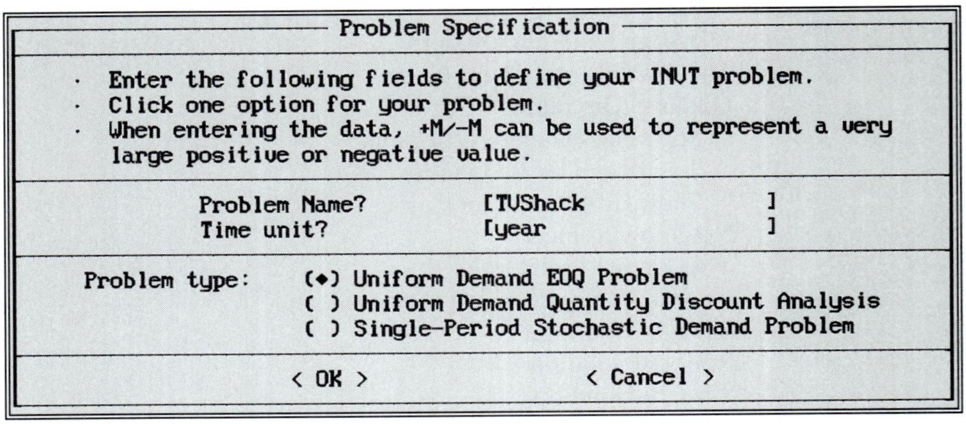

Figure 14-1. Problem specification for the EOQ problem.

Solve the Problem

1. Select "Solve the EOQ" from the "Solution" menu to solve the problem. The message "Please standby . . ." will display for a short period while the problem is being solved.

```
                         EOQ Data for TUShack
  . You may enter M/-M to represent positive/negative infinity.

[600        ] Demand per year
[50         ] Order or setup cost per order
[60         ] Holding cost per unit per year
[M          ] Shortage cost per unit per year (default = M)
[           ] Lost-sale cost per unit (default = 0)
[M          ] Replenishment or production rate per year (default = M)
[           ] Lead time for a new order in year (default = 0)
[300        ] Unit cost without discount

        < OK >              < Print >              < Cancel >
```

Figure 14-2. Entry for the EOQ problem.

2. After the problem is solved, select "Show the Solution" from the "Solution" menu to display the EOQ analysis. Fig. 14-3 shows the result.
3. You may choose "Show Inventory Cost Curve" from the "Solution" menu to display the inventory cost curve. Fig. 14-4 shows the specification of figure scales. Assume the default is specified. Fig. 14-5 shows the result. Note that in Fig. 14-5 each slot of the horizontal dimension represents 2 units. You may press the "P" key to print the figure to the printer (make sure the printer is on and select the right printer from "Options" menu).
4. You can also choose "Assign an Order Quantity" from the "Solution" menu to analyze the inventory cost with an assigned order quantity.

```
                 Inventory Cost Analysis for TUShack
08-23-1993 16:36:25                                       Page: 1 of 1

        Input Data              Value      Inventory and Cost         Value

Demand per year                   600   Order quantity (EOQ)       31.62278
Order (setup) cost                 50   Maximum inventory          31.62278
Holding cost per year              60   Maximum backorder                 0
Shortage cost per year              M   Order interval in year     0.052704
Lost-sale cost per unit             0   Reorder point                     0
Replenishment/production                  Total setup or
     rate per year                  M         ordering cost        948.6833
Lead time in year                   0     Total holding cost       948.6833
Unit cost                         300     Total shortage cost             0
                                          Total lost-sales cost           0
                                        Subtotal                   1897.367
                                        Total material cost          180000
                                        Grand total cost           181897.4
                                        Elapsed CPU seconds         .046875

    < PageDown >       < PageUp >       < Hardcopy >       < Cancel >
```

Figure 14-3. EOQ analysis for TVSHK.

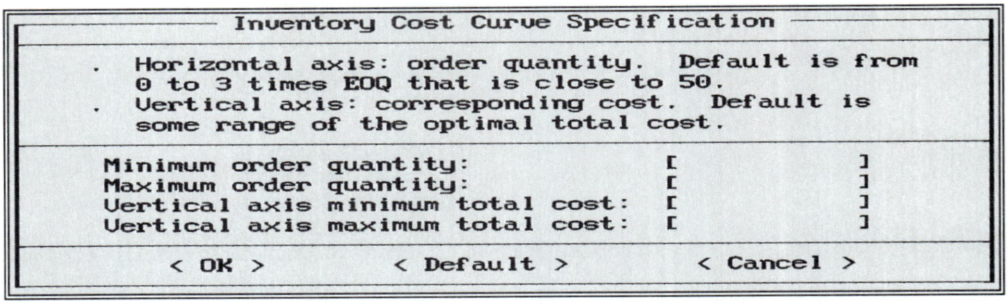

Figure 14-4. Inventory cost curve specification for TVSHK.

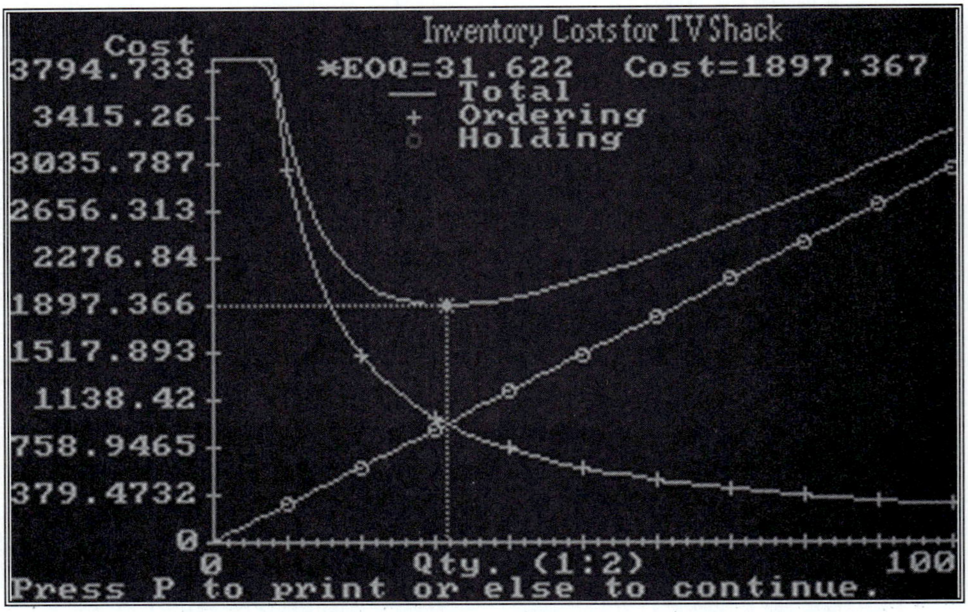

Figure 14-5. Inventory cost curves for TVSHK.

Example - Quantity Discounts

If the wholesaler offers 2% and 5% discounts if TV Shack orders more than or equal to 50 sets and 80 sets, respectively, what is the best order strategy for TV Shack?

Enter the Problem

1. Select "Data Entry" from the "Input Data" menu.
2. Fig. 14-6 shows the problem specification. Note that "Uniform Demand Quantity Discount Analysis" is selected for the problem type.
3. Fig. 14-7 shows the basic data entry. Note that the unit holding cost is equal to $60, which is 20% of $300, discount type is set to "All unit", and holding, shortage, and lost-sales costs, if any, are set to constant. You can change the setting later on.
4. Fig. 14-8 shows the entry of quantity breaks and discount percentages.

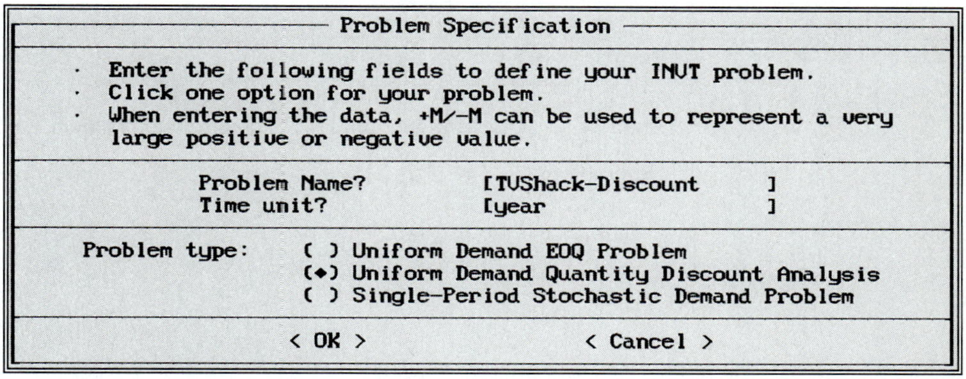

Figure 14-6. Problem specification for TV Shack discount problem.

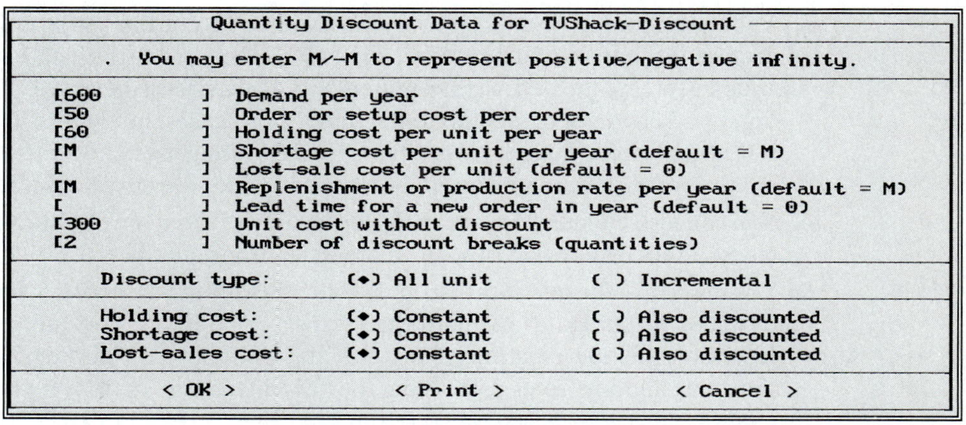

Figure 14-7. Entry for TV Shack discount problem.

Discount Quantities and % for TVShack-Discount

Break	Quantity (≥)	Discount %
1	[50]	[2]
2	[80]	[5]

< OK > < PgUp > < PgLt > < PgRt > < Help > < Print > < Cancel >

Figure 14-8. Discount data for TV Shack discount problem.

Solve the Problem

1. Select "Solve the Quantity Discounts" from the "Solution" menu to solve the problem.
2. After the problem is solved, select "Show the Solution" from the "Solution" menu to display the discount analysis. Figs. 14-9 and 14-10 show the results.
3. You may choose "Show Inventory Cost Curve" from the "Solution" menu to display the inventory cost curve. Fig. 14-11 shows the specification of figure scales. Assume the default is specified. Fig. 14-12 shows the curve. Note that in Fig. 14-12 each slot of the horizontal dimension represents 2 units. The "*" represents the order quantity. Specifying the right range is important when showing the cost curve. Inappropriate range may make the curve obscure.
4. You can also choose "Assign an Order Quantity" from the "Solution" menu to analyze the inventory cost with an assigned order quantity.
5. You may solve the quantity discounts with other options. Choose "Modify Data" from the "Input Data" menu to change discount options. For example, Fig. 14-13 shows the specification of incremental discount and discounted holding, shortage, and lost-sales costs using the "Modify Data" option. If you solve the quantity discounts based on these options, Figs. 14-14 and 14-15 show the new results, and Figs. 14-16 and 14-17 demonstrate the new cost curve.

Quantity Discount Analysis for TVShack-Discount

08-23-1993 16:42:51 Page: 1 of 1

Break Qty.	Discount %	EOQ	Total Cost	Status	Order Qty.	Total Cost
0	0	31.62	181897.4	Feasible	31.62	181897.4
50.00	2.00	31.62	178297.4	Infeasible	50.00	178500.0
80.00	5.00	31.62	172897.4	Infeasible	80.00	173775.0

Recommended Order Qty.= 80.00 Total Cost = 173775.0 Discount = 5%
All units discounts Elapsed CPU seconds = 0
Holding cost: constant

< PageDown > < PageUp > < Hardcopy > < Cancel >

Figure 14-9. Discount analysis for TVShack-Discount.

Inventory Cost Analysis for TVShack-Discount

08-23-1993 16:43:27 Page: 1 of 1

Input Data	Value	Inventory and Cost	Value
Demand per year	600	Order quantity	80
Order (setup) cost	50	Maximum inventory	80
Holding cost per year	60	Maximum backorder	0
Shortage cost per year	M	Order interval in year	.1333333
Lost-sale cost per unit	0	Reorder point	0
Replenishment/production rate per year	M	Total setup or ordering cost	375
Lead time in year	0	Total holding cost	2400
Unit cost	300	Total shortage cost	0
		Total lost-sales cost	0
		Subtotal	2775
		Total material cost	171000
		Grand total cost	173775
		Elapsed CPU seconds	0

< PageDown > < PageUp > < Hardcopy > < Cancel >

Figure 14-10. Inventory cost for TVShack-Discount.

Inventory Cost Curve Specification

- Horizontal axis: order quantity. Default is from 0 to 1.2 times the largest break quantity.
- Vertical axis: corresponding cost. Default is some range of the optimal total cost.

Minimum order quantity: [ ]
Maximum order quantity: [ ]
Vertical axis minimum total cost: [ ]
Vertical axis maximum total cost: [ ]

< OK > < Default > < Cancel >

Figure 14-11. Inventory cost curve specification for TVShack-Discount.

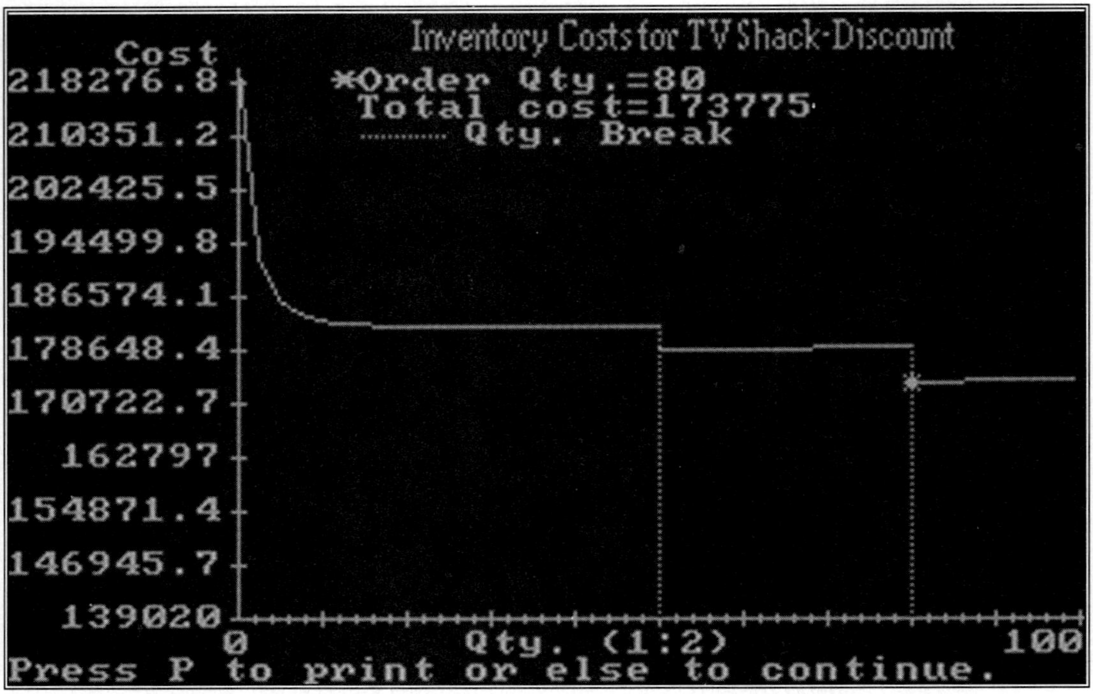

Figure 14-12. Inventory cost curves for TVShack-Discount.

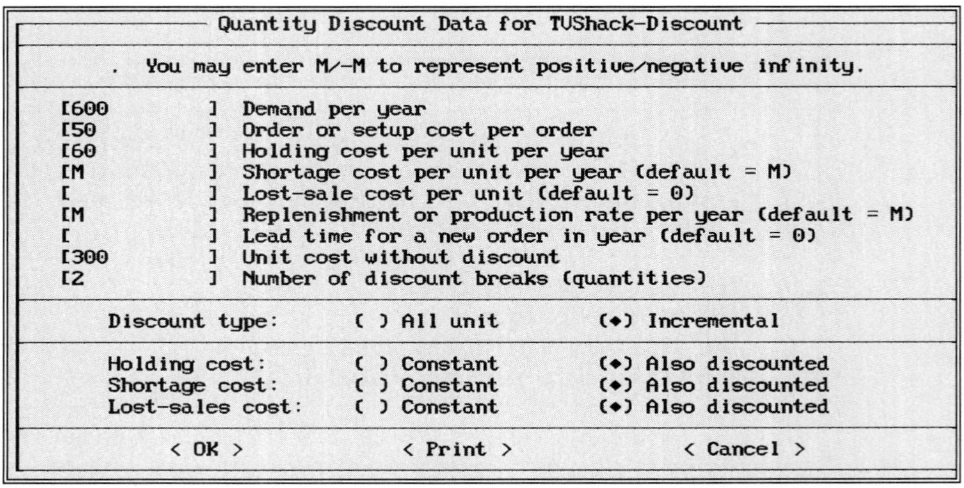

Figure 14-13. Another discount option for TVShack-Discount.

Quantity Discount Analysis for TVShack-Discount

08-23-1993 16:52:42 Page: 1 of 1

Break Qty.	Discount %	EOQ	Total Cost	Status	Order Qty.	Total Cost
0	0	31.62	181897.4	Feasible	31.62	181897.4
50.00	2.00	84.52	181081.0	Infeasible	80.00	181377.0
80.00	5.00	150.09	179555.0	Feasible	150.09	179555.0

Recommended Order Qty.= 150.09 Total Cost = 179555.0 Discount = 5%
Incremental discounts Elapsed CPU seconds = 0
Holding cost: discounted

< PageDown > < PageUp > < Hardcopy > < Cancel >

Figure 14-14. Discount analysis for TVShack-Discount with incremental discounts.

Inventory Cost Analysis for TVShack-Discount

08-23-1993 16:53:21 Page: 1 of 1

Input Data	Value	Inventory and Cost	Value
Demand per year	600	Order quantity	150.0877
Order (setup) cost	50	Maximum inventory	150.0877
Holding cost per year	60	Maximum backorder	0
Shortage cost per year	M	Order interval in year	.2501462
Lost-sale cost per unit	0	Reorder point	0
Replenishment/production rate per year	M	Total setup or ordering cost	199.8831
Lead time in year	0	Total holding cost	4277.499
Unit cost	300	Total shortage cost	0
		Total lost-sales cost	0
		Subtotal	4477.382
		Total material cost	175077.6
		Grand total cost	179555
		Elapsed CPU seconds	0

< PageDown > < PageUp > < Hardcopy > < Cancel >

Figure 14-15. Inventory cost for TVShack-Discount with incremental discounts.

Inventory Cost Curve Specification

- Horizontal axis: order quantity. Default is from 0 to 1.2 times the largest break quantity.
- Vertical axis: corresponding cost. Default is some range of the optimal total cost.

Minimum order quantity: [ ]
Maximum order quantity: [200]
Vertical axis minimum total cost: [170000]
Vertical axis maximum total cost: [190000]

< OK > < Default > < Cancel >

Figure 14-16. Inventory cost curve specification.

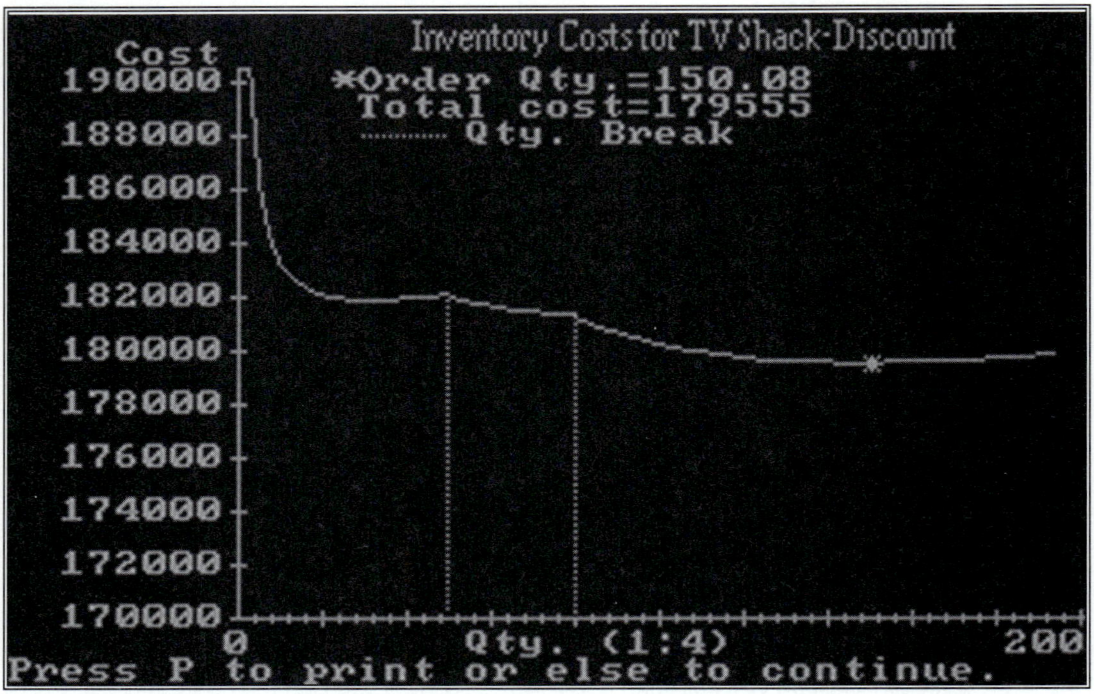

Figure 14-17. Inventory cost curves for TVShack-Discount with incremental discounts.

Example - Newsboy Problem

Mayflower for Mother is a major flower chain store in Atlanta. The company is preparing flowers for the coming Mother's Day. From experience, roses packaged in a dozen are the best seller during Mother's Day week. A dozen roses usually sell for \$30 with cost at \$20. It is estimated that a shortage will cost the company on average about \$10 in good will and special handling (shipped from other franchise stores). However, the left-over roses after Mother's Day will be sold at only \$15 per dozen. The company has estimated the demand will be normal distributed with mean 1000 dozens and standard deviation 100 dozens. Order cost is estimated at \$300, including all paperwork and handling. If you are asked to recommend the rose purchase for this coming Mother's Day, what is the best order quantity? If 90% service level is desired, what is the order quantity? Service level in this case is considered to be the probability of roses being available when a customer arrives.

Enter the Problem

1. Select "Data Entry" from the "Input Data" menu.
2. Fig. 14-18 shows the problem specification. Note that "Single-Period Stochastic Demand Problem" is selected for the problem type.

3. Fig. 14-19 shows the data entry. The demand distribution is normal, the parameter 1 is the mean, and parameter 2 is the standard deviation.

```
──────────── Problem Specification ────────────
 · Enter the following fields to define your INUT problem.
 · Click one option for your problem.
 · When entering the data, +M/-M can be used to represent a very
   large positive or negative value.

        Problem Name?           [Mayflower          ]
        Time unit?              [period             ]

   Problem type:     ( ) Uniform Demand EOQ Problem
                     ( ) Uniform Demand Quantity Discount Analysis
                     (•) Single-Period Stochastic Demand Problem

              < OK >                       < Cancel >
```

Figure 14-18. Selection of the newsboy problem.

```
──────── Single-Period Stochastic Demand Data Entry ────────
 . Default will be assumed if you do not enter a value.
 . Allowed demand distributions are normal(u,sd), uniform(LB,UB),
   exponential(u), Laplace(u,b), triangular(LB,MD,UB), Poisson(u),
   binomial(n,p), geometric(p), and discrete(u,n), where () contains
   the required parameters for each distribution.
 . The first three letters are required to specify a distribution.

    [20         ] Unit acquisition cost
    [30         ] Unit selling price
    [10         ] Unit shortage cost
    [15         ] Unit salvage value
    [300        ] Order or setup cost
    [           ] Initial inventory
    [Normal     ] Demand distribution (default = Normal)
    [1000       ] Demand parameter 1
    [100        ] Demand parameter 2
    [           ] Demand parameter 3

      < OK >            < Print >            < Cancel >
```

Figure 14-19. Data entry for Mayflower.

Solve the Problem

1. Select "Solve the Problem" from the "Solution" menu to solve the problem.
2. After the problem is solved, select "Show the Solution" from the "Solution" menu to display the analysis. Fig. 14-20 shows the result. Note that the optimal service level is at 80.23% with an order quantity of 1085 and an expected maximum profit of $9000.07.

3. You can also choose "Assign Order Quantity/Service Level" from the "Solution" menu to analyze the problem with an assigned order quantity or service level. Note that you need only one of them. If you enter an order quantity, the program will compute the service level, and vice versa. In this case, we enter a service level of 90%. Fig. 14-21 shows the entry, and Fig. 14-22 shows the result of ordering for 90% service level.

Stochastic Demand Analysis for Mayflower

08-23-1993 16:57:59 Page: 1 of 1

Input Data	Value	Input Data	Value
Unit acquisition cost	20	Unit shortage cost	10
Unit selling price	30	Unit salvage value	15
Order or setup cost	300	Initial inventory	0
Demand distribution	Normal		
Average demand	1000	Standard deviation	100
Optimal Inventory Level =	1085	Reorder Point =	999
Order Quantity =	1085	Expected Profit =	$9000.07
Expected Service Level =	80.23%	Elapsed CPU Seconds =	0

< PageDown > < PageUp > < Hardcopy > < Cancel >

Figure 14-20. Analysis for Mayflower.

Enter Order Quantity/Service Level

. Enter either order quantity or service level (one only). The program will compute the other one.
. Default is the optimal order quantity.

Enter your order quantity: [ ]
Enter desired service level (%): [90]

< OK > < Default > < Cancel >

Figure 14-21. Enter an order quantity for Mayflower.

Stochastic Demand Analysis for Mayflower

08-23-1993 16:59:15 Page: 1 of 1

Input Data	Value	Input Data	Value
Unit acquisition cost	20	Unit shortage cost	10
Unit selling price	30	Unit salvage value	15
Order or setup cost	300	Initial inventory	0
Demand distribution	Normal		
Average demand	1000	Standard deviation	100
Optimal Inventory Level =	1085	Reorder Point =	999
Order Quantity =	1085	Expected Profit =	$9000.07
Expected Service Level =	80.23%	Elapsed CPU Seconds =	0
Your Order Quantity =	1129	Maximum Inventory Level =	1129
Expected Service Level =	90.15%	Expected Profit =	$8938.707

< PageDown > < PageUp > < Hardcopy > < Cancel >

Figure 14-22. About 90% service level for Mayflower.

EXERCISES

1. Assume that a production system has the following related information:

   Annual demand = 1800 units
   Setup cost = \$120
   Holding cost per year per unit = 20% of unit production cost
   Unit production cost = \$40
   Shortage cost per year per unit = \$10
   Lead time = 0.01 year

   a. What is the EOQ?
   b. What are the related inventory costs?

2. Assume that the production (replenishment) rate is 300 units per month for exercise 1. What are the effects on the questions of exercise 1?

3. Given an inventory system with the following information:

   Annual demand = 120 units
   Ordering cost = \$45
   Annual carrying cost per unit= \$48
   Unit cost = \$200

   a. What is the EOQ?
   b. What is the total inventory cost?
   c. The supplier offers a 2% discount on the unit price if the items are purchased in lots of 100 or more at one time. Should management accept the offer? Assume all units are discounted.

4. To produce a tape recorder doll, Educational Toy Company purchases all the doll material from the same vendor. The annual demand is 10,000 units, ordering cost is \$10, and the holding cost per year is 20% of the purchase cost.

   a. If the purchase cost is \$2 per unit, what is the EOQ? What is the annual inventory-relevant cost?
   b. Suppose that the purchase cost falls to \$1.75 per unit for an order size of 500 or more. Now what is the EOQ? What is the annual inventory-relevant cost? Assume all unit discount is used.
   c. What should the company decide for the order size? What happens if the vendor offers more attractive discounts, such as:

   Order $<$ 500 units: \$2 per unit
   Order $<$ 1000 units and $\geq$ 500 units: \$1.75 per unit
   Order $\geq$ 1000 units: \$1.5 per unit

5. A single-period product is priced to sell at \$100 per unit, and its cost is \$70 per unit. Each unsold unit has a salvage value of \$30. Demand is normally distributed with a mean of 1000 units and a standard deviation of 100 units.

   a. How many units should be stocked in order to optimize the profit?
   b. If a 90% service level is desired, what should the stock level be?

6. The Supermart Store is about to place an order for Valentine's Day candy. The candy can be bought for $1.40 per box, and it is sold for $2.90 per box up to Valentine's Day. After Valentine's Day, any remaining boxes of candy are sold for $1 per box. All surplus candy can be sold at this reduced price. Demand for the candy at the regular retail price is a random variable with the following discrete probability distribution:

Demand (boxes)	Probability
100	.15
150	.15
180	.15
200	.20
250	.15
300	.10
330	.10

a. Determine the expected demand for boxes of candy at the regular retail price.
b. Determine the optimal number of boxes of candy to stock.
c. If the cost of loss of goodwill, $2.10, is incurred when a potential customer cannot buy a box, what is the optimal number of boxes of candy to stock?

15

INVENTORY THEORY 2 (INVT2)

OVERVIEW OF THE INVT2 DECISION SUPPORT SYSTEM

This program solves three inventory control problems: continuous review fixed-order-quantity (FOQ) system, fixed-order-interval (FOI) order-up-to-level system, and optional replenishment (OR) system (also called [s,S] system). All three systems assume demand uncertainty. In INVT2, the allowed demand distributions are normal, uniform, exponential, triangular, Poisson, binomial, geometric, discrete, and Laplace.

FOQ continuously monitors the inventory level. When it hits the designated reorder point (R), order a designated fixed quantity (Q). R and Q can be optimally determined by the program. In a FOI system, inventory (y) is checked at the end of each interval, then you order up to the designated level (S), that is, to order S-y quantity. S can be optimally determined. In an OR system, inventory (y) is also checked at the end of each interval, but you order up to S only when y is less than or equal to a prescribed s. You may also assign values for the decision parameters of any of the three systems and let the program perform analysis.

A spreadsheet is used for entering the data. The program has options to save, read, modify, and print the input data. After the solution has been obtained, you may display, print, or save it.

TECHNICAL NOTES ON THE INVT2 PROGRAM

1. INVT2 assumes that demand is stochastic and uncertain and may follow any of the distributions in Table 15-1. Unless specified, the rest of the system parameters are assumed deterministic. For example, lead time of order or setup is assumed constant. When specifying a demand distribution in data entry, the first three letters are required. In particular, the Laplace probability density function is given as follows:

   $f(x) = e^{-|x-\mu|/b}/(2b)$, where x is the demand, μ is the mean, and variance $= 2b^2$.

Table 15-1. Possible demand distributions.

Distribution	Parameters 1, 2, and/or 3
Normal	Mean, standard deviation
Uniform	Lower bound, upper bound
Exponential	Mean
Triangular	Lower bound, mode, upper bound
Poisson	Mean
Binomial	n, p
Geometric	p
Discrete	Mean, number of discrete values
Laplace	Mean, b

2. We will use the following notations to describe the three inventory system.

x: Random number for demand
f(x): Density function of x
F(X): Cumulative probability function of x, $F(X) = Pr(x \leq X)$
E(z): Expected value of variable z over the density function f(x)
y: Inventory level
Q: Order quantity
R: Reorder point
T: Review cycle time for FOI and OR systems
M: Order-up-to-level for FOI and OR systems
D: Average demand in a period, i.e., $D = E(x)$
C: Unit acquisition cost
H: Unit holding cost
K: Order or setup cost
S: Unit shortage cost
V: Inventory review cost for FOI and OR systems
L: Order or setup lead time
EOQ: Economic order quantity

3. Continuous review fixed-order-quantity (FOQ) system is also called order-point, order-quantity (R,Q) system, reorder point (ROP) system, or simply Q system. It continuously monitors the inventory position (y); when y becomes less than or equal to R, order the fixed quantity Q. The major parameters of the FOQ are Q and R. The goal of the system is to find appropriate Q and R in order to minimize the inventory related costs. For the FOQ system, INVT2 computes the following performance measures for a planning period:

N: Expected shortage during the lead time (L)
SL: Service level, i.e., the probability of serving customer during lead time

OC: Total expected ordering or setup cost, OC = K * D/Q

HC: Total expected holding cost, HC = H * (Q/2+R-D*L) if shortage is backordered, HC = H * (Q/2+R-D*L+N) if shortage is lost

SC: Total expected shortage cost, SC = S * N * D/Q

MC: Total expected material acquisition cost, MC = C * D if shortage is backordered, MC = C * (D − N * D/Q) if shortage is lost

SS: Safety stock, SS = R − D * L

Expected maximum inventory = Q + R − D * L

Expected minimum inventory = SS

TC: Total cost = OC + HC + SC + MC

The procedure to obtain the optimal Q and R for the FOQ system works as follows:

Step 0. Set Q = EOQ, ε = a small tolerance.

Step 1. Let F(R) = 1 − (H*Q)/(S*D) if shortage is backordered, or F(R) = 1/(1+(H*Q)/(S*D)) if shortage is lost.

Step 2. Solve R, determine N.

Step 3. Compute Q′ = SQR(2*D*(K+S*N)/H), where SQR represents square root.

Step 4. If $|Q-Q'| \le \varepsilon$, stop; otherwise, let Q = Q′ and go to step 1.

4. Periodic review fixed-order-interval (FOI) system is also called replenishment cycle system, or simply P system. Each T period, it periodically checks the inventory position (y) and orders up to the level of M, that is, order quantity equals to M−y. The major parameters of the FOI are M and T. The goal of the system is to find appropriate T and M in order to minimize the inventory related costs. For the FOI system, INVT2 computes the following performance measures for a planning period:

N: Expected shortage during the cycle + lead time (T+L)

SL: Service level, i.e., the probability of serving customer during cycle + lead time

OC: Total expected ordering or setup cost, OC = K/T

VC: Total review cost, VC = V/T

HC: Total expected holding cost, HC = H * (M−D*L−D*T/2) if shortage is backordered, HC = H * (M−D*L−D*T/2+N) if shortage is lost

SC: Total expected shortage cost, SC = S * N / T

MC: Total expected material acquisition cost, MC = C * D if shortage is backordered, MC = C * (D − N / T) if shortage is lost

SS: Safety stock, SS = M − D * (T+L)

Expected maximum inventory = M − D * L

Expected minimum inventory = SS

TC: Total cost = OC + VC + HC + SC + MC

The procedure to obtain the optimal M and T for the FOI system works as follows:

Step 0. Set Q = EOQ, T = EOQ/D.

Step 1. Let $F_{L+T}(M) = 1-$ (H*T)/S if shortage is backordered, or $F_{L+T}(M)$ = 1/(1+(H*T)/S) if shortage is lost.

Step 2. Solve M, determine N, compute TC.

Step 3. Let $T_1 = 0.01T$ and $T_2 = 10T$.

Step 4. Search between T_1 and T_2 to obtain the best set of M and T that minimizes the total cost TC.

INVT2 uses a golden section search method in Step 4 to find the optimal M and T.

5. Optional replenishment (OR) system is also called optional review, min-max, or simply (s,S) system. Each T period, it periodically checks the inventory position (y) and if y is less than or equal to the reorder point R, then you order up to the level of M, that is, order quantity equals to M−y; otherwise, do nothing. The major parameters of the OR are M, R, and T. The goal of the system is to find appropriate M, R, and T in order to minimize the inventory related costs. For the OR system, INVT2 computes the following performance measures for a planning period:

N: Expected shortage

SL: Service level, i.e., the probability of inventory available when a customer arrives

OC: Total expected ordering or setup cost

VC: Total review cost, VC = V/T

HC: Total expected holding cost, HC = H * (M−D*L+R−D*T/2)/2 if shortage is backordered, HC = H * (M−D*L+R−D*T/2+2N)/2 if shortage is lost

SC: Total expected shortage cost, SC = S * N / T

MC: Total expected material acquisition cost, MC = C * D if shortage is backordered, MC = C * (D − N / T) if shortage is lost

SS: Safety stock to maintain service level SL

R: Reorder point, R = SS + D * T / 2

M: Order-up-to-level, M = Q + SS

Expected maximum inventory = M − D * L

Expected minimum inventory = SS

TC: Total cost = OC + VC + HC + SC + MC

The procedure to obtain the optimal M, R, and T for the OR system works as follows:

Step 0. Set Q = EOQ, T = EOQ/D.

Step 1. Let $F_{L+T}(R) = 1-$ (H*T)/S if shortage is backordered, or $F_{L+T}(R)$ = 1/(1+(H*T)/S) if shortage is lost.

Step 2. Solve R, SS = R− D*T/2, M = Q + SS, determine N, compute TC.

Step 3. Let T_1 = 0.01T and T_2 = 10T.

Step 4. Search between T_1 and T_2 to obtain the best set of M, T, and R (Q = D*T) to minimize the total cost TC.

INVT2 uses a golden section search method in Step 4 to find the optimal M, R, and T.

6. Input data for the three inventory systems include:
— Demand distribution and parameters
— Unit acquisition cost
— Order or setup cost
— Unit holding cost per period
— Unit shortage cost
— Lead time
— Review cost per review for FOI and OR systems

MENU STRUCTURE

The functions and options in each of the pull-down menus are hierarchically listed as follows:

- Modules
  - Linear Programming (LP)
  - Integer Linear Programming (ILP)
  - Goal Programming (GP)
  - Quadratic Programming (QP)
  - Nonlinear Programming (NLP)
  - Dynamic Programming (DP)
  - Transportation and Transshipment (TRP)
  - Assignment and Traveling Salesman (ASTS)
  - Specialized Network Modeling (SNET)
  - Capacitated Network Flow Modeling (CNET)
  - Project Scheduling: CPM/PERT
  - Inventory Theory (INVT)
  - Inventory Theory 2 (INVT2)
  - Queuing Theory (QUEUE)
  - Queuing System Simulation (QSIM)
  - Decision Analysis (DA)
  - Markov Process (MKV)
  - Time Series Forecasting (TSFC)
  - Financial Analysis (FA)
  - Exit from QSB
- Input Data
  - Data Entry

- Read a File
- Show Data
- Print Data
- Modify Data
- Save
- Save As
- Exit from QSB

Solution
- Solve the Problem
- Assign Decision Values
- Show the Solution
- Print the Solution
- Save the Solution

Options
- Color
- Monochrome
- Printer Selection

Help — INVT2
- About INVT2
- About the User Interface
- About the Edit Keys

SOLVING PROBLEMS WITH INVT2

In the following sections, we will use example problems to show how to enter and solve the problems. The general procedure and menu options are described in detail in the tutorial sections of Chapter 2.

Example—Continuous Review Fixed-Order-Quantity (FOQ)

Consider a continuously reviewed electronic item MZ586. The cost information follows: unit cost = \$50, holding cost = \$10 per unit per year, shortage cost = \$20 per unit, and order cost = \$100. Shortages are backordered and delivered later on. Annual demand of the item is normally distributed with mean 1000 units and standard deviation of 100 units. It takes about a month to receive the shipment of an order; that is, the lead time is a month, or 0.083333 (1/12) year. Determine the reorder point and order quantity to minimize the total costs. With the optimal reorder point and order quantity, what is the expected service level?

Enter the Problem

1. Select "Data Entry" from the "Input Data" menu (refer to Chapter 2 for selecting a menu item).

2. Fig. 15-1 shows the problem specification. Note that "Continuous Review Fixed-Order-Quantity System" is selected for the problem type.
3. Fig. 15-2 shows the data entry. Note that the shortage item is specified to be backordered (backlogged).

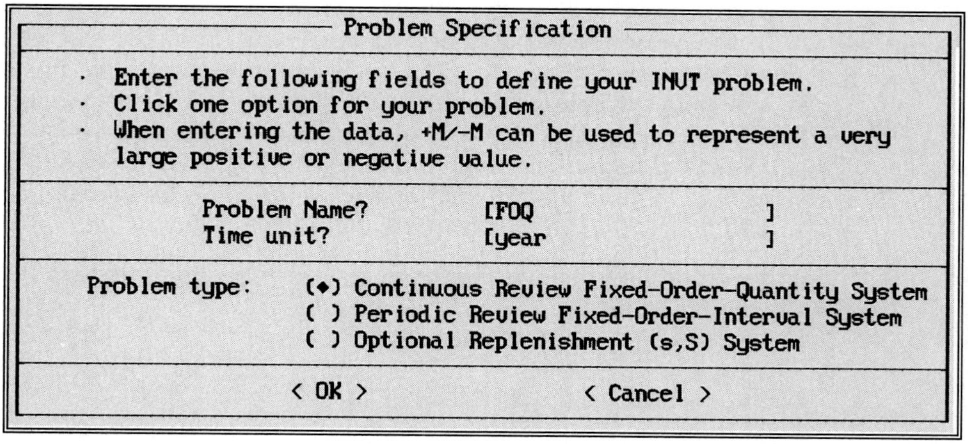

Figure 15-1. Problem specification for the FOQ problem.

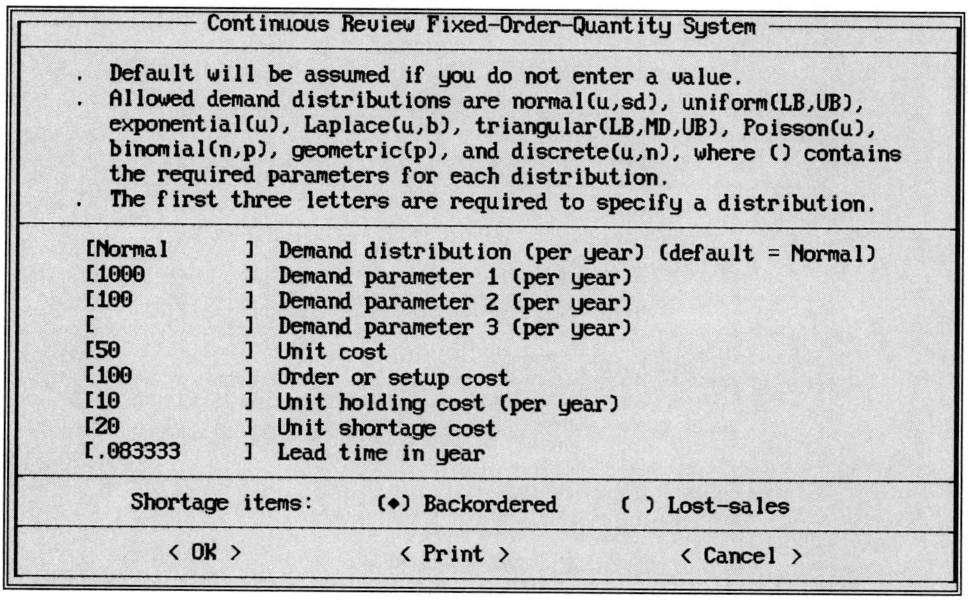

Figure 15-2. Entry for the FOQ problem.

Solve the Problem

1. Select "Solve the Problem" from the "Solution" menu to solve the problem. The message "Please standby . . ." will display for a short period while the problem is being solved.
2. After the problem is solved, select "Show the Solution" from the "Solution" menu to display the FOQ analysis. Fig. 15-3 shows the result. Note that the expected service level is about 92.09%.
3. You can also choose "Assign Decision Values" from the "Solution" menu to analyze the inventory cost with assigned decision parameters. Fig. 15-4 demonstrates an example to assign the order quantity of 200 and the reorder point of 100. After pressing the "OK" button, then select "Show the Solution" from the "Solution" menu to display the analysis (Fig. 15-5). The service level is obtained at 71.81%. Note that you may assign a service level and order quantity in Fig. 15-4 and let the program compute the reorder point.

FOQ Analysis for FOQ – Optimal

08-23-1993 17:02:30 Page: 1 of 1

Input Data	Value	Input Data	Value
Demand distribution	Normal		
Average demand per year	1000	Standard deviation	100
Unit acquisition cost	50	Order or setup cost	100
Unit shortage cost	20	Shortage are	Backlogged
Unit holding cost	10	Lead time in year	.083333
Average lead time demand	83.333	Standard deviation	28.86746

Optimal Order Qty. =	154.8005	Cost per year:	
Reorder Point =	124.3248	Order/Setup Cost =	645.9929
Minimum Inventory =	40.99178	Holding Cost =	1183.92
Maximum Inventory =	195.7923	Shortage Cost =	130.8855
Safety Stock =	40.99178	Subtotal =	1960.799
Expected Shortage Qty. =	1.013057	Material Cost =	50000
Service Level (%) =	92.08915	Total Cost =	51960.8

Elapsed CPU seconds = 0.058593

< PageDown > < PageUp > < Hardcopy > < Cancel >

Figure 15-3. FOQ analysis.

Enter Decision Values for FOQ

- Default is the optimal value.
- Enter the reorder point (R) or service level, but not both. If you enter the reorder point, the program will calculate the service level and vice versa.

Enter your order quantity: [200]
Enter the reorder point: [100]
Enter the desired service level (%): [ ]

< OK > < Default > < Cancel >

Figure 15-4. Decision parameters for FOQ.

FOQ Analysis for FOQ – Assigned Qty.

08-23-1993 17:03:49 Page: 1 of 1

Input Data	Value	Input Data	Value
Demand distribution	Normal		
Average demand per year	1000	Standard deviation	100
Unit acquisition cost	50	Order or setup cost	100
Unit shortage cost	20	Shortage are	Backlogged
Unit holding cost	10	Lead time in year	.083333
Average lead time demand	83.333	Standard deviation	28.86746

Assigned Order Qty. =	200	Cost per year:	
Assigned Reorder Point =	100	Order/Setup Cost =	500
Minimum Inventory =	16.667	Holding Cost =	1166.67
Maximum Inventory =	216.667	Shortage Cost =	505.0662
Safety Stock =	16.667	Subtotal =	2171.736
Expected Shortage Qty. =	5.050662	Material Cost =	50000
Service Level (%) =	71.81418	Total Cost =	52171.73

Elapsed CPU seconds = 0

< PageDown > < PageUp > < Hardcopy > < Cancel >

Figure 15-5. Revised FOQ analysis.

Example—Periodic Review Fixed-Order-Interval (FOI)

Suppose the review process of the item MZ586 has been changed to periodic review. Assuming that the review costs very little (almost nothing), determine the order-up-level and the review interval to minimize the total cost.

Enter the Problem

1. Select "Data Entry" from the "Input Data" menu.
2. Fig. 15-6 shows the problem specification. Note that "Periodic Review Fixed-Order-Interval System" is selected for the problem type.

Problem Specification

- Enter the following fields to define your INUT problem.
- Click one option for your problem.
- When entering the data, +M/-M can be used to represent a very large positive or negative value.

Problem Name? [FOI]
Time unit? [year]

Problem type: ( ) Continuous Review Fixed-Order-Quantity System
(•) Periodic Review Fixed-Order-Interval System
( ) Optional Replenishment (s,S) System

< OK > < Cancel >

Figure 15-6. Problem specification for the FOI problem.

3. Fig. 15-7 shows the data entry. Note that the shortage item is specified to be backordered (backlogged).

```
Periodic Review Fixed-Order-Interval System

 . Default will be assumed if you do not enter a value.
 . Allowed demand distributions are normal(u,sd), uniform(LB,UB),
   exponential(u), Laplace(u,b), triangular(LB,MD,UB), Poisson(u),
   binomial(n,p), geometric(p), and discrete(u,n), where () contains
   the required parameters for each distribution.
 . The first three letters are required to specify a distribution.

[Normal      ] Demand distribution (per year) (default = Normal)
[1000        ] Demand parameter 1 (per year)
[100         ] Demand parameter 2 (per year)
[            ] Demand parameter 3 (per year)
[50          ] Unit cost
[100         ] Order or setup cost
[10          ] Unit holding cost (per year)
[20          ] Unit shortage cost
[.083333     ] Lead time in year
[            ] Review cost per review

   Shortage items:      (•) Backordered      ( ) Lost-sales

        < OK >            < Print >            < Cancel >
```

Figure 15-7. Entry for the FOI problem.

Solve the Problem

1. Select "Solve the Problem" from the "Solution" menu to solve the problem.The message "Please standby . . ." will display for a short period while the problem is being solved.
2. After the problem is solved, select "Show the Solution" from the "Solution" menu to display the FOI analysis. Fig. 15-8 shows the result. The expected service level is 93.29%, and the review cycle is 0.134 year, or 1.61 month. The total cost is higher than that of FOQ.
3. You can also choose "Assign Decision Values" from the "Solution" menu to analyze the inventory cost with assigned decision parameters. Fig. 15-9 demonstrates an example that reviews the inventory every month (0.08333 year) and requires 90% service level. After pressing the "OK" button, select "Show the Solution" from the "Solution" menu to display the analysis (Fig. 15-10). The new order-up-to-level is 219.33. Note that you may assign the order-up-to-level and order cycle in Fig. 15-9 and let the program compute the service level.

FOI Analysis for FOI - Optimal

08-23-1993 17:06:02 Page: 1 of 1

Input Data	Value	Input Data	Value
Demand distribution	Normal		
Average demand per year	1000	Standard deviation	100
Unit acquisition cost	50	Order + review cost	100
Unit shortage cost	20	Shortage are	Backlogged
Unit holding cost	10	Lead time in year	.083333
Cycle+lead time demand	217.5103	Standard deviation	46.63799

Best Order-Up-To Qty. =	287.4673	Cost per year:	
Review Cycle in year =	.1341773	Order + Review Cost =	745.2828
Minimum Inventory =	69.957	Holding Cost =	1370.456
Maximum Inventory =	204.1342	Shortage Cost =	203.7874
Safety Stock =	69.957	Subtotal =	2319.527
Expected Shortage Qty. =	1.367182	Material Cost =	50000
Service Level (%) =	93.29114	Total Cost =	52319.53

Elapsed CPU seconds = .109375

< PageDown > < PageUp > < Hardcopy > < Cancel >

Figure 15-8. FOI analysis.

Enter Decision Values for FOI

- Default is the optimal value.
- Enter the order-up-to-level (M) or service level, but not both. If you enter the order-up-to-level, the program will calculate the service level and vice versa.

Enter the review cycle in year: [.083333]
Enter the order-up-to-level: [ ]
Enter the desired service level (%): [90]

< OK > < Default > < Cancel >

Figure 15-9. Decision parameters for FOI.

FOI Analysis for FOI - Assigned Qty.

08-23-1993 17:07:17 Page: 1 of 1

Input Data	Value	Input Data	Value
Demand distribution	Normal		
Average demand per year	1000	Standard deviation	100
Unit acquisition cost	50	Order + review cost	100
Unit shortage cost	20	Shortage are	Backlogged
Unit holding cost	10	Lead time in year	.083333
Cycle+lead time demand	166.666	Standard deviation	40.82475

Assigned Order-Up-To =	219.3299	Cost per year:	
Review Cycle in year =	.083333	Order + Review Cost =	1200.005
Minimum Inventory =	52.66393	Holding Cost =	943.3042
Maximum Inventory =	135.9969	Shortage Cost =	455.7758
Safety Stock =	52.66393	Subtotal =	2599.085
Expected Shortage Qty. =	1.899058	Material Cost =	50000
Service Level (%) =	90	Total Cost =	52599.09

Elapsed CPU seconds = 0

< PageDown > < PageUp > < Hardcopy > < Cancel >

Figure 15-10. Revised FOI analysis.

Example—Optional Replenishment (s,S) System (ORsS)

If the inventory management of the item MZ586 has been changed to optional replenishment system, which means periodic review and order only when inventory is below the reorder point, determine the order-up-level, the reorder point, and the review interval to minimize the total cost.

Enter the Problem

1. Select "Data Entry" from the "Input Data" menu.
2. Fig. 15-11 shows the problem specification. Note that "Optional Replenishment (s,S) System" is selected for the problem type.
3. Fig. 15-12 shows the data entry. Note that the shortage item is specified to be backordered (backlogged).

```
                         Problem Specification

  .  Enter the following fields to define your INVT problem.
  .  Click one option for your problem.
  .  When entering the data, +M/-M can be used to represent a very
     large positive or negative value.

          Problem Name?          [ORsS                  ]
          Time unit?             [year                  ]

  Problem type:    ( ) Continuous Review Fixed-Order-Quantity System
                   ( ) Periodic Review Fixed-Order-Interval System
                   (•) Optional Replenishment (s,S) System

                   < OK >                  < Cancel >
```

Figure 15-11. Problem specification for the ORsS problem.

```
                  Optional Replenishment (s,S) System

  .  Default will be assumed if you do not enter a value.
  .  Allowed demand distributions are normal(u,sd), uniform(LB,UB),
     exponential(u), Laplace(u,b), triangular(LB,MD,UB), Poisson(u),
     binomial(n,p), geometric(p), and discrete(u,n), where () contains
     the required parameters for each distribution.
  .  The first three letters are required to specify a distribution.

  [Normal      ]  Demand distribution (per year) (default = Normal)
  [1000        ]  Demand parameter 1 (per year)
  [100         ]  Demand parameter 2 (per year)
  [            ]  Demand parameter 3 (per year)
  [50          ]  Unit cost
  [100         ]  Order or setup cost
  [10          ]  Unit holding cost (per year)
  [20          ]  Unit shortage cost
  [.083333     ]  Lead time in year
  [            ]  Review cost per review

     Shortage items:      (•) Backordered        ( ) Lost-sales

        < OK >              < Print >              < Cancel >
```

Figure 15-12. Entry for the ORsS problem.

Solve the Problem

1. Select "Solve the Problem" from the "Solution" menu to solve the problem. The message "Please standby . . ." will display for a short period while the problem is being solved.
2. After the problem is solved, select "Show the Solution" from the "Solution" menu to display the ORsS analysis. Fig. 15-13 shows the result. The expected service level is 97.81%, the review cycle is 0.103 year or 1.24 month, and the reorder point is 256.92. The total cost is the highest among the three systems.
3. You can also choose "Assign Decision Values" from the "Solution" menu to analyze the inventory cost with assigned decision parameters. Fig. 15-14 demonstrates an example to review the inventory every month (0.08333 year) and set the order-up-to-level at 300 and the reorder point at 150. After pressing the "OK" button, then select "Show the Solution" from the "Solution" menu to display the analysis (Fig. 15-15). The service level is only 65.35%.

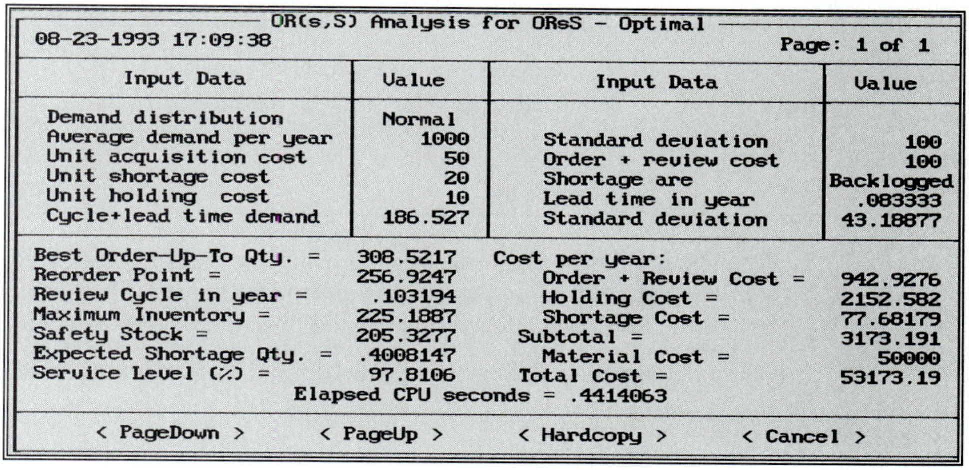

OR(s,S) Analysis for ORsS – Optimal

08-23-1993 17:09:38 Page: 1 of 1

Input Data	Value	Input Data	Value
Demand distribution	Normal		
Average demand per year	1000	Standard deviation	100
Unit acquisition cost	50	Order + review cost	100
Unit shortage cost	20	Shortage are	Backlogged
Unit holding cost	10	Lead time in year	.083333
Cycle+lead time demand	186.527	Standard deviation	43.18877

Best Order-Up-To Qty. =	308.5217	Cost per year:	
Reorder Point =	256.9247	Order + Review Cost =	942.9276
Review Cycle in year =	.103194	Holding Cost =	2152.582
Maximum Inventory =	225.1887	Shortage Cost =	77.68179
Safety Stock =	205.3277	Subtotal =	3173.191
Expected Shortage Qty. =	.4008147	Material Cost =	50000
Service Level (%) =	97.8106	Total Cost =	53173.19

Elapsed CPU seconds = .4414063

< PageDown > < PageUp > < Hardcopy > < Cancel >

Figure 15-13. ORsS analysis.

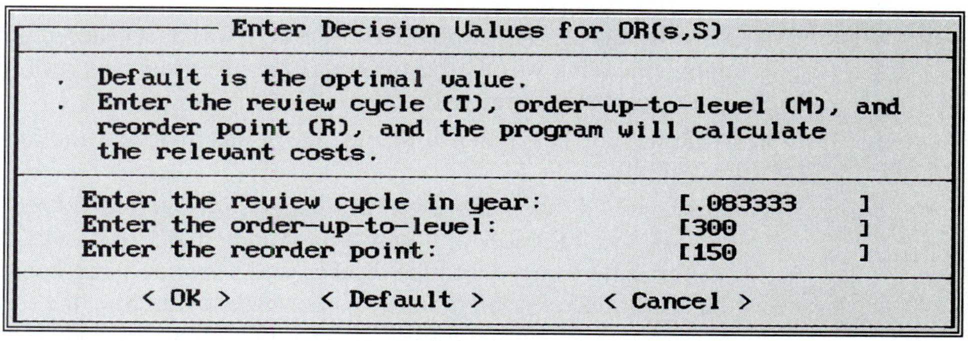

Enter Decision Values for OR(s,S)

. Default is the optimal value.
. Enter the review cycle (T), order-up-to-level (M), and reorder point (R), and the program will calculate the relevant costs.

Enter the review cycle in year:	[.083333]
Enter the order-up-to-level:	[300]
Enter the reorder point:	[150]

< OK > < Default > < Cancel >

Figure 15-14. Decision parameters for ORsS.

OR(s,S) Analysis for ORsS - Assigned Qty.

08-23-1993 17:10:54 Page: 1 of 1

Input Data	Value	Input Data	Value
Demand distribution	Normal		
Average demand per year	1000	Standard deviation	100
Unit acquisition cost	50	Order + review cost	100
Unit shortage cost	20	Shortage are	Backlogged
Unit holding cost	10	Lead time in year	.083333
Cycle+lead time demand	166.666	Standard deviation	40.82475

Assigned Order-Up-To =	300	Cost per year:	
Assigned Reorder Point =	150	Order + Review Cost =	544.0161
Review Cycle in year =	.083333	Holding Cost =	1625.002
Maximum Inventory =	216.667	Shortage Cost =	1850.809
Safety Stock =	108.3335	Subtotal =	4019.827
Expected Shortage Qty. =	7.711672	Material Cost =	50000
Service Level (%) =	65.35375	Total Cost =	54019.83

Elapsed CPU seconds = 0

< PageDown > < PageUp > < Hardcopy > < Cancel >

Figure 15-15. Revised ORsS analysis.

EXERCISES

1. Intelligent Satellite (IS) was the only company that supplied satellite receiver service to households in the Atlanta metropolitan area. Management had estimated the following information related to satellite receiver inventory:

Annual demand = 5000, normally distributed with standard deviation of 500

Order cost = \$250

Unit acquisition cost = \$200

Annual holding cost per unit = \$48

Unit shortage cost = \$30

Order lead time = 0.08333 year (one month)

a. Since IS was the only supplier, the shortage was backordered until the next shipment. What was the best policy if the inventory was reviewed and ordered every fixed time interval?

b. What was the best policy if the inventory was reviewed and ordered every half month?

c. After the FCC opened a few more channels for satellite TV program transmission, satellite receiver business has boomed in recent years. Many competitors have jumped into the local as well as national markets. Therefore, the unsatisfied customers can go somewhere to purchase the receiver. That is, the shortage will no longer be backordered and will cost the company \$300 in lost sales. If the demand remains almost the same as before, determine a new inventory policy to maintain a 95% service level if the inventory is still reviewed every half month.

d. Management has learned that air cargo shipping has become cheaper and more available recently. Almost all satellite receivers are made in the Far East. If shipped by air flight, it is estimated the lead will be reduced by half. However, the order cost, which includes shipping cost will be doubled too. Following (c), what is the best inventory policy?

e. Following (d), if a computer system is proposed for real time inventory monitoring, what is the best inventory policy?

f. Following (e), if the order quantity obtained in (e) is maintained and service level is set at 95%, what is the reorder point?

2. As the manager of Super Teen Hot Shop, Pete Montro manages popular items for teens with a very simple mechanism. For example, he checks the Bugle Bingo T-shirts every half month. If the inventory is lower than 100, he orders up to 150; otherwise, he does nothing. Below is the information related to Bugle Bingo T-shirts.

Monthly demand = uniform distribution from 75 to 150

Order cost = $100

Unit acquisition cost = $30

Monthly holding cost per unit = $8

Unit shortage cost = $50

Order lead time = half month

a. Determine the inventory related costs and service level for Pete Montro's current method if shortages can not be backordered.

b. If Pete is willing to change his method to a pure FOI mechanism, recommend a new inventory policy for him.

c. A computer system that can monitor the inventory instantly and order as necessary is proposed. If it is adopted, Bugle Bingo T-shirts may need to share the cost of the system estimated at about $100 a month. Compared to (b), how much is the saving if the computer system is used to review the inventory continuously and Bugle Bingo T-shirts are the only concern?

16

QUEUING THEORY (QUEUE)

OVERVIEW OF THE QUEUE DECISION SUPPORT SYSTEM

This program analyzes several popular queuing problems. For example, a single or multiple server system with an infinite or a finite queue, with an infinite or a finite population, and with various service-time distributions can be analyzed. The program will display the analysis using conventional queuing terminology and performance measures: arrival rate, service rate, utilization rate, average number of customers in the system, average number of customers in the queue, average time a customer spends in the system, average time a customer waits in the queue, and probabilities related to the system status. The program also computes the queuing system costs including server, waiting, and balking costs.

You may enter a problem from the keyboard or read the problem from a disk(ette). QUEUE enables you to display, save, modify, and solve your queuing problem. After the model has been solved, the results can be displayed, printed, or saved.

TECHNICAL NOTES ON THE QUEUE PROGRAM

1. The queuing problems that can be solved by QUEUE are *M/M/1, M/G/1, D/M/1, M/M/s, M/M/s/K, M/M/s/N, M/M/s/K/N, M/G/Infinity, M(b)/M/1,* and *M/M/s/s* problems.
2. The pressure service and discouraged arrival are allowed for any of the *M/M/s* and *M/M/s/K/N* systems. Let a represent the pressure coefficient and b represent the discourage coefficient, then the service rate and arrival rate will be as follows:

   $u = s*u_0*(n/s)^a$, for $n \geq s$

   $\lambda = \lambda_0*(s/(n+1))^b$, for $n \geq s$

   where s is the number of servers, u_0 is the individual service rate without pressure, n is the number of customers, and λ_0 is the arrival rate without discouragement.

3. Bulk arrival (i.e., arrival with more than one customer at the same time) is allowed only for the M/M/1 system.
4. Poisson, constant, and general distributions are allowed to define the service or arrival pattern. General distribution means that only its mean and standard deviation are known; its distribution pattern is unknown. Based on the entry of service and arrival distributions, the program will classify the problem and check if a close form solution is available. If not, no queuing analysis will be provided in this program. For the queuing system without a theoretical close form solution, we recommend to use the queuing simulation (QSIM) program described in Chapter 17 to analyze it.
5. When the maximum number of customers allowed in the system is more than 10,000, it is assumed that the system has an infinite queue. When the maximum number of customers in the population is more than 10,000, it is assumed that the system has an infinite population.
6. When the queuing system has a finite input source, the arrival rate is correspondent to the individual customer arrival rate, not to the population arrival rate.
7. After the problem is solved, the program can display up to 200 probabilities.
8. Balking occurs when the system has a finite queue and when all the queue spaces are occupied. Let k represent the maximum number of customers allowed in the system, that is, the queue length plus the number of servers. The arrival customer will be balked with the probability of P_k, which is the probability of k customers in the system.
9. Let

C_s:	Average server cost per unit time
C_w:	Average customer cost per unit time in the system
C_b:	Average cost of a balked customer
L:	Average number of customers in the system
TC:	Total queuing system cost per unit time

then

$$TC = C_s * s + C_w * L + C_b * P_k * \lambda$$

MENU STRUCTURE

The functions and options in each of the pull-down menus are hierarchically listed as follows:

Modules
- Linear Programming (LP)
- Integer Linear Programming (ILP)
- Goal Programming (GP)
- Quadratic Programming (QP)

- Nonlinear Programming (NLP)
- Dynamic Programming (DP)
- Transportation and Transshipment (TRP)
- Assignment and Traveling Salesman (ASTS)
- Specialized Network Modeling (SNET)
- Capacitated Network Flow Modeling (CNET)
- Project Scheduling: CPM/PERT
- Inventory Theory (INVT)
- Inventory Theory 2 (INVT2)
- Queuing Theory (QUEUE)
- Queuing System Simulation (QSIM)
- Decision Analysis (DA)
- Markov Process (MKV)
- Time Series Forecasting (TSFC)
- Financial Analysis (FA)
- Exit from QSB

Input Data
- Data Entry
- Read a File
- Show Data
- Print Data
- Modify Data
- Save
- Save As
- Exit from QSB

Solution
- Solve the Problem
- Show the Solution
- Print the Solution
- Save the Solution

Options
- Color
- Monochrome
- Printer Selection

Help — QUEUE
- About QUEUE
- About the User Interface
- About the Edit Keys

SOLVING PROBLEMS WITH QUEUE

In the following sections, we will use example problems to show how to enter and solve the problems. The general procedure and menu options are described in detail in the tutorial sections of Chapter 2.

Example—*M/M/1* System

A transportation company has a load/unload team to serve its truck fleet. The service time of load/unload is exponentially distributed with a mean of 20 minutes per truck. The trucks arrive at the load/unload area in a Poisson distribution with a mean of two trucks per hour. Management wants to evaluate the expected performance of the load/unload system. Assume that the team costs $200 per hour. A truck in the process of load or unload or in waiting will lose its productivity, and it is estimated to cost $50 per hour.

Enter the Problem

1. Select "Data Entry" from the "Input Data" menu (refer to Chapter 2 for selecting a menu item).
2. Fig. 16-1 shows the problem specification. Note that "hour" has been entered for the time unit.
3. Fig. 16-2 shows the data entry. Note that the default has been used for many data items.

Arrival rate (λ) = 2 per hour

Service rate (u) = 3 per hour

Number of servers (s) = 1

```
                        Problem Specification
 . Enter the following fields to define your queuing problem.
 . When entering the data, +M/M can be used to represent a very
   large positive or infinite value.

      Problem Name?            [Truck                 ]
      Time unit?               [hour                  ]

      < OK >             < Print >             < Cancel >
```

Figure 16-1. Problem specification of Truck.

```
                   Queuing Data Entry for Truck
 . Default will be assumed if you do not enter a value.
 . For the distribution, enter 1 for Poisson (exponential time),  2 for
   constant, and 3 for general with a specified standard deviation.

 [1          ] Number of servers
 [3          ] Service rate (mu) per server per hour
 [1          ] Distribution of service time
 [           ] Standard deviation of service time in hours
 [           ] Service pressure coefficient
 [2          ] Arrival rate (lambda) per hour
 [1          ] Distribution of interarrival time
 [           ] Standard deviation of interarrival time in hours
 [           ] Arrival discouraged coefficient
 [1          ] Bulk arrival size
 [           ] Standard deviation of bulk arrival size
 [M          ] Maximum number of customers allowed in the system
 [M          ] Number of customers in the population
 [200        ] Average cost per server per hour
 [50         ] Average waiting cost per customer per hour
 [           ] Average cost a customer can not enter the queue (balking)

      < OK >             < Print >             < Cancel >
```

Figure 16-2. Data entry for problem Truck.

Solve the Problem

1. Select "Solve the Problem" from the "Solution" menu to solve the problem. The message "Please standby . . ." will display for a short period while the problem is being solved.
2. After the problem is solved, select "Show the Solution" from the "Solution" menu to display the queuing analysis. Fig. 16-3 shows the result. No balking cost is incurred since the system is assumed to have infinite space.
3. From Fig. 16-3, you may choose "Show Probabilities" to display the probabilities of the queuing system. Fig. 16-4 illustrates the probabilities of 0 to 29 customers in the system.

Queuing Performance for Truck

08-23-1993 17:13:47

The System is M/M/1

Customer arrival rate (lambda)	=	2 per hour
Service rate per server (mu)	=	3 per hour
Overall system effective arrival rate	=	2 per hour
Overall system effective service rate	=	2 per hour
Overall system effective utilization factor	=	.6666667
Average number of customers in the system (L)	=	2
Average number of customers in the queue (Lq)	=	1.333333
Average time of a customer in the system (W)	=	1 hour
Average time of a customer in the queue (Wq)	=	.6666666 hours
The probability that all servers are idle (Po)	=	33.33333 %
The probability an arriving customer waits (Pw)	=	66.66667 %
The total server cost (Cs)	=	$200 per hour
The total customer waiting cost (Cw)	=	$100 per hour
The total customer balking cost (Cb)	=	$0 per hour
The overall total cost	=	$300 per hour

< OK > < Show Probabilities > < HardCopy >

Figure 16-3. Queuing analysis for Truck.

Probability of n Customer in The System

08-23-1993 17:14:30 Page: 1 of 7

Number of Customers(n)	Probability P(n)	Cumulated Probability	Number of Customers(n)	Probability P(n)	Cumulated Probability
0	.333333	.333333	15	0.000761	.998478
1	.222222	.555556	16	0.000507	.998985
2	.148148	.703704	17	0.000338	.999323
3	0.098765	.802469	18	0.000226	.999549
4	0.065844	.868313	19	0.000150	.999699
5	0.043896	.912209	20	0.000100	.999800
6	0.029264	.941472	21	0.000067	.999866
7	0.019509	.960982	22	0.000045	.999911
8	0.013006	.973988	23	0.000030	.999941
9	0.008671	.982658	24	0.000020	.999960
10	0.005781	.988439	25	0.000013	.999974
11	0.003854	.992293	26	0.000009	.999982
12	0.002569	.994862	27	0.000006	.999988
13	0.001713	.996575	28	0.000004	.999992
14	0.001142	.997716	29	0.000003	.999995

< PageDown > < PageUp > < Hardcopy > < Cancel >

Figure 16-4. Probability analysis for Truck.

Example — *M/M/2* System with Finite Queue Space

If the transportation company splits the load/unload team into two identical teams with a service rate of 1.5 trucks per hour each, the *M/M/2* model can be used to solve this problem. However, the company realizes that the space is limited. Only 5 trucks are allowed to enter the system, including 2 trucks in service and 3 waiting for service. The truck that cannot get into the system needs to go to nearby public parking; that is, it is balked. Each balked truck will cost about $60 per hour including parking fee, loss of productivity, and hassle of handling. Determine the system performance.

Enter the Problem

1. Select "Data Entry" from the "Input Data" menu and enter the problem name "Truck2" (Fig. 16-5).
2. Fig. 16-6 shows the data entry. Note that the server cost is $100 per server per hour because of splitting.

Arrival rate (λ) = 2 per hour

Service rate (u) = 1.5 per hour per server

Number of servers (s)= 2

```
                     Problem Specification
 .  Enter the following fields to define your queuing problem.
 .  When entering the data, +M/M can be used to represent a very
    large positive or infinite value.

          Problem Name?          [Truck2               ]
          Time unit?             [hour                 ]

       < OK >               < Print >               < Cancel >
```

Figure 16-5. Problem specification of Truck2.

```
                   Queuing Data Entry for Truck2
 .  Default will be assumed if you do not enter a value.
 .  For the distribution, enter 1 for Poisson (exponential time),  2 for
    constant, and 3 for general with a specified standard deviation.

 [2            ]  Number of servers
 [1.5          ]  Service rate (mu) per server per hour
 [1            ]  Distribution of service time
 [             ]  Standard deviation of service time in hours
 [             ]  Service pressure coefficient
 [2            ]  Arrival rate (lambda) per hour
 [1            ]  Distribution of interarrival time
 [             ]  Standard deviation of interarrival time in hours
 [             ]  Arrival discouraged coefficient
 [1            ]  Bulk arrival size
 [             ]  Standard deviation of bulk arrival size
 [5            ]  Maximum number of customers allowed in the system
 [M            ]  Number of customers in the population
 [100          ]  Average cost per server per hour
 [50           ]  Average waiting cost per customer per hour
 [60           ]  Average cost a customer can not enter the queue (balking)

       < OK >               < Print >               < Cancel >
```

Figure 16-6. Data entry for problem Truck2.

Solve the Problem

1. Select "Solve the Problem" from the "Solution" menu to solve the problem.
2. After the problem is solved, select "Show the Solution" from the "Solution" menu to display the queuing analysis. Fig. 16-7 shows the result.
3. From Fig. 16-7, you may choose "Show Probabilities" to display the probabilities of the queuing system. Fig. 16-8 illustrates the probabilities. Note that the probability of an arrival truck being balked is P_5, which is 0.058878.

```
                    Queuing Performance for Truck2
 08-23-1993 17:16:58

                       The System is M/M/2/5

                  Customer arrival rate (lambda) =          2 per hour
                    Service rate per server (mu) =        1.5 per hour
             Overall system effective arrival rate =   1.882245 per hour
             Overall system effective service rate =   1.882245 per hour
        Overall system effective utilization factor =   .6274149
      Average number of customers in the system (L) =    1.74057
      Average number of customers in the queue (Lq) =   .4857406
       Average time of a customer in the system (W) =   .9247313 hours
       Average time of a customer in the queue (Wq) =   .2580645 hours
     The probability that all servers are idle (Po) =    22.3551 %
   The probability an arriving customer waits (Pw) =   47.83809 %
                        The total server cost (Cs) =       $200 per hour
             The total customer waiting cost (Cw) =   $87.0285 per hour
             The total customer balking cost (Cb) =   $7.06532 per hour
                            The overall total cost =   $294.093 per hour

      < OK >          < Show Probabilities >          < HardCopy >
```

Figure 16-7. *M/M/2/5* queuing performance for problem Truck2.

Probability of n Customer in The System

08-23-1993 17:17:40 Page: 1 of 7

Number of Customers(n)	Probability P(n)	Cumulated Probability	Number of Customers(n)	Probability P(n)	Cumulated Probability
0	.223551	.223551	15	0	1.000000
1	.298068	.521619	16	0	1.000000
2	.198712	.720331	17	0	1.000000
3	.132475	.852806	18	0	1.000000
4	0.088316	.941122	19	0	1.000000
5	0.058878	1.000000	20	0	1.000000
6	0	1.000000	21	0	1.000000
7	0	1.000000	22	0	1.000000
8	0	1.000000	23	0	1.000000
9	0	1.000000	24	0	1.000000
10	0	1.000000	25	0	1.000000
11	0	1.000000	26	0	1.000000
12	0	1.000000	27	0	1.000000
13	0	1.000000	28	0	1.000000
14	0	1.000000	29	0	1.000000

< PageDown > < PageUp > < Hardcopy > < Cancel >

Figure 16-8. *M/M/2/5* probabilities for problem Truck2.

EXERCISES

1. Determine the queuing performance for the following queuing system:

Arrival rate = 5 per hour, Poisson distributed
Number of servers = 1
Service rate = 7 per hour, Poisson distributed
Number of waiting spaces = 10

2. An *M/G/1* queuing system has the following information:

Arrival rate = 1 per minute
Service rate = 1.2 per minute
Standard deviation of service time = 0.9 minute

a. What is the L_q and W_q for this system?

b. What is the probability that an arrival customer will need to wait?

3. NODE Computer Service, Inc., has four engineers to service its 10 mainframes in town. The required service from each mainframe arrives with the mean time of five days exponentially distributed. The expected service time for each service is one day and is exponentially distributed. The company considers adding more engineers when the waiting time for each service is expected to be more than half a day. Should the company add engineers and, if so, how many?

4. Top Bank wants to build a teller service near a downtown area. The company is considering two alternatives. One is to build a booth and hire a clerk. The clerk can serve 30 customers per hour with a Poisson distribution. The other choice is to build an automatic teller machine that can serve almost 30 customers per hour constantly. The clerk is salaried at $5 per hour; the machine costs $7 per hour. The customers will arrive at the teller station with a mean of 20 per hour, Poisson distributed. Assume that a waiting customer will cost the company a $4 loss in good will. Determine the best choice.

5. A new fast-food restaurant has one cash register in operation. On the average, customers arrive at the register at the rate of 10 per hour. The arrival rate is assumed to follow the Poisson distribution. The cashier spends an average of five minutes per customer, with a standard deviation of one minute per customer. Assume an arbitrary distribution for service time.

a. Determine the average waiting time in the queue.

b. Assume that the cashier can service customers at a constant rate of six per half hour. What is the average number of customers in the system?

c. Now assume that the time required to service a customer follows the exponential distribution. The cashier can service six customers per half hour on the average. What is the probability of having fewer than two customers in the system?

6. Video Games, Inc., owns hundreds of video games that are strategically located at stores and shopping malls throughout Houston. When video game machines break down, a maintenance worker is dispatched. Broken machines are fixed on a first-come, first-served basis. Assume that machines break down at an average rate of one per hour, Poisson distributed. Also assume that a broken machine costs the company $4 per hour (lost sales), and a maintenance worker is salaried at $15 per hour.

a. Assume that there is only one maintenance worker, and that the average service time is 30 minutes per machine, with a standard deviation of 6 minutes. On the average, how long will a broken machine be inoperable?

b. Now assume that service time averages 30 minutes and is exponentially distributed. What is the probability of having more than three machines inoperable at one time?

c. Assume that a second maintenance worker is employed who services machines at the same average rate as the first worker. For both workers, the service time averages 30 minutes and is exponentially distributed. What is the total average hourly cost of this system? When compared with the original one-worker system, which is better?

d. Assume now that the workers work together as a single team so that the average service time is 15 minutes per machine (exponentially distributed). What is the total average cost of this system?

7. The Southern Independent Venders Company (SIV) supplies vended food to a large university. Because students kick the machines at every opportunity, management has a constant repair problem. Machines break down at an average rate of four per hour, Poisson distributed. Downtime costs an average of $20 per machine per hour. Each maintenance worker makes $6 per hour. One worker can service a machine in an average of 12 minutes; two workers together can service a machine in an average of 10 minutes; three workers together can service a machine in an average of 6 minutes. All service times are exponentially distributed.

a. On the average, how long would a broken machine be out of service for each crew size (assume workers work together)?

b. If workers work individually, what will be the out-of-service time for a broken machine?

c. What is the optimal work crew size and work relationship?

17

QUEUING SYSTEM SIMULATION (QSIM)

OVERVIEW OF THE QSIM DECISION SUPPORT SYSTEM

This program performs Monte Carlo simulation for multi-stage queuing systems. The stage represents sequential service or operations. You may specify multiple customer types which may require different service times on each stage. Service time may follow different distribution such as exponential, Erlang, uniform, normal, constant, discrete, and so on. When a server finishes with a customer, it sends that customer to the next queue or server and serves another customer waiting in the preceding queue. Each queue has its dispatching rule such as first-in-first-out (FIFO), last-in-first-out (LIFO), random, shortest process time (SPT), and others.

Three types of servers can be specified. A regular server has one input and one output. An assembly server receives multiple inputs and returns one output. A disassembly server decomposes one input into multiple outputs. Use the input/output selection rule to specify the design of server. Customers may arrive in batches or as individuals and follow a specified distribution pattern.

You may enter, read, save, modify, and print the problem and choose to display, print, or save the final analysis. You can choose to run simulation with displaying the system status. However, it will take longer to finish.

TECHNICAL NOTES ON THE QSIM PROGRAM

1. The QSIM program can simulate a multi-stage queuing system with multiple customer types and multiple queues. Each customer type may go through the system with different arrival, waiting, and service patterns. A stage in QSIM represents a service. A multi-stage queuing system has sequential service stations (servers) which customers need to go through.
2. Customers arrive at the queuing system with prescribed interarrival time distribution. QSIM allows you to specify the arrival in individual or in bulk. For bulk arrival, which means multiple customers arrive at the system in bundle at

the same time, you may define a distribution for the batch size. The default batch size is constant 1, that is, arriving singly. QSIM assumes that the customer population is unlimited.

3. QSIM allows you to define different service time distributions for different customer types, if any, at different service stations (servers).
4. Any queuing system in QSIM is defined as a queuing network containing customers (entities), queues, service stations (servers), and connections. An arrival enters a queue or is balked. An available or idle server chooses a customer from a queue or queues that connect to it. A customer who has finished a service from a server enters a followed queue or leaves the system. To define a queuing network, QSIM allows you to specify the arrival to queue connections, queue to server connections, and server to queue connections. These connections uniquely define the possible customer flows in the queuing network. When entering your queuing problem into QSIM, it is recommended to draw a schematic network diagram to help you define the connections.
5. Queue is an important component to define a queuing network. It represents a buffer between the arrival and the first server and between successive servers. There is no queue after the last service station (server) in the network. The default queue capacity is 100 in QSIM. However, you may specify the capacity from 0 to a large number. For the purpose of memory saving, use as small a queue capacity as possible. A queue with capacity 0 represents a direct connection without a buffer.
6. After a customer finishes service at a server, it will leave the system if the server is the last sequence, or it will join a queue waiting for the next server, or it will be balked and stay at the current server if the next queue is full. If the served customer is going to join the next queue, you may assign a fixed transfer time before it arrives at the next queue. The default transfer time of the server to queue connections is 0.
7. QSIM always assumes two components, fixed and deviation, to define an interarrival time, service time, or batch size. The fixed component (d) usually is non-negative and represents a constant component for the interarrival time, service time, or batch size. The deviation (x) follows a probability distribution. Therefore, a sample or observation of an interarrival time, a service time, or a batch size is equal to $d + x$.
8. The probability functions allowed in QSIM and their parameters are listed in Table 17-1. The probability density function, f(x), is briefly defined below.

Table 17-1. Possible distribution functions and parameters.

Distribution	Parameter 1	Parameter 2	Parameter 3
Beta	a	b	
Binomial	n	p	
Constant	c (constant)		
Discrete	n (number of values)		

Table 17-1. Possible distribution functions and parameters (continued).

Distribution	Parameter 1	Parameter 2	Parameter 3
Erlang	k	b	
Exponential	μ		
Gamma	a	b	
Geometric	p		
Laplace	μ	q	
Lognormal	μ	σ	
Normal	μ	σ	
Poisson	μ		
Triangular	a (lower bound)	b (mode)	c (upper bound)
Uniform	a (lower bound)	b (upper bound)	
Weibull	v	a	b

a. Beta

$f(x) = (\Gamma(a+b)/(\Gamma(a) * \Gamma(b))) * x^{a-1} * (1-x)^{b-1}$

b. Binomial

$f(x) = (n!/((x!) * ((n-x)!))) * p^x * (1-p)^{n-x}$

c. Erlang

$f(x) = e^{-x/b} * x^{k-1} / (\Gamma(k) * b^k)$

d. Exponential

$f(x) = e^{-x/\mu} / \mu$

e. Gamma

$f(x) = e^{-x/b} * x^{a-1} / (\Gamma(a) * b^a)$

f. Geometric

$f(x) = p * (1-p)^{x-1}$

g. Laplace

$f(x) = e^{-|x-\mu|/q} / (2q)$

h. Lognormal

$f(x) = e^{-((\log(x)-\mu)/\sigma)^2/2} / (2.5066\sigma)$

i. Normal

$f(x) = e^{-((x-\mu)/\sigma)^2/2} / (2.5066\sigma)$

j. Poisson

$f(x) = e^{-\mu} * \mu^x / x!$

k. Triangular

$f(x) = 2(x-a)/((b-a)*(c-a)) \text{ for } a \leq x \leq b$

$\quad = 2(c-x)/((c-b)*(c-a)) \text{ for } b < x \leq c$

l. Uniform

$f(x) = 1/(b-a)$

m. Weibull

$f(x) = (b/a) * ((x-v)/a)^{b-1} * e^{-((x-v)/a)b}$

9. Let F(x) represent the cumulative distribution function. To generate a random sample of deviation for an interarrival time, service time, or batch size, QSIM generates a random number r and solves the equation below. The method is usually called inverse transformation.

$F(x) = r$

10. The congruential method is used to generate any random number in QSIM. Given a random number seed (−32768 to 32767), QSIM will generate a random number sequence.

11. QSIM uses the following selection rules for a choice situation. The default is Random.

Random:	Randomly choose
Probability:	Choose based on the probability
RoundRobin:	Choose in round robin order
Assembly:	Choose all from predecessors (for server only)
DisAssembly:	Choose all for descendents (for server only)
LongestQueue:	Choose the queue with the longest line
ShortestQueue:	Choose the queue with the shortest line
MaxQueueCapacity:	Choose the queue with the largest capacity
MinQueueCapacity:	Choose the queue with the smallest capacity

12. The following queue disciplines are available in QSIM to define how a customer waits when it enters a queue. The default is FIFO.

FIFO:	First in first out (served)
LIFO:	Last in first out (served)
Random:	Served in random sequence
PriorityIndex:	Higher priority index first
SPT	Shortest process time (fixed component) first
LPT:	Longest process time (fixed component) first
MaxWorkDone:	Maximum total process time has been done first
MinWorkDone:	Minimum total process time done first
MostWait:	Maximum total waiting has been first
EarliestEntering:	Earliest entering the system first

13. QSIM performs discrete-event simulation. The discrete events to trigger the simulation operations are customer arrival and server finishing a customer.

14. The operating rules of a queuing network in QSIM work as follows:

a. The arrival customer will enter a queue based on the specified arrival to queue connections and the defined selection rule. No transfer is imposed between arrival and queue. If the queue is full, the arriving customer is balked.

b. When a server becomes available, choose a customer from the connected preceding queues based on the defined input selection rule. If "Assembly" is the input rule, the server will wait until all preceding queues have at least a customer. The assembled customer will carry the combined information of its predecessors and keep it with the lowest number customer name.

c. When a server finishes the service for a customer, it will send the served customer to the succeeding queues based on the defined output selection rule. If "DisAssembly" is the output rule, a copy of the served customer will be sent to each succeeding queue. If the server is the last in sequence, the served customer will leave the system. A fixed transfer time, if you have entered, is required before the customer joins the next queue. The default transfer time is 0.

d. If the succeeding queue is full, the served customer will occupy the current server until the queue has a space. This is called a balked idle situation.

e. If the selected succeeding queue is not full, after spending the transfer time on the move, the served customer will enter the queue based on the defined queuing discipline.

15. Before performing the simulation, it is recommended to specify the total simulation time (default is 100 time units), the data collection start time (default is 0), the random number seed (default is 27437, a prime number), and the maximum number of observations to collect. Note that the same random number seed will create the same random number stream. If you are to compare different queuing configurations, it is recommended to use the same random seed and run the simulation long enough. The simulation will end when either simulation time expires or maximum number of observations is reached. One finished customer is counted as one observation.

16. QSIM collects the customer information when the customer leaves the system and collects the server information when the server finishes a service. The arrival information is collected when the customer arrives.

17. If you find out that the simulation results are irrational or too far from expectation, check the problem entry to see whether the parameters or the network connections are entered correctly.

18. QSIM program has the option to interactively display the Monte Carlo discrete-event simulation.

19. The following notations are used to show the simulation results.

L	Average number of customers in the system
L_q	Average number of customers in the queue
W	Average time a customer spends in the system
W_q	Average time a customer spends in the queue
PT	Process time for a customer
Utilization =	Total process time of a machine / simulation time (for the data collection period only)

MENU STRUCTURE

The functions and options in each of the pull-down menus are hierarchically listed as follows:

- Modules
  - Linear Programming (LP)
  - Integer Linear Programming (ILP)
  - Goal Programming (GP)
  - Quadratic Programming (QP)
  - Nonlinear Programming (NLP)
  - Dynamic Programming (DP)
  - Transportation and Transshipment (TRP)
  - Assignment and Traveling Salesman (ASTS)
  - Specialized Network Modeling (SNET)
  - Capacitated Network Flow Modeling (CNET)
  - Project Scheduling: CPM/PERT
  - Inventory Theory (INVT)
  - Inventory Theory 2 (INVT2)
  - Queuing Theory (QUEUE)
  - Queuing System Simulation (QSIM)
  - Decision Analysis (DA)
  - Markov Process (MKV)
  - Time Series Forecasting (TSFC)
  - Financial Analysis (FA)
  - Exit from QSB
- Input Data
  - Data Entry
  - Read a File
  - Show Data
  - Print Data
  - Modify Data
  - Save
  - Save As
  - Exit from QSB
- Solution
  - Simulation Specification
  - Simulation
  - Show the Result
  - Print the Result
  - Save the Result
- Options
  - Color
  - Monochrome
  - Printer Selection
- Help - QSIM
  - About QSIM

About the User Interface
About the Edit Keys

SOLVING PROBLEMS WITH QSIM

In the following sections, we will use example problems to show how to enter and solve the problems. The general procedure and menu options are described in detail in the tutorial sections of Chapter 2.

Example - Single Stage

To demonstrate the use of QSIM, consider the following sample problem. A local bank has to decide whether to hire two clerks or lease two automatic teller machines. Assume the two alternatives have the same cost. Table 17-2 shows the service rates and distributions. Customers arrive at the bank with a Poisson distribution with a mean of 50 per hour. The manager of the bank wants to know which alternative will provide a higher service level, that is, lower customer average waiting time. Because of different service rates for the two clerks, the Monte Carlo simulation is appropriate to analyze the problem. Also, assume that the arrival customers form a single waiting line. The schematic diagram of the bank service is depicted in Fig. 17-1.

Table 17-2. Service rates of the two alternatives.

Alternative		Service rate per hour	Distribution
1	Clerk 1	35	Poisson
	Clerk 2	30	Poisson
2	Machine 1	30	Constant
	Machine 2	30	Constant

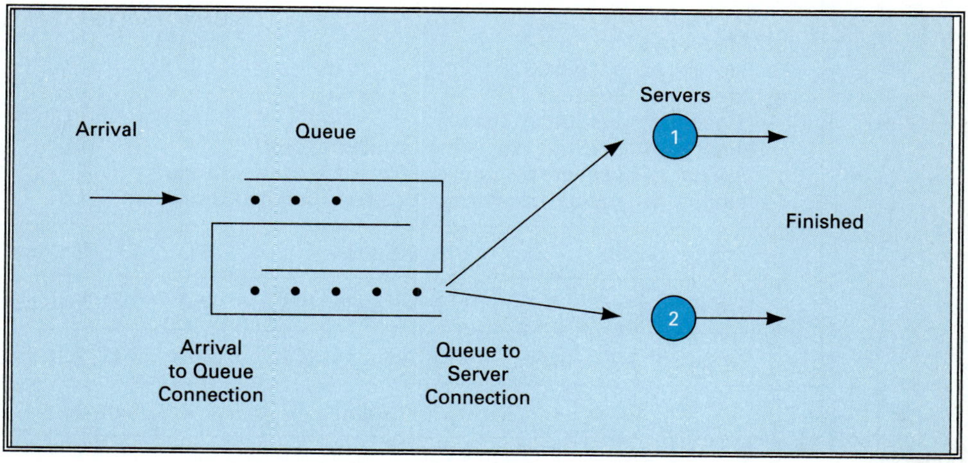

Figure 17-1. Schematic diagram of the bank service.

Enter the Problem - Alternative 1

1. Select "Data Entry" from the "Input Data" menu (refer to Chapter 2 for selecting a menu item).
2. Fig. 17-2 shows the problem specification for alternative 1. From the schematic diagram of Fig. 17-1, there is one arrival to queue connection and there are two queue to server connections.
3. Fig. 17-3 shows the server entry. The input and output rules are assumed to be the default.
4. Fig. 17-4 shows the queue entry. Only one queue which is in front of the two clerks is designed in Fig. 17-1. The default dispatching discipline is FIFO and capacity is 100.
5. Fig. 17-5 shows the customer arrival entry. Only one customer is specified. Arrival rate (λ) of 50 per hour Poisson distributed is equal to 1.2 minutes mean interarrival time exponentially distributed. The batch size is constantly equal to 1. No queue selection rule is required since only one queue exists.
6. Fig. 17-6 shows the arrival to queue connection, and Fig. 17-7 shows the queue to server connections. Note that in Fig. 17-7, the queue to server connection is entered in server sequence. The "From Queue" is entered in the second column.
7. Fig. 17-8 shows the service time distributions. Both are exponential distributions. Mean service time for clerk 1 = 1/35 hour = 1.7142857 minutes, and mean service time for clerk 2 = 1/30 hour = 2 minutes.

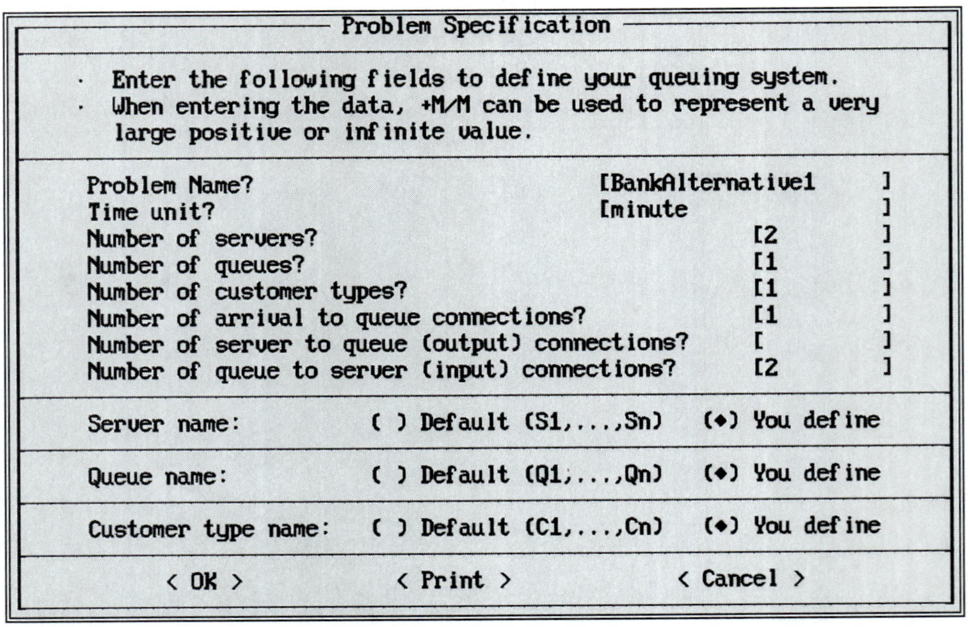

Figure 17-2. Problem specification for BankAlternative1.

```
──────────── Server Entry for BankAlternative1 ────────────
 Number        Name      Input Rule   Output Rule

 1         [Clerk 1    ][           ][           ]  NOTE:
 2         [Clerk 2    ][           ][           ]    Server follows input
                                                      rule to select custo-
                                                      mer and uses output
                                                      rule to deliver.

                                                      Possible rules:
                                                        Random
                                                        Probability
                                                        RoundRobin
                                                        Assembly
                                                        DisAssembly
                                                        LongestQueue
                                                        ShortestQueue
                                                        MaxQueueCapacity
                                                        MinQueueCapacity
                                                      First 3 letters are
                                                      required.

 < OK >  < PgUp >  < PgLt >  < PgRt >  < Help >  < Print >  < Cancel >
```

Figure 17-3. Server information for BankAlternative1.

```
──────────── Queue Entry for BankAlternative1 ────────────
 Number        Name        Discipline   Capacity

 1         [Queue 1    ][FIFO       ][100        ]  Enter M for infinite
                                                    or large capacity.

                                                    Possible disciplines:
                                                        FIFO
                                                        LIFO
                                                        Random
                                                        PriorityIndex
                                                        SPT
                                                        LPT
                                                        MaxWorkDone
                                                        MinWorkDone
                                                        MostWait
                                                        EarliestEntering

                                                    The first 3 letters are
                                                    required.

 < OK >  < PgUp >  < PgLt >  < PgRt >  < Help >  < Print >  < Cancel >
```

Figure 17-4. Queue information for BankAlternative1.

```
                     Customer Type Entry for BankAlternative1
 Data Item      Customer Type 1

Name           [Customer    ]   Queue selection rules are as in server entry.
Q. Sel. Rule   [            ]   Priority index represents an attribute value.
PriorityIdx.   [            ]   Interarrival time = fixed component + deviation
Arrival Dis.   [Exp         ]   Deviation follows a probability distribution
Fixed Comp.    [            ]   with up to three parameters (see below).
Parameter 1    [1.2         ]   The first 3 letters are required to define
Parameter 2    [            ]   the distribution.
Parameter 3    [            ]   Arrival batch size = fixed component + deviation
BatchSize D.   [Constant    ]   Deviation follows a probability distribution.
Fixed Comp.    [1           ]
Parameter 1    [            ]   Possible probability distributions include:
Parameter 2    [            ]     Beta(a, b), Binomial(n, p), Erlang(k, b)
Parameter 3    [            ]     Exponential(u), Gamma(a, b), Geometric(p)
                                  Laplace(u, q), LogNormal(u, s), Normal(u, s)
                                  Poisson(u), Triangular(a, b, c), Uniform(a, b)
                                  Weibull(v, a, b), and user defined Discrete(n).

                                () contains the required parameters.

   < OK >  < PgUp >  < PgLt >  < PgRt >  < Help >  < Print >  < Cancel >
```

Figure 17-5. Arrival information for BankAlternative1.

```
                     Customer Arrival to Queue Connections
  Number       CustomerType    To Queue    Probability (if any)

   1           [Customer    ][Queue 1    ][            ]          Probability
                                                                  is required
                                                                  only when
                                                                  the rule of
                                                                  PROBABILITY
                                                                  is selected.

   < OK >  < PgUp >  < PgLt >  < PgRt >  < Help >  < Print >  < Cancel >
```

Figure 17-6. Arrival to queue connection for BankAlternative1.

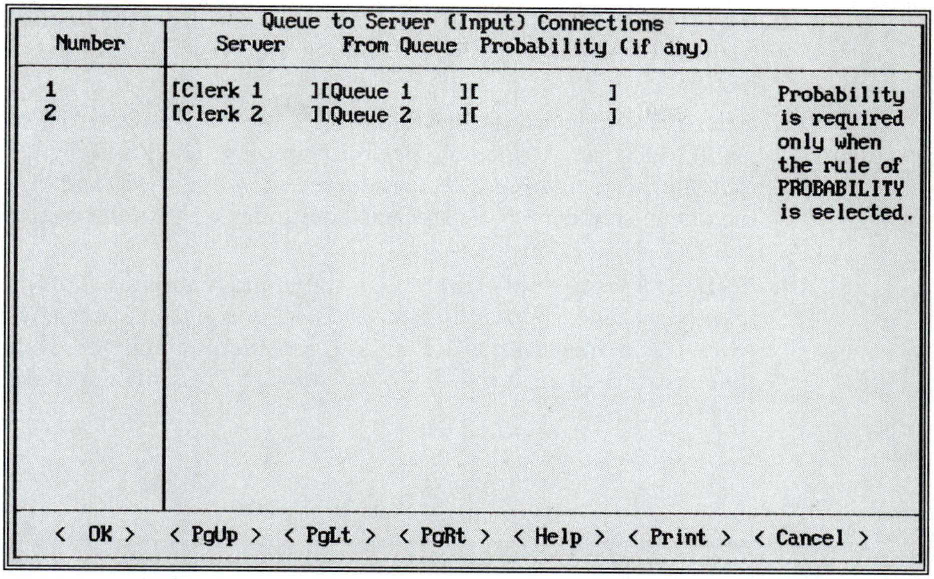

Figure 17-7. Queue to server connections for BankAlternative1.

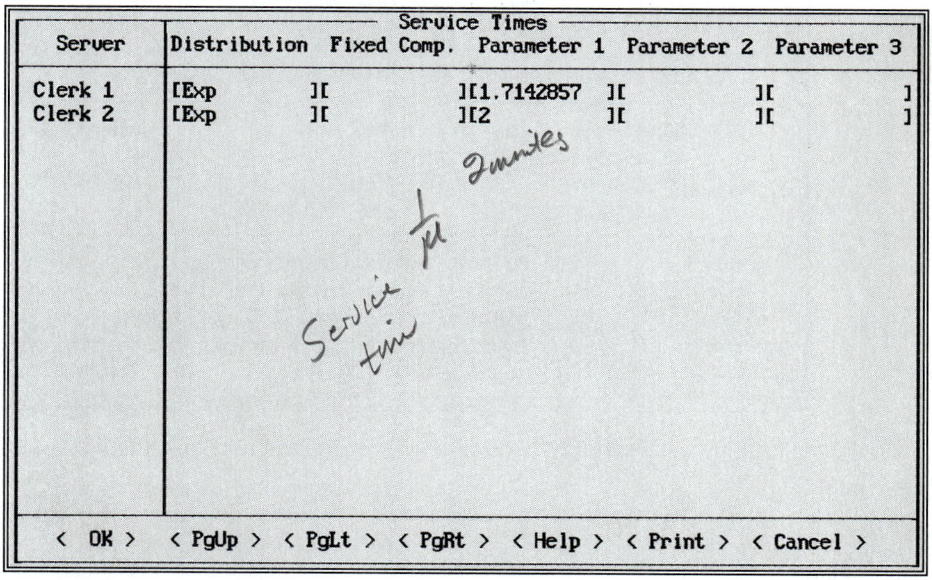

Figure 17-8. Service times for BankAlternative1.

Simulate the Alternative 1

1. Before performing the simulation, select "Simulation Specification" from the "Solution" menu to specify the simulation setup. Fig. 17-9 shows the setup of simulating 10,000 minutes, collecting data from time 0, random seed 27437 (default), and unlimited observation (M).

2. After the setup is specified, select "Simulation" from the "Solution" menu to perform the simulation. Fig. 17-10 shows the Gantt chart of the real-time completion of the simulation.
3. After the simulation is done, choose "Show the Result" from the "Solution" menu to display the queuing performance. Fig. 17-11 and Fig. 17-12 show the customer statistics, Fig. 17-13 shows the server analysis, and Fig. 17-14 shows the queue summary. Note that each customer waits in the queue (Wq) an average of about 2.55634 minutes.
4. You may want to display the system status and real-time events during the simulation process. Choose the button "Display and stop at each event" from the "Simulation Specification" (Fig. 17-9) and then simulate the system. The real-time status such as in Fig. 17-15 will appear. Press the appropriate button to proceed.

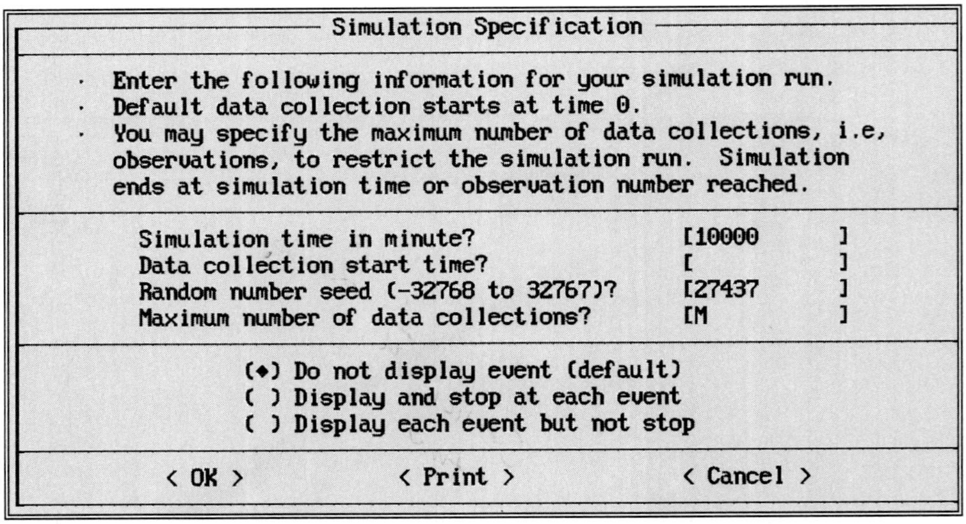

Figure 17-9. Simulation specification for BankAlternative1.

Figure 17-10. Gantt chart of simulation completion for BankAlternative1.

Customer Summary for BankAlternative1

08-23-1993 17:29:13 Page: 1 of 1

Customer Type	Total Arrival	Total Balked	Mean No. in System (L)	Max. No. in System	Current in System
Customer	8326	0	3.655799	26	5

Data Collection: 0 to 10000.00 minutes CPU Seconds = 38.99

< PageDown > < PageUp > < Hardcopy > < Cancel >

Figure 17-11. Customer summary for BankAlternative1.

Customer Summary (Continued) for BankAlternative1

08-23-1993 17:29:55 Page: 1 of 1

Customer Type	Number Finished	Av.Process Time	Av.Waiting Time (Wq)	Av. Transfer Time	Av. Flow Time (W)	Max. Flow Time
Customer	8321	1.83538	2.55634	0	4.391721	27.2309
Std. Dev.		1.831397	3.554511	0	3.985337	

Data Collection: 0 to 10000.00 minutes CPU Seconds = 38.99

< PageDown > < PageUp > < Hardcopy > < Cancel >

Figure 17-12. Customer summary for BankAlternative1 (continued).

Server Summary for BankAlternative1

08-23-1993 17:30:24 Page: 1 of 1

Server Name	Utilization %	Av.Process Time	Std. Dev. of PT	Maximum of PT	Blocked %	# Customer Processed
Clerk 1	75.64644	1.73104	1.708937	16.66602	0	4370
Clerk 2	77.07572	1.95079	1.951466	15.9426	0	3951
Overall	76.36108	1.835382	1.831402	16.66602	0	8321

Data Collection: 0 to 10000.00 minutes CPU Seconds = 38.99

< PageDown > < PageUp > < Hardcopy > < Cancel >

Figure 17-13. Server summary for BankAlternative1.

Queue Summary for BankAlternative1

08-23-1993 17:31:04 Page: 1 of 1

Queue Name	Av. Queue Length(Lq)	Current Lq	Maximum Lq	Av.Waiting Time (Wq)	Std. Dev. of Wq	Maximum of Wq
Queue 1	2.128361	3	24	2.55678	3.554249	23.52393

Data Collection: 0 to 10000.00 minutes CPU Seconds = 38.99

< PageDown > < PageUp > < Hardcopy > < Cancel >

Figure 17-14. Queue summary for BankAlternative1.

0 [progress bar] 100

↑ Data collection time

Queuing System Status for BankAlternative1

Time: 42.60603 Event: Customer Customer Arrives Simulation time: 100

Server	Status	Queue	Q. Length	Customer	# Arrived	# Balked
Clerk 1 Clerk 2	Busy Busy	Queue 1	2	Customer	41	0

< NextEvent > < NonStop > < StopDisplaying > < Hardcopy > < Cancel >

Figure 17-15. Display of system status for BankAlternative1.

Enter the Problem - Alternative 2

The procedure to enter alternative 2 is similar to that of alternative 1 except that the service times are constant. Constant service time for both machines is 60/30 = 2 minutes.

Simulate the Alternative 2

Again, define the same "Simulation Specification" as that of alternative 1 and perform the simulation. Figs. 17-16 to 17-19 show the results. Note that each customer waits in the queue (W_q) an average of about 2.726912 minutes.

Example - Multiple Stages

A production system has five workstations depicted in Fig. 17-20. Component A arrives at buffer 1 and goes through stations 1 and 2. Component B arrives at buffer 3

Customer Summary for BankAlternative2

08-23-1993 17:36:14 Page: 1 of 1

Customer Type	Total Arrival	Total Balked	Mean No. in System (L)	Max. No. in System	Current in System
Customer	8346	0	3.944856	22	2

Data Collection: 0 to 10000.00 minutes CPU Seconds = 15.11

< PageDown > < PageUp > < Hardcopy > < Cancel >

Figure 17-16. Customer summary for BankAlternative2.

Customer Summary (Continued) for BankAlternative2
08-23-1993 17:36:47 Page: 1 of 1

Customer Type	Number Finished	Av.Process Time	Av.Waiting Time (Wq)	Av. Transfer Time	Av. Flow Time (W)	Max. Flow Time
Customer	8344	2	2.727341	0	4.727345	21.02637
Std. Dev.		0.00000000	3.356782	0	3.356783	

Data Collection: 0 to 10000.00 minutes CPU Seconds = 15.11

< PageDown > < PageUp > < Hardcopy > < Cancel >

Figure 17-17. Customer summary for BankAlternative2 (continued).

Server Summary for BankAlternative2
08-23-1993 17:37:19 Page: 1 of 1

Server Name	Utilization %	Av.Process Time	Std. Dev. of PT	Maximum of PT	Blocked %	# Customer Processed
Clerk 1	83.76	2	0.00068290	2.000488	0	4188
Clerk 2	83.12	2	9.2457E-10	2.000061	0	4156
Overall	83.44	2	0.00000000	2.000488	0	8344

Data Collection: 0 to 10000.00 minutes CPU Seconds = 15.11

< PageDown > < PageUp > < Hardcopy > < Cancel >

Figure 17-18. Server summary for BankAlternative2.

Queue Summary for BankAlternative2
08-23-1993 17:37:54 Page: 1 of 1

Queue Name	Av. Queue Length(Lq)	Current Lq	Maximum Lq	Av.Waiting Time (Wq)	Std. Dev. of Wq	Maximum of Wq
Queue 1	2.275871	0	20	2.726912	3.356525	19.02637

Data Collection: 0 to 10000.00 minutes CPU Seconds = 15.11

< PageDown > < PageUp > < Hardcopy > < Cancel >

Figure 17-19. Queue summary for BankAlternative2.

and goes through stations 3 and 4. Station 5 assembles the two components together. Each buffer has a capacity to store 50 units of component A or B. The operational data is shown in Table 17-3. Transfer times between stations are shown in Table 17-4. Component A arrives at the buffer with a mean of 30 units per hour Poisson distributed, while component B arrives at the buffer with a mean interarrival time of 2 minutes and standard deviation of 1 minute normally distributed. Perform the simulation up to 10,000 minutes to evaluate the system performance.

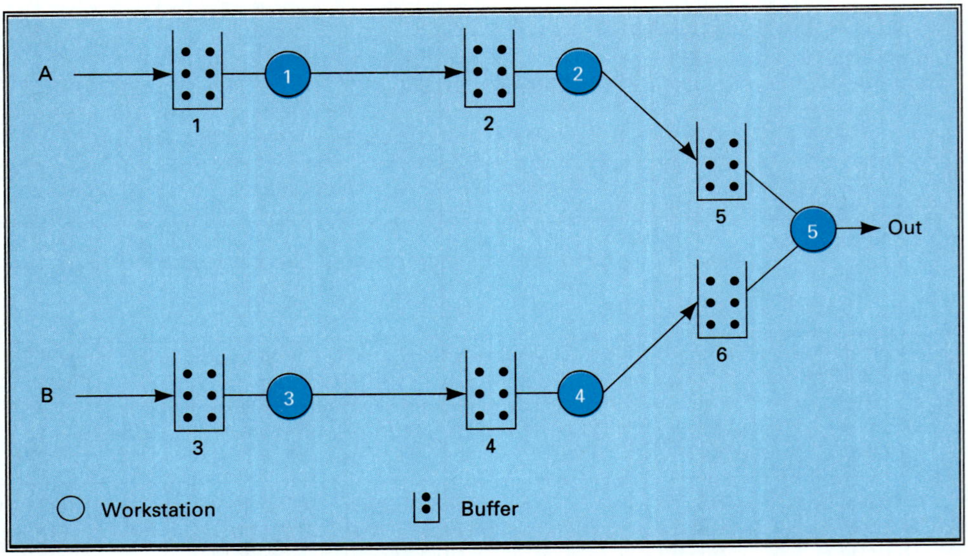

Figure 17-20. Schematic diagram of the production system.

Table 17-3. Operational data for the production system.

Workstations (Servers)	Operation times (in minutes)	
	Fixed component	Deviation
1		Exponential (1.8)
2	1	Exponential (1)
3	1	Uniform (0.5, 1)
4	1.5	0
5	0.5	Triangular (0.5, 1, 1.5)

Table 17-4. Transfer times between stations.

Transfer		
From	To	Time (in minutes)
Station 1	Buffer 2	.2
Station 2	Buffer 5	.2
Station 3	Buffer 4	.1
Station 4	Buffer 6	.3

Enter the Problem

Select "Data Entry" from the "Input Data" menu. Figs. 17-21 to 17-30 show the sequence of the data entry.

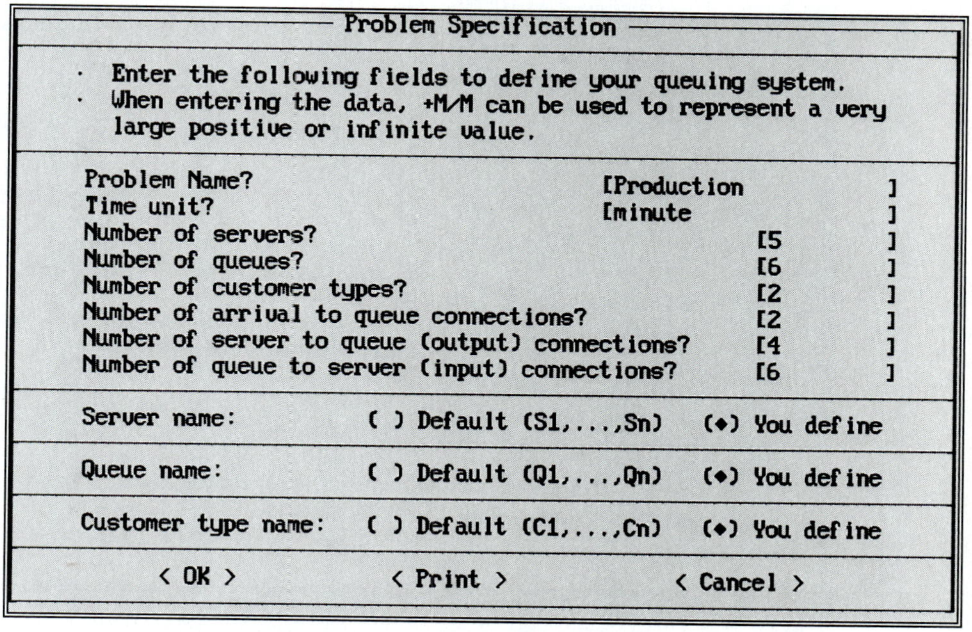

Figure 17-21. Problem specification for the production system.

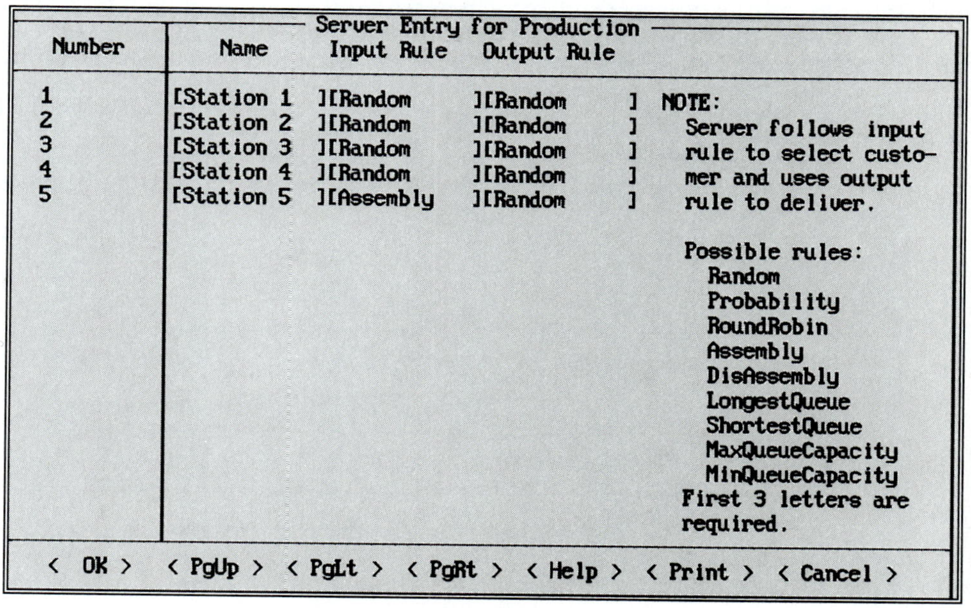

Figure 17-22. Server entry for Production.

```
                    Queue Entry for Production
 Number         Name        Discipline   Capacity

   1       [Buffer 1   ][FIFO        ][50          ]  Enter M for infinite
   2       [Buffer 2   ][FIFO        ][50          ]  or large capacity.
   3       [Buffer 3   ][FIFO        ][50          ]
   4       [Buffer 4   ][FIFO        ][50          ]  Possible disciplines:
   5       [Buffer 5   ][FIFO        ][50          ]     FIFO
   6       [Buffer 6   ][FIFO        ][50          ]     LIFO
                                                         Random
                                                         PriorityIndex
                                                         SPT
                                                         LPT
                                                         MaxWorkDone
                                                         MinWorkDone
                                                         MostWait
                                                         EarliestEntering

                                                      The first 3 letters are
                                                      required.

   < OK >  < PgUp >  < PgLt >  < PgRt >  < Help >  < Print >  < Cancel >
```

Figure 17-23. Queue entry for Production.

```
                  Customer Type Entry for Production
 Data Item    Customer Type 1

Name         [A          ]  Queue selection rules are as in server entry.
Q. Sel. Rule [Random     ]  Priority index represents an attribute value.
PriorityIdx. [           ]  Interarrival time = fixed component + deviation
Arrival Dis. [Exp        ]  Deviation follows a probability distribution
Fixed Comp.  [           ]  with up to three parameters (see below).
Parameter 1  [2          ]  The first 3 letters are required to define
Parameter 2  [           ]  the distribution.
Parameter 3  [           ]  Arrival batch size = fixed component + deviation
BatchSize D. [Constant   ]  Deviation follows a probability distribution.
Fixed Comp.  [1          ]
Parameter 1  [           ]  Possible probability distributions include:
Parameter 2  [           ]    Beta(a, b), Binomial(n, p), Erlang(k, b)
Parameter 3  [           ]    Exponential(u), Gamma(a, b), Geometric(p)
                              Laplace(u, q), LogNormal(u, s), Normal(u, s)
                              Poisson(u), Triangular(a, b, c), Uniform(a, b)
                              Weibull(v, a, b), and user defined Discrete(n).

                            () contains the required parameters.

   < OK >  < PgUp >  < PgLt >  < PgRt >  < Help >  < Print >  < Cancel >
```

Figure 17-24. Component A entry for Production.

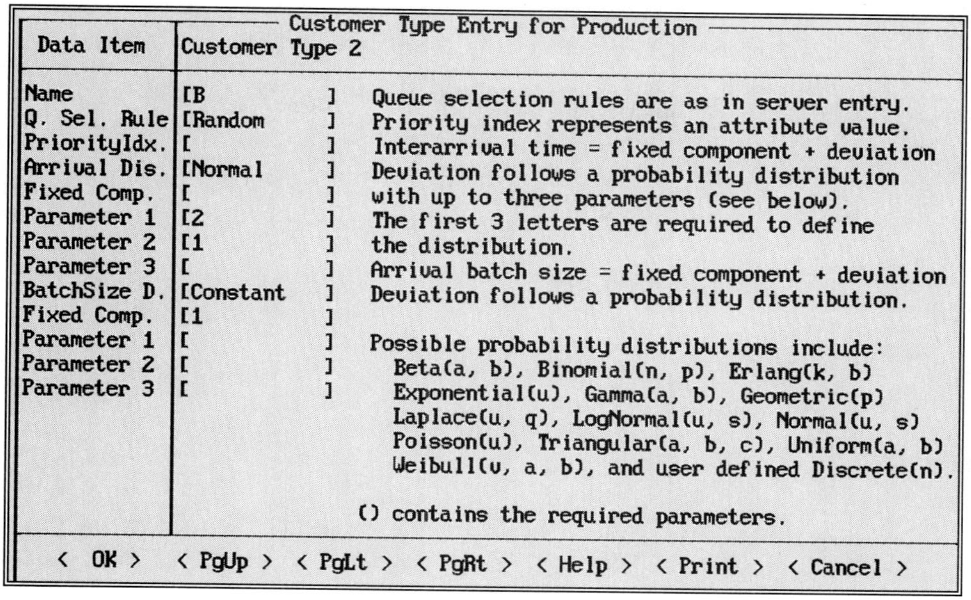

Figure 17-25. Component B entry for Production.

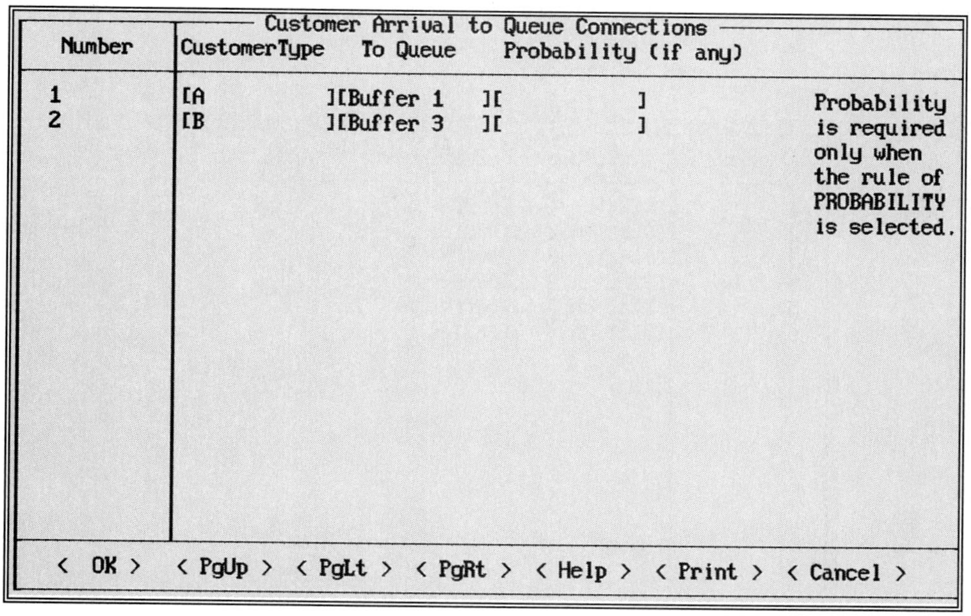

Figure 17-26. Customer arrival to queue connections for Production.

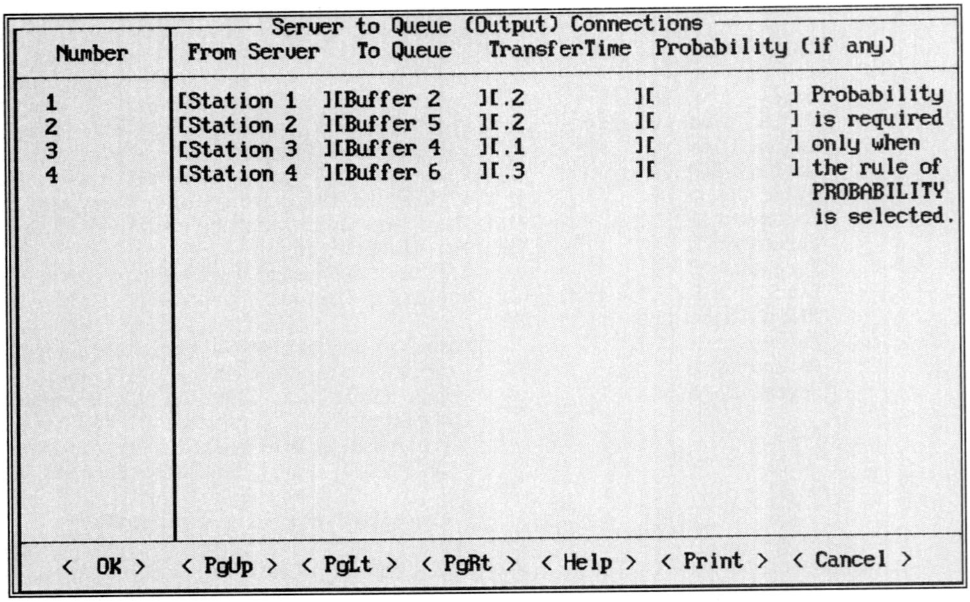

Figure 17-27. Server to queue connections for Production.

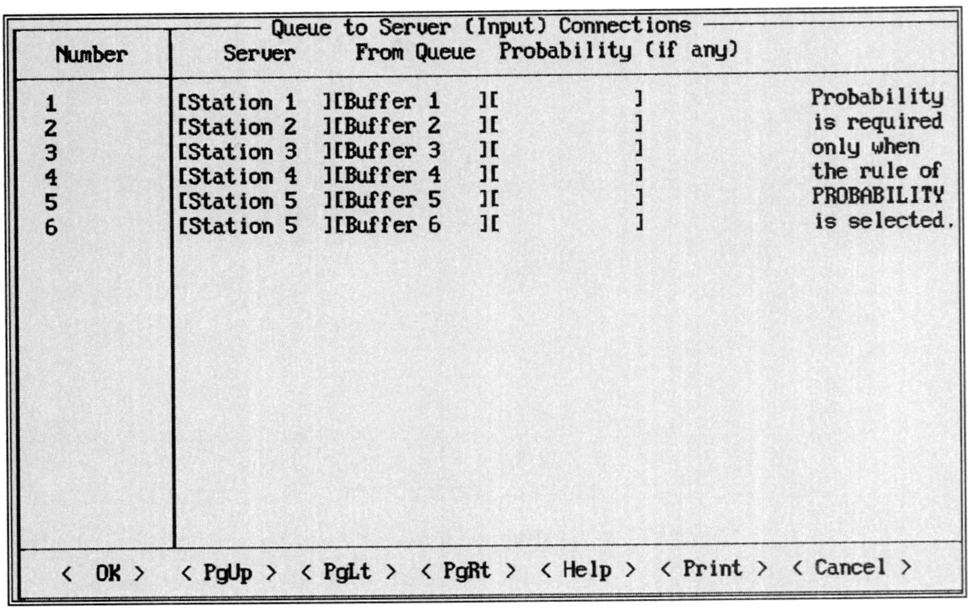

Figure 17-28. Queue to server connections for Production.

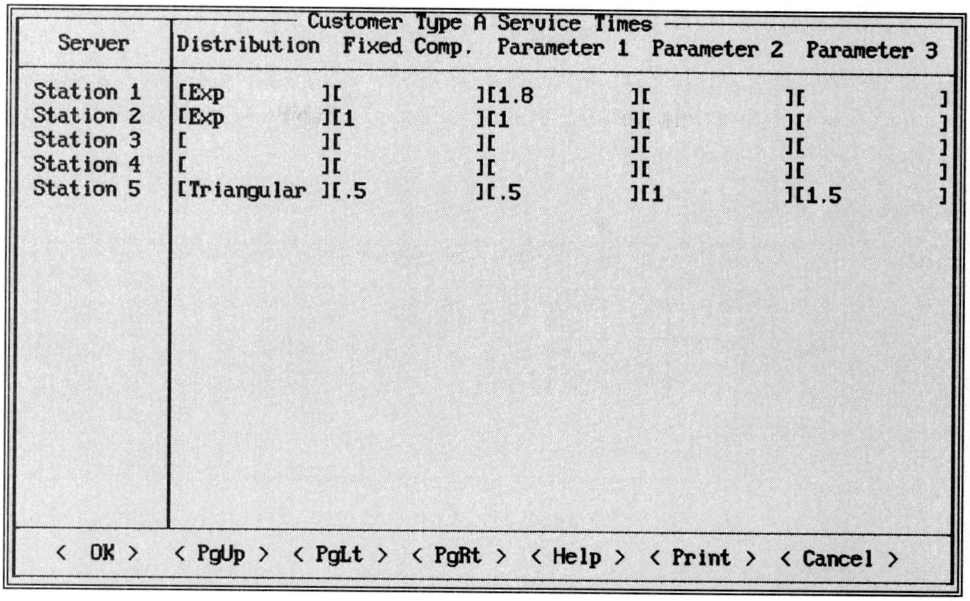

Customer Type A Service Times

Server	Distribution	Fixed Comp.	Parameter 1	Parameter 2	Parameter 3
Station 1	Exp		1.8		
Station 2	Exp	1	1		
Station 3					
Station 4					
Station 5	Triangular	.5	.5	1	1.5

< OK > < PgUp > < PgLt > < PgRt > < Help > < Print > < Cancel >

Figure 17-29. Component A operation times for Production.

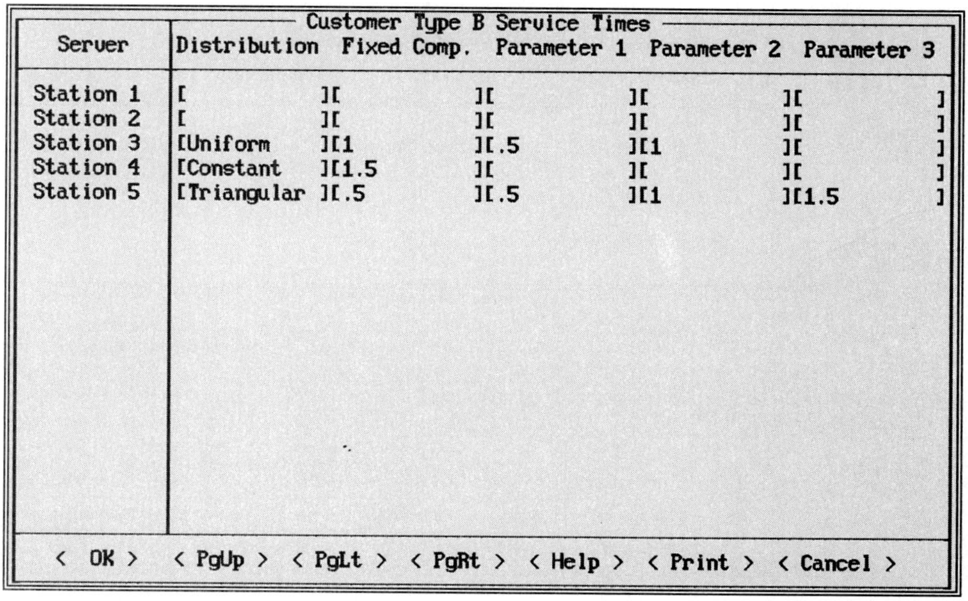

Customer Type B Service Times

Server	Distribution	Fixed Comp.	Parameter 1	Parameter 2	Parameter 3
Station 1					
Station 2					
Station 3	Uniform	1	.5	1	
Station 4	Constant	1.5			
Station 5	Triangular	.5	.5	1	1.5

< OK > < PgUp > < PgLt > < PgRt > < Help > < Print > < Cancel >

Figure 17-30. Component B operation times for Production.

Simulate the Problem

Again, select "Simulation Specification" from the "Solution" menu to specify the simulation time of 10,000 minutes. Figs. 17-31 to 17-34 show the queuing performance after the simulation finishes.

Customer Summary for Production

08-23-1993 17:56:48 Page: 1 of 1

Customer Type	Total Arrival	Total Balked	Mean No. in System (L)	Max. No. in System	Current in System
A	5079	19	49.36674	114	113
B	4951	0	19.88665	52	3
Overall	10030	19	69.25339	166	116

Data Collection: 0 to 10000.00 minutes CPU Seconds = 42.79

< PageDown > < PageUp > < Hardcopy > < Cancel >

Figure 17-31. Customer summary for Production.

Customer Summary (Continued) for Production

08-23-1993 17:57:24 Page: 1 of 1

Customer Type	Number Finished	Av.Process Time	Av.Waiting Time (Wq)	Av. Transfer Time	Av. Flow Time (W)	Max. Flow Time
A	4947	8.585905	128.5837	.8000339	101.9894	209.8428
Std. Dev.		2.1222	52.4738	0	46.48281	
B	0	0	0	0	0	0
Std. Dev.		0	0	0	0	
Overall	4947	8.585905	128.5837	.8000339	101.9894	209.8428
Std. Dev.		2.1222	52.4738	0	46.48281	

Data Collection: 0 to 10000.00 minutes CPU Seconds = 42.79

< PageDown > < PageUp > < Hardcopy > < Cancel >

Figure 17-32. Customer summary for Production (continued).

Server Summary for Production

08-23-1993 17:58:04 Page: 1 of 1

Server Name	Utilization %	Av.Process Time	Std. Dev. of PT	Maximum of PT	Blocked %	# Customer Processed
Station 1	92.35376	1.843756	1.867527	18.7832	1.59668	5009
Station 2	99.36401	2.000081	.9938241	9.613525	0	4968
Station 3	86.53105	1.748455	.1452195	2	0	4949
Station 4	74.22	1.5	0.00044425	1.500244	0	4948
Station 5	74.07175	1.497306	.2054572	1.984375	0	4947
Overall	85.30811	1.718467	.9760206	18.7832	.3193359	24821

Data Collection: 0 to 10000.00 minutes CPU Seconds = 42.79

< PageDown > < PageUp > < Hardcopy > < Cancel >

Figure 17-33. Server summary for Production.

Queue Summary for Production

08-23-1993 17:58:34 Page: 1 of 1

Queue Name	Av. Queue Length(Lq)	Current Lq	Maximum Lq	Av.Waiting Time (Wq)	Std. Dev. of Wq	Maximum of Wq
Buffer 1	17.09393	50	50	33.7584	26.03577	110.0591
Buffer 2	25.80629	40	51	51.56441	30.28524	122.2246
Buffer 3	.6269436	1	6	1.266542	1.568986	10.26953
Buffer 4	0	0	1	0	0	0
Buffer 5	3.597135	19	27	7.199978	13.67006	50.38574
Buffer 6	17.45435	0	48	35.2756	26.22415	94.19244
Overall	64.57864	110	51	21.55544	28.27421	122.2246

Data Collection: 0 to 10000.00 minutes CPU Seconds = 42.79

< PageDown > < PageUp > < Hardcopy > < Cancel >

Figure 17-34. Queue summary for Production.

EXERCISES

1. Compare the following three queuing systems. Assume that the mean interarrival time is 8 minutes and the mean service time is 10 minutes. Simulate up to 2000 minutes. Single queue with infinite length (Hint: Specifying 500 for the queue length is usually enough) and FIFO dispatching are also assumed.

a. *M/M/2* system (solvable by QUEUE).

b. Two servers, both have uniform service time from 8 minutes to 12 minutes.

c. *M/D/2* system.

2. Compare the following *M/M/1* queuing systems, assuming that the mean interarrival time = 15 minutes and mean service time = 10 minutes. Simulate up to 2000 minutes.

a. Dispatching rule is FIFO (solvable by QUEUE).

b. Dispatching is LIFO.

c. Dispatching is random.

3. Compare the following four three server systems, assuming that the mean interarrival time = 2 minutes and the mean service time = 5 minutes. Simulate up to 10 hours. Single queue with infinite length and FIFO dispatching are also assumed.

a. *M/M/3* (solvable by QUEUE).

b. Normal interarrival time with standard deviation of 1 minute and exponentially distributed service time.

c. Normal interarrival time with standard deviation of 1 minute and constant service time.

d. Constant interarrival time and service time.

4. Buck Stadium has five clerks and five automatic machines to sell tickets for the upcoming football season. Each clerk can sell 60 tickets per hour with a Poisson distribution, and each machine can sell 50 tickets per hour constantly. In general, jockeying is not allowed. What is the expected time you will spend as a ticket buyer? Assume there are 10 lines and the arrival rate is 500 per hour,

Poisson distributed. Also assume that the arriving ticket buyers enter the line with shortest length. Each buyer can buy only one ticket. Simulate up to 1200 minutes.

5. A supercomputer system has four processors. According to their configuration, each processor can process jobs at different speeds. Expected process times for incoming jobs on each processor are 10, 12, 13, and 15 seconds, respectively. Assume that the process times are exponentially distributed. The jobs arrive at the system with a mean of 10 per minute, Poisson distributed. Simulate up to 100 minutes.
   - **a.** If there is only one queue and the system applies the FIFO rule, what is the expected number of jobs in the queue? How long does each job stay in the system?
   - **b.** Do part (a) using the LIFO rule.
6. Job batches arrive at a machining center in an exponential interarrival time with a mean value of 20 minutes per batch. Each job requires operation time with a mean value of 2 minutes and exponentially distributed. Batch size ranges from 5 to 10 jobs, uniform distributed. What is the mean flow time of each job going through the machining center? Simulate up to 24 hours.
7. Assume that the multiple stage production system of Fig. 17-20 has been improved by implementing a synchronous just-in-time type of operations. Transfer times between stations have been reduced to 0.05 minutes. Buffer sizes are trimmed down to 10 per buffer. Operation times on each workstation have been reallocated and streamlined to uniform distribution between 1.5 and 1.7 minutes. Components A and B are transferred from upstream production every 1.6 minutes. Perform the simulation up to 10,000 minutes to evaluate the system performance.

18

DECISION ANALYSIS (DA)

OVERVIEW OF THE DA DECISION SUPPORT SYSTEM

This program contains three basic decision analysis methods: Bayesian, payoff table, and decision tree analyses. With Bayesian analysis, you provide the prior probabilities of the states of nature and the conditional probabilities of the outcomes; the program computes the joint probabilities, marginal probabilities, and posterior probabilities.

With payoff table analysis, you provide the probabilities of the states of nature, the conditional probabilities of the experimental outcomes or indicators, and the payoffs for each alternative; the program analyzes the decision under the criteria of maximin, maximax, minimax regret, expected value, principle of insufficient reason, and expected regret, and computes the values of perfect and sample information.

With decision tree, you can define three different nodes (events): decision, chance, and end (terminal) nodes. A decision node has multiple alternatives for selection; a chance node has many succeeding branches with specified probabilities; and an end node has no branches. After specifying the node information, the program provides a matrix to specify the linkages between nodes. The program analyzes backward from end node to origin to determine the expected values and/or decisions.

You may save, read, modify, or print the input data as well as to display, print, or save the solution.

TECHNICAL NOTES ON THE DA PROGRAM

1. A state of nature in DA usually represents the happening of a particular situation for the problem. It may be a situation in the market, a temperature for a chemical process, an attitude of a person, or a possible orientation of a population. For example, possible states of nature are demand levels, consumer's choices, income levels, economic status, and the like.
2. The prior probability of the state of nature represents the possibility that a state will occur in a general sense. It usually comes from historical data or human estimate.
3. The conditional probability represents the possibility of a particular activity or event given that another activity or event occurs. In Bayesian and payoff analyses, it usually represents the conditional probability of the experiment out-

come/indicator given a particular state of nature. That is to represent the reliability of the experiment.

4. In Bayesian or payoff analysis, the posterior or revised probability is another kind of conditional probability that represents the possibility of the state of nature given a particular survey or experiment outcome or indication.
5. Let

S:	State of nature
I:	Survey or experiment outcome/indicator
P(S):	Prior probability of the state of nature S
P(I/S):	Conditional probability of I given S
P(I,S):	Joint probability of I and S, which is P(S) * P(I/S)
P(I):	Marginal probability of I
P(S/I):	Posterior or revised probability of S given I, which is P(I,S)/P(I)

6. In payoff table analysis, the decision rules include:

   Maximin: Choose the decision alternative that has the best of the worst possible outcomes.

   Maximax: Choose the decision alternative that has the best of the best possible outcomes.

   Minimax regret: A regret value represents the opportunity loss if you don't choose the best alternative given that a particular state of nature occurs. Minimax regret rule chooses the decision alternative that has the least of the maximum possible regrets.

   Expected value: Choose the decision alternative that has the best expected value.

   Principle of insufficient reason: Choose the decision alternative that has the best expected value assuming all states of nature are equal.

   Expected regret: Choose the decision alternative that has the least expected regret.

7. In payoff table analysis, DA computes the expected value of perfect information (EVPI) and expected value of sample information (EVSI). EVPI is the difference between the expected value when the perfect information (about the states of nature) is known and the expected value from the above "Expected Value" rule. EVSI is the difference between the expected value after the sample/survey/experiment information (revised probabilities of the states of nature) is known and the expected value from the above "Expected Value" rule. The efficiency of the sample/survey/experiment is equal to EVSI/EVPI.
8. For decision tree analysis, you may define three types of nodes: decision (1), chance (2), and terminal (3). A terminal node has no descendant node. You may name each node up to 10 characters. Each node, especially a terminal node, may have a payoff value (net cost or profit) with it.
9. To specify the connections of the decision tree, DA provides a spreadsheet matrix to define the linkages between nodes. Any non-empty entry of the connection represents a direct linkage between two nodes. Usually, you enter a non-empty probability for the connection from a chance node to another node,

and you enter a non-empty letter such as "x" for the connection from a decision node to another node.

MENU STRUCTURE

The functions and options in each of the pull-down menus are hierarchically listed as follows:

- Modules
  - Linear Programming (LP)
  - Integer Linear Programming (ILP)
  - Goal Programming (GP)
  - Quadratic Programming (QP)
  - Nonlinear Programming (NLP)
  - Dynamic Programming (DP)
  - Transportation and Transshipment (TRP)
  - Assignment and Traveling Salesman (ASTS)
  - Specialized Network Modeling (SNET)
  - Capacitated Network Flow Modeling (CNET)
  - Project Scheduling: CPM/PERT
  - Inventory Theory (INVT)
  - Inventory Theory 2 (INVT2)
  - Queuing Theory (QUEUE)
  - Queuing System Simulation (QSIM)
  - Decision Analysis (DA)
  - Markov Process (MKV)
  - Time Series Forecasting (TSFC)
  - Financial Analysis (FA)
  - Exit from QSB
- Input Data
  - Data Entry
  - Read a File
  - Show Data
  - Print Data
  - Modify Data
  - Save
  - Save As
  - Exit from QSB
- Solution
  - Solve the Problem
  - Show the Solution
  - Print the Solution
  - Save the Solution
- Options
  - Color

Monochrome
Printer Selection

Help - DA
About DA
About the User Interface
About the Edit Keys

SOLVING PROBLEMS WITH DA

In the following sections, we will use example problems to show how to enter and solve the problems. The general procedure and menu options are described in detail in the tutorial sections of Chapter 2.

Example - Bayesian Analysis

The following example demonstrates the process of Bayesian analysis using DA. The marketing department is considering the options to market a product for the coming winter season. Table 18-1 shows the prior probabilities of the states of nature (consumer demand) for the product based on the past experience. In Table 18-2, the market survey division provides the conditional probabilities of the survey outcomes given the states of nature. Bayesian analysis can be used to find the probabilities, that is, the posterior or revised probabilities, of the states of consumer demand with respect to the survey outcomes.

Table 18-1. Prior probabilities of the states of nature.

Consumer demand	Probability
High	.2
Medium	.5
Low	.3

Table 18-2. Conditional probabilities of the survey outcomes given the states of nature.

State of nature	Survey outcome		
	Favorable	Unfavorable	Neutral
High	.6	.2	.2
Medium	.3	.3	.4
Low	.2	.55	.25

Enter the Problem

1. Select "Data Entry" from the "Input Data" menu (refer to Chapter 2 for selecting a menu item).
2. Figs. 18-1 to 18-6 show the entry for the Bayesian analysis.

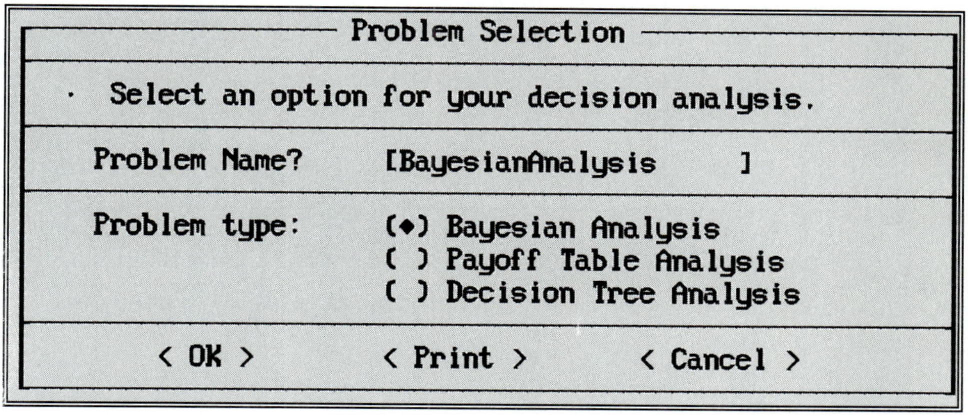

Figure 18-1. Selection of Bayesian analysis.

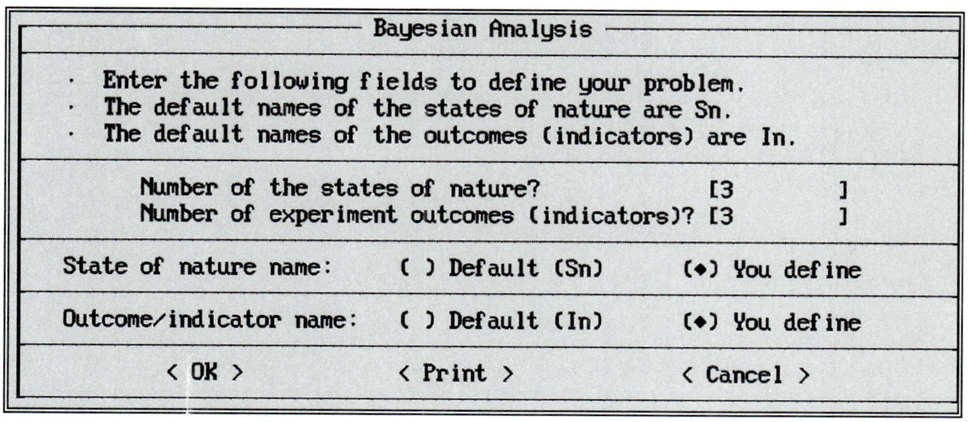

Figure 18-2. Problem specification for BayesianAnalysis.

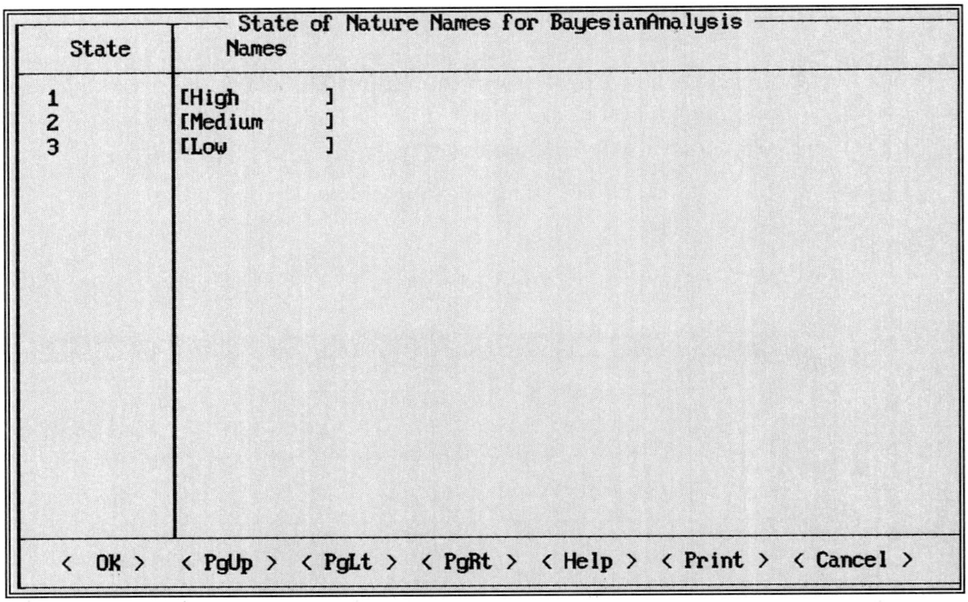

Figure 18-3. State of nature names for BayesianAnalysis.

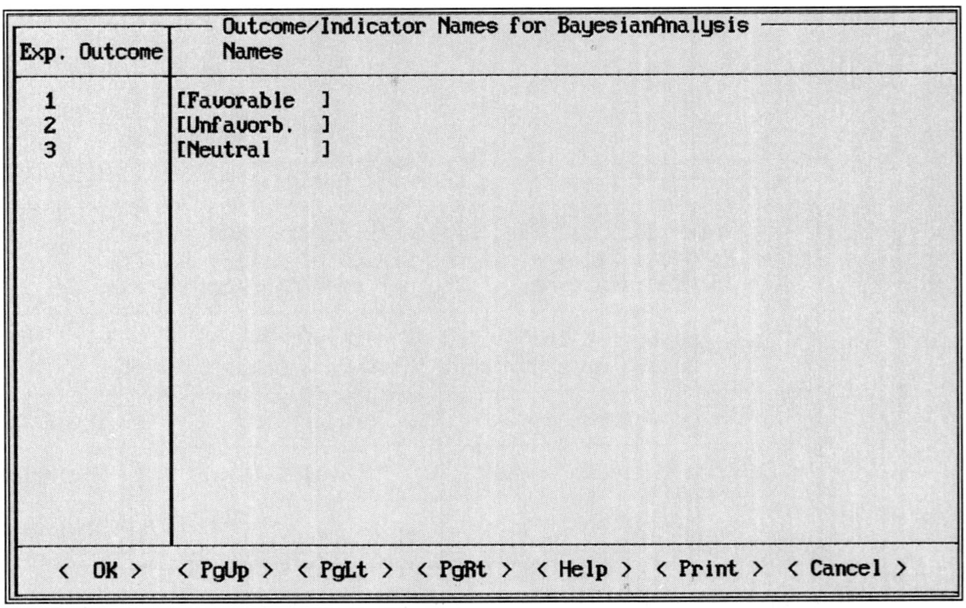

Figure 18-4. Experiment/survey outcome/indicator names for BayesianAnalysis.

Prior Probabilities of the States of Nature

State	Probability
High	[.2]
Medium	[.5]
Low	[.3]

< OK > < PgUp > < PgLt > < PgRt > < Help > < Print > < Cancel >

Figure 18-5. Prior probabilities for BayesianAnalysis.

Conditional Probabilities for BayesianAnalysis

State\Outco.	Favorable	Unfavorb.	Neutral
High	[.6]	[.2]	[.2]
Medium	[.3]	[.3]	[.4]
Low	[.2]	[.55]	[.25]

< OK > < PgUp > < PgLt > < PgRt > < Help > < Print > < Cancel >

Figure 18-6. Conditional probabilities for BayesianAnalysis.

Solve the Problem

1. Select "Solve the Problem" from the "Solution" menu to solve the problem.The message "Please standby . . ." will display for a short period while the problem is being solved.
2. After the problem is solved, select "Show the Solution" from the "Solution" menu to display the Bayesian analysis. Fig. 18-7 shows the joint probabilities, Fig. 18-8 shows the marginal probabilities of the survey outcomes, and Fig. 18-9 shows the posterior or revised probabilities, which are the probabilities of the consumer demands given the outcomes of the survey.

Joint Probabilities for BayesianAnalysis

08-23-1993 18:55:09 Page: 1 of 1

State	Outcome or Indicator	Joint Probability	State	Outcome or Indicator	Joint Probability
High	Favorable	.120000	Medium	Neutral	.200000
High	Unfavorb.	.040000	Low	Favorable	.060000
High	Neutral	.040000	Low	Unfavorb.	.165000
Medium	Favorable	.150000	Low	Neutral	.075000
Medium	Unfavorb.	.150000			

< PageDown > < PageUp > < Hardcopy > < Cancel >

Figure 18-7. Joint probabilities for BayesianAnalysis.

Marginal Probabilities for BayesianAnalysis

08-23-1993 18:55:41 Page: 1 of 1

Outcome or Indicator	Marginal Probability	Outcome or Indicator	Marginal Probability	Outcome or Indicator	Marginal Probability
Favorable	.330000	Unfavorb.	.355000	Neutral	.315000

< PageDown > < PageUp > < Hardcopy > < Cancel >

Figure 18-8. Marginal probabilities for BayesianAnalysis.

Posterior/Revised Probabilities for BayesianAnalys

08-23-1993 18:56:08 Page: 1 of 1

Outcome or Indicator	State	Posterior Probability	Outcome or Indicator	State	Posterior Probability
Favorable	High	.363636	Unfavorb.	Low	.464789
Favorable	Medium	.454546	Neutral	High	.126984
Favorable	Low	.181818	Neutral	Medium	.634921
Unfavorb.	High	.112676	Neutral	Low	.238095
Unfavorb.	Medium	.422535			

< PageDown > < PageUp > < Hardcopy > < Cancel >

Figure 18-9. Posterior/revised probabilities for BayesianAnalysis.

Example - Payoff Table Analysis

The options that the marketing department is considering are advertisement, do-nothing, and pricing strategies. Table 18-3 shows the potential payoffs of the decision alternatives. Perform a decision analysis.

Table 18-3. Payoffs (profits) of the marketing options.

State of nature	Marketing alternatives		
	Advertise	Do nothing	Pricing
High	$100,000	$35,000	$84,000
Medium	52,000	−10,000	55,000
Low	30,000	−30,000	40,000

Enter the Problem

1. Select "Data Entry" from the "Input Data" menu.
2. Figs. 18-10 to 18-17 show the entry for the payoff table analysis. Note that if there is no survey or experiment information, you enter one pseudo experiment outcome with all conditional probabilities equal to 1.

Problem Selection

· Select an option for your decision analysis.

Problem Name? [PayoffAnalysis]

Problem type: ( ) Bayesian Analysis
(•) Payoff Table Analysis
( ) Decision Tree Analysis

< OK > < Print > < Cancel >

Figure 18-10. Selection of Payoff table analysis.

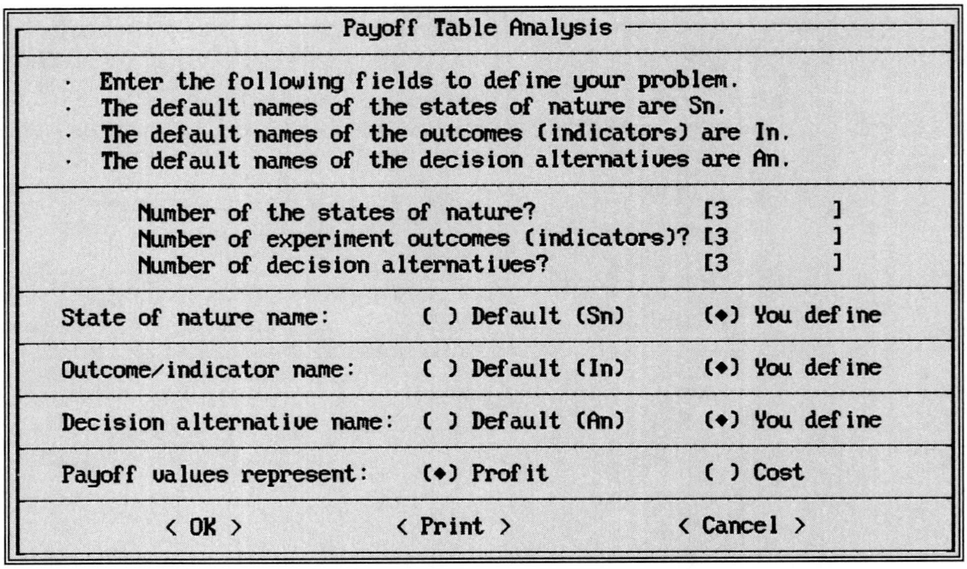

Figure 18-11. Problem specification for PayoffAnalysis.

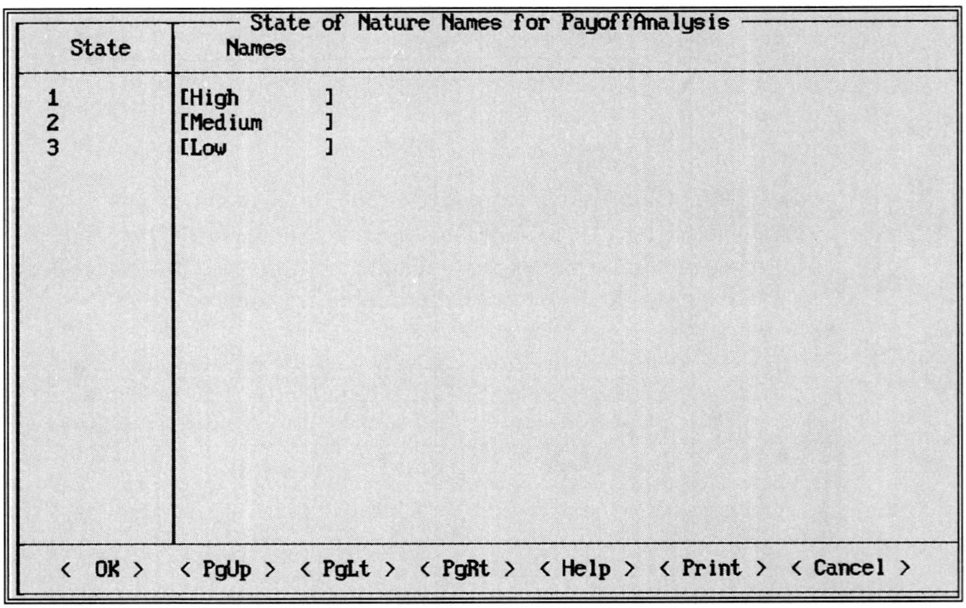

Figure 18-12. State of nature names for PayoffAnalysis.

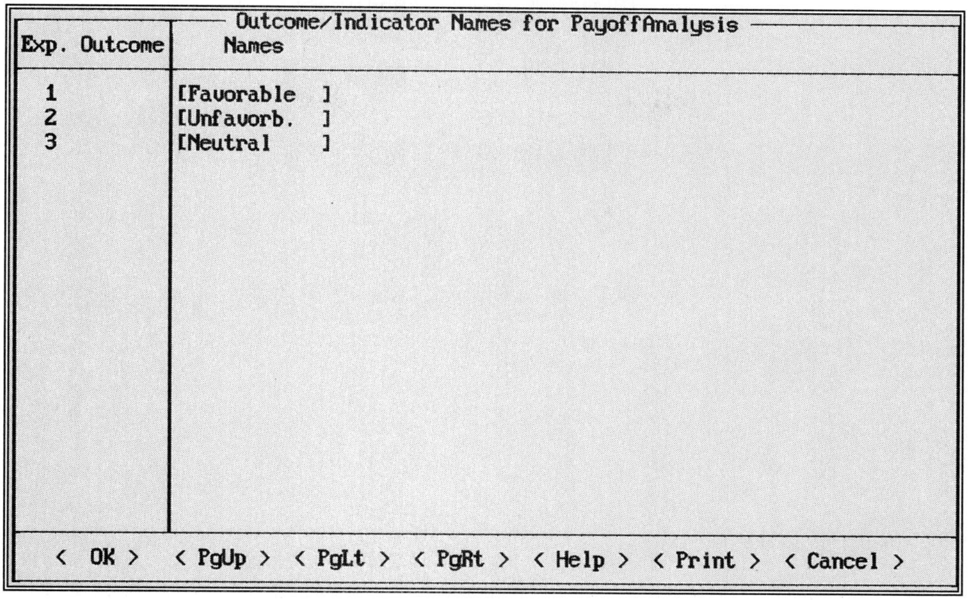

Figure 18-13. Experiment outcome/indicator names for PayoffAnalysis.

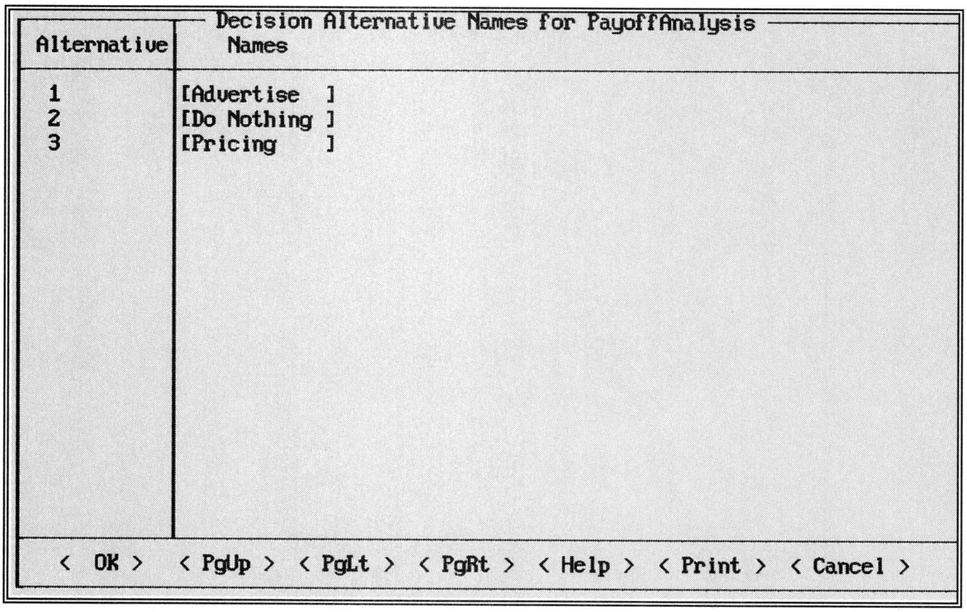

Figure 18-14. Decision alternative names for PayoffAnalysis.

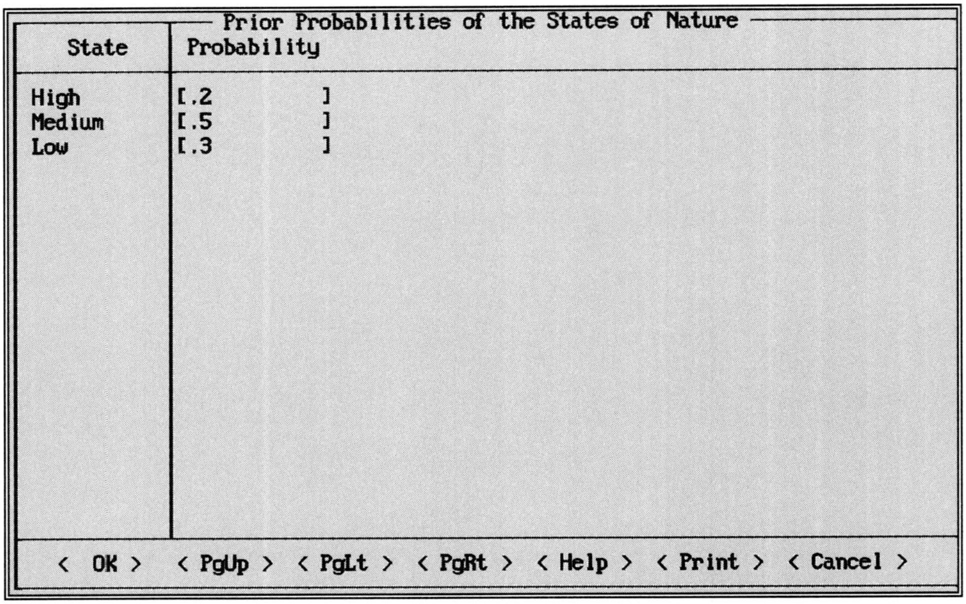

Figure 18-15. Prior probabilities for PayoffAnalysis.

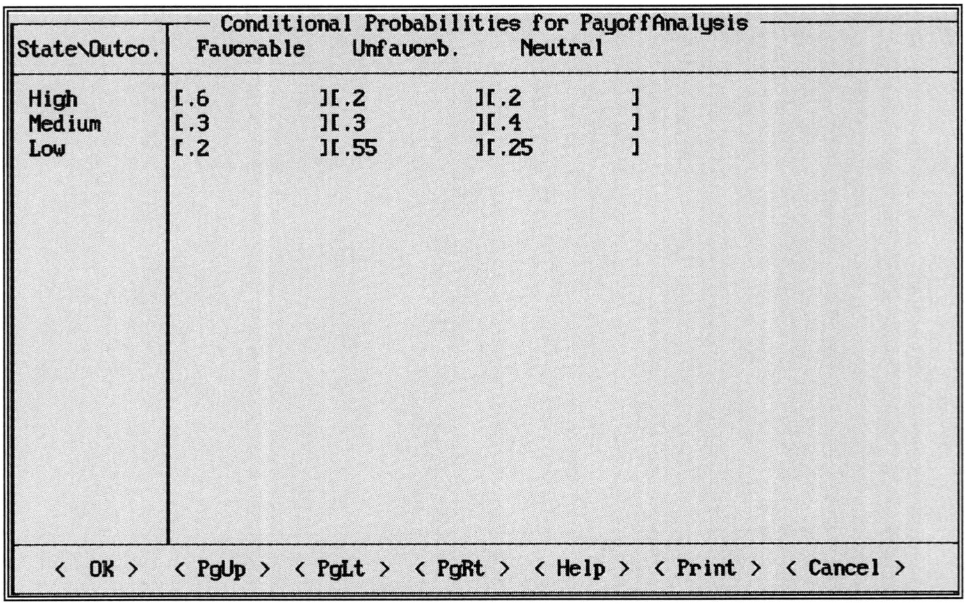

Figure 18-16. Conditional probabilities for PayoffAnalysis.

Payoff Values for PayoffAnalysis

State\Alter.	Advertise	Do Nothing	Pricing
High	[100000	][35000	][84000]
Medium	[52000	][-10000	][55000]
Low	[30000	][-30000	][40000]

< OK > < PgUp > < PgLt > < PgRt > < Help > < Print > < Cancel >

Figure 18-17. Payoff values for PayoffAnalysis.

Solve the Problem

1. Select "Solve the Problem" from the "Solution" menu to solve the problem.
2. After the problem is solved, select "Show the Solution" from the "Solution" menu to display the payoff analysis. Fig. 18-18 shows the joint probabilities; Fig. 18-19 shows the marginal probabilities of the survey outcomes; Fig. 18-20 shows the posterior or revised probabilities, which are the probabilities of the consumer demands given the outcomes of the survey; and Fig. 18-21 shows the decision analysis. Note that the expected value of perfect information (EVPI) is \$3200, and the expected value of the sample/experiment (survey) information is about \$870.

Joint Probabilities for PayoffAnalysis

08-23-1993 19:02:31 Page: 1 of 1

State	Outcome or Indicator	Joint Probability	State	Outcome or Indicator	Joint Probability
High	Favorable	.120000	Medium	Neutral	.200000
High	Unfavorb.	.040000	Low	Favorable	.060000
High	Neutral	.040000	Low	Unfavorb.	.165000
Medium	Favorable	.150000	Low	Neutral	.075000
Medium	Unfavorb.	.150000			

< PageDown > < PageUp > < Hardcopy > < Cancel >

Figure 18-18. Joint probabilities for PayoffAnalysis.

Marginal Probabilities for PayoffAnalysis
08-23-1993 19:02:58 Page: 1 of 1

Outcome or Indicator	Marginal Probability	Outcome or Indicator	Marginal Probability	Outcome or Indicator	Marginal Probability
Favorable	.330000	Unfavorb.	.355000	Neutral	.315000

< PageDown > < PageUp > < Hardcopy > < Cancel >

Figure 18-19. Marginal probabilities for PayoffAnalysis.

Posterior/Revised Probabilities for PayoffAnalysis
08-23-1993 19:03:21 Page: 1 of 1

Outcome or Indicator	State	Posterior Probability	Outcome or Indicator	State	Posterior Probability
Favorable	High	.363636	Unfavorb.	Low	.464789
Favorable	Medium	.454546	Neutral	High	.126984
Favorable	Low	.181818	Neutral	Medium	.634921
Unfavorb.	High	.112676	Neutral	Low	.238095
Unfavorb.	Medium	.422535			

< PageDown > < PageUp > < Hardcopy > < Cancel >

Figure 18-20. Posterior/revised probabilities for PayoffAnalysis.

Payoff Table Decision Given Outcomes for PayoffAna
08-23-1993 19:03:48 Page: 1 of 1

Outcome or Indicator	Maximin	Maximax	Minimax Regret	Expected Value	Insufficient Reason	Expected Regret
Favorable	Pricing	Advertise	Advertise	Advertise	Advertise	Advertise
(value)	40000	100000	10000	65454.55	60666.66	3181.818
Unfavorb.	Pricing	Advertise	Advertise	Pricing	Advertise	Pricing
(value)	40000	100000	10000	51295.78	60666.66	1802.817
Neutral	Pricing	Advertise	Advertise	Pricing	Advertise	Pricing
(value)	40000	100000	10000	55111.11	60666.66	2031.746

Expected Value without Sample (Experiment) = 56300 Decision: Pricing
Expected Value with Perfect Information = 59500
Expected Value with Sample (Experiment) Information = 57170
EVPI = 3200 EVSI = 870.0039 Sample Information Efficiency = 27.187%

< PageDown > < PageUp > < Hardcopy > < Cancel >

Figure 18-21. Decision analysis for PayoffAnalysis.

Example - Decision Tree Analysis

The above situation can be represented by the decision tree shown in Fig. 18-22. Note that circles represent chance nodes, squares represent decision nodes, and dots are terminal nodes. Nodes are numbered from 1 to 40, including terminal nodes. The payoff values in the tree are in thousands.

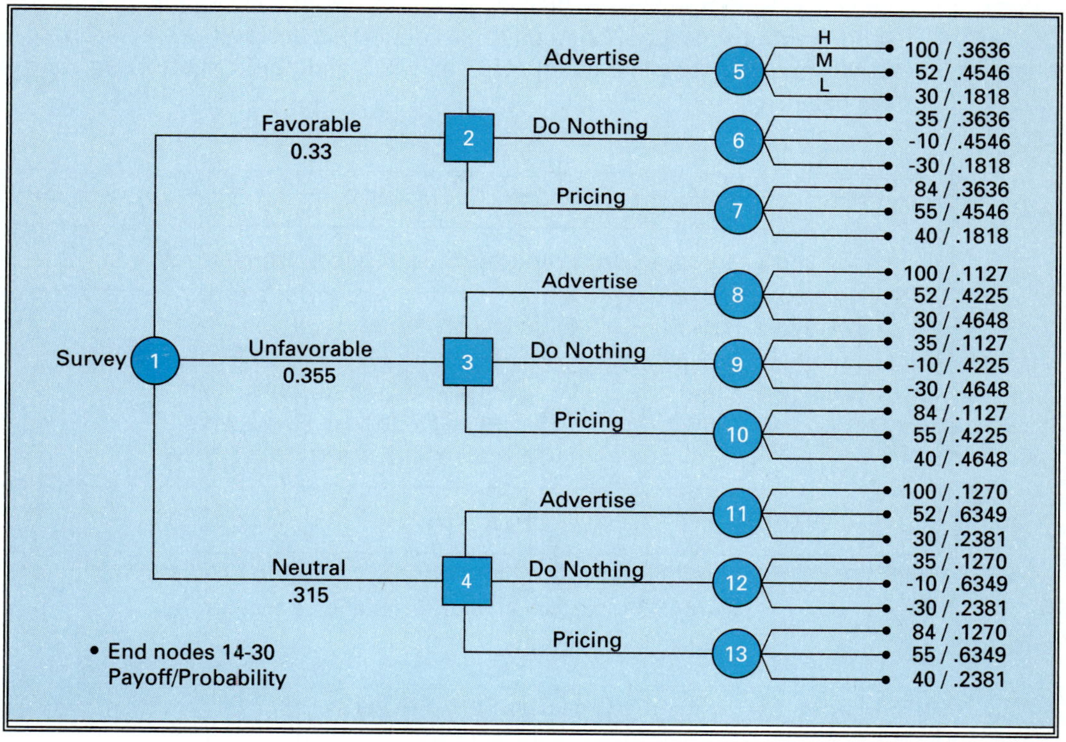

Figure 18-22. Decision tree.

Enter the Problem

1. Select "Data Entry" from the "Input Data" menu.
2. Fig. 18-23 selects the decision tree problem, and Fig. 18-24 specifies the problem. Note that "Maximization" (profit) is specified for the objective.
3. Figs. 18-25 to 18-27 show the data entry for the nodes. Node types 1, 2, and 3 represent decision, chance, and terminal, respectively. You may enter a payoff value (cost or profit) for each node. For a maximization problem such as this one, positive values represent net profits and negative values represent net costs or losses. The reverse is true for the minimization problem. Note that if you have more than 18 nodes, use the "PgDn" and "PgUp" buttons to control the pages.

4. Figs. 18-28 to 18-35 enter the connections between nodes. Any non-blank entry represents a valid connection between two nodes. Usually, we use a fractional number to represent a probability connection from one chance node to another, and a non-empty letter to represent a pure connection from one decision node to another. For example, in Fig. 18-28, .33 is the probability from node 1-Survey to node 2-Favor., and .355 is the probability from node 1-Survey to node 3-Unfavor. A non-empty letter "x" in Fig. 18-28 from node 2-Favor. to node 5-Adver. or in Fig. 18-29 from node 2-Favor. to node 6-DoNothng represents a pure connection. For a multiple connection decision tree problem such as this one, use the "PgDn", "PgUp", "PgRt", and "PgLt" buttons to control the pages.

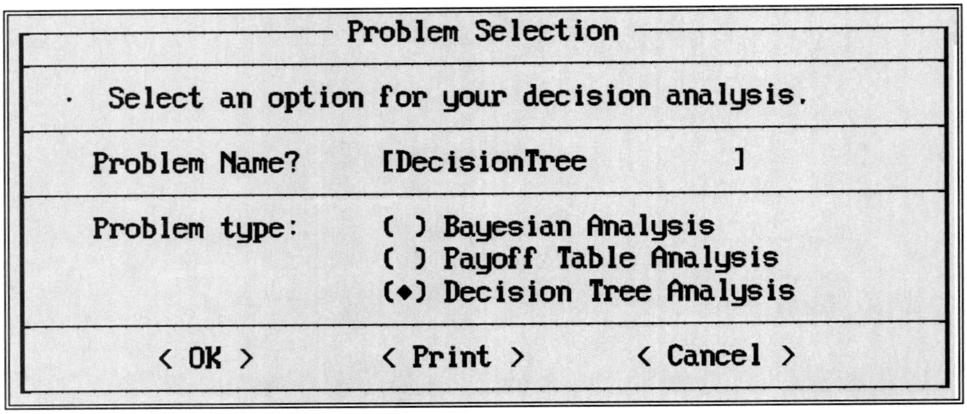

Figure 18-23. Selection of the decision tree analysis.

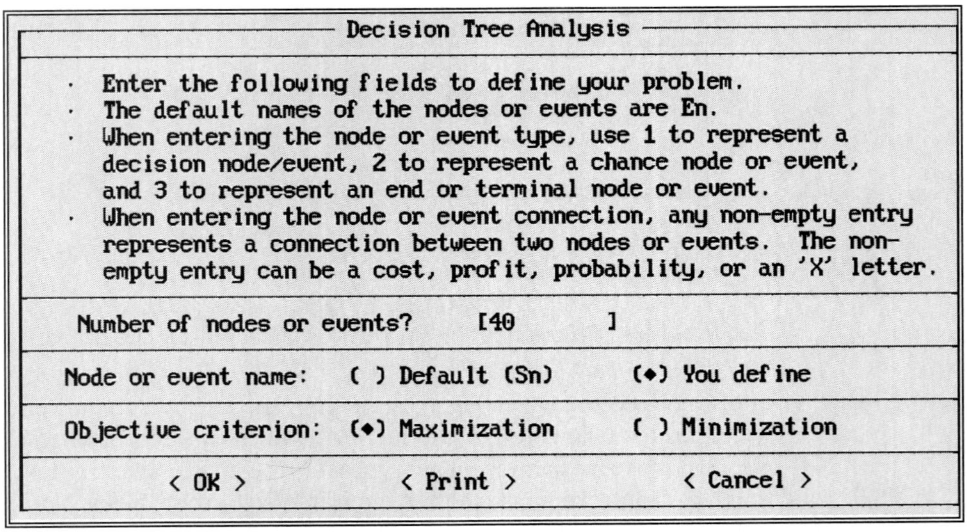

Figure 18-24. Specification of the decision tree.

```
Decision Tree Nodes or Events for DecisionTree
Node/Event    Names          Type        Direct Cost/Profit

  1           [1-Survey    ][2          ][              ]
  2           [2-Favor.    ][1          ][              ]
  3           [3-Unfavor.  ][1          ][              ]
  4           [4-Neutral   ][1          ][              ]
  5           [5-Adver.    ][2          ][              ]
  6           [6-DoNothng  ][2          ][              ]
  7           [7-Pricing   ][2          ][              ]
  8           [8-Adver.    ][2          ][              ]
  9           [9-DoNothng  ][2          ][              ]
  10          [10-Pricing  ][2          ][              ]
  11          [11-Adver.   ][2          ][              ]
  12          [12-DoNoth.  ][2          ][              ]
  13          [13-Pricing  ][2          ][              ]
  14          [14-High     ][3          ][100000        ]
  15          [15-Medium   ][3          ][52000         ]
  16          [16-Low      ][3          ][30000         ]
  17          [17-High     ][3          ][35000         ]
  18          [18-Medium   ][3          ][-10000        ]

  < PgDn >  < PgUp >  < PgLt >  < PgRt >  < Help >  < Print >  < Cancel >
```

Figure 18-25. Node/event definition for DecisionTree.

```
Decision Tree Nodes or Events for DecisionTree
Node/Event    Names          Type        Direct Cost/Profit

  19          [19-Low      ][3          ][-30000        ]
  20          [20-High     ][3          ][84000         ]
  21          [21-Medium   ][3          ][55000         ]
  22          [22-Low      ][3          ][40000         ]
  23          [23-High     ][3          ][100000        ]
  24          [24-Medium   ][3          ][52000         ]
  25          [25-Low      ][3          ][30000         ]
  26          [26-High     ][3          ][35000         ]
  27          [27-Medium   ][3          ][-10000        ]
  28          [28-Low      ][3          ][-30000        ]
  29          [29-High     ][3          ][84000         ]
  30          [30-Medium   ][3          ][55000         ]
  31          [31-Low      ][3          ][40000         ]
  32          [32-High     ][3          ][100000        ]
  33          [33-Medium   ][3          ][52000         ]
  34          [34-Low      ][3          ][30000         ]
  35          [35-High     ][3          ][35000         ]
  36          [36-Medium   ][3          ][-10000        ]

  < PgDn >  < PgUp >  < PgLt >  < PgRt >  < Help >  < Print >  < Cancel >
```

Figure 18-26. Node/event definition for DecisionTree (continued).

Decision Tree Nodes or Events for DecisionTree

Node/Event	Names	Type	Direct Cost/Profit
23	23-High	3	100000
24	24-Medium	3	52000
25	25-Low	3	30000
26	26-High	3	35000
27	27-Medium	3	-10000
28	28-Low	3	-30000
29	29-High	3	84000
30	30-Medium	3	55000
31	31-Low	3	40000
32	32-High	3	100000
33	33-Medium	3	52000
34	34-Low	3	30000
35	35-High	3	35000
36	36-Medium	3	-10000
37	37-Low	3	-30000
38	38-High	3	84000
39	39-Medium	3	55000
40	40-Low	3	40000

< OK > < PgUp > < PgLt > < PgRt > < Help > < Print > < Cancel >

Figure 18-27. Node/event definition for DecisionTree (continued).

Decision Tree Connection Values for DecisionTree

From / To	1-Survey	2-Favor.	3-Unfavor.	4-Neutral	5-Adver.
1-Survey		.33	.355	.315	
2-Favor.					x
3-Unfavor.					
4-Neutral					
5-Adver.					
6-DoNothng					
7-Pricing					
8-Adver.					
9-DoNothng					
10-Pricing					
11-Adver.					
12-DoNoth.					
13-Pricing					
14-High					
15-Medium					
16-Low					
17-High					
18-Medium					

< PgDn > < PgUp > < PgLt > < PgRt > < Help > < Print > < Cancel >

Figure 18-28. Node connection values for DecisionTree.

Decision Tree Connection Values for DecisionTree

From / To	6-DoNothng	7-Pricing	8-Adver.	9-DoNothng	10-Pricing
1-Survey					
2-Favor.	x	x			
3-Unfavor.			x	x	x
4-Neutral					
5-Adver.					
6-DoNothng					
7-Pricing					
8-Adver.					
9-DoNothng					
10-Pricing					
11-Adver.					
12-DoNoth.					
13-Pricing					
14-High					
15-Medium					
16-Low					
17-High					
18-Medium					

< PgDn > < PgUp > < PgLt > < PgRt > < Help > < Print > < Cancel >

Figure 18-29. Node connection values for DecisionTree (continued).

Decision Tree Connection Values for DecisionTree

From / To	11-Adver.	12-DoNoth.	13-Pricing	14-High	15-Medium
1-Survey					
2-Favor.					
3-Unfavor.					
4-Neutral	x	x	x		
5-Adver.				.3636	.4546
6-DoNothng					
7-Pricing					
8-Adver.					
9-DoNothng					
10-Pricing					
11-Adver.					
12-DoNoth.					
13-Pricing					
14-High					
15-Medium					
16-Low					
17-High					
18-Medium					

< PgDn > < PgUp > < PgLt > < PgRt > < Help > < Print > < Cancel >

Figure 18-30. Node connection values for DecisionTree (continued).

Decision Tree Connection Values for DecisionTree

From / To	16-Low	17-High	18-Medium	19-Low	20-High
1-Survey					
2-Favor.					
3-Unfavor.					
4-Neutral					
5-Adver.	.1818				
6-DoNothng		.3636	.4546	.1818	
7-Pricing					.3636
8-Adver.					
9-DoNothng					
10-Pricing					
11-Adver.					
12-DoNoth.					
13-Pricing					
14-High					
15-Medium					
16-Low					
17-High					
18-Medium					

< PgDn > < PgUp > < PgLt > < PgRt > < Help > < Print > < Cancel >

Figure 18-31. Node connection values for DecisionTree (continued).

Decision Tree Connection Values for DecisionTree

From / To	21-Medium	22-Low	23-High	24-Medium	25-Low
1-Survey					
2-Favor.					
3-Unfavor.					
4-Neutral					
5-Adver.					
6-DoNothng					
7-Pricing	.4546	.1818			
8-Adver.			.1127	.4225	.4648
9-DoNothng					
10-Pricing					
11-Adver.					
12-DoNoth.					
13-Pricing					
14-High					
15-Medium					
16-Low					
17-High					
18-Medium					

< PgDn > < PgUp > < PgLt > < PgRt > < Help > < Print > < Cancel >

Figure 18-32. Node connection values for DecisionTree (continued).

Decision Tree Connection Values for DecisionTree

From / To	26-High	27-Medium	28-Low	29-High	30-Medium
1-Survey					
2-Favor.					
3-Unfavor.					
4-Neutral					
5-Adver.					
6-DoNothng					
7-Pricing					
8-Adver.					
9-DoNothng	.1127	.4225	.4648		
10-Pricing				.1127	.4225
11-Adver.					
12-DoNoth.					
13-Pricing					
14-High					
15-Medium					
16-Low					
17-High					
18-Medium					

< PgDn > < PgUp > < PgLt > < PgRt > < Help > < Print > < Cancel >

Figure 18-33. Node connection values for DecisionTree (continued).

Decision Tree Connection Values for DecisionTree

From / To	31-Low	32-High	33-Medium	34-Low	35-High
1-Survey					
2-Favor.					
3-Unfavor.					
4-Neutral					
5-Adver.					
6-DoNothng					
7-Pricing					
8-Adver.					
9-DoNothng					
10-Pricing	.4648				
11-Adver.		.1270	.6349	.2381	
12-DoNoth.					.1270
13-Pricing					
14-High					
15-Medium					
16-Low					
17-High					
18-Medium					

< PgDn > < PgUp > < PgLt > < PgRt > < Help > < Print > < Cancel >

Figure 18-34. Node connection values for DecisionTree (continued).

Decision Tree Connection Values for DecisionTree

From / To	36-Medium	37-Low	38-High	39-Medium	40-Low
1-Survey					
2-Favor.					
3-Unfavor.					
4-Neutral					
5-Adver.					
6-DoNothng					
7-Pricing					
8-Adver.					
9-DoNothng					
10-Pricing					
11-Adver.					
12-DoNoth.	.6349	.2381			
13-Pricing			.1270	.6349	.2381
14-High					
15-Medium					
16-Low					
17-High					
18-Medium					

< PgDn > < PgUp > < PgLt > < PgRt > < Help > < Print > < Cancel >

Figure 18-35. Node connection values for DecisionTree (continued).

Solve the Problem

1. Select "Solve the Problem" from the "Solution" menu to solve the problem.
2. After the problem is solved, select "Show the Solution" from the "Solution" menu to display the decision tree analysis. Fig. 18-36 shows the analysis. Node

Decision Tree Analysis for DecisionTree

08-23-1993 19:27:27 Page: 1 of 1

Node/Event	Type	Expected Value	Decision
1-Survey	Chance	57169.86	
2-Favor.	Decision	65453.2	5-Adver.
3-Unfavor.	Decision	51296.3	10-Pricing
4-Neutral	Decision	55111.5	13-Pricing
5-Adver.	Chance	65453.2	
6-DoNothng	Chance	2725.999	
7-Pricing	Chance	62817.4	
8-Adver.	Chance	47184	
9-DoNothng	Chance	-14224.5	
10-Pricing	Chance	51296.3	
11-Adver.	Chance	52857.8	
12-DoNoth.	Chance	-9047	
13-Pricing	Chance	55111.5	

Overall Value = 57169.86 Elapsed CPU seconds = .0546875

< PageDown > < PageUp > < Hardcopy > < Cancel >

Figure 18-36. Decision-tree analysis.

1-Survey has expected value $57,169.86; node 2-Favor. is a decision node and has the decision to go to 5-Adver. with the expected value of $65,453.20, and so on.

EXERCISES

1. The following matrix gives the posterior probabilities for three states of nature (A, B, and C) and three survey results (a, b, and c). The marginal probabilities associated with a, b, and c are .24, .31, and .45, respectively.

Survey result	State of nature A	B	C
a	.67	.12	.21
b	.07	.77	.16
c	.04	.07	.89

a. Determine the joint probabilities associated with each survey result and state of nature.

b. What are the conditional probabilities (i.e, the probabilities of each survey result) under the conditions of each state of nature?

2. Consider the following profit table, where I to V are alternatives and S1 to S5 are states of nature. The prior probabilities associated with S1 to S5 are .3, .2, .1, .15, and .25, respectively. (Hint: Use one outcome or indicator.)

State of nature	Alternative I	II	III	IV	V
S1	$10,000	$17,000	$5,000	$35,000	$45,000
S2	31,000	67,000	45,000	19,000	51,000
S3	11,000	13,000	13,000	9,000	8,000
S4	39,000	22,000	18,000	29,000	40,000
S5	54,000	43,000	32,000	35,000	45,000

a. Which alternative maximizes expected monetary value?

b. Which is the best decision if you use minimax regret as the criterion?

c. What if you use maximin as the criterion?

3. The following payoff matrix indicates the monetary values that would be realized for each of the three alternatives (A1, A2, A3) and the three states of nature (S1, S2, S3). All dollar amounts are in thousands.

Probability	State of nature	A1	A2	A3
.3	S1	$1000	$0	$−400
.5	S2	−200	0	100
.2	S3	−2000	0	500

a. Use the expected value to choose an alternative.

b. A market analyst offers to conduct a survey to determine which state of nature might occur. The analyst indicates that the survey will be 80% accurate; that is, if S1 will occur, there is an 80% chance that the survey will indicate this, whereas there is a 10% chance that it will indicate each of the other two states. The same is true if S2 occurs or if S3 occurs. If you go ahead with the survey, then either A1 or A3 must be chosen.

i. Determine the posterior probabilities.

ii. Draw a decision tree to represent these situations and find the best strategy.

4. The following questions relate to the decision tree shown in Fig. 18-37. Note that the cost of the survey ($100) has not been subtracted from the terminal values. Nodes 14 to 25 are terminal nodes. The numbers in parentheses are probabilities.

a. What is the recommended strategy?

b. What is the most you would be willing to pay for the survey information?

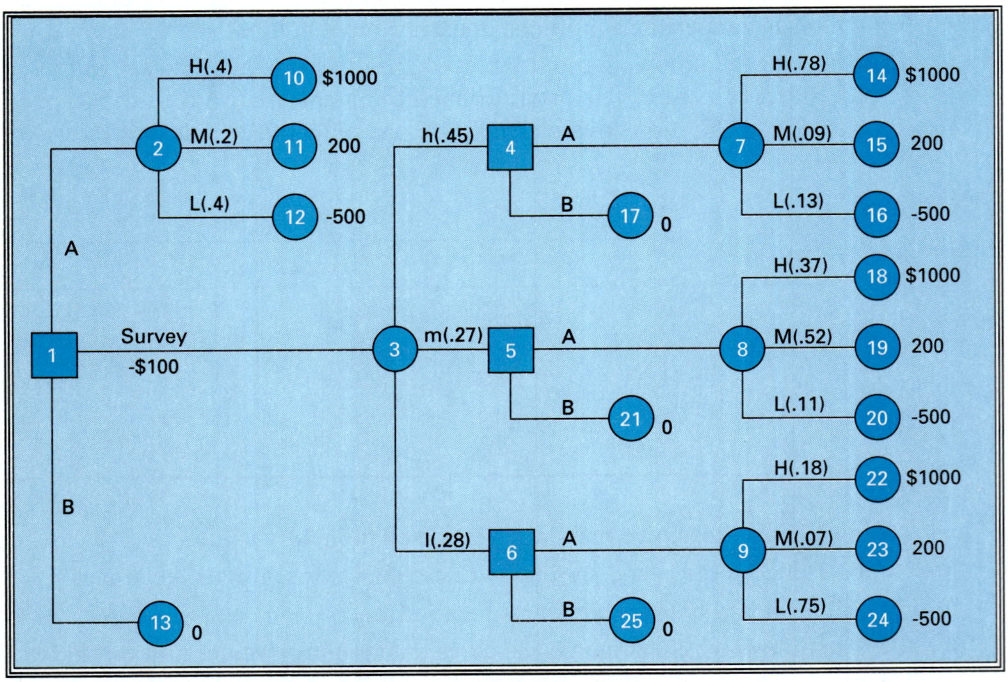

Figure 18-37. Decision tree for exercise 4.

5. Joe Stingy needed a camera. The model that appealed to him had a firm retail price of \$420 at local camera stores. On the chance that he could save some money, Joe called on Slippery Jim, the proprietor of a discount store that specialized in "seconds" - articles that had been rejected for retail sale. Sure enough, Slippery Jim had just the camera Joe wanted, and he was offering it for \$270. Looking it over, Joe thought that the camera body seemed fine, but he was not sure about the lens. From experience, he felt there was a .3 probability that a new lens would have to be purchased at a cost of \$240. Joe had a "friend" who, for \$20, could tell for certain whether the lens was acceptable or not. A local lens-testing service would charge only \$12, but the probability that the test results would be accurate was .9. Slippery Jim would allow Joe to test the camera only if he left a \$10 nonrefundable deposit.

a. Assume that Joe will not use the testing services and that he will make a decision immediately. Construct the payoff table that describes the alternatives, states of nature, and associated monetary values. What is the decision by expected value?

b. Now assume that Joe either decides immediately or uses the testing services. Construct a decision tree that describes the sequence of alternatives available to Joe and analyze it to determine the best decision for Joe.

19

MARKOV PROCESS (MKV)

OVERVIEW OF THE MKV DECISION SUPPORT SYSTEM

This program solves the probability of a system in a particular state at a particular time period by using the Markov process model. You may also let the program solve the steady-state probabilities, if they exist. The program will analyze the expected cost if the cost information is provided, and find the first passage times from state to state, if they exist.

The inputs include the initial state probabilities and the transition probabilities from one state to the others, and the cost or profit associated with each state, if available. If the initial state probabilities are not known, the program will assume equal probability for each state. You may name each state up to ten characters.

You may save, read, modify, or print the input data as well as to display, print, or save the solution.

TECHNICAL NOTES ON THE MKV PROGRAM

1. Let T represent the transition probability matrix, π represent the probability vector for the states, and i represent period. Therefore, π_0 is the initial state probability vector, and $\pi_{i+1} = T\,\pi_i$. The steady-state exists if there is a solution for the equation $\pi = T\,\pi$.
2. If you choose to solve the state probabilities by steps, the program will end when the specific iteration number reaches or the differences of state probabilities for the consecutive period all are less than 10^{-6}.
3. The first passage time of state p to state q is defined as after the expected number of transitions (periods), the system will go from state p to state q for the first time. If $p = q$, it is called recurrence time, that is, the length of time it takes for the process to come back to the original state.

MENU STRUCTURE

The functions and options in each of the pull-down menus are hierarchically listed as follows:

Modules
- Linear Programming (LP)
- Integer Linear Programming (ILP)
- Goal Programming (GP)
- Quadratic Programming (QP)
- Nonlinear Programming (NLP)
- Dynamic Programming (DP)
- Transportation and Transshipment (TRP)
- Assignment and Traveling Salesman (ASTS)
- Specialized Network Modeling (SNET)
- Capacitated Network Flow Modeling (CNET)
- Project Scheduling: CPM/PERT
- Inventory Theory (INVT)
- Inventory Theory 2 (INVT2)
- Queuing Theory (QUEUE)
- Queuing System Simulation (QSIM)
- Decision Analysis (DA)
- Markov Process (MKV)
- Time Series Forecasting (TSFC)
- Financial Analysis (FA)
- Exit from QSB

Input Data
- Data Entry
- Read a File
- Show Data
- Print Data
- Modify Data
- Save
- Save As
- Exit from QSB

Solution
- Solve the Steady-state
- Solve and Display Steps
- Solve up to a Specific Period
- Show the Solution
- Print the Solution
- Save the Solution

Options
- Color
- Monochrome
- Printer Selection

Help - MKV
- About MKV
- About the User Interface
- About the Edit Keys

SOLVING PROBLEMS WITH MKV

In the following sections, we will use example problems to show how to enter and solve the problems. The general procedure and menu options are described in detail in the tutorial sections of Chapter 2.

Example

To demonstrate the use of MKV, consider the following sample problem. Market survey concluded that a customer who buys product brand A now will have a .2 probability of buying brand A again, a .3 probability of buying product brand B, and a .5 probability of buying product brand C. Similarly, a customer who buys brand B or C will have different probabilities of buying different brands next time. Table 19-1 shows these transition probabilities. Jimmy is the average customer who just bought brand B this time. What is the probability that he will buy brand A the next two times? What are the probabilities that Jimmy will buy brand A, B, or C in the long run?

Table 19-1. Transition probabilities.

This time	Next time A	Next time B	Next time C
A	.2	.3	.5
B	.4	.3	.3
C	.2	.4	.4

Enter the Problem

1. Select "Data Entry" from the "Input Data" menu (refer to Chapter 2 for selecting a menu item).
2. Fig. 19-1 shows the problem specification. Note that costs or profits of the states are unknown.

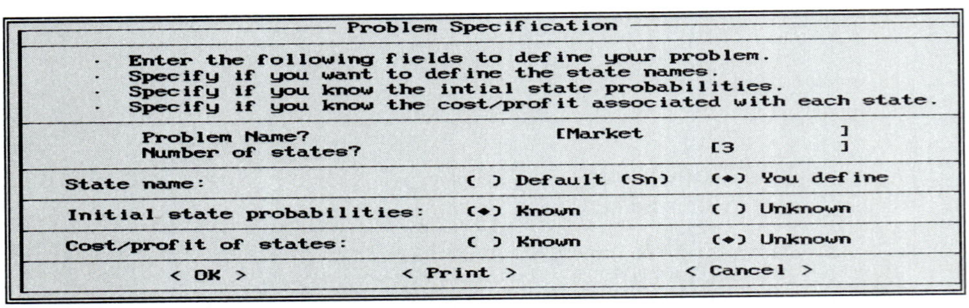

Figure 19-1. Problem specification for the problem Market.

3. Fig. 19-2 shows the state names, Fig. 19-3 shows the initial state probability (Jimmy bought product B), and Fig. 19-4 shows the transition probabilities.

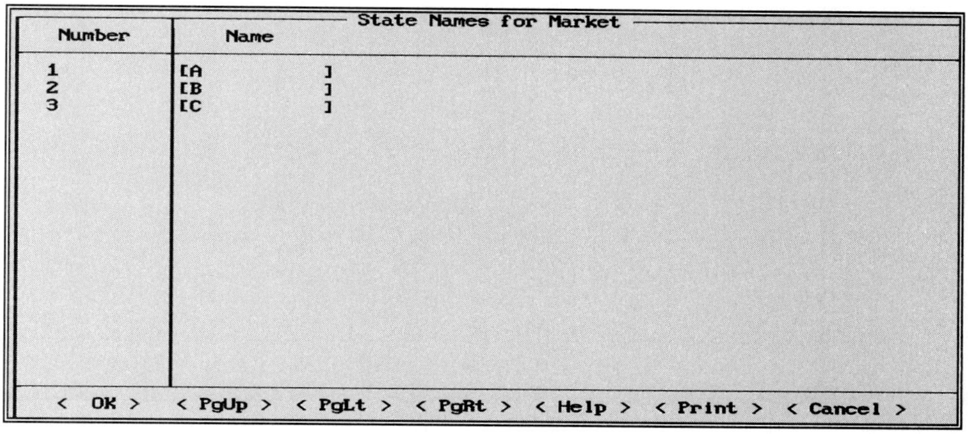

Figure 19-2. Entry of the state names.

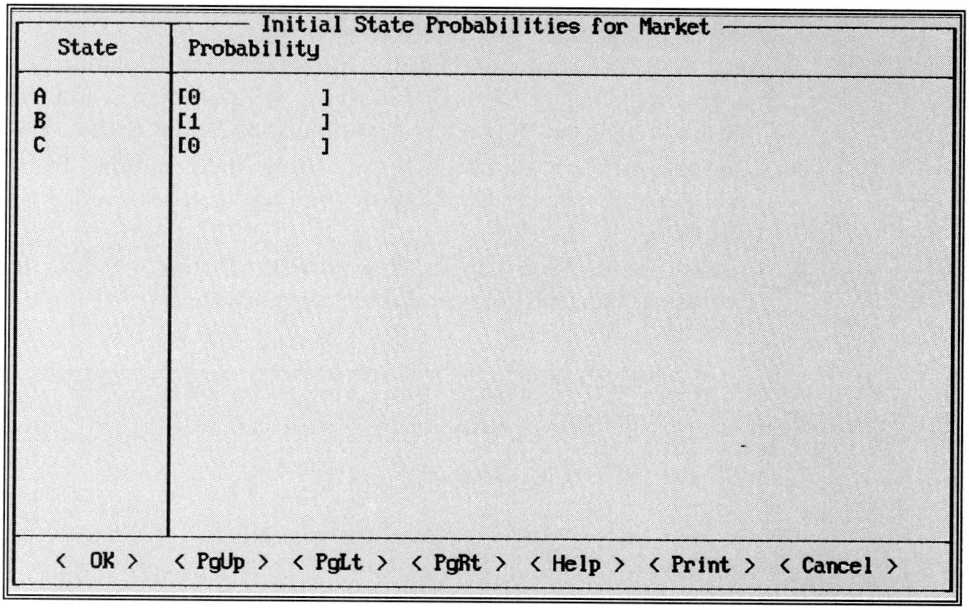

Figure 19-3. Entry of the initial state probabilities.

Transition Probabilities for Market

From \ To:	A	B	C
A	[.2	][.3	][.5]
B	[.4	][.3	][.3]
C	[.2	][.4	][.4]

< OK > < PgUp > < PgLt > < PgRt > < Help > < Print > < Cancel >

Figure 19-4. Entry of the state transition probabilities.

Solve the Problem

1. Select "Solve the Steady-state" from the "Solution" menu to solve the problem. The message "Please standby..." will display for a short period while the problem is being solved.
2. You may choose "Solve and Display Steps" from the "Solution" menu to show the iterations. Figs. 19-5 to 19-7 illustrate iteration 0 to 2. Jimmy will have .4 chance to buy brand A product next time and .26 chance the following time.
3. After the problem is solved, select "Show the Solution" from the "Solution" menu to display the Markov analysis. Fig. 19-8 and Fig. 19-9 show the results.
4. You may choose "Solve up to a Specific Period" from the "Solution" menu to perform only specific iterations of the Markov process.

State Probabilities of Period 0

08-23-1993 19:31:06 Page: 1

State	Probability	State	Probability	State	Probability
A	0	B	1	C	0

< Next Period > < Non Stop > < PageDown > < PageUp > < Hardcopy > < Cancel >

Figure 19-5. Iteration 0.

State Probabilities of Period 1

08-23-1993 19:31:33 Page: 1

State	Probability	State	Probability	State	Probability
A	.4	B	.3	C	.3

< Next Period > < Non Stop > < PageDown > < PageUp > < Hardcopy > < Cancel >

Figure 19-6. Iteration 1.

State Probabilities of Period 2

08-23-1993 19:31:58 Page: 1

State	Probability	State	Probability	State	Probability
A	.26	B	.33	C	.41

< Next Period > < Non Stop > < PageDown > < PageUp > < Hardcopy > < Cancel >

Figure 19-7. Iteration 2.

Steady State Solution for Market

08-23-1993 19:36:02 Page: 1 of 1

State Name	State Probability	Recurrence Time	State Name	State Probability	Recurrence Time
A	.2678571	3.733333	C	.3928572	2.545455
B	.3392857	2.947368			

Expected Cost/Profit = 0 Elapsed CPU Seconds = 0

< PageDown > < PageUp > < Hardcopy > < Cancel >

Figure 19-8. Steady-state probabilities.

First Passage Times for Market

08-23-1993 19:33:05 Page: 1 of 1

From State	To State	First Passage Time	From State	To State	First Passage Time
A	A	3.733333	B	C	2.727273
A	B	2.894737	C	A	3.666667
A	C	2.272727	C	B	2.631579
B	A	3	C	C	2.545454
B	B	2.947368			

< PageDown > < PageUp > < Hardcopy > < Cancel >

Figure 19-9. First passage times.

Example - Cost Data Known

If the prices of the brands A, B, and C are \$3.50, \$4.00, and \$3.95, respectively, how much we can expect a customer will spend on this kind of product each time? For this problem, specify the cost known in Fig. 19-1, and besides state names, initial probabilities, and transition probabilities, enter the state costs as shown in Fig. 19-10. Solve the steady-state; Fig. 19-11 shows the expected spending for this product is about \$3.85.

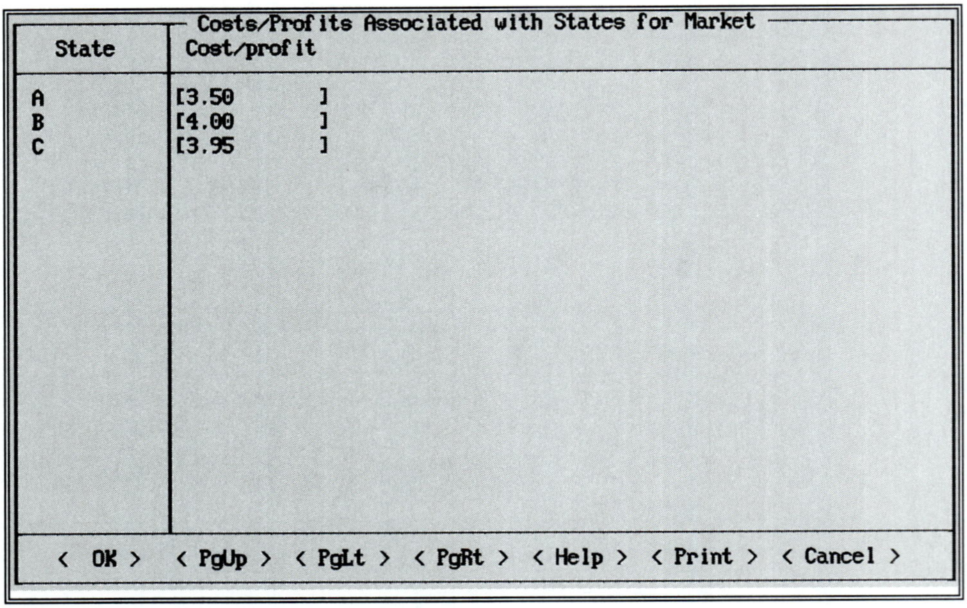

Figure 19-10. State costs for Market.

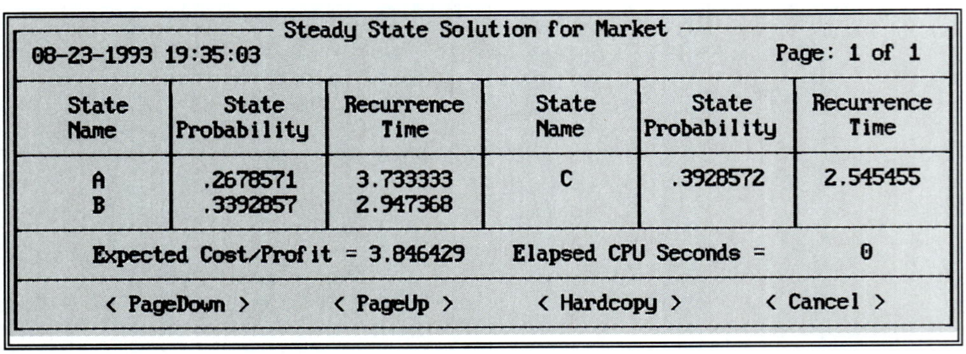

Figure 19-11. Steady-state solution with costs.

EXERCISES

1. A laboratory has conducted an experiment about the random walk of an animal. From some preliminary tests, if the animal goes to the right this time, the probabilities that it will go to the right, left, up, or down next time are .2, .4, .4, and 0, respectively. The following table summarizes these probabilities. What is your prediction concerning how many times the animal will turn to the right or left in 100 walks? Assume the animal's first turn is right.

Transition probability

	Right	Left	Up	Down
Right	.2	.4	.4	0
Left	.1	.3	.4	.2
Up	.7	.1	.1	.1
Down	.2	.3	.1	.4

2. Consider the system with the following initial probability vector and transition probability matrix.

Initial probability vector:

<.1 .2 .3 .05 .05 .1 .05 .15 0>

Transition probability matrix:

	S1	S2	S3	S4	S5	S6	S7	S8	S9
S1	.1	.05	.1	.2	.05	.3	.1	.1	0
S2	.05	.05	.1	.15	.15	.1	.2	.1	.1
S3	.15	.15	.05	.05	.15	.2	.05	.1	.1
S4	.2	.3	.05	.15	0	0	0	.1	.2
S5	.1	.2	.05	.05	.15	.2	.05	0	.2
S6	0	.3	.1	.2	.1	.1	.05	.15	0
S7	.5	.1	.05	.05	.05	.1	0	0	.15
S8	.2	.1	.05	.15	.15	.15	0	.1	.1
S9	.1	0	.2	.1	.15	.1	.05	.2	.1

a. What is the probability that S5 occurs at the fifth period?

b. What is the probability that S3 occurs at the tenth period?

c. What are the probabilities of each state in the long run?

3. In a certain state, a voter is allowed to change his or her party affiliation (for primary elections) only by abstaining from voting in the primary for at least one year. Let D, R, and A, respectively, indicate that a person votes Democratic, votes Republican, or abstains from primary voting in any given year.

a. If the following one-step transition probability matrix represents general voting behavior in the state, what is the probability that a person abstaining this year will abstain two years from now?

	D	R	A
D	1/2	0	1/2
R	0	3/4	1/4
A	1/2	1/2	0

b. Last year, one half of the population voted Democratic, one quarter Republican, and the remainder abstained. What do you expect to be the voting proportions in the next primary, given the same transition matrix?

c. In the long run, what proportion of the population will be voting Democratic, Republican, or abstaining in the primary elections? Again, assume the one-step transition matrix just used.

20

TIME SERIES AND FORECASTING (TSFC)

OVERVIEW OF THE TSFC DECISION SUPPORT SYSTEM

This program performs time series forecasting and linear regression. Time series methods include simple average, moving average with or without trend, single and double exponential smoothing with or without trend, adaptive exponential smoothing, linear regression, and Winter's model. The program can handle more than 1000 historical data depending on the computer memory. You may add or delete historical data for the time moving on by choosing to modify the original data. Save the data after making any change. When performing time series forecasting, you may be asked to provide parameters for the specific model you choose, or let TSFC search for the best parameters based on the specified performance measure. TSFC also allows you to define the initial values such as the initial forecast and the seasonality index. You can choose the option of plotting the forecasting results.

For linear regression, you can enter multiple variable observations. By specifying a dependent variable, the program performs regression analysis, analysis of variance (ANOVA), correlation analysis, and predictions. You may add or delete any observations. After performing regression, you can display, save, or print the result.

TECHNICAL NOTES ON THE TSFC PROGRAM

1. For time series, TSFC computes the forecast based on the historical data, that is, time series data. Available forecasting models are:

- **a.** Simple average
- **b.** Weighted moving average
- **c.** Moving average with linear trend
- **d.** Single exponential smoothing
- **e.** Exponential smoothing with linear trend
- **f.** Double exponential smoothing
- **g.** Double exponential smoothing with linear trend
- **h.** Adaptive exponential smoothing

i. Linear regression

j. Winter's model

2. Some of the methods require users to enter additional parameters. For example, the moving average requires the number of moving periods, and the exponential smoothing requires a smoothing constant and/or trend constant. Refer to the formula shown later.
3. Four performance measures are provided in TSFC for time series forecasting. They are the mean absolute deviation (MAD), mean square deviation (MSD), bias, and R_2 (multiple correlation coefficient or coefficient of determination). They are defined later.
4. Based on one of the four performance measures, you may let the program search the best parameters for the specific model based on provided parameter ranges. TSFC uses a golden section type of line search to find the best parameters. It usually obtains a very good solution but does not guarantee the global optimal. If you are not satisfied with the obtained parameters, try to search with a different parameter range.
5. For time series forecasting, you have the option to plot the forecasts on the screen with different scales.
6. Notation and formula for time series forecasting:

t:	Time or period, t = 1,2, . . . ,n
τ:	Time from t
m:	Moving average periods or seasonal cycle length
α:	First smoothing parameter
β:	Trend smoothing parameter
γ:	Seasonal smoothing parameter
A(t):	Actual data in period t
f(t):	Forecast for period t
T(t):	Trend for period t
F(t):	Smoothed value for period t
W(t):	Weight for period t
I(t):	Seasonal index for period t
e(t):	Error (deviation) for period t, which is f(t) − A(t)
N:	Number of periods that e(t) can be found, i.e., have both f(t) and A(t)
A:	Average of actual data
V:	Variance of actual data for the N periods
MAD:	Mean absolute error (deviation), MAD $= \Sigma_t \lvert e(t) \rvert / N$
MSD:	Mean square error (deviation), MSD $= \Sigma_t e(t)^2 / N$
Bias:	Mean error (deviation), Bias $= \Sigma_t e(t) / N$
R^2:	Multiple correlation coefficient, $R^2 = 1 - N * MSD / ((N-1) V)$

a. Simple average:

$$F(t) = A$$

$f(t+\tau) = F(t)$

b. Weighted moving average:

$F(t) = \Sigma\, W(i)A(i) / \Sigma\, W(i)$ where $i = (t-m+1)$ to t
$f(t + \tau) = F(t)$
The default value of each weight is 1/m.

c. Moving average with linear trend:

$F(t) = \Sigma\, A(i)/m$ where $i = (t-m+1)$ to t,
$T(t) = 12\, \Sigma\, (i\, A(t-(m-1)/2+i) / m / (m^2-1))$, where $i = -(m-1)/2$ to $(m-1)/2$
$f(t+\tau) = F(t) + T(t)(t+\tau)$

d. Single exponential smoothing:

$F(0) = A(1)$
$F(t) = \alpha\, A(t) + (1-\alpha)\, F(t-1)$
$f(t+\tau) = F(t)$

e. Single exponential smoothing with linear trend:

$F(0) = A(1)$
$T(0) = 0$
$F(t) = \alpha\, A(t) + (1-\alpha)\, (F(t-1) + T(t-1))$
$T(t) = \beta\, (F(t)-F(t-1)) + (1-\beta)\, T(t-1)$
$f(t+\tau) = F(t) + \tau T(t)$

f. Double exponential smoothing:

$F(0) = F'(0) = A(1)$
$F(t) = \alpha\, A(t) + (1-\alpha)\, F(t-1)$
$F'(t) = \alpha\, F(t) + (1-\alpha)\, F'(t-1)$
$f(t+\tau) = F'(t)$

g. Double exponential smoothing with linear trend:

$F(0) = F'(0) = A(1)$
$F(t) = \alpha\, A(t) + (1-\alpha)\, F(t-1)$
$F'(t) = \alpha\, F(t) + (1-\alpha)\, F'(t-1)$
$\gamma = \tau\, \alpha / \beta$
$f(t+\tau) = (2+\gamma)\, F(t) - (1+\gamma)\, F'(t)$

h. Adaptive exponential smoothing:

The method starts from an assigned smoothing constant (a). In each period, check which of the three values, $\alpha-0.05$, α, and $\alpha+0.05$, creates the F(t) with the least absolute error. Then assign that value as the new smoothing parameter.

$F(0) = A(1)$

$F(t) = \alpha\, A(t) + (1-\alpha)\, F(t-1)$

i. Linear regression:

$b = [\Sigma_i\, A(i)\, i - n\, A\, (n+1)/2] / [\Sigma_i\, i^2 - n\, (n+1)^2/4]$, where $i = 1$ to n
$a = A - b\,(n+1)/2$
$f(t) = a + b\,t$

j. Winter's model:

$F(0) = A(1)$
$T(0) = 0$
$F(t) = \alpha\, A(t)/I(t-m) + (1-\alpha)\, (F(t-1) + T(t-1))$
$T(t) = \beta\, (F(t)-F(t-1)) + (1-\beta)\, T(t-1)$
$I(t) = \gamma\, A(t)/F(t) + (1-\gamma)\, I(t-m)$
$f(t+\tau) = (F(t) + \tau\, T(t))\, I(t+\tau-m)$

If you do not enter the seasonal factors, then the default seasonal factors are initially set to the following values:

$I(t) = m\, A(t) / \Sigma_i\, A(i)$, where $i=1$ to m, $t = 1, \ldots, m$

7. For linear regression, TSFC obtains the least square solution for the general linear model:

$Y = b_0 + b_1 X_1 + b_2 X_2 + \ldots + b_n X_n + \varepsilon$

where Y is the dependent variable; $X_1, X_2, \ldots, X_n$ are independent variables; $b_0, b_1, b_2, \ldots, b_n$ are regression parameters; and ε is the random deviation.

MENU STRUCTURE

The functions and options in each of the pull-down menus are hierarchically listed as follows:

Modules
- Linear Programming (LP)
- Integer Linear Programming (ILP)
- Goal Programming (GP)
- Quadratic Programming (QP)
- Nonlinear Programming (NLP)
- Dynamic Programming (DP)
- Transportation and Transshipment (TRP)
- Assignment and Traveling Salesman (ASTS)
- Specialized Network Modeling (SNET)
- Capacitated Network Flow Modeling (CNET)
- Project Scheduling: CPM/PERT

- Inventory Theory (INVT)
- Inventory Theory 2 (INVT2)
- Queuing Theory (QUEUE)
- Queuing System Simulation (QSIM)
- Decision Analysis (DA)
- Markov Process (MKV)
- Time Series and Forecasting (TSFC)
- Financial Analysis (FA)
- Exit from QSB

Input Data
- Data Entry
- Read a File
- Show Data
- Print Data
- Modify Data
- Save
- Save As
- Exit from QSB

Solution
- Time Series and Forecasting
  - Perform Forecasting
  - Select Forecasting Model
  - Show the Forecasting Result
  - Print the Forecasting Result
  - Save the Forecasting Result
  - Plot the Forecasting Result
- Linear Regression
  - Perform Linear Regression
  - Select Dependent Variable
  - Perform Estimate and Prediction
  - Show the Forecasting Result
  - Print the Forecasting Result
  - Save the Forecasting Result

Options
- Color
- Monochrome
- Printer Selection
- Refresh the Module Menu

Help - TSFC
- About TSFC
- About the User Interface
- About the Edit Keys

SOLVING PROBLEMS WITH TSFC

In the following sections, we will use an example problem to show how to enter and solve the problem. The general procedure and menu options are described in detail in the tutorial sections of Chapter 2.

Example-Time Series

A company's sales volume for the last 24 months is shown in Table 20-1. By using the single exponential smoothing with smoothing constant $\alpha = 0.3$, and Winter's model with seasonal cycle = 12 and $\alpha = .3$, $\beta = .2$, and $\gamma = .4$, forecast the next 12 month sales.

Table 20-1. Sales volume for the last 24 months.

Month	Sales	Month	Sales	Month	Sales
1	$398	9	$430	17	$487
2	395	10	460	18	500
3	290	11	465	19	530
4	400	12	473	20	500
5	410	13	480	21	505
6	425	14	465	22	550
7	450	15	435	23	555
8	440	16	470	24	580

Enter the Problem

1. Select "Data Entry" from the "Input Data" menu (refer to Chapter 2 for selecting a menu item).
2. Fig. 20-1 shows the problem specification.
3. Fig. 20-2 and Fig. 20-3 show the historical data. Note that you can use the "PgDn" and "PgUp" buttons to control the entry pages.

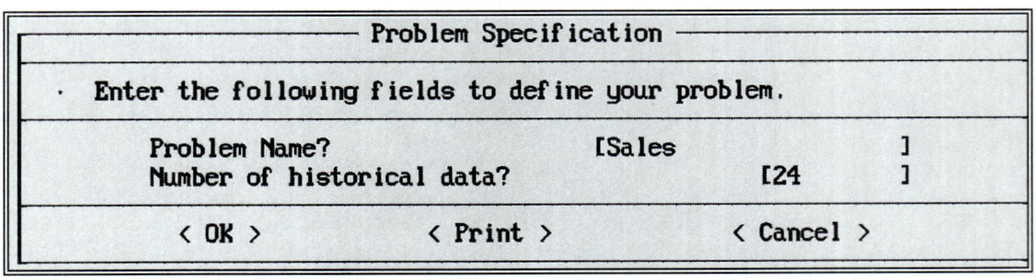

Figure 20-1. Problem specification for Sales.

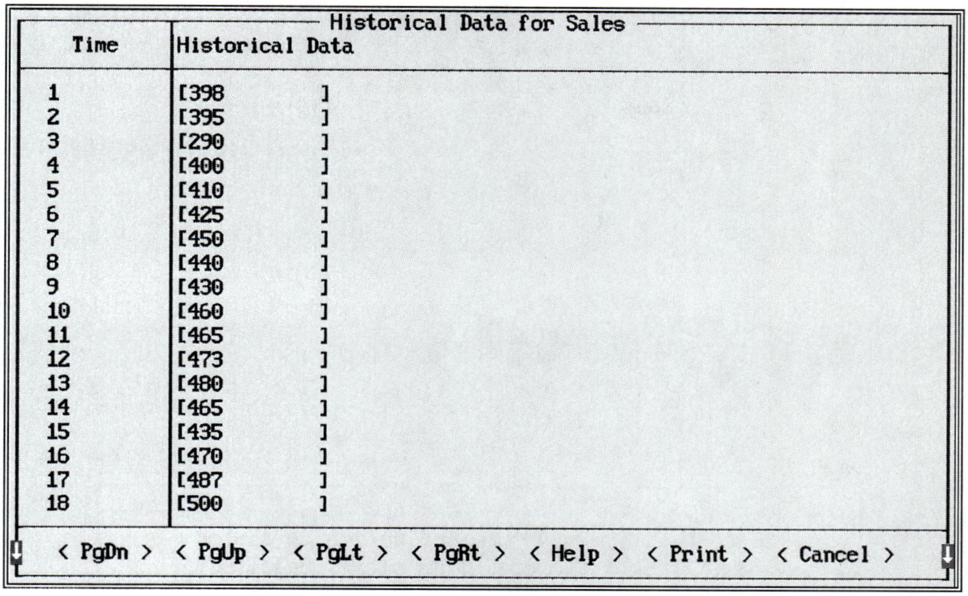

Figure 20-2. Entry of the historical data.

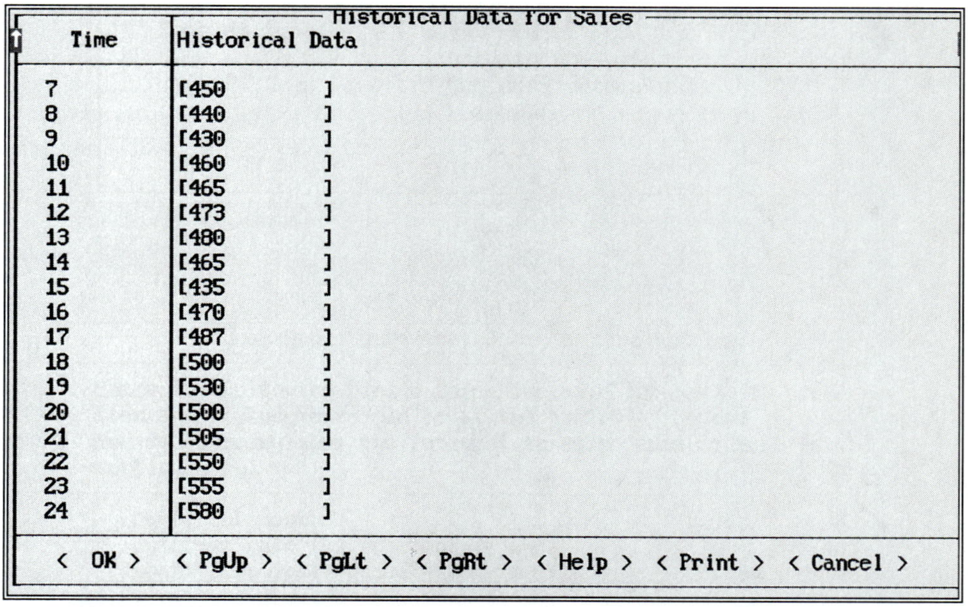

Figure 20-3. Entry of the historical data (continued).

Forecasting by Single Exponential Smoothing

1. Choose "Select Forecasting Model" from the "Solution" menu. Fig. 20-4 will display the forecasting models. Click the "Single exponential smoothing" option and then click the "OK" button. If you do not have a mouse with your com-

```
Simple average
Weighted moving average
Moving average with linear trend
Single exponential smoothing
Exponential smoothing with linear trend
Double exponential smoothing
Double exponential smoothing with linear trend
Adaptive exponential smoothing
Linear regression
Winter's model

< OK >                                        < Cancel >
```

Figure 20-4. Forecast models.

puter, use the "Tab" and arrow key combination to make the choice. Refer to Chapter 2 for the list box selection.

2. Select "Perform Forecasting" from the "Solution" menu. The program will ask you to specify some parameters. Fig. 20-5 shows the interaction. Note that the initial value is defaulted. After a few seconds, the forecasting should be completed.
3. After the forecasting is done, select "Show the Forecasting Result" from the "Solution" menu to display the result. Figs. 20-6 to 20-8 show the forecasting results. Note that the forecasting errors are available only from periods 2 to 24.
4. You may also choose "Plot the Forecasting Result" from the "Solution" menu to plot the result. Fig. 20-9 shows the specification for the chart. Assuming the default is selected, Fig. 20-10 shows the chart. If the plot has more than one page, use the left and right arrow keys to change pages. You may press the "P" key to print the chart.

```
You have chosen to forecast by Single exponential smoothing

For how many periods do you want to forecast ? 12
Do you want TSFC to search the best parameters (Y/N) ? n
Do you want to enter the initial forecast or trend (Y/N, N for default) ? n
What is the smoothing constant (α (alpha) ≤ 1.0) ? 0.3
```

Figure 20-5. Forecast by single exponential smoothing.

Forecast Results for Sales

08-23-1993 19:42:59 Page: 1 of 3

Period	Actual	F(t)			Forecast	Error
1	398	398				
2	395	397.1			398	3
3	290	364.97			397.1	107.1
4	400	375.479			364.97	-35.03
5	410	385.8353			375.479	-34.521
6	425	397.5847			385.8353	-39.1647
7	450	413.3093			397.5847	-52.41528
8	440	421.3165			413.3093	-26.6907
9	430	423.9215			421.3165	-8.683502
10	460	434.7451			423.9215	-36.07846
11	465	443.8216			434.7451	-30.25491
12	473	452.5751			443.8216	-29.17844

Single exponential smoothing: CPU Seconds = .06
MAD = 32.83 MSD = 1562.63 Bias = -20.90 R-square = .58
Alpha = .30000

< PageDown > < PageUp > < Hardcopy > < Cancel >

Figure 20-6. Single exponential smoothing forecasts for Sales.

Forecast Results for Sales

08-23-1993 19:43:37 Page: 2 of 3

Period	Actual	F(t)			Forecast	Error
13	480	460.8026			452.5751	-27.4249
14	465	462.0618			460.8026	-4.197418
15	435	453.9433			462.0618	27.0618
16	470	458.7603			453.9433	-16.05673
17	487	467.2322			458.7603	-28.23972
18	500	477.0626			467.2322	-32.76779
19	530	492.9438			477.0626	-52.93744
20	500	495.0606			492.9438	-7.056213
21	505	498.0424			495.0606	-9.939362
22	550	513.6297			498.0424	-51.95755
23	555	526.0408			513.6297	-41.3703
24	580	542.2285			526.0408	-53.95923

Single exponential smoothing: CPU Seconds = .06
MAD = 32.83 MSD = 1562.63 Bias = -20.90 R-square = .58
Alpha = .30000

< PageDown > < PageUp > < Hardcopy > < Cancel >

Figure 20-7. Single exponential smoothing forecasts for Sales (continued).

Forecast Results for Sales

08-23-1993 19:44:05 Page: 3 of 3

Period	Actual	F(t)			Forecast	Error
25					542.2285	
26					542.2285	
27					542.2285	
28					542.2285	
29					542.2285	
30					542.2285	
31					542.2285	
32					542.2285	
33					542.2285	
34					542.2285	
35					542.2285	
36					542.2285	

Single exponential smoothing: CPU Seconds = .06

MAD = 32.83 MSD = 1562.63 Bias = -20.90 R-square = .58

Alpha = .30000

< PageDown > < PageUp > < Hardcopy > < Cancel >

Figure 20-8. Single exponential smoothing forecasts for Sales (continued).

Forecasting Plot Specification

. Vertical axis: forecast value. Default is from minimum data to 1.1 times maximum data.

. Horizontal axis: time period.

Minimum vertical value: [ ]

Maximum vertical value: [ ]

< OK > < Default > < Cancel >

Figure 20-9. Forecasting plot specification.

Forecasting by Winter's Model

1. Choose "Select Forecasting Model" from the "Solution" menu and select the "Winter's Model" (refer to Fig. 20-4).
2. Select "Perform Forecasting" from the "Solution" menu. The program will ask you to specify some parameters. Fig. 20-11 shows the interaction. Note that the seasonal index and initial values are defaulted.

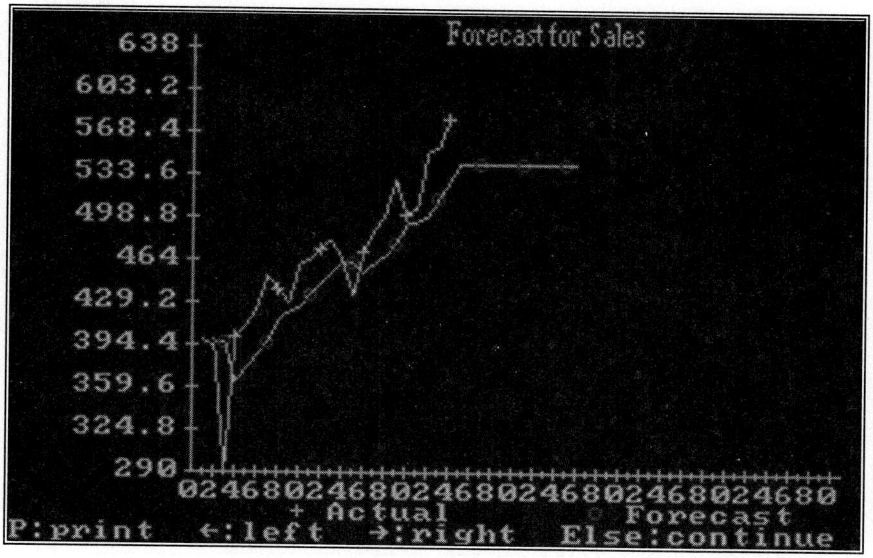

Figure 20-10. Plot the single exponential smoothing forecasts for Sales.

```
You have chosen to forecast by Winter's model

For how many periods do you want to forecast ? 12
Do you want TSFC to search the best parameters (Y/N) ? n
How many periods has the length of the seasonal cycle ? 12
Do you want to enter the estimated seasonal index (factors) (Y/N) ? n
Do you want to enter the initial forecast or trend (Y/N, N for default) ? n
What is the smoothing constant (α (alpha) ≤ 1.0) ? .3
What is the trend smoothing constant (β (beta) ≤ 1.0) ? .2
What is the seasonal smoothing constant (Γ (gamma) ≤ 1.0) ? .4
```

Figure 20-11. Winter's model parameters.

3. After the forecasting is done, select "Show the Forecasting Result" from the "Solution" menu to display the result. Figs. 20-12 to 20-14 show the forecasting results.
4. You may also choose "Plot the Forecasting Result" from the "Solution" menu to plot the result. Assuming the default is specified for the plot, Fig. 20-15 shows the chart.

Forecast Results for Sales

08-23-1993 19:47:58 Page: 1 of 3

Period	Actual	F(t)	T(t)	I(t)	Forecast	Error
1	398	398	0	.9483718		
2	395	397.1	-.1799988	.9412232	398	3
3	290	364.844	-6.595201	.6910247	396.92	106.92
4	400	370.7741	-4.090132	.9531375	358.2488	-41.75122
5	410	379.6788	-1.491173	.9769658	366.684	-43.31598
6	425	392.2313	1.317566	1.012709	378.1876	-46.81238
7	450	410.4842	4.704632	1.07228	393.5489	-56.45111
8	440	422.6322	6.193302	1.048451	415.1888	-24.81116
9	430	429.1779	6.263772	1.024623	428.8255	-1.1745
10	460	442.8091	7.737275	1.096108	435.4416	-24.55838
11	465	454.8825	8.604493	1.108022	450.5464	-14.45358
12	473	466.3409	9.175276	1.127085	463.487	-9.513

Winter's model: CPU Seconds = 0

MAD = 35.70 MSD = 2040.87 Bias = 1.89 R-square = .45

Alpha = .30000 Beta = .20000 Gamma = .40000

< PageDown > < PageUp > < Hardcopy > < Cancel >

Figure 20-12. Winter's model forecast for Sales.

Forecast Results for Sales

08-23-1993 19:48:39 Page: 2 of 3

Period	Actual	F(t)	T(t)	I(t)	Forecast	Error
13	480	484.7005	11.01214	.9735766	450.9661	-29.03387
14	465	495.2103	10.91166	.9485478	466.5763	1.576263
15	435	543.1353	18.31434	.7413986	349.7427	-85.25726
16	470	540.9473	14.21386	.9274542	535.1387	65.13867
17	487	538.1574	10.81312	.9564397	542.3735	55.37347
18	500	532.397	7.498419	.9918758	555.9471	55.94714
19	530	526.209	4.761138	1.055391	578.9189	48.91888
20	500	514.7473	1.516564	1.026502	556.6963	56.69629
21	505	509.244	.1125921	1.020277	528.9758	23.97577
22	550	507.0822	-.3422872	1.101056	558.3099	8.309875
23	555	504.9857	-.6931351	1.114079	561.4791	6.479126
24	580	507.3853	-0.0745764	1.143401	568.3806	-11.61945

Winter's model: CPU Seconds = 0

MAD = 35.70 MSD = 2040.87 Bias = 1.89 R-square = .45

Alpha = .30000 Beta = .20000 Gamma = .40000

< PageDown > < PageUp > < Hardcopy > < Cancel >

Figure 20-13. Winter's model forecast for Sales (continued).

Forecast Results for Sales

08-23-1993 19:49:10

Page: 3 of 3

Period	Actual	F(t)	T(t)	I(t)	Forecast	Error
25					493.9059	
26					481.1378	
27					376.0089	
28					470.3	
29					484.9268	
30					502.8194	
31					534.9389	
32					520.2197	
33					516.989	
34					557.8388	
35					564.3536	
36					579.1216	

Winter's model: CPU Seconds = 0

MAD = 35.70 MSD = 2040.87 Bias = 1.89 R-square = .45

Alpha = .30000 Beta = .20000 Gamma = .40000

< PageDown > < PageUp > < Hardcopy > < Cancel >

Figure 20-14. Winter's model forecast for Sales (continued).

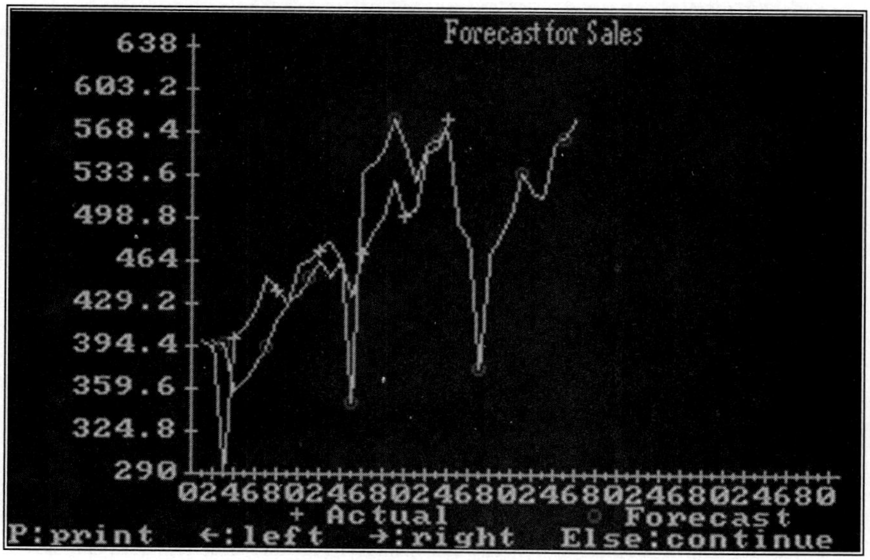

Figure 20-15. Plot the Winter's model forecast for Sales.

Searching for the Best Parameters

Assume that we are not satisfied with the forecasting result from the above Winter's model. The MSD is a little bit too large (larger than that of the single exponential smoothing) and the seasonality does not seem obvious. We can try other parameter sets and rerun the forecasting to obtain other results. However, TSFC provides a line search to find the best parameters. In the following, we demonstrate the search process.

1. Choose "Select Forecasting Model" from the "Solution" menu and select the "Winter's Model" (refer to Fig. 20-4).
2. Select "Perform Forecasting" from the "Solution" menu. Fig. 20-16 shows the interaction to perform the search. After specifying "y" for the search, the program requests the search parameter range and performance measure. Fig. 20-17 shows the specification of parameter range, and Fig. 20-18 specifies the per-

```
You have chosen to forecast by Winter's model

For how many periods do you want to forecast ? 12
Do you want TSFC to search the best parameters (Y/N) ? y
How many periods has the length of the seasonal cycle ? 12
Do you want to enter the estimated seasonal index (factors) (Y/N) ? y
Do you want to enter the initial forecast or trend (Y/N, N for default) ? n
```

Figure 20-16. Interaction for the search of parameters.

Specifying Search Parameters

Parameter	Start From	End At
α (Alpha)	[0]	[1]
β (Beta)	[0]	[1]
Γ (Gamma)	[0]	[1]

< OK > < PgUp > < PgLt > < PgRt > < Help > < Print > < Cancel >

Figure 20-17. Specification of the parameter search range.

formance measure MSD. Since the seasonality is not obvious, answer "y" for the question of entering the seasonal indexes, and enter the seasonal indexes with value 1 as shown in Fig. 20-19. The unity indexes erase the effect of seasonality. After the interaction finishes, the program will search the best parameters for the specified performance measure.

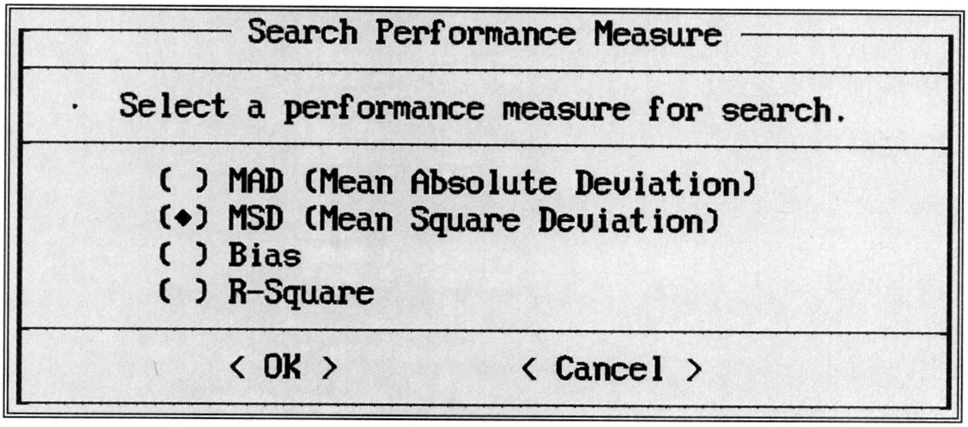

Figure 20-18. Performance measure for the parameter search.

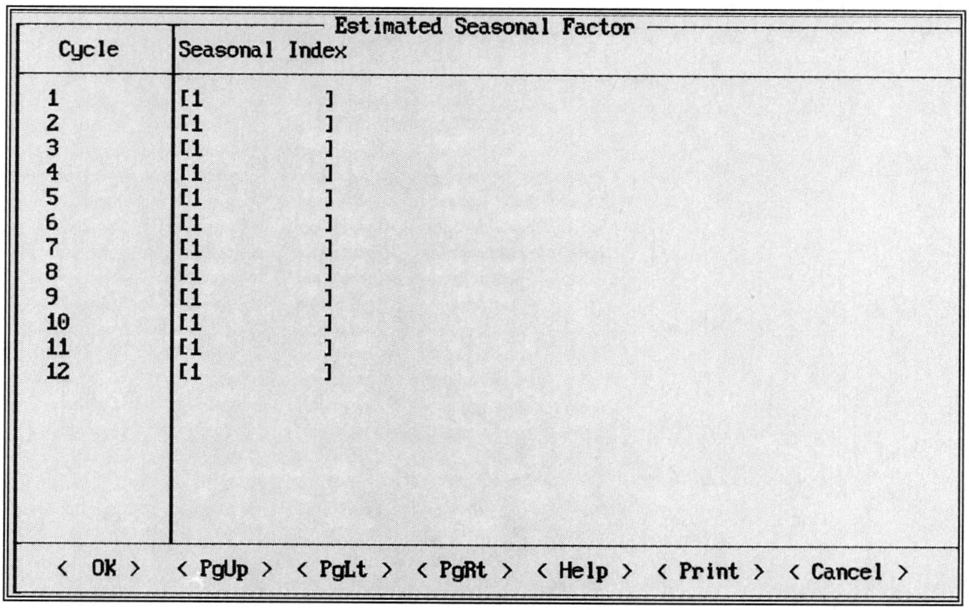

Figure 20-19. Estimated initial seasonal indexes.

3. After the search is done, select "Show the Forecasting Result" from the "Solution" menu to display the result. Figs. 20-20 to 20-22 show the forecasting results. The new MSD is 1205.43, a 41% improvement.

Forecast Results for Sales

08-23-1993 19:58:53 Page: 1 of 3

Period	Actual	F(t)	T(t)	I(t)	Forecast	Error
1	398	398	0	1		
2	395	396.5517	-.126983	1	398	3
3	290	345.0449	-4.63172	1	396.4247	106.4247
4	400	369.1805	-2.109532	1	340.4131	-59.58685
5	410	387.7963	-.2924383	1	367.071	-42.92899
6	425	405.6063	1.294694	1	387.5038	-37.49615
7	450	427.7084	3.118989	1	406.901	-43.09903
8	440	435.2557	3.507247	1	430.8274	-9.172638
9	430	434.5324	3.136328	1	438.763	8.76297
10	460	448.4498	4.081565	1	437.6687	-22.3313
11	465	458.551	4.609335	1	452.5314	-12.4686
12	473	467.9107	5.025828	1	463.1603	-9.839661

Winter's model: CPU Seconds = .43

MAD = 26.53 MSD = 1205.43 Bias = -8.59 R-square = .67

Alpha = .48278 Beta = 0.08768 Gamma = .50000 Search criterion: MSD

< PageDown > < PageUp > < Hardcopy > < Cancel >

Figure 20-20. Forecasting result after the search.

Forecast Results for Sales

08-23-1993 19:59:25 Page: 2 of 3

Period	Actual	F(t)	T(t)	I(t)	Forecast	Error
13	480	476.3466	5.324808	1.00084	472.9366	-7.063446
14	465	473.6228	4.61914	.9879413	481.6714	16.67145
15	435	457.3656	2.7888	.9726396	478.2419	43.24194
16	470	464.9077	3.205545	1.002478	460.1544	-9.845642
17	487	477.2314	4.004984	1.007221	468.1132	-18.88681
18	500	490.2951	4.799211	1.006885	481.2364	-18.76364
19	530	511.9461	6.276695	1.014597	495.0943	-34.90567
20	500	509.4252	5.505361	.9877939	518.2228	18.22278
21	505	510.1363	5.085022	.991998	514.9305	9.930542
22	550	532.0118	6.557132	1.013873	515.2213	-34.77869
23	555	546.5015	7.252626	1.004769	538.5689	-16.43109
24	580	566.4252	8.363561	1.008964	553.7542	-26.24585

Winter's model: CPU Seconds = .43

MAD = 26.53 MSD = 1205.43 Bias = -8.59 R-square = .67

Alpha = .48278 Beta = 0.08768 Gamma = .50000 Search criterion: MSD

< PageDown > < PageUp > < Hardcopy > < Cancel >

Figure 20-21. Forecasting result after the search (continued).

Forecast Results for Sales

08-23-1993 19:59:57 Page: 3 of 3

Period	Actual	F(t)	T(t)	I(t)	Forecast	Error
25					575.2718	
26					576.1202	
27					575.3317	
28					601.3656	
29					612.6353	
30					620.8516	
31					634.0929	
32					625.6031	
33					636.5623	
34					659.0788	
35					661.5645	
36					672.7652	

Winter's model: CPU Seconds = .43

MAD = 26.53 MSD = 1205.43 Bias = -8.59 R-square = .67

Alpha = .48278 Beta = 0.08768 Gamma = .50000 Search criterion: MSD

< PageDown > < PageUp > < Hardcopy > < Cancel >

Figure 20-22. Forecasting result after the search (continued).

4. You may also choose "Plot the Forecasting Result" from the "Solution" menu to plot the result. Assuming the default is specified for the plot, Fig. 20-23 shows the chart. Note that the forecast is much closer to the actual.

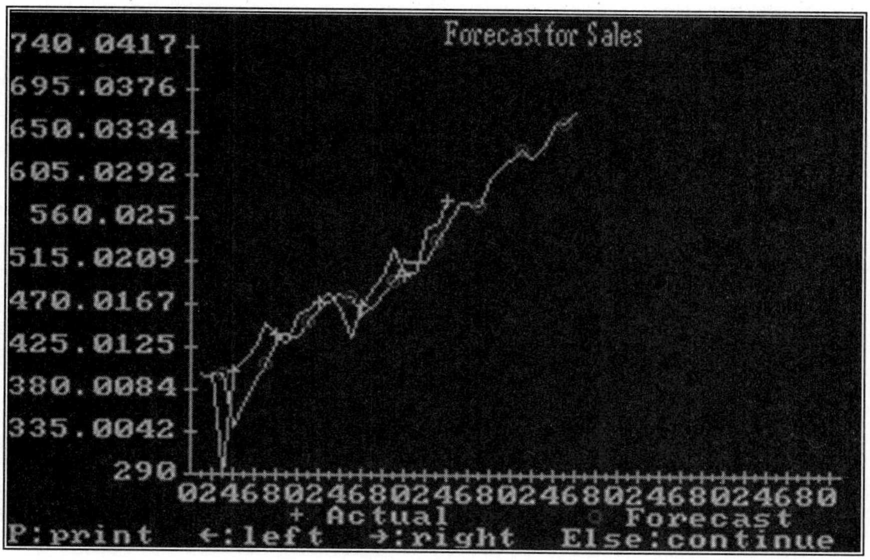

Figure 20-23. Plot the forecasting result after the search.

Example - Linear Regression

Table 20-2 shows the monthly utility costs of 15 families randomly chosen in Metro Atlanta. Column 2 represents the average temperature in a particular month and column 3 contains the attic insulation inches of the surveyed families. Perform the linear regression analysis and predict the utility cost of a typical family house with 5 inch attic insulation in the summer with average temperature 95oF. Assume that the confidence level is set at 95%, that is, $\alpha = 5\%$.

Table 20-2. Utility costs of 15 families randomly chosen from Metro Atlanta.

Family	Monthly utility cost	Average temperature (°F)	Attic insulation in inches
1	$200.50	90	3
2	178.40	85	4
3	180.86	92	10
4	182.20	87	8
5	140.10	70	4
6	120.54	65	3
7	182.60	85	2
8	156.45	77	4
9	225.34	95	7
10	212.18	94	10
11	193.44	89	10
12	161.21	80	6
13	169.44	84	8
14	179.54	88	5
15	184.72	91	7

Enter the Problem

1. Select "Data Entry" from the "Input Data" menu (refer to Chapter 2 for selecting a menu item).

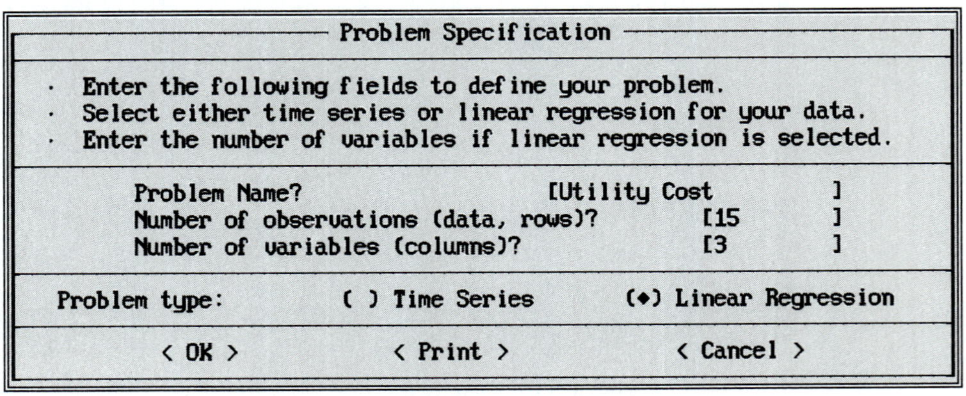

Figure 20-24. Problem specification for Utility Cost.

2. Fig. 20-24 shows the problem selection. Note that the "Linear Regression" is selected and three variables are specified.
3. Fig. 20-25 shows the variable names and Fig. 20-26 shows the observations.

Variable Names for Utility Cost

Variable	Name
1	Utility
2	Temp.(F)
3	Insulation

< OK > < PgUp > < PgLt > < PgRt > < Help > < Print > < Cancel >

Figure 20-25. Variable names for Utility Cost.

Observation Data for Utility Cost

Observation	Utility	Temp.(F)	Insulation
1	200.5	90	3
2	178.4	85	4
3	180.86	92	10
4	182.2	87	8
5	140.1	70	4
6	120.54	65	3
7	182.6	85	2
8	156.45	77	4
9	225.34	95	7
10	212.18	94	10
11	193.44	89	10
12	161.21	80	6
13	169.44	84	8
14	179.54	88	5
15	184.72	91	7

< OK > < PgUp > < PgLt > < PgRt > < Help > < Print > < Cancel >

Figure 20-26. Observation data for Utility Cost.

Regression Analysis

1. Choose "Select Dependent Variable" from the "Solution" menu and select "Utility" as the dependent variable as shown in Fig. 20-27.
2. Select "Perform Linear Regression" from the "Solution" menu. The message "Please standby . . ." will display for a short period while the problem is being solved.
3. After the regression is done, select "Show the Forecasting Result" from the "Solution" menu to display the result. Fig. 20-28 shows the correlation analysis. Note that the utility cost and temperature have high correlation (.9453434). Fig. 20-29 shows the regression summary. Fig. 20-30 shows the ANOVA. Fig. 20-31 shows the regression equation. Fig. 20-32 shows the prediction and residual analysis.
4. Choose "Perform Estimate and Prediction" from the "Solution" menu to perform point estimate. Fig. 20-33 shows the specification with $\alpha = 5\%$. Fig. 20-34 shows the entry of the particular observation of independent variables. After the entry, the message "Please standby . . ." will display for a short period while the problem is being solved. Fig. 20-35 shows the point estimate and its confidence and prediction intervals.

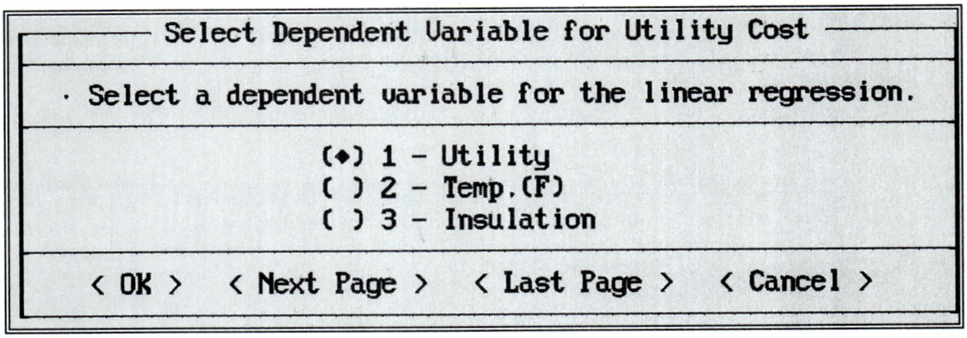

Figure 20-27. Select dependent variable for Utility Cost.

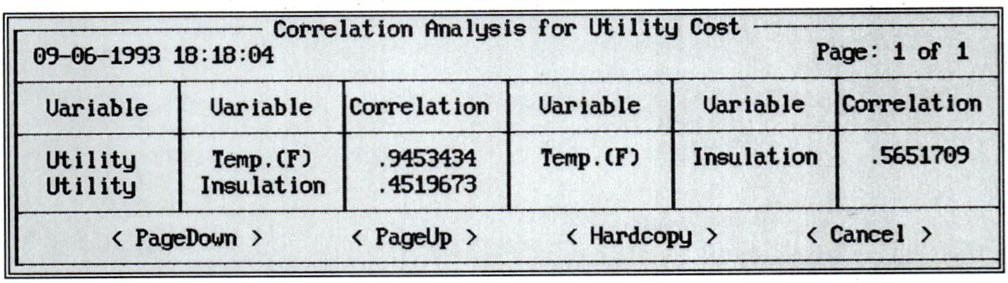

Correlation Analysis for Utility Cost

09-06-1993 18:18:04 Page: 1 of 1

Variable	Variable	Correlation	Variable	Variable	Correlation
Utility	Temp.(F)	.9453434	Temp.(F)	Insulation	.5651709
Utility	Insulation	.4519673			

< PageDown > < PageUp > < Hardcopy > < Cancel >

Figure 20-28. Correlation analysis for Utility Cost.

Regression Summary for Utility Cost

09-06-1993 18:18:34 Page: 1 of 1

Variable	Mean	Standard Deviation	Regression Coefficient	Standard Error	t	Prob.> !t!
Utility	177.8347	26.46548	Dependent	Variable		
Constant			-79.7438	25.4179	-3.13731	0.008574
Temp.(F)	84.8	8.595648	3.121087	.3344743	9.331321	0.000000
Insulation	6.066667	2.737743	-1.16915	1.050145	-1.11333	.2873709

Se = 8.874556 R-square = .90362 R-adjusted = .88755 CPU Seconds = 0

< PageDown > < PageUp > < Hardcopy > < Cancel >

Figure 20-29. Regression summary for Utility Cost.

Analysis of Variance for Utility Cost

09-06-1993 18:19:04 Page: 1 of 1

Source	Degree of Freedom	Sum of Square	Mean Square	F value	Prob. > F
Regression	2	8860.813	4430.406	56.2536	0.00000080
Error	12	945.0928	78.75774		
Total	14	9805.905			

< PageDown > < PageUp > < Hardcopy > < Cancel >

Figure 20-30. ANOVA for Utility Cost.

Regression Equation for Utility Cost

09-06-1993 18:19:34 Page: 1 of 1

Utility = - 79.74384 + 3.121087 Temp.(F) - 1.169159 Insulation

< PageDown > < PageUp > < Hardcopy > < Cancel >

Figure 20-31. Regression equation for Utility Cost.

Prediction and Residual Analysis for Utility Cost

09-06-1993 18:19:59 Page: 1 of 1

Number	Actual	Prediction	Std. Dev. Prediction	Residual	% Residual	Standardized Residual
1	200.5	197.6465	4.9978	2.853485	1.443732	.3472981
2	178.4	180.8719	3.18264	-2.47192	-1.36667	-.300858
3	180.86	195.7046	4.10703	-14.8445	-7.58519	-1.80673
4	182.2	182.4375	2.867965	-.237457	-.130158	-0.02890
5	140.1	134.0556	4.724567	6.044388	4.508866	.7356634
6	120.54	119.6193	5.947509	.9206619	.7696598	.1120539
7	182.6	183.2102	4.880139	-.610229	-.333076	-0.07427
8	156.45	155.9032	3.219766	.5467682	.35071	0.066547
9	225.34	208.5753	3.751085	16.76468	8.03771	2.040431**
10	212.18	201.9467	4.172988	10.23325	5.067299	1.24549
11	193.44	186.3413	4.210294	7.098679	3.809503	.8639812
12	161.21	162.9282	2.775939	-1.71815	-1.05454	-.209116
13	169.44	173.0742	3.171454	-3.63420	-2.09979	-.442319
14	179.54	189.066	3.00099	-9.52603	-5.03846	-1.15941
15	184.72	196.091	2.866007	-11.3709	-5.79882	-1.38396

< PageDown > < PageUp > < Hardcopy > < Cancel >

Figure 20-32. Prediction and residual analysis for Utility Cost.

Perform Estimate and Prediction

- To obtain the confidence interval and prediction interval for a particular response of the dependent variable Utility, enter the probability α (Prob. > |t|), and press the OK button to go to the next screen to enter a set of independent variable values.
- The default probability α is 5%.

Enter the probability α (%)? [5]

< OK > < Cancel >

Figure 20-33. Estimate and prediction specification for Utility Cost.

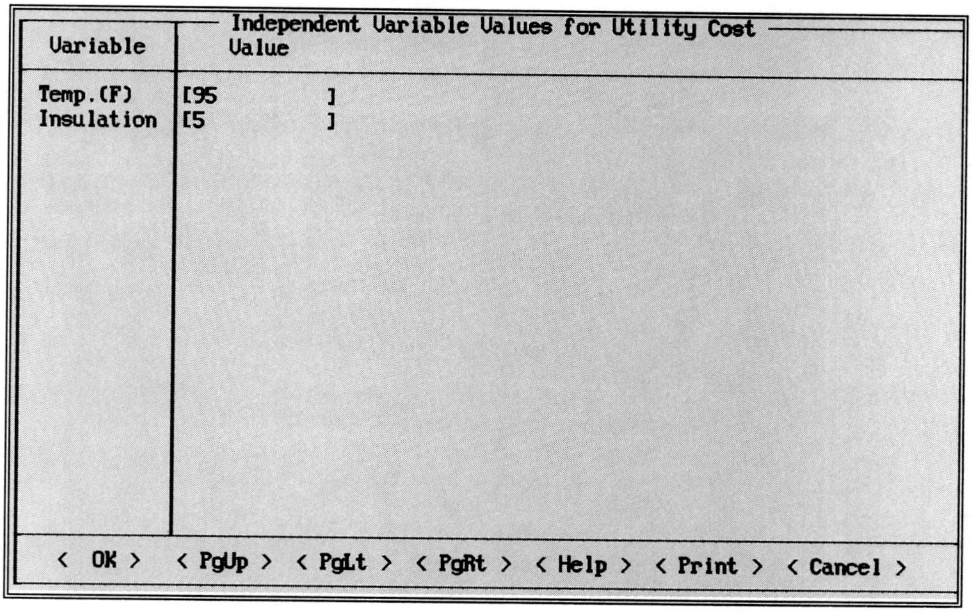

Independent Variable Values for Utility Cost

Variable	Value
Temp.(F)	[95]
Insulation	[5]

< OK > < PgUp > < PgLt > < PgRt > < Help > < Print > < Cancel >

Figure 20-34. One observation of independent variables for Utility Cost.

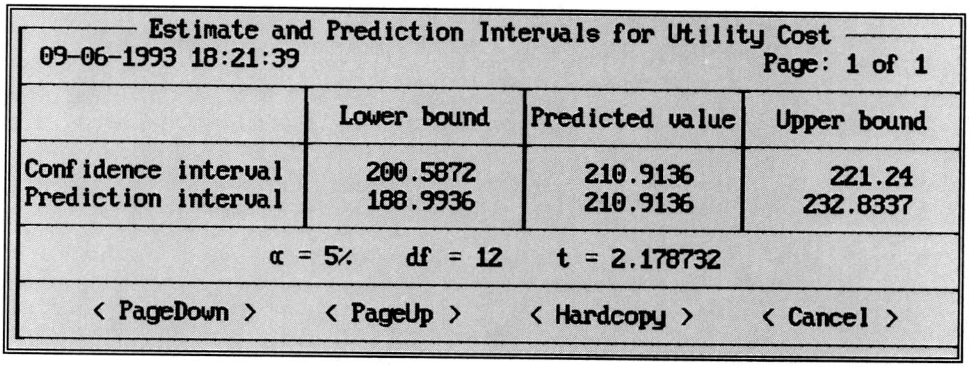

Estimate and Prediction Intervals for Utility Cost

09-06-1993 18:21:39 Page: 1 of 1

	Lower bound	Predicted value	Upper bound
Confidence interval	200.5872	210.9136	221.24
Prediction interval	188.9936	210.9136	232.8337

α = 5% df = 12 t = 2.178732

< PageDown > < PageUp > < Hardcopy > < Cancel >

Figure 20-35. Point estimate and intervals for Utility Cost.

EXERCISES

1. Forecast the sales volume for the next three years. Sales volumes for the last 24 years are:

Year	Sales	Year	Sales	Year	Sales
1	48,123	9	52,010	17	62,111
2	47,560	10	54,101	18	63,567
3	48,535	11	56,888	19	61,256
4	49,638	12	59,346	20	60,355
5	47,215	13	57,215	21	63,578
6	46,222	14	55,333	22	67,999
7	44,333	15	58,999	23	69,356
8	50,135	16	61,256	24	71,976

a. Use the linear regression to perform the forecasting.
b. Use the adaptive exponential smoothing with $\alpha = .3$ to perform the forecasting.
c. Use the three-year moving average to perform the forecasting.
d. Compare the performance for the above methods.

2. For the following historical data, forecast the next five-period sales by using the following methods:
a. Three-year moving average.
b. Three-year moving average with trend.
c. Exponential smoothing with $\alpha = .5$.
d. Compare the performance for the above method.

Period	Sales	Period	Sales
1	\$390,150	7	\$378,652
2	430,253	8	373,439
3	390,158	9	356,215
4	380,139	10	312,059
5	385,125	11	336,025
6	380,125	12	311,038

3. Repeat exercise 2 by using the following data:

Period	Data	Period	Data	Period	Data
1	415	6	398	11	411
2	386	7	365	12	432
3	435	8	421	13	405
4	535	9	374	14	379
5	437	10	395	15	397

4. Based on the following two-year data, use the Winter's model to forecast the next two years' sales volume. Assume the seasonal cycle is 12 months and the seasonal factors are unknown.

No	Month	Sales	No	Month	Sales
1	January	189,000	13	January	259,000
2	February	177,050	14	February	247,050
3	March	210,000	15	March	270,000
4	April	236,500	16	April	286,500
5	May	260,645	17	May	295,645
6	June	246,580	18	June	316,580
7	July	230,569	19	July	280,569
8	August	251,759	20	August	271,759
9	September	285,675	21	September	305,675
10	October	303,450	22	October	353,450
11	November	281,230	23	November	312,330
12	December	260,876	24	December	305,676

a. Use $\alpha = .3, \beta = .5, \gamma = .1$.

b. Find the best parameters for the Winter's model based on the MAD performance.

21

FINANCIAL ANALYSIS (FA)

OVERVIEW OF THE FA DECISION SUPPORT SYSTEM

This program contains four basic financial analysis methods: investment analysis, annuity analysis, compounding analysis, and loan annuity payment analysis. For a specific investment alternative, you enter a series of investments, revenues, and expenses, and an interest rate. The program then computes the following evaluation criteria: payback period, discounted payback period, accounting rate of return, profitability index, internal rate of return, net present value, and net future or end value.

Annuity analysis computes the annuity's present and future values, including perpetuity. Compounding analysis computes the present and future values for a series of cash inflows and outflows. Given the initial loan and interest rate, the loan analysis computes the annuity payment and associated interest and principal information.

The cash flows can be specified to occur at the beginning or at the end of each period. The compounding can be periodically or continuously. You may save, read, modify, or print the input data as well as to display, print, or save the final analysis.

TECHNICAL NOTES ON THE FA PROGRAM

1. Let n: Number of periods
   r: Interest rate per period

   The compounding factor for the future value is $(1+r)^n$ for periodic compounding, e^{rn} for continuous compounding, where e is equal to 2.71828. The conversion factor for the present value is $(1+r)^{-n}$ for periodic compounding, e^{-rn} for continuous compounding.

2. For investment analysis, the following criteria are computed for both the periodic and continuous compounding:

   <u>Payback period</u>: The time when the total cash inflow is greater than or equal to the total cash outflow.

Discounted payback period: The time when the total discounted cash inflow is greater than or equal to the total discounted cash outflow.

Accounting rate of return: The ratio of the average accounting profit to the average investment.

Profitability index: The ratio of the present value of the future net cash inflows to the present value of all investments.

Internal rate of return: The discount rate that equates the present value of the cash inflows with the present value of the cash outflows.

Net present value: The present value of the net cash flows.

Net future/end value: The future value of the net cash flows.

3. A perpetuity is an annuity with an infinite number of periods.

MENU STRUCTURE

The functions and options in each of the pull-down menus are hierarchically listed as follows:

- Modules
  - Linear Programming (LP)
  - Integer Linear Programming (ILP)
  - Goal Programming (GP)
  - Quadratic Programming (QP)
  - Nonlinear Programming (NLP)
  - Dynamic Programming (DP)
  - Transportation and Transshipment (TRP)
  - Assignment and Traveling Salesman (ASTS)
  - Specialized Network Modeling (SNET)
  - Capacitated Network Flow Modeling (CNET)
  - Project Scheduling: CPM/PERT
  - Inventory Theory (INVT)
  - Inventory Theory 2 (INVT2)
  - Queuing Theory (QUEUE)
  - Queuing System Simulation (QSIM)
  - Decision Analysis (DA)
  - Markov Process (MKV)
  - Time Series Forecasting (TSFC)
  - Financial Analysis (FA)
  - Exit from QSB
- Input Data
  - Data Entry
  - Read a File
  - Show Data
  - Print Data
  - Modify Data

- Save
- Save As
- Exit from QSB

Solution
- Solve the Problem
- Show the Solution
- Print the Solution
- Save the Solution

Options
- Color
- Monochrome
- Printer Selection

Help - FA
- About FA
- About the User Interface
- About the Edit Keys

SOLVING PROBLEMS WITH FA

In the following sections, we will use example problems to show how to enter and solve the problems. The general procedure and menu options are described in detail in the tutorial sections of Chapter 2.

Example - Investment Analysis

A company is considering two projects for expanding the production and market. Table 21-1 shows the related investment data for both projects. The initial investment for Project A is $1,000,000 and for Project B is $1,500,000. Both projects have no salvage value. Assume that the interest rate is 10% and that both the revenues and expenses are incurred at the end of year. Compare the two investments.

Table 21-1. Investment data for projects A and B.

	Project A		Project B	
Year	Revenue	Expense	Revenue	Expense
1	$200,000	$50,000	$250,000	$70,000
2	300,000	55,000	300,000	80,000
3	400,000	60,000	400,000	85,000
4	500,000	65,000	450,000	90,000
5	500,000	70,000	500,000	95,000
6	400,000	75,000	600,000	100,000
7			650,000	100,000
8			500,000	105,000

Project A

1. Select "Data Entry" from the "Input Data" menu (refer to Chapter 2 for selecting a menu item).
2. Fig. 21-1 shows the problem selection.
3. Fig. 21-2 and Fig. 21-3 show the investment data for project A. No additional investment is involved after the initial investment.
4. Select "Solve the Problem" from the "Solution" menu to solve the problem. The message "Please standby . . ." will display for a short period while the problem is being solved.
5. After the problem is solved, select "Show the Solution" from the "Solution" menu to display the result. Fig. 21-4 shows the investment analysis, and Fig. 21-5 shows the cash flow for the investment.

```
                    Problem Selection

   · Select an option for your financial analysis.
   · The default time unit (period) name is year.

       Problem name?     [Project A              ]
       Time unit name?        [year              ]

  Problem type:       (•) Investment Analysis
                      ( ) Annuity Analysis
                      ( ) Compounding Analysis
                      ( ) Loan/Annuity Payment Analysis

        < OK >            < Print >          < Cancel >
```

Figure 21-1. Problem selection for Project A.

```
                  Investment Data for Project A

   · Enter the following fields to define your investment problem.
   · Revenues or expenses can be paid at the beginning or at the
     end of each period. However, all additional investments are
     assumed to be at the beginning of each period.

       Investment time span (number of years)?   [6          ]
       Interest rate (%) per year?               [10         ]
       Initial investment (outlay)?              [1000000    ]
       Salvage value?                            [0          ]

 Revenue timing:   ( ) Beginning of year          (•) End of year

 Expense timing:   ( ) Beginning of year          (•) End of year

       < OK >              < Print >              < Cancel >
```

Figure 21-2. Investment data for Project A.

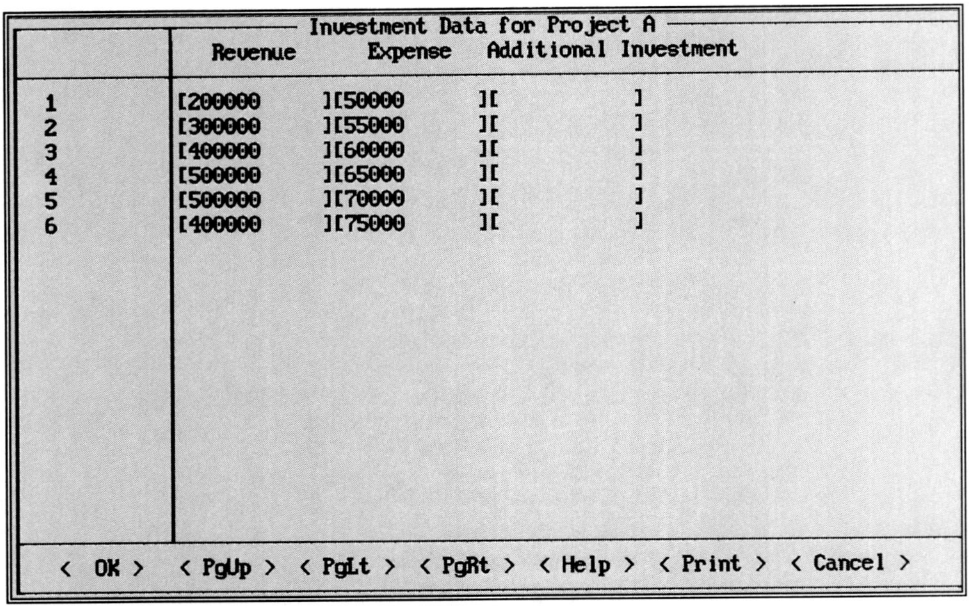

Figure 21-3. Revenues and expenses for Project A.

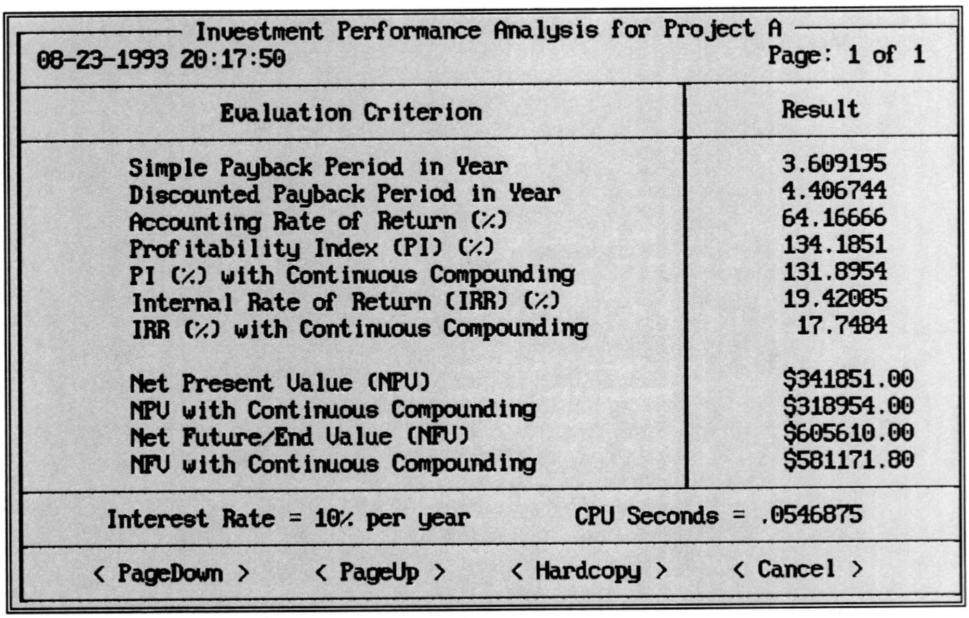

Figure 21-4. Investment analysis for Project A.

Investment Cash Flow for Project A

08-23-1993 20:18:30 Page: 1 of 1

Year	Revenue	Expense	Additional Investment	Cumulative Cash Flow	Compounded Cash Flow
Initial			$1000000.00	$-1000000.00	$-1000000.00
1	$200000.00	$50000.00	$0	$-850000.00	$-950000.00
2	$300000.00	$55000.00	$0	$-605000.00	$-800000.00
3	$400000.00	$60000.00	$0	$-265000.00	$-540000.00
4	$500000.00	$65000.00	$0	$170000.00	$-159000.00
5	$500000.00	$70000.01	$0	$600000.00	$255100.00
6	$400000.00	$75000.01	$0	$925000.00	$605610.00
Salvage	$0			$925000.00	$605610.00

< PageDown > < PageUp > < Hardcopy > < Cancel >

Figure 21-5. Cash flow for Project A.

Project B

1. Similarly, the investment data of project B is entered in Figs. 21-6 to 21-8.
2. Solve the problem and show the solution. Fig. 21-9 shows the investment analysis, and Fig. 21-10 shows the cash flow for the investment.

```
Problem Selection

· Select an option for your financial analysis.
· The default time unit (period) name is year.

Problem name?      [Project B          ]
Time unit name?        [year           ]

Problem type:      (◆) Investment Analysis
                   ( ) Annuity Analysis
                   ( ) Compounding Analysis
                   ( ) Loan/Annuity Payment Analysis

< OK >       < Print >       < Cancel >
```

Figure 21-6. Problem selection for Project B.

```
Investment Data for Project B

 · Enter the following fields to define your investment problem.
 · Revenues or expenses can be paid at the beginning or at the
   end of each period.  However, all additional investments are
   assumed to be at the beginning of each period.

     Investment time span (number of years)?     [8          ]
     Interest rate (%) per year?                 [10         ]
     Initial investment (outlay)?                [1500000    ]
     Salvage value?                              [0          ]

 Revenue timing:   ( ) Beginning of year          (•) End of year

 Expense timing:   ( ) Beginning of year          (•) End of year

        < OK >             < Print >            < Cancel >
```

Figure 21-7. Investment data for Project B.

```
                        Investment Data for Project B
    Year        Revenue       Expense    Additional Investment

     1        [250000    ][70000     ][            ]
     2        [300000    ][80000     ][            ]
     3        [400000    ][85000     ][            ]
     4        [450000    ][90000     ][            ]
     5        [500000    ][95000     ][            ]
     6        [600000    ][100000    ][            ]
     7        [650000    ][100000    ][            ]
     8        [500000    ][105000    ][            ]

 < OK >  < PgUp >  < PgLt >  < PgRt >  < Help >  < Print >  < Cancel >
```

Figure 21-8. Revenues and expenses for Project B.

Investment Performance Analysis for Project B

08-23-1993 20:21:44 Page: 1 of 1

Evaluation Criterion	Result
Simple Payback Period in Year	5.04
Discounted Payback Period in Year	6.489965
Accounting Rate of Return (%)	48.75
Profitability Index (PI) (%)	121.8814
PI (%) with Continuous Compounding	119.2215
Internal Rate of Return (IRR) (%)	14.81667
IRR (%) with Continuous Compounding	13.81665
Net Present Value (NPV)	$328221.00
NPV with Continuous Compounding	$288322.30
Net Future/End Value (NFV)	$703571.00
NFV with Continuous Compounding	$641672.30

Interest Rate = 10% per year CPU Seconds = .046875

< PageDown > < PageUp > < Hardcopy > < Cancel >

Figure 21-9. Investment analysis for Project B.

Investment Cash Flow for Project B

08-23-1993 20:22:12 Page: 1 of 1

Year	Revenue	Expense	Additional Investment	Cumulative Cash Flow	Compounded Cash Flow
Initial			$1500000.00	$-1500000.00	$-1500000.00
1	$250000.00	$70000.01	$0	$-1320000.00	$-1470000.00
2	$300000.00	$80000.01	$0	$-1100000.00	$-1397000.00
3	$400000.00	$85000.01	$0	$-785000.00	$-1221700.00
4	$450000.00	$90000.01	$0	$-425000.00	$-983870.00
5	$500000.00	$95000.01	$0	$-20000.01	$-677257.00
6	$600000.00	$100000.00	$0	$480000.00	$-244982.70
7	$650000.00	$100000.00	$0	$1030000.00	$280519.00
8	$500000.00	$105000.00	$0	$1425000.00	$703570.90
Salvage	$0			$1425000.00	$703570.90

< PageDown > < PageUp > < Hardcopy > < Cancel >

Figure 21-10. Cash flow for Project B.

Example - Annuity Analysis

In preparation for your child's higher education, you want to invest $3000 in a mutual fund specialized in corporate bonds at the beginning of each year for the next 10 years. The fund has performed reasonably well and has been stable in the past with an average annual return of 12%. Estimate how much you will have 10 years from now.

1. Select "Data Entry" from the "Input Data" menu.
2. Fig. 21-11 shows the problem selection.
3. Fig. 21-12 shows the data entry.
4. Select "Solve the Problem" from the "Solution" menu to solve the problem.
5. After the problem is solved, select "Show the Solution" from the "Solution" menu to display the result. Fig. 21-13 shows the annuity analysis, and Fig. 21-14 shows the cash flow.

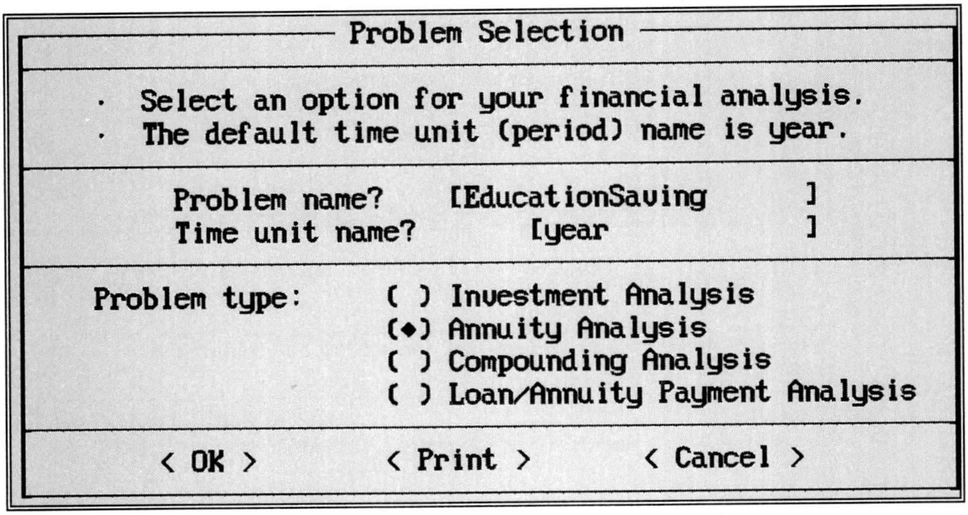

Figure 21-11. Select the annuity analysis.

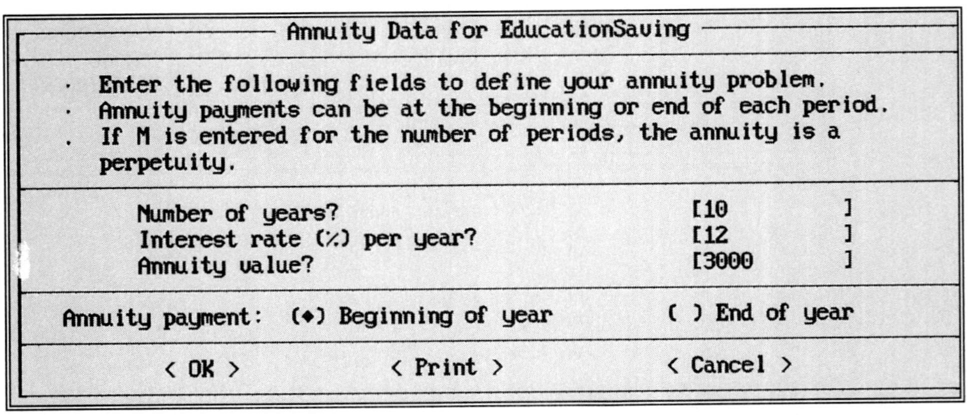

Figure 21-12. Annuity data for EducationSaving.

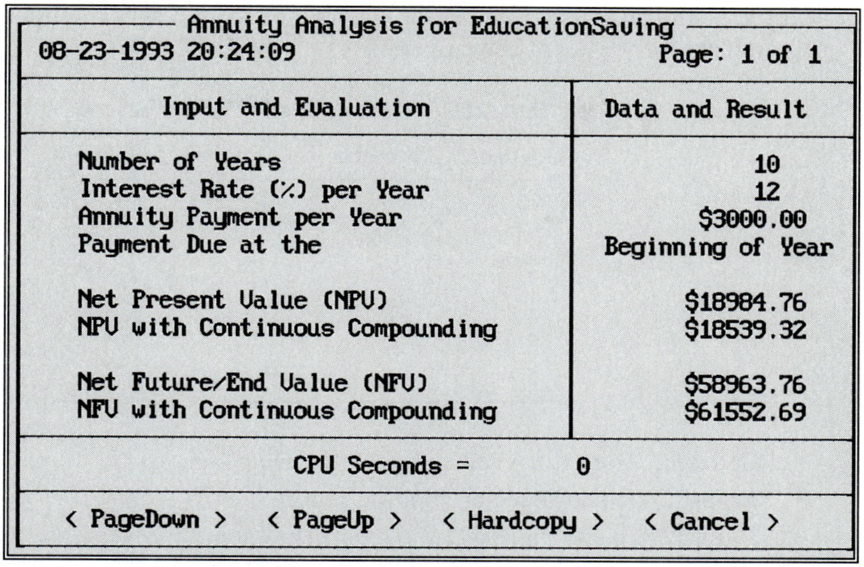
Annuity Analysis for EducationSaving
08-23-1993 20:24:09 Page: 1 of 1

Input and Evaluation	Data and Result
Number of Years	10
Interest Rate (%) per Year	12
Annuity Payment per Year	$3000.00
Payment Due at the	Beginning of Year
Net Present Value (NPV)	$18984.76
NPV with Continuous Compounding	$18539.32
Net Future/End Value (NFV)	$58963.76
NFV with Continuous Compounding	$61552.69

CPU Seconds = 0

< PageDown > < PageUp > < Hardcopy > < Cancel >

Figure 21-13. Annuity analysis for EducationSaving.

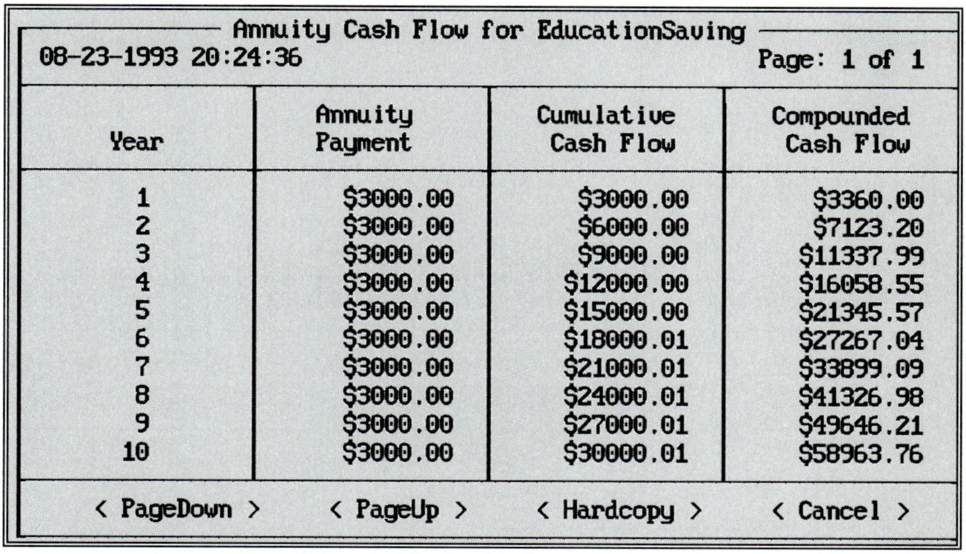
Annuity Cash Flow for EducationSaving
08-23-1993 20:24:36 Page: 1 of 1

Year	Annuity Payment	Cumulative Cash Flow	Compounded Cash Flow
1	$3000.00	$3000.00	$3360.00
2	$3000.00	$6000.00	$7123.20
3	$3000.00	$9000.00	$11337.99
4	$3000.00	$12000.00	$16058.55
5	$3000.00	$15000.00	$21345.57
6	$3000.00	$18000.01	$27267.04
7	$3000.00	$21000.01	$33899.09
8	$3000.00	$24000.01	$41326.98
9	$3000.00	$27000.01	$49646.21
10	$3000.00	$30000.01	$58963.76

< PageDown > < PageUp > < Hardcopy > < Cancel >

Figure 21-14. Cash flow for EducationSaving.

Example - Compounding Analysis

Tom owns a townhouse which he will rent to John for the next twelve months. Payments are due at the beginning of each month. The payment schedule is shown in Table 21-2. Assume that Tom will deposit the payment right after it is received into a local bank savings account which pays about 1% interest per month. Compute Tom's cash flow for the next twelve months.

Table 21-2. Rent payment schedule for John.

Month	Payment	Month	Payment
1	$500	7	$400
2	500	8	400
3	550	9	400
4	550	10	600
5	600	11	650
6	600	12	650

1. Select "Data Entry" from the "Input Data" menu.
2. Fig. 21-15 shows the problem selection.
3. Fig. 21-16 and Fig. 21-17 show the data entry.
4. Select "Solve the Problem" from the "Solution" menu to solve the problem.
5. After the problem is solved, select "Show the Solution" from the "Solution" menu to display the result. Fig. 21-18 shows the compounding analysis, and Fig. 21-19 shows the cash flow.

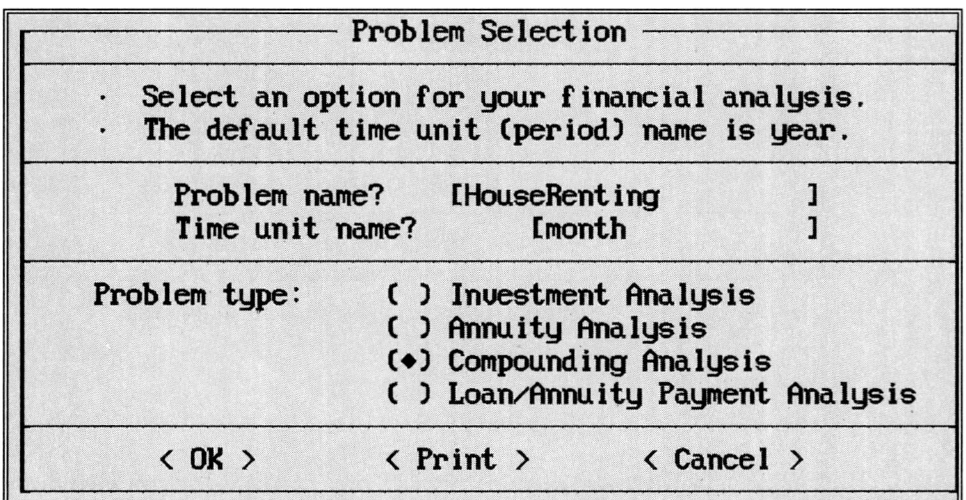

Figure 21-15. Select the compounding analysis.

Compounding Data for HouseRenting

- Enter the following fields to define your compounding problem.
- Cash flows can be at the beginning or the end of each period.
- When entering cash flows, + values represent inflows, while
  − values represent outflows.

Number of months?	[12]
Interest rate (%) per month?	[1]

Cash flow at: (◆) Beginning of month ( ) End of month

< OK > < Print > < Cancel >

Figure 21-16. Compounding data for HouseRenting.

Compounding Data for HouseRenting

Year	Cash Flow
1	[500]
2	[500]
3	[550]
4	[550]
5	[600]
6	[600]
7	[400]
8	[400]
9	[400]
10	[600]
11	[650]
12	[650]

< OK > < PgUp > < PgLt > < PgRt > < Help > < Print > < Cancel >

Figure 21-17. Compounding data for HouseRenting (continued).

Compounding Analysis for HouseRenting

08-23-1993 20:27:12 Page: 1 of 1

Input and Compounding	Data and Result
Number of Months	12
Interest Rate (%) per Month	1
Cash Flow at the	Beginning of Month
Net Present Value (NPV)	$6054.45
NPV with Continuous Compounding	$6052.80
Net Future/End Value (NFV)	$6822.31
NFV with Continuous Compounding	$6824.51

CPU Seconds = 0

< PageDown > < PageUp > < Hardcopy > < Cancel >

Figure 21-18. Compounding analysis for HouseRenting.

Cash Flow for HouseRenting

08-23-1993 20:27:36 Page: 1 of 1

Month	Cash In/Outflow	Cumulative Cash Flow	Compounded Cash Flow
1	$500.00	$500.00	$505.00
2	$500.00	$1000.00	$1015.05
3	$550.00	$1550.00	$1580.70
4	$550.00	$2100.00	$2152.01
5	$600.00	$2700.00	$2779.53
6	$600.00	$3300.00	$3413.32
7	$400.00	$3700.00	$3851.46
8	$400.00	$4100.00	$4293.97
9	$400.00	$4500.00	$4740.91
10	$600.00	$5100.00	$5394.32
11	$650.00	$5750.00	$6104.76
12	$650.00	$6400.00	$6822.31

< PageDown > < PageUp > < Hardcopy > < Cancel >

Figure 21-19. Cash flow for HouseRenting.

Example - Loan/Annuity Payment Analysis

A 15-year 12% annual interest rate home mortgage is offered to you when you are buying a house. You plan to borrow $200,000 and the interest is compounded each month. Compute the payment schedule.

1. Select "Data Entry" from the "Input Data" menu.
2. Fig. 21-20 shows the problem selection.
3. Fig. 21-21 shows the data entry.
4. Select "Solve the Problem" from the "Solution" menu to solve the problem.
5. After the problem is solved, select "Show the Solution" from the "Solution" menu to display the result. Fig. 21-22 and Fig. 21-23 illustrate the first two years' payments and interest amounts.

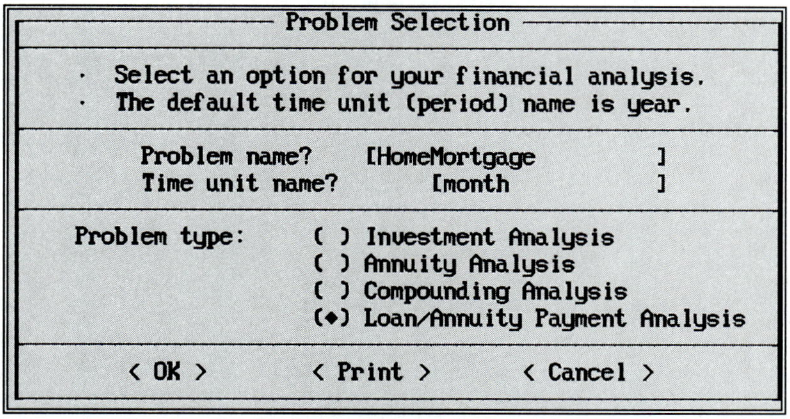

Figure 21-20. Select loan payment analysis.

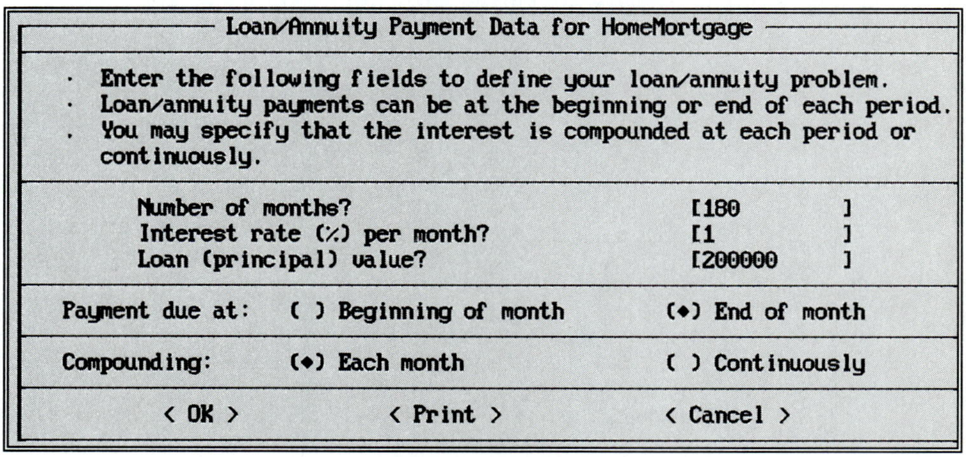

Figure 21-21. Information for HomeMortgage.

Loan/Annuity Payment for HomeMortgage

08-23-1993 20:29:36 Page: 1 of 15

Month	Annuity Payment	Cumulative Payment	Principal Portion	Cumulative Principal	Interest Portion	Cumulative Interest
1	$2400.34	$2400.34	$400.34	$400.34	$2000.00	$2000.00
2	$2400.34	$4800.67	$404.34	$804.68	$1996.00	$3995.99
3	$2400.34	$7201.01	$408.39	$1213.07	$1991.95	$5987.94
4	$2400.34	$9601.35	$412.47	$1625.54	$1987.87	$7975.81
5	$2400.34	$12001.69	$416.59	$2042.13	$1983.74	$9959.56
6	$2400.34	$14402.03	$420.76	$2462.89	$1979.58	$11939.14
7	$2400.34	$16802.37	$424.97	$2887.86	$1975.37	$13914.51
8	$2400.34	$19202.70	$429.22	$3317.08	$1971.12	$15885.63
9	$2400.34	$21603.04	$433.51	$3750.59	$1966.83	$17852.45
10	$2400.34	$24003.38	$437.84	$4188.43	$1962.49	$19814.95
11	$2400.34	$26403.71	$442.22	$4630.65	$1958.11	$21773.06
12	$2400.34	$28804.05	$446.65	$5077.30	$1953.69	$23726.75

Interest Rate = 1% per month CPU Seconds = .0625
Payment at the End of Month Interest Compounding Periodically

< PageDown > < PageUp > < Hardcopy > < Cancel >

Figure 21-22. Payments for HomeMortgage.

Loan/Annuity Payment for HomeMortgage

08-23-1993 20:30:17 Page: 2 of 15

Month	Annuity Payment	Cumulative Payment	Principal Portion	Cumulative Principal	Interest Portion	Cumulative Interest
13	$2400.34	$31204.38	$451.11	$5528.41	$1949.23	$25675.97
14	$2400.34	$33604.72	$455.62	$5984.03	$1944.71	$27620.69
15	$2400.34	$36005.06	$460.18	$6444.21	$1940.16	$29560.85
16	$2400.34	$38405.39	$464.78	$6908.99	$1935.56	$31496.40
17	$2400.34	$40805.73	$469.43	$7378.42	$1930.91	$33427.31
18	$2400.34	$43206.07	$474.12	$7852.54	$1926.21	$35353.52
19	$2400.34	$45606.41	$478.86	$8331.41	$1921.47	$37275.00
20	$2400.34	$48006.74	$483.65	$8815.06	$1916.68	$39191.68
21	$2400.34	$50407.08	$488.49	$9303.55	$1911.85	$41103.53
22	$2400.34	$52807.42	$493.37	$9796.92	$1906.96	$43010.49
23	$2400.34	$55207.75	$498.31	$10295.24	$1902.03	$44912.52
24	$2400.34	$57608.09	$503.29	$10798.53	$1897.05	$46809.56

Interest Rate = 1% per month CPU Seconds = .0625
Payment at the End of Month Interest Compounding Periodically

< PageDown > < PageUp > < Hardcopy > < Cancel >

Figure 21-23. Payments for HomeMortgage (continued).

EXERCISES

1. Consider the following two investment projects (all numbers are in thousands):

	Mass automation			Flexible manufacturing system		
Year	Investment	Revenue	Expense	Investment	Revenue	Expense
Initial	$20,000			$12,000		
1		$2,000	$500		$2,000	$350
2		4,000	550		4,000	400
3		5,000	600	4,000	5,000	450
4		7,000	650		6,000	500
5	5,000	7,000	700	4,000	7,000	500
6		8,000	750		8,000	500
7		8,000	800	4,000	9,000	550
8		10,000	850		9,000	600
9		10,000	900	1,000	9,000	600
10		8,000	950		9,000	650

a. Compare the simple and discounted payback period if the interest rate is 10%.

b. Compare the net present value if the interest rate is 10%.

c. Compare the net present value if the interest rate is 12%.

2. You are considering buying a new car. The salesman has proposed three financial methods: Pay $22,000 cash right now, pay four equal installments of $6000 each for now and three for every three months, or lease for $399 each month for the next five years. It is estimated that the car will be worth $8000 after five years. The car will be yours if you take the first two options; however, you will walk away with nothing if you take the leasing option.

a. If your savings interest rate is 12% per year (or 1% per month), which option is the best? (Assume that all payments are at the beginning of the month.)

b. What if the interest rate is 15%?

3. A retirement plan puts $500 into a mutual fund which carries an average return of 12% a year (or 1% per month). Assume that all payments are at the end of the month.

a. How much will the plan accumulate if you retire after 30 years?

b. After retirement, if the money will be taken out equally each month for five years, how much will the before-tax payment be? Assume that the return rate remains the same.

Appendix EXERCISE SOLUTIONS

Chapter 3 (LP)

1. **a.** $X_1 = 35.1351$, $X_2 = 35.9459$, OBJ = 712.4324.
   b. C1: 4.8 to 14.6667, C2: 6.5455 to 20, B1: 129.0909 to 394.4445, B2: 450 to 1375.
2. **a.** A = 87.85714, B = 62.142857, C = 0, OBJ = 274.2857.
   b. 0, 0, 2.85714.
3. $X_1 = 0$, $X_2 = 99.35$, $X_3 = 0$, $X_4 = 66.6125$, $X_5 = 0$, $X_6 = 34.0375$, OBJ = 1694.962.
4. X = 276.9231, Y = 54.6154, Z = 70, OBJ = 6716.154.
5. Clerks for shifts 1 to 6 are 9, 2, 10, 5, 0, 1, respectively. Total = 27.
6. AS (grade A to super) = 37,500, AH = 35,000, CS = 12,500, CH = 35,000, CR = 40,000, OBJ = 86,500.

Chapter 4 (ILP)

1. X_1 5 35, $X_2 = 36$, OBJ = 712.
2. $X_1 = 1$, $X_2 = 98$, $X_4 = 67$, $X_6 = 34$, OBJ = 1694.
3. $X_1 = 1$, $X_2 = 3$, OBJ = 5.
4. **a.** $X_1 = 1$, $X_2 = 1$, $X_3 = 1$, $X_4 = 0$, $X_5 = 1$, OBJ = 115.
   b. $X_1 = 1$, $X_2 = 1$, $X_3 = 1$, $X_4 = 1$, $X_5 = 0$, OBJ = 103.
5. X_c (coal) = 1100, $Y_c = 1$, $Y_n = 1$, $X_h = 400$, $Y_h = 1$, OBJ = 597.
6. $X_1 = 200$, $X_3 = 200$, OBJ = 199100.
7. $X_{11} = 1$, $X_{13} = 1$, $X_{22} = 1$, $X_{24} = 1$, $Y_1 = 1$, $Y_2 = 1$, OBJ = 130.
8. $X_{11} = 500$, $X_{22} = 500$, $P_1 = P_2 = 1$, A = B = 1, OBJ = 27750 + 2800.
9. $TW_1 = 80$, $TW_2 = 78$, $O_1 = O_2 = 0$, $H_1 = H_2 = 0$, $P_1 = 332$, $P_2 = 468$,Inv = 32, OBJ = 190080.

Chapter 5 (GP)

1. A = 87.85714, B = 62.142857, OBJ1 = 0, OBJ2 = 274.28571.
2. $X_4 = 141.125$, $X_6 = 58.875$, OBJ1 = 3152.375, OBJ2 = 1670.125.

Chapter 6 (QP)

1. $X_1 = 2$, $X_2 = 2$, OBJ = 20.
2. A = 56.80811, B = 31.54369, C = 23.51171, OBJ = −5355.865. Note that the objective function is negative definite.
3. $X_1 = 10.0408$, $X_3 = 36.24476$, $X_6 = 4.77855$, OBJ = − 900.7231.

Chapter 7 (NLP)

1. X = .7851939, OBJ = 1.414214.
2. $X_1 = 0.9986992$, X2 = 0.9993755, OBJ = −0.9999993.
3. X = 21.07235, OBJ = 205617.1.
4. A = 99.9997, B = 4.98922, C = 99.97733, OBJ = 28762.35.
5. A = 0, B = 0.09913043, OBJ = 1.055072.

Chapter 8 (DP)

1. 1-2-5-9-13-16, OBJ = 50.
2. 1-2-5-9-14-18-21-24-25, OBJ = 106.
3. Display items 4, 5, 8, and 9, total return = 24.
4. Buy stock 1: 4 thousands, 2: 4 thousands, 3: 2 thousands, total return = 15 thousands.
5. Production schedule: 8, 14, 13, 13, 0, 8, total cost = 18,610.
6. Production schedule: 0, 2, 6, 6, 6, 7, 0, 6, 4, 2, total cost = 12,240.

Chapter 9 (TRP)

1. OBJ = 2,790.
2. OBJ = 4,780,000.
3. OBJ = 77.
4. OBJ = 81,800.
5. 316,700.
6. 1R1 (month 1, regular production for month 1 demand) = 1000, 2R2 = 1000, 2O2 (month 2, overtime production for month 2 demand) = 200, 3R3 = 1000, 3O3 = 500, 4R4 = 1000, 4O4 = 800, 5R4 = 200, 5R5 = 800, 5O5 = 800, 6R6 = 1000, 6O5 = 200, 6O6 = 500, OBJ = 102800.
7. OBJ = 21,220.
8. OBJ = 324,200.

Chapter 10 (ASTS)

1. OBJ = 47.
2. OBJ = 78.
3. OBJ = 77.
4. OBJ = 18.
5. OBJ =80.
6. Child 1: F & D, 2: C & G, 3:E, 4:B, 5:A, OBJ = 47.4.
7. OBJ = 130, 1 - 5 - 4 - 6 - 2 - 3 - 1.
8. OBJ = 9000, LA - Houston - DC - Boston - NY - SL - Seattle - SF - LA.

Chapter 11 (SNET)

1. 1 - 2 - 5 - 8 - 11, distance = 32.
2. OBJ = 67.
3. 1 - 2 - 5 - 9 - 13 - 15, distance = 52.
4. OBJ = 122.
5. Maximal flow = 39.
6. Link 1-2, 1-3, 2-4, 3-6, 3-7, 7-5, OBJ = 9600.

Chapter 12 (CNET)

1. **a.** OBJ = 2960.
   b. OBJ = 3120.
   c. Infeasible.
2. OBJ = 30180.

Chapter 13 (CPM/PERT)

1. CP: A-D-G-K-M, Tcp = 31.
2. CP: A-C-E-H-K-L-N & B-D-E-H-K-L-N, Tcp = 53.
3. CP: A-D-G-J, Tcp = 13.
4. **a.** CP: A-E, Tcp = 11, total cost = 24,000 + (2500)(3) = 31,500.
   b. Crash: C one day, E two days, Tcp = 9, total cost = 26,500 + 2,500 = 29,000.
5. **b.** CP: A-E-H-K, Tcp = 26, total cost = 45,300 + 9,000 = 54,300.
   c. Tcp = 22 or 21, total cost = 52,200, CP: A-E-H-K, A-E-J-M, C-F-J-M, and C-F-H-K.
6. CP: B-D-H-J-K, Tcp = 45.

7. CP: B-D-E-H-K-L-N, Tcp = 53.
8. CP: A-B-D-G-K-O-T-W-Z, Tcp = 67.3333.
9. **b.** CP: B-E-H, Tcp = 16.
   c. C. 87.37%.
10. **a.** CP:A2-A6-A8-A10, Tcp = 12.
    b. 2.28 %.
    c. Decision: renegotiate, expected cost = 700.
11. **a.** CP: D-H-J, Tcp = 15.
    b. 0.1933.
    c. Decision: extend, expected cost = 325.
    d. 17 days.

Chapter 14 (INVT)

1. EOQ = 311.769, TC = 73,385.641.
2. EOQ = 440.908, TC = 72,979.797.
3. EOQ = 15, TC = 24720.
4. **a.** EOQ = 707.1072, inventory cost = 282.842.
   c. Order 1000, total cost = 15,250.
5. **a.** Order 985.
   b. Order 1128.
6. **a.** 205.
   b. 250.
   c. 300.

Chapter 15 (INVT2)

1. **a.** FOI M = 923.935, T = 0.049973, SL = 92.00427%, TC = 1,027,287.
   b. FOI M = 891.9308, SL = 93.33334%, TC = 1,027,460.
   c. FOI M = 916.6795, TC = 1,033,932.
   d. FOI M = 777.9459, T = 0.053468, SL = 97.45065%, TC = 1,033,066.
   e. FOQQ = 357.85, R = 396.1275, SL = 96.65286%, TC = 1,026,490.
   f. FOQQ = 357.85, R = 376.7357, SL = 95%, TC = 1,026,702.
2. **a.** OR SL = 77.77777%, TC = 4404.167.
   b. FOI M = 124.1443, T = .3872749, SL = 86.55523%, TC = 4037.967.
   c. FOQQ = 54.29314, R = 68.92552, SL = 83.80138%, TC = 3925.11. Saving = 4037.967 − 3925.11 − 100 = 12.857.

Chapter 16 (QUEUE)

1. L = 2.2845, W = .4602.
2. a. Lq = 4.513, Wq = 4.513.
   b. 0.83333.
3. No.
4. Cost for clerk = 5 + 1.33(4) = 10.333. Cost for machine = 7 + 0.66(4) = 9.64. Decision: machine.
5. a. Wq = 0.2167 hour.
   b. L = 2.9167.
   c. 0.3055.
6. a. W = 0.76.
   b. 0.125.
   c. TC = 2(15) + 4(.5333) = 32.1332.
   d. TC = 30 + 4(.3333) = 31.3332.
7. 1.0, .5, .16667.

Chapter 17 (QSIM)

7. Average Process Time = 7.999364, Average Flow Time = 13.50127, Max. Flow Time = 17.71289; Overall utilization = 99.90121%; Overall average Lq = 10.74565.

Chapter 18 (DA)

2. a. A5, $41,750.
   b. A5, $16,000.
   c. A2, $13,000.
3. A3, 30.
4. a. A (no survey), EV = 390.
   b. 442.98 − 390 = $52.98.
5. a. Buy the second, expected cost = 342.
   b. Buy the second - test by friend, expected cost = 338.

Chapter 19 (MKV)

1. R: 0.3103, L: 0.2759, U: 0.2759, D: 0.1379.
2. a. S5: 0.1036.

b. S3: 0.0857.

c. .1321, .1448, .0857, .1332, .1036, .1370, .0635, .1001, .0999.

3. **a.** .375.

b. .375, .3125, .3125.

c. .25, .5, .25.

Chapter 21 (FA)

1. **a.** Simple payback: MA: 5.413793 FMS: 4.723077.
Discounted payback: MA: 6.961647 FMS: 5.555464.

b. MA: $10,987,610 FMS: $14,194,114.

c. MA: $7,831,158 FMS: $11,336,382.

2. **a.** Cash option: NPV = $17,596.41

b. Lease option: NPV = $16,981.44.

3. **a.** $1,747,478.

b. $38,871.71.

INDEX